Tourism and Economic Development in Eastern Europe and the Soviet Union

Tourism and Economic Development in Eastern Europe and the Soviet Union

Edited by Derek R. Hall

Belhaven Press
London

HALSTED PRESS

WILEY

Halsted Press, an Imprint of John Wiley & Sons, Inc.
New York Toronto

First published in Great Britain in 1991 by
Belhaven Press (a division of Pinter Publishers),
25 Floral Street, London WC2E 9DS

British Library Cataloguing in Publication Data

A CIP catalogue record for this book is available from the British Library

ISBN 1 85293 098 5

Copublished in the Western Hemisphere by
Halsted Press, an Imprint of John Wiley & Sons, Inc.
605 Third Ave, New York, NY 10158-0012

Library of Congress Cataloging-in-Publication Data

Tourism and economic development in Eastern Europe and the Soviet Union / edited by Derek R. Hall.
p. cm.
Includes bibliographical references and index.
ISBN 0-470-21758-8
1. Tourist trade—Soviet Union. 2. Tourist trade—Europe, Eastern. I. Hall, Derek R.
G155.S59T68 1991
338.4'79147—dc20 91-9122
CIP

Typeset by Florencetype Ltd, Kewstoke, Avon
Printed and bound by Biddles Ltd, Guildford and Kings Lynn

To Ann

List of contributors

John B. Allcock	Research Unit in Yugoslav Studies, University of Bradford
Frank W. Carter	Department of Social Sciences, School of Slavonic and East European Studies, University of London
Paul A. Compton	School of Geosciences, the Queen's University of Belfast
Andrew H. Dawson	Department of Geography, University of St. Andrews
Derek R. Hall	School of Environmental Technology, Sunderland Polytechnic
Roy E.H. Mellor	Department of Geography, University of Aberdeen
Denis J.B. Shaw	Department of Geography, University of Birmingham
David Turnock	Department of Geography, University of Leicester

acknowledges the willing cooperation and good natured efficiency of the volume's authors in this undertaking.

Continuing events have been by no means clear cut. While Hungary, Poland, Czechslovakia and the former GDR have led the return, along a relatively direct path, to 'Western'-style market economies, the position of those countries without a Westward-looking tradition has been more ambivalent. Bulgaria's way forward was still unclear at the time of writing, Yugoslavia seemed to be moving in a number of different directions at the same time and a big question mark still hung over Romania. In the Soviet Union the Shatalin Plan for a 500-day economic restructuring programme had just begun to be debated as this text was being submitted for publication. Albania remained reliably steadfast in its Stalinism until early in 1990, when a series of damage limitation exercises was attempted to forestall major upheaval, a possible foretaste of which came with the mass occupation of foreign embassies and subsequent exodus out of the country in early July.

For Eastern Europe and the Soviet Union, the political and economic transformation processes now under way are likely to telescope the time-scale and intensity of structural change, and certainly to stimulate an expansion of the service economy. The relatively labour-intensive nature of the tourism industry, and the limited scope for capital substitution in the production of tourism services (Gershuny and Miles, 1983) may be particularly compelling for these societies which are experiencing, for the first time in half a century, significant and increasing unemployment problems.

Having become a major component of economic strategies in many parts of Western Europe, the signs are that tourism could represent at least one economic escape route for the beleaguered economies of the newly emergent democratic Eastern European societies. It is not, however, a path devoid of dangers.

1.2 Structure

The first four overview chapters, written by the editor, attempt to place tourism and economic development in Eastern Europe and the Soviet Union within both theoretical and empirical contexts. They provide an introduction, within that wider perspective, to the nature and role of tourism within the processes of economic development of the Soviet Union and societies of erstwhile socialist Eastern Europe. In evaluating these characteristics, emphasis has been placed upon recent political and economic change, and the significance of these new environments for both domestic and international tourism development.

The second half of the work complements and exemplifies the first by undertaking a country-by-country evaluation of tourism and economic development: both the commonality and diversity of the approaches to tourism taken by these countries is analysed. This is essential given the enormous range in scale—from the Soviet Union to Albania—and relative levels of development of the societies concerned.

This second major section of the book contains nine commissioned chapters on the Soviet Union and the individual countries of Eastern Europe. These case studies have been written by acknowledged experts who are currently undertaking research in these areas. Each contributor was asked to consider the relevance of a number of topics in structuring and preparing their chapters. While a degree of overall coherence for the text was sought, providing comparability between individual countries and between the country chapters and the introductory overview, the intrinsic diversity of the societies addressed has inevitably required differing emphases for each country.

Authors therefore remained relatively free to organise and develop their arguments as appropriate, adding and deleting themes in accordance with the needs of their particular country. However, consideration of the topics listed below, and the use of main sections broadly following along these lines, was sought to enhance the value of the volume and to provide a reasonable degree of overall coherence.

1. Historical aspects of tourism and recreation: a summary sketch of the evolution of tourism and recreation, from pre-socialist times to the present day. Changing scale, location, nature and administration of activities, and role of tourism and recreation within processes of economic, social and cultural development. Data sources and the degree of reliability and availability of tourism-related data.
2. The role and impact of tourism in economic development planning: a brief examination of economic development planning in the post-war period; the nature of, and priority given to, tourism policies at a national scale. The administration of such policies and their local and regional impacts as a framework for subsequent sections. The nature of available labour markets, appropriate training, infrastructural investment, and regional differences in perceived developmental priorities and opportunities. The range of constraints operating on the development of tourism at the national level. The extent to which tourism development policies expressed elements of erstwhile socialism and/or national individual character. How was tourism now being employed as a (welcome/unwelcome) generator of market forces?
3. Domestic tourism and recreation: the scale, location and nature of activities and flows, and their local and regional economic, spatial, social, cultural and environmental impacts. Changing national circumstances, such as improved transport provision and increasing personal mobility, decreasing bureaucratic controls, rising second-home ownership, privatisation and abolition of controls on personal mobility and property ownership.
4. International tourism: the scale, location and nature of activities and flows, and their local and regional economic, spatial, social, cultural and environmental impacts. Source countries and the overall characteristics of foreign tourists.
5. Tourism relations with the other erstwhile socialist countries viewed within the context of the changing economic and political relations between the states. Tourism cooperation and development in relation to the availability, or otherwise, of appropriate CMEA (Council for Mutual Economic Assistance, or COMECON) mechanisms. The nature and extent of tourist and migratory flows as an indication of the international division of labour within the socialist world.
6. Tourism relations with the West: viewed within a context of changing East–West economic and political relations. International frameworks for

tourism cooperation and development transcending ideological boundaries. The role of joint ventures and inward investment in the tourist industry. Asymmetry of tourist flows and the international division of labour expressed in tourism. The appropriateness of dependency frameworks for analytical purposes.

7. Impacts of *glasnost* and *perestroika*: changing official attitudes to the role of tourism in economic development in the light of contemporary changing values and practices, with a projection of future trends. The role of these forces grew to a dominant position during the production of the volume and varying degrees of rewriting were required to address the new, albeit ever-changing political and economic conditions.
8. Conclusions: how important is tourism in the economic development of the specific country? What are the economic, spatial, social, cultural and environmental consequences of that role? Has that role changed significantly in recent years and/or is it likely to in the future? Some of these questions began to be dramatically answered during the drafting period.

A final concluding section (Chapter 14) evaluates the likely roles and paths of tourism development in the foreseeable future under the new conditions and suggests future research agendas to take forward the analysis of tourism and economic development within such societies.

This volume is also intended to provide some degree of complementarity with two other Belhaven edited volumes on tourism and development: Williams and Shaw's (1988) *Tourism and economic development: West European experiences* and Harrison's (forthcoming) *International tourism in the Third World*, although of course, the emphases and content of the material vary in response to the particular requirements of the societies addressed.

1.3 The geographical focus

Too often in the recent past, the geographical term 'Europe' has been used by politicians and the media to refer only to the west of the continent and often specifically to European Community (EC) members. Europe east of the Elbe was a blind spot. However, the events of 1989 coupled to and stimulated by Mikhail Gorbachev's reforms and notion of the 'common European home' put Eastern Europe firmly back on the map.

The whole continent is now in flux, with moves towards the Single European Market in the EC, momentous political and economic change in the East, German unification and a drawing closer together of Europe's economic and political component parts. Indeed, recent European events have moved so swiftly that the very geographical parameters of this work may appear anachronistic and divisive: that is emphatically not the intention. But the irony has to be admitted: the very processes which have brought Eastern Europe back on to the Western political, economic and media agenda are also undermining the very concept of 'Eastern Europe', which had become defined by political rather than geographical dimensions. On the one hand there is a resurgence of the use of the term 'Central Europe', particularly underscored by attempts to establish new international political groupings there, while on the other, the continuing instability and relative detachment of 'the Balkans' from the rest of the new Europe is tending to reinforce the use of that regional term: pre-war distinctions are beginning to reassert themselves. For the present at least, the Soviet Union is quite another entity.

Nevertheless, the former (and persisting) state socialist societies of Eastern Europe and the Soviet Union form the focus of this particular enquiry, an unequal and anachronistic partnership though they may now appear (Fig. 1.1, Table 1.1). As a shorthand, the term 'the region'—geographically imprecise as that is—will be used by the editor when referring to these societies as a whole.

1.3.1 1989 and beyond

Up to mid-1989, the states of Eastern Europe were governed by communist parties, often with hard-line pseudo-'Stalinist' leaders incapable of tolerating opposition and still pursuing inflexible economic and political policies after several decades of relative inertia. Five-year economic plans and large-scale state ownership of the means of production and distribution dictated development processes. Full employment was still largely guaranteed—indeed considered a mutual obligation between state and citizen—while personal mobility was generally constrained. Across a divided continent, two implicitly opposing military, ideological and economic systems faced each other, perpetuating antagonisms which had none the less maintained a degree of stability in Europe over the previous 40 years.

Yet, by the end of 1989, most communist parties had lost power or had 'reformed' themselves. The old leaders had been swept away, 'people power' had established itself in a European context and, in the ruins of the Berlin Wall, both German states were set on an inexorable path towards unification within a year (Elkins 1990; Hall 1990e). In the Soviet Union, Mikhail Gorbachev, the inspiration for much of the transformation, was himself being overtaken by events, with nationalism and inter-ethnic rivalry fomenting instability in the Soviet rimlands and mounting dissatisfaction with economic and social conditions generating considerable unease within the Union's heartlands. Soviet spokesmen articulated the relative detachment with which Eastern Europe's transformations were viewed from Moscow by emphasising that the 'Sinatra doctrine' (letting Eastern European societies do it 'their way') had irreversibly replaced the 'Brezhnev doctrine' (symbolising Soviet military intervention). Indeed, the Soviet bloc supranational institutions—COMECON (CMEA—Council for Mutual Economic Assistance) and the Warsaw Pact (WTO—Warsaw Treaty Organisation)—now appeared irrelevant, with the Cold War institutions of the West—notably NATO and CoCom (Coordinating Committee for Strategic Exports to Communist Countries)—appearing only marginally less so.

However, much of the early euphoria expressed in the West over the 'defeat of communism' appeared to be based upon the simplistic notion that East European 'freedom' was predicated on the region's adopting fullblooded Western market capitalism. No doubt this line of thinking would anticipate Eastern Europe, under the influence of Western market forces, succumbing to an economic-cultural dependency. Tourism could so easily be placed in the forefront of such a process, reducing Eastern Europe to an inexpensive playground for leisured Westerners and an economic plaything for transnational corporations.

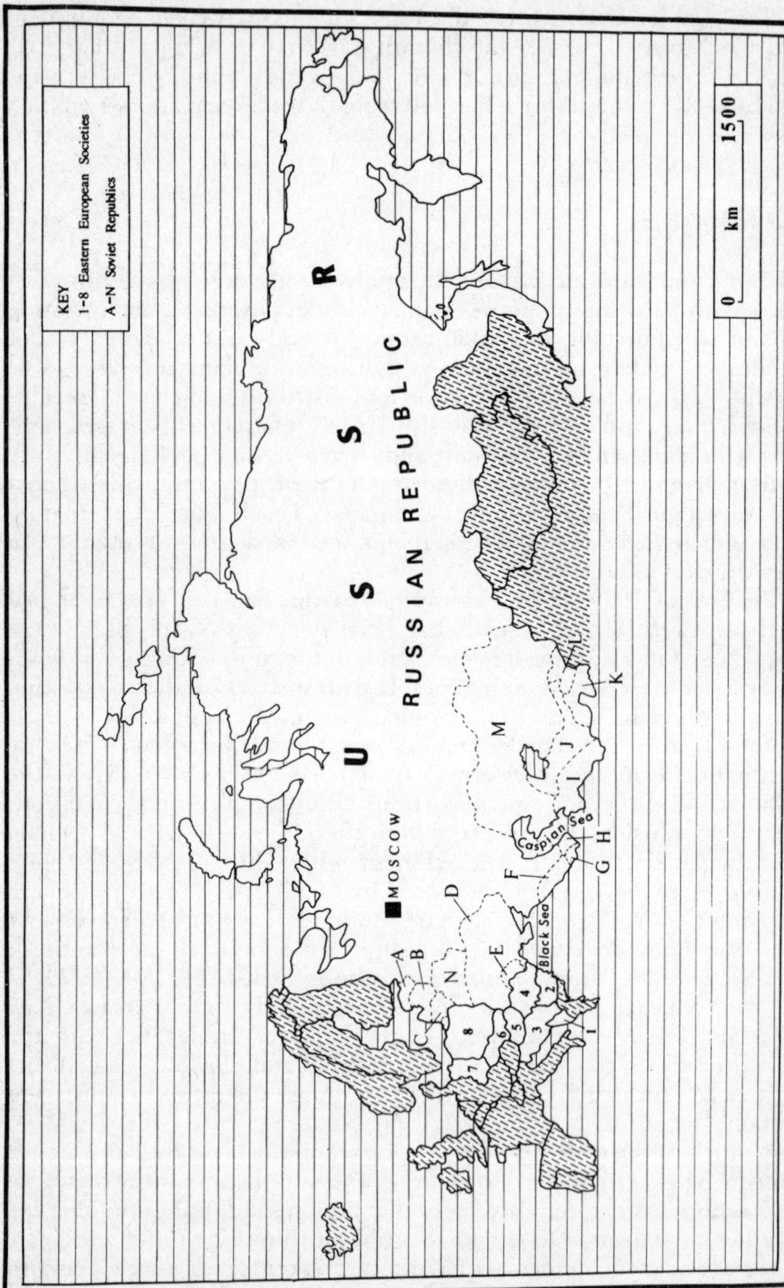

Figure 1.1 Eastern Europe and the Soviet Union

Key to Figure 1.1

East European societies	*Soviet Republics*	
1. Albania	A. Estonia	H. Azerbaijan
2. Bulgaria	B. Latvia	I. Turkmenistan
3. Yugoslavia	C. Lithuania	J. Uzbekistan
4. Romania	D. Ukraine	K. Tadjikistan
5. Hungary	E. Moldavia	L. Kirgizia
6. Czechoslovakia	F. Georgia	M. Kazakhstan
7. Former German Democratic Republic (GDR)	G. Armenia	N. Belorussia
8. Poland		

Table 1.1 Eastern Europe and the Soviet Union: some basic dimensions

Country	Area sq kms (000s)	Population				$ per caput GNP based on purchasing power parity (1988)
		Total (millions) (1988)	Density per sq. km.	(%) Annual rate of increase (1980–8)	(%) Ethnic minorities	
Albania	28.7	3.15	110	2.3	2	2,000★
Bulgaria	110.9	8.96	81	0.1	13	5,633
Czechoslovakia	127.9	15.62	122	0.2	5.3†	7,603
Former GDR	107.8	16.60	154	−0.1	1	9,361
Hungary	93.4	10.59	113	−0.1	1.2	6,491
Poland	312.7	37.96	121	0.8	1.5	5,453
Romania	237.5	23.04	97	0.4	12	4,117
USSR	22,402.2	285.20	13	0.9	48‡	5,552
Yugoslavia	255.8	23.58	92	0.7	27§	4,898
EC	2,261.0	327.0	145	–	–	12,515

Source: Various national and international statistical yearbooks; Bebbington, 1990, p. 77.

★ 1987 per capita GDP estimate, purchasing power adjusted
† Neither Czech nor Slovak
‡ Non-Russian
§ Non-south Slav

After World War I, warnings were voiced of the need to establish a strong federation of the then newly created Central and Eastern European 'succession states' to act as a buffer against Bolshevik expansion in the East, against German resurgence in Central Europe and to overcome the potentially divisive disposition of ethnic minorities and latent irredentism. Such warnings then went largely unheeded. However, having been suppressed for half a century, several ancient territorial and ethnic disputes are being rekindled by the new freedoms. As a counter-balance, therefore, new structures are required for the region, and Havel's call for a joint approach in Central Europe and the emergence of the Pentagon regional grouping of Italy, Austria, Yugoslavia, Czechoslovakia and Hungary could act as a first-stage vehicle for eventual East–West European integration, perhaps within a European Community framework. Linkages through new patterns of international tourism relationships could certainly help this process along, although both transport and accommodation infrastructures are in desperate need of upgrading. The imminent demise of the CMEA, which did little to provide a supranational framework for tourism development within the region, will be little mourned.

The impact of change in Eastern Europe and the Soviet Union has had significant consequences for the developing world. Many African and Arab leaders had close links with the former socialist regimes and patterns of travel, at least of economic and political elites, students and 'solidarity' delegations, reflected this relationship. Most of those relationships are now severed, while such developing countries have further suffered from the fact that at least some of the financial aid offered to Eastern Europe from Western nations was diverted from funds previously earmarked for the Third World. At the time of writing, the longer-term impacts of the mid-1990 Gulf crisis could not be foreseen.

The region's image of considerable environmental degradation—a potential major constraint on tourism expansion programmes—embodies a half-century's interplay of ideological dogma, economic mismanagement, inefficient technology and poor fuel resources. In a number of Eastern European countries and in the Baltic republics, environmental pressure groups provided a driving force within the popular movements for change, even though ecological concerns tended to become overshadowed by, albeit interrelated with, the pressure for political and economic change. Subsequently, several new governments, notably the Polish and Bulgarian, began to respond to environmental challenges by upgrading state responsibility for environmental matters to ministerial status. Yet environmental problems in the region are enormous, with one estimate putting the cost of arresting environmental damage in Eastern Europe alone at over $200 billion. In the absence of more efficient indigenous fuel sources, most thermal power stations in the region burn lignite, disgorging huge quantities of sulphurous pollutants into the atmosphere, damaging human health, vegetation and architectural treasures alike. Much media publicity given to this element in the first post-revolutionary year may impose medium-term constraining effects on tourism to the region. Yet, the eager pursuit of nuclear energy programmes by a number of countries, despite the Chernobyl accident, has reflected attempts to move away from this situation. This has, ironically, tended to receive the implicit support of ecological groups who are both opposed to the continuation of widespread lignite burning and to large-scale hydro-electric schemes such as the Gabcikovo–Nagymaros project on the Danube (now part-abandoned), with their long-term adverse environmental impacts.

Heavily polluting and archaic smokestack industries are being closed in response to Western pre-conditions for assistance in economic restructuring. But the consequences of such policies, while bringing long-term environmental enhancement, are also likely to stimulate short-term social unrest and extremist political reaction, as unemployment is accompanied by fiscal measures inducing high food prices and declining living standards. International tourism, so sensitive to social and political upheavals, could well by-pass the region if such instability persists or if the problem of environmental degradation is not adequately addressed.

At the time of writing, however, the region is witnessing a massive post-revolutionary upsurge in international tourism. An ability to sustain and consolidate this growth depends upon a wide range of factors, which, as these words are being written, are still high on policy agendas but are still far from being resolved.

1.4 Tourism and the new democracies

During the state-socialist period, tourism posed something of a philosophical problem. Neither Marx nor Lenin provided any guidelines for its development, and while there appeared to be a number of 'socialist' objectives towards which a tourism programme could strive (for example, see Hall, 1990c), centralised bureaucratic organisation, inflexibility and often sheer hostility shown to foreign visitors tended to render such programmes counterproductive and severely limited. The basic requirement of a tourism industry, as understood in the West—the availability of a flexible, entrepreneurial service sector responsive to changing demands and fashions—was the very antithesis of the centralised socialist economy based upon heavy industry.

Not surprisingly, most studies of tourism activity and its impact had been confined to the world's capitalist, market economies and as such failed to recognise the particular structural circumstances of tourism under state socialism. As Allcock and Przecławski (1990, p. 1) point out:

> the definition of the central intellectual and practical issues in the field has come to reflect this capitalist context; and one result is a misunderstanding about the nature of the economic and social environment of tourism development in those countries which do not follow this model.

Since those words were written, however, history has moved on, such that most of the societies within this volume are, at different speeds and in varying ways, adopting the key elements of a market economy. This does not mean that they will represent a homogenous grouping, just as the 'Soviet bloc' under communism was never an economic, cultural or even ideological monolith. Yet tourism development here within a market-orientated, politically pluralistic framework presents a whole new learning environment for the industry's recruits. Economic restructuring will prove to be a long-term and painful process. Tourism's role in this transformation can be many-sided, acting as:

1. A means of gaining hard currency and improving balance of payments/indebtedness problems, through admitting much larger numbers of Western tourists.
2. A catalyst of social change, by permitting greater and closer interaction between host populations and those from the outside world, particularly as constraints on tourist accommodation and itineraries are eased.
3. A symbol of new found freedoms by permitting the region's citizens to travel freely both within and outside of their own countries, albeit initially constrained by financial considerations.
4. A means of improving local infrastructures by upgrading tourist facilities, with or without foreign assistance.
5. An integral part of economic restructuring, with the freeing of service industries through privatisation, exposure to national and international market forces, Western transnational corporations' expansion within the region's tourism industry, and through the elimination of centralisation, subsidy and bureaucratisation.

6. A complement to commercial development through a growth of business and conference tourism, reflecting the region's entry/return into the (essentially capitalist) world economic system.

With genuine freedom for indigenous privately owned companies to enter into the tourist industry and to undertake joint ventures with foreign interests in a wide range of tourism and leisure activities, an enormous absolute increase in both foreign and domestic tourism could be absorbed, drawing upon local entrepreneurial skills and stimulating a provision of facilities on a scale not previously witnessed in the region. Unless carefully planned, however, this process could witness rapid overcrowding, infrastructural strains and environmental deterioration. Further, unless current tourism popularity is consolidated and developed, the whims of tourist fashionability could easily move elsewhere, leaving the region with substantial infrastructural overcapacity, badly skewed employment structures and devastated local economies. This is the challenge awaiting the region's tourism managers.

1.5 Statistical data sources and problems

1.5.1 Data inconsistency

Although national statistical yearbooks have been produced by all of the countries of the region, a number of problems are presented by them. Differing definitions, methods of data collection, computation, compilation and statistical presentation render comparability between countries sometimes difficult. Often, figures provided are estimates, perhaps based on sample surveys with likely substantial grossing-up errors. Problems of changing definitions and methods of presentation within individual countries' statistical compilations have often produced discontinuities, thereby considerably reducing the value of time-series data: this has been the case for figures from Czechoslovakia and the Soviet Union in recent years. Moreover, some countries, notably Albania, publish virtually no tourism data at all.

Because of such problems, international organisations have found it difficult to produce meaningful comparative statistical compilations of tourism-related data. The most comprehensive is the annual *Yearbook* of the World Tourism Organisation (WTO) in their series World Tourism Statistics. As an intergovernmental organisation, the WTO compiles and circulates travel statistics made available by member and some non-member states. Although the WTO provides technical guidelines for the collection of these data in an attempt to provide internationally uniform and accurate figures (WTO 1978, 1981), it is ultimately dependent upon the respective national governments' data collecting agencies and statistics departments for the nature and quality of the material used (Pearce 1987b, p. 35). The *United Nations Statistical Yearbook* abstracts tourism-related data from the WTO and other sources and is thus equally prone to inconsistencies.

The very nature of the populations under scrutiny poses problems: tourists are, by definition, highly mobile (Latham 1989, p. 55). Different ways of enumerating arrivals are undertaken: census points may be located at international frontiers or at places of accommodation. Data tend to be most reliable for hotels and large camping sites and least reliable for privately rented rooms and small camping sites. Data on the economic aspects of tourism are, given the wide range of tourism-related economic activities, incomplete, under-recorded and often unhelpfully categorised. Domestic tourism tends to be heavily underestimated by national governments and thus under-represented in international statistical compilations.

1.5.2 *Definitional problems*

'Tourism' is normally understood to constitute travelling away from home for periods of more than 24 hours, for recreation or business purposes; family visits, educational or health reasons may also be included. 'Excursionists' are those staying for a visit of less than 24 hours, although they cannot be ignored since both the development and economic impact of tourism are often closely linked with excursionism. 'Visitor' tends to cover those persons visiting another country for any reason other than taking up employment remunerated from the country visited.

Travel statistics are most frequently expressed in terms of 'frontier arrivals'. These represent the number of visitors who enter a country and are subject to a frontier check. These data take no account of purpose of visit nor length of stay, such that 'excursionists' are often included in visitor frontier (VF) arrivals data. Vuoristo (1981 p. 238), points to the potential confusion arising from the fact that the internationally recommended 'tourist' definition (OECD 1978, pp. 7–9) ignores 'excursionists' (EF: excursionist frontier arrivals), and that, in WTO and United Nations' published data, short-term visitors may be included among the published number of tourists which only footnotes may (or may not) reveal.

The term 'tourist arrivals' refers to visitors staying at least 24 hours. Where the majority of arrivals are by air through a limited number of points of entry, the degree of control is usually very high and statistics are normally considered relatively reliable (TF: tourist frontier arrivals). This is particularly the case where immigration procedures require the completion of an arrival/departure (A/D) card. From this, a range of information can be obtained including nationality, age, occupation, purpose of visit and intended length of stay. In other instances, where there is a large volume of traffic arriving overland through a number of entry points, the degree of control may be less, with some form of estimate being employed, although in the case of Eastern Europe one would have expected a high degree of control. In countries not requiring the completion of an A/D card, periodic surveys may be employed to provide additional information.

Accommodation returns provide a second common source of tourism data: most countries of the region require international visitors to complete registration cards in hotels and other tourist accommodation. Such data are then collated and analysed. 'Arrivals' data for Yugoslavia, for example, are only derived from tourists recorded at registered accommodation (TA). Increasingly, problems of underestimation will now grow as 'unofficial' accommodation increases in importance, since visitors not staying in any form of officially recognised accommodation are more likely to go unenumerated. This is already a major problem in Hungarian data.

Inconsistencies in both the recording and definition of tourism data for Eastern Europe and the Soviet Union can be briefly exemplified from the most recent international compilation available at the time of writing (WTO

Table 1.2 Eastern Europe and the Soviet Union: inconsistencies in arrivals data

Country	1987	1988
Albania	nd	nd
Bulgaria	7.59*‡	8.30*‡
Czechoslovakia	6.13*	14.03*
	15.63§	10.57§
	21.76‡	24.59‡
Former GDR	1.12†	1.21†
	2.10*	2.23*
Hungary	3.28§	3.62§
	11.83*†	10.56*†
Poland	2.48*	2.50*
	4.78‡	6.20‡
Romania	5.14*‡	5.51*‡
Soviet Union	5.25*‡	6.01*‡
Yugoslavia	8.91*±	9.02*±
Eastern Europe	18.91§	14.19§
	40.52*	49.13*

Source: WTO *Yearbook* (1990)

* Table 9.1, Volume 1: Arrivals of tourists from abroad
† Table 1, Volume 2: Arrivals of tourists at frontiers
‡ Table 2, Volume 2: Arrivals of visitors at frontiers
§ Table 11.1, Volume 1: Arrivals of excursionists
± Table 4, Volume 2: Tourists at all accommodation

Yearbook, 1990—2 volumes, 1,300pp). Table 1.2 identifies the range of arrivals data for the region for 1987 and 1988 presented in the WTO compendium. Discrepancies and inconsistencies include:

1. The WTO's Table 9.1 (vol. 1) compiles tourist arrivals data from (at least) three inconsistent bases—visitor arrivals at frontiers (VF: Bulgaria, the former GDR, Romania, the Soviet Union), tourist arrivals at frontiers (TF: Czechoslovakia, Hungary, Poland) and tourists recorded at all accommodation (TA: Yugoslavia).
2. The GDR data list different totals for tourist arrivals in Table 1 (volume 2) (1.21 million for 1988) and in Table 9.1 (volume 1) (2.23 million). The difference is not to be found in the table of excursionists: the Eastern European total for this category includes only the Czechoslovak and Hungarian figures. Is the higher figure therefore either due to a changing location point of enumeration (ie, at accommodation as well as at the frontier), or, more likely, is it based on visitor arrivals data? No other table in the compendium quotes this figure to allow greater elucidation.
3. The GDR VF(?) figure is never quoted again, the TF figure being substituted; for Czechoslovakia and Poland, perversely, the reverse is the case, with TF data being replaced by VF figures.
4. Excursionist arrivals (EF) in Czechoslovakia (Table 11.1) represent the difference between VF (Table 2) and TF arrivals (Table 9.1). But while the

Table 1.3 Eastern Europe and the Soviet Union: arrivals from abroad by purpose of visit (1988)

Country	Purpose of visit										Total
	Holidays/ recreation		Business		VFR		Transit		Other		
	a	*b*	*a*	*b*	*a*	*b*	*a*	*b*	*a*	*b*	
Albania	nd		nd		nd		nd		nd		
Bulgaria†	3.2	39.0	0.5	6.5	0.6	7.5	4.3	52.2	0.2	2.3	8.3
Czechoslovakia†	11.9	85.1	1.2	8.4	nd		9.1	36.8	nd		24.6
Former GDR	nd		nd		nd		nd		nd		
Hungary*	9.6	90.6	0.1	1.0	0.9	8.1	nd		nd		10.6
Poland	nd		nd		nd		nd		nd		
Romania	nd		nd		nd		nd		nd		
Soviet Union	nd		nd		nd		nd		nd		
Yugoslavia	nd		nd		nd		nd		nd		

Source: WTO *Yearbook* (1990).

a numbers in millions
b percentage of country's total arrivals
VFR visiting friends and relatives
* arrivals of tourists from abroad
† arrivals of visitors from abroad

only other country in the region recording EF data is Hungary, only TF data are otherwise listed for that country elsewhere (Tables 1 and 9.1), leaving one to assume that the unlisted total arrivals' figure must equal the combination of the TF and EF figures. By contrast, that figure is listed for Czechoslovakia.

The combined effect of these basic data anomalies is to render the analysis and interpretation of arrivals' data somewhat less effective than might otherwise have been the case.

A further shortcoming in the WTO statistics is that they do not usually take into account the purpose of visit, as all foreigners are usually recorded under 'frontier arrivals' and no distinctions are made in the accommodation figures. The original source of such national data may provide some functional breakdown into such categories as 'holiday and vacation', 'business', 'visiting friends and relations (VFR)', 'education', and 'sport'. Within the region such data are provided for the WTO by only three countries—Bulgaria, Czechoslovakia and Hungary—and none of these are compiled in a manner which makes them directly comparable for purposes of analysis. Some brief observations, however, can be made on the data in Table 1.3:

1. The importance of transit traffic for Bulgaria, representing over half (52.2 per cent) of the recorded arrivals is notable and complements observations made in respect of the data in Table 1.4 below. The transit figures for Czechoslovakia account for most, but not all, of the recorded difference between visitor arrivals and tourist arrivals, and as such—adding to the

above inconsistencies—are slightly less than the excursionist figures for that country (9.1 and 10.57 million respectively for 1988).
2. Within the 'visitors' figures, Czechoslovakia has a higher proportion of business arrivals compared to Bulgaria, as one might expect given the two countries' relative levels of economic development and relative orientations towards Western business opportunities.
3. The Bulgarian and Hungarian VFR figures are relatively similar in terms of both relative and absolute numbers.

While knowledge of absolute numbers of travellers, particularly if they can be classified by purpose of visit, is useful, such elements as length of stay are decisive in determining the impact of any one market on a particular destination. Certain groups of tourists also spend more money than others. Increases in total tourist traffic are often the result of destinations becoming accessible to tourists of more modest means, such that, as the number of visitors increased, their average expenditure may decrease. This, for example, is a situation that the Albanian authorities have set their faces against, not only by severely limiting tourist numbers but by also maintaining relatively high prices: this was forcefully reflected in a 43 per cent price rise for the 1989 tourist season. These factors tend to be interrelated: daily expenditure, for example, may decline with increasing length of stay so that the overall impact of high-spending short-stay visitors may be comparable to or greater than tourists spending more time but less money per day (see Chapter 4).

Few data are collected on a systematic basis showing the extent to which international tourists engage in 'circuit tourism', visits to more than one country or region. This is unfortunate as this would appear to be a significant aspect of tourism within the region, both internationally within Eastern Europe and internally within the Soviet Union (for example, the 'Golden Ring'). Individual countries record visitor arrivals in isolation and take account only of the part of any trip spent within their frontiers, and information on departing nationals is usually recorded only in terms of a single 'main destination'. Globally, information made available on circuit tourism tends to come from more extensive visitor surveys, undertaken on either a regular or *ad hoc* basis. Reviewing a survey on United States' tourist flows to 16 European countries, O'Hagan (1979) found that the characteristic of 'circuit tourism' had been considerably reduced, with the average number of countries visited per trip declining from 3.9 in 1967 to only 1.9 ten years later, thereby belying the 'if it's Thursday it must be Belgium' syndrome.

Improved access to and quality of data on Eastern Europe and the Soviet Union, with regimes no longer obsessed with secrecy and security but with a vested interest in portraying an open and accurate self-image, should encourage the production of appropriate data in this field.

In terms of data on tourism employment, the nature and utility of statistics is very limited. As Williams and Shaw (1988, p. 2) have pointed out in the context of Western Europe, while defining the nature and extent of the tourism industry is crucially important: 'In most countries it is "statistically invisible" and usually, only the most obvious sectors or those devoted exclusively to tourists are enumerated in official tourism data. Inevitably, this tends to be the accommodation sector, and perhaps, cafes and restaurants . . .'
The position regarding such data in the region under review here is no less difficult.

In summary, a wide range of data problems exist in the analysis of tourism on a comparative international level to render the task often difficult and sometimes less than meaningful (for example, see Chib 1977). Many commentators (for example, Baron 1983) have argued for the need to develop reliable and internationally acceptable methods of data collection and presentation. While international organisations such as the OECD and WTO have been active towards this end, the data problems for Eastern Europe and the Soviet Union—societies which until very recently tended to provide limited and not always helpful data and which generally considered tourism to be of minor importance—remain considerable.

1.6 Tourism measurement

1.6.1 Tourism trip generation

International tourism markets and destinations can be examined in relative as well as in absolute terms. Hudman (1979, 1980), for example, employed a country potential generation index (CPGI) to assess the relative capability of countries to generate tourism trips whereby (a) the number of international trips generated by a country is divided by the global total number of international trips; (b) the country's population is divided by the total global population figure; and (c) (a) is then divided by (b). Thus an index of 1.0 indicates a globally average generation capacity, while values greater or lesser than unity show a country is generating respectively more or fewer trips than its population would suggest.

Hudman (1979) calculated the CPGI for a range of countries using 1974 data from the *UN Statistical Yearbook*. The former West and East Germany took first and second ranking, representing divided spheres of European tourism influence at the time, with indices of 11.9 and 11.7 respectively. The United States came 25th with a CPGI of 2.1. Of the countries in the region thus enumerated, Czechoslovakia, Hungary and Poland, interestingly, were clustered, just below Austria at eleventh, twelfth and thirteenth rankings with 6.1, 5.9 and 5.7 respectively; representing the less developed but tourist receiving rather than generating economies, Yugoslavia ranked 24th with 2.3 and Bulgaria 27th at 1.9. Hudman attributed countries' roles as generators of international visitors to three major factors: wealth, size, and access—geographical (in terms of propinquity) and ideological (in terms of commonality). He noted that the small size of several of the high-ranking countries limited the potential for domestic tourism but conversely permitted relative ease of access to neighbouring countries: certainly a characteristic of Czechoslovakia, Hungary and Poland in recent years, further emphasised by the first two countries' land-locked situation.

An early attempt at 'uncovering a few major patterns of flow', was that by Williams and Zelinsky (1970, p. 549), who derived a relative acceptance (RA) index to measure the relative success of a destination in attracting tourists from a generating country. Developed from transaction-flow analysis, the RA index was obtained by dividing the difference between actual and expected flows by the expected flow. Examining fourteen 'Western' countries (West European, the United States, Japan and South Africa), Williams and Zelinsky were constrained by the availability and quality of comparable data. They were obliged to deal with a relatively closed system, taking little account of other, often major flows. By using the RA index, the authors were able to establish the comparative strength and weakness of flows between the pairs of countries examined and to advance a number of 'tentative hypotheses' to account for these patterns. These included distance and the resulting inequalities in travel time and costs, international connectivity (such as commercial and cultural ties), 'general touristic "appeal"', relative tourist costs at the destination, strength and nature of the mental image held of the potential tourist destination.

1.6.2 Concentration ratio

To gain some idea of the level of tourist economies' dependence upon a limited number of markets, a simple measure of concentration has been employed, whereby numbers of arrivals from each host country's three most important tourist sources can be combined to present a percentage of total arrivals for that country. These can then be employed for comparative purposes.

Table 1.4 Eastern Europe and the Soviet Union: concentration ratios, with Western comparisons

Country	Concentration ratio (Arrivals from three most important sources as a percentage of all arrivals)		
	1979	1986	1988
Ireland★	82.0	85.6	86.1
Poland†	80.5	64.3	68.4
Austria‡	74.6	69.0	67.5
USA★	70.1	71.7	70.5
Former GDR†	65.5	nd	nd
Czechoslovakia†	64.9	84.2	83.6
Bulgaria†	58.8	70.6	70.6
Hungary★	nd	62.6	52.0
Switzerland‡	55.6	49.0	51.8
Yugoslavia‡	51.0	53.1	53.1
Romania†	47.3	49.5	51.7
(FR) Germany‡	44.4	39.2	37.7
United Kingdom†	37.1	40.8	40.6
Albania	nd	nd	nd
Soviet Union	nd	nd	nd

Source: Pearce (1987b, p. 45); WTO *Yearbook* (1988, 1990).

★ tourist frontier arrivals
† visitor frontier arrivals
‡ tourist arrivals in all accommodation

Table 1.5 Eastern Europe and the Soviet Union: concentration ratios for 1988 comparing arrivals and tourist nights data

Country	Arrivals			Tourist nights§		
	CR	Three most important sources	% of total	CR	Three most important sources	% of total
Albania	nd			nd		
Bulgaria	67.6†	Turkey	38.9	54.0	Soviet Union	19.0
		Yugoslavia	17.5		Poland	18.4
		Poland	11.1		Czechoslovakia	16.5
Czechoslovakia	83.6†	Former GDR	38.2	nd		
		Hungary	26.0			
		Poland	16.3			
Former GDR	nd			nd		
Hungary	52.0*	Czechoslovakia	21.2	48.1	(FR) Germany	24.4
		Poland	18.0		Former GDR	14.7
		Former GDR	12.9		Czechoslovakia	9.0
Poland	68.4†	Soviet Union	28.1	nd		
		Czechoslovakia	22.9			
		Former GDR	17.5			
Romania	51.7†	Yugoslavia	24.2	nd		
		Poland	14.9			
		Bulgaria	12.7			
Soviet Union	nd			nd		
Yugoslavia	53.1‡	(FR) Germany	30.5	59.2	(FR) Germany	37.8
		Italy	13.7		United Kingdom	11.2
		Austria	8.9		Italy	10.2

Source: WTO *Yearbook* (1990).

* tourist frontier arrivals
† visitor frontier arrivals
‡ tourist arrivals in all accommodation
§ tourist nights in all accommodation

While limited by the nature and availability of data, Pearce (1987b, p. 45) compiled a table of the concentration ratios of visitors for 122 destination countries based on 1979 WTO data. The range of concentration extended from a high of 97.4 for Bermuda, closely followed by Bahamas at 96.3 (both dominated by the American market), down to Ethiopia at 16.8. Of the 122 destination countries used, only six countries featured in this present volume were enumerated, but the current writer updated this analysis using 1986 and 1988 data, and the consequent ratios are indicated in Table 1.4.

No clear trend or regional patterns appear to emerge from these data in isolation: between 1979 and 1988 ratios increased significantly for Bulgaria and Czechoslovakia and gradually for Romania. They diminished for Hungary and Poland and remained relatively constant for Yugoslavia. When compared with tourist nights data, which are unfortunately only available for a limited set of countries, a number of the region's characteristics become better illuminated (Table 1.5):

1. The enormous influence exerted on Bulgarian arrivals data by transiting Turkish and Yugoslav migrant workers. These two groups of nationals represented no less than 56.4 per cent of all arrivals for 1988 (63.6 in 1986), yet in terms of tourist nights made up a mere 0.83 per cent (Turkish 0.05, Yugoslav 0.78 per cent). One assumes ethnic Turkish Bulgarian passport holders would be (very explicitly) regarded by the Bulgarian authorities at that time as Bulgarians, and their movements therefore would not add to the 'Turkish' total.
2. The dominance of Western tourists in Yugoslavia, and in particular the strong showing of West Germans, representing almost a third of total arrivals and well over a third of all tourist nights.
3. The significance of contiguity and the relatively shorter stays of near neighbours. Contiguous neighbours provided the three largest arrivals groups for Czechoslovakia and Poland and two of the top three for Bulgaria and Romania. However, while the data are only fragmentary, the pattern observable from the Hungarian figures (and incidentally, much clearer from the 1986 than from the 1988 data) suggests that Western tourists stay longer than those from the East and provide, as embodied in the figures of West Germans, the most tourist nights for any one group (24.4 per cent, but only 10.7 per cent of arrivals: see also Tables 4.8, 4.9 below). By contrast, neighbouring Czechoslovaks were relatively short stayers, representing only 9.0 per cent of tourist nights (as in 1986) (the fourth highest group) despite comprising the most numerous arrivals group with 21.1 per cent of the total (29.8 in 1986): this may suggest the significance of short cross-border excursions. Unfortunately, insufficiently comprehensive tourist nights data are available to further examine the nearest-neighbour effect within the region.

What these static data do not reveal is the increasing mobility of Poles within Eastern Europe from the mid-1980s, for reasons not necessarily concerned with recreational tourism (see Gołembski, 1990). For example, their tourist nights in Hungary increased by 22 per cent from 1985 to 1986, and in Yugoslavia by no less than 67 per cent, by far the highest increase for any group to that country. However, their preferred destinations appeared to change fashion rapidly. For the 1987–8 period, Polish arrivals in Czechoslovakia increased by 55.8 per cent and in Romania by 14.4 per cent, while for Hungary Poles recorded a 58.5 per cent decrease in tourist nights, moving down from first to fifth position of importance along this dimension (see also Tables 4.5, 4.6).

1.6.3 The tourist exposure rate

This measure attempts to represent the quantitative impact of tourism levels on the host population. It is computed by dividing the number of yearly tourist arrivals by the size of the local population (Böröcz, 1990). Reviewing data for Eastern Europe and the Soviet Union from 1965 to 1988, Table 1.6 reveals groups of tourist destinations:

Table 1.6 Eastern Europe and the Soviet Union: tourist exposure rates

Country	Tourist exposure rates (number of annual arrivals as a % of the destination country's population total)						
	1965	1970	1975	1980	1986	1988	TIR* 1988
Albania	nd	nd	nd	nd	nd	nd	nd
Bulgaria	13.4	29.4	46.0	61.8	85.0	92.6	0.61
Czechoslovakia	20.8	24.4	nd	33.3	34.2	89.6	nd
Former GDR	nd	nd	6.5	9.0	9.0	13.3	nd
Hungary	12.9	38.7	47.2	87.9	100.0	100.1	0.41
Poland	3.6	5.8	10.5	16.0	6.7	6.6	nd
Romania	1.6	11.4	15.0	30.2	19.4	23.9	nd
Soviet Union	0.6	0.9	1.4	2.1	2.8	2.1	nd
Yugoslavia	14.2	23.1	21.4	28.6	36.1	38.2	0.61

Sources: UN *Statistical Yearbooks*; WTO *Yearbooks*.

* Tourist Intensity Rate (see text)
nd no data

1. Relatively small countries with annual numbers of arrivals which grew dramatically over the period and which in 1988 were comparable to or approaching comparability with their own populations. Interestingly, the two countries falling into this category—Bulgaria (92.6 for 1988) and Hungary (100.1) reveal very different tourism characteristics—the first offering Black Sea coastal resorts in summer and winter sports mountain resorts in winter, and the second land-locked and relatively flat, with the city of Budapest, the Danube Bend and the Lake Balaton area offering the major tourist attractions. Both country's exposure rates were, however, far below those for one of the most popular West European tourism economies and comparably small country, Austria (218.4 in 1988), but they were catching up with Spain (111.1), and exceeded the figure for Greece (77.8).
2. Medium-sized countries with strong tourist attractions with annual arrivals representing about a third of the countries' total populations. Yugoslavia had gradually improved its rate to 38.2 by 1988, while Romania had actually peaked in 1981 with a rate of around 31, its 1980 figure being 30.2. Particularly after 1984, the regime and conditions within the country became increasingly repellent to large numbers of tourists, such that even by 1986 Romania's exposure rate had fallen to 19.4, although it had recovered to 23.9 for 1988. Overall, these rates were somewhat higher than those for both the UK (27.8) and West Germany (21.4).
3. Third, the group with single- or near-single-figure exposure rates are somewhat disparate. Relatively small East Germany, with very questionable statistical reliability, had been essentially, as noted earlier, a strong tourist generator. Poland's index actually peaked in 1979, before the disruption of the Solidarność period and the subsequent imposition of martial law in the country in 1981: the 1980 rate of 16.0 is in marked contrast to the 1988 figure of just 6.6. However, as explained by

Gołembski (1990), from about 1984, Poland became an important 'tourist'-generating country. The third country of this group, the Soviet Union, much of which still remains closed to foreigners, received a small number of foreign arrivals compared to its large population. Ironically of course, such tourist arrivals tended to be concentrated into a relatively few locations—Moscow and Leningrad being the most obvious—which have experienced extreme problems of infrastructural under-capacity and overcrowding.

4. Last, Czechoslovakia had experienced rates similar to those of the second group until an enormous increase in tourist arrivals for 1988—portending future trends in the region—brought it within range of the first category. Ironically, until very recently the country's tourism performance had been rather sluggish.

Table 1.7 Global tourism growth figures

Year	Arrivals		Receipts		Tourism receipts as % of world exports of goods
	Number (millions)	% annual growth	US$ billion	% annual growth	
1950	25.3	—	2.1	—	—
1960	69.3	10.6*	6.9	2	5.3
1970	159.7	8.8*	17.9	10.1*	5.8
1980	284.8	6.0*	102.4	19.2*	5.1
1981	288.8	1.4	104.3	1.9	5.3
1982	286.8	−0.7	98.6	−5.4	5.3
1983	284.2	0.9	98.4	0.2	5.2
1984	312.4	9.9	109.8	11.6	5.8
1985	326.5	4.5	115.0	4.7	6.0
1986	334.5	2.5	138.7	20.6	6.6
1987	361.2	8.0	169.5	22.2	6.8
1988	393.2	8.9	194.2	14.5	6.9
1989	403.8	2.6	208.7	6.9	nd

Source: WTO (1988), p. 23, *Yearbook* (1990), pp. 1, 13.

* annual average over ten years
† estimate

1.6.4 *The Tourist Intensity Rate (TIR)*

This measure represents the number of tourist nights in a year as a percentage of total population nights in the country in the same year (total annual tourist nights divided by the size of the local population and further divided by 365). It has been employed (Hoivik and Heiberg, 1980; Böröcz, 1990) to provide a more precise measure of the substantive presence of tourists in a country (or a region, and for quantifiable periods other than one year). Given the inadequate tourist nights data cover for the region, however, such an indicator cannot be gainfully employed in a comparative context. Those rates which can be computed from available data for 1988 (Table 1.6) show Bulgaria and

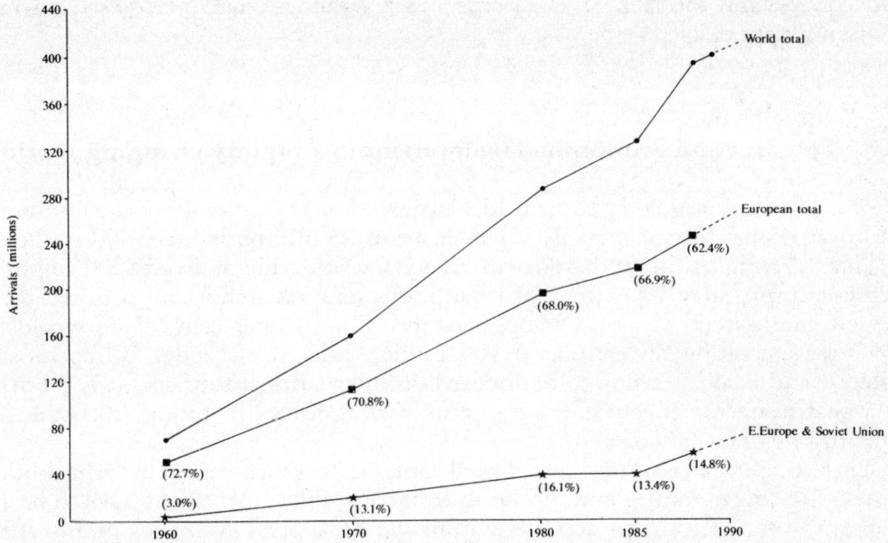

Figure 1.2 World, European and East European tourism growth
Source: WTO *Yearbook* (1990)

Table 1.8 Tourist arrivals by region

Region	1960		1970		1980		1985		1988	
	a	*b*	*a*	*b*	*a*	*b*	*a*	*b*	*a*	*b*
Africa	0.7	1.0	2.4	1.5	7.1	2.5	9.8	3.0	14.6	3.7
America	16.7	24.1	36.6	22.9	53.7	18.9	58.6	18.0	74.3	18.9
Asia and Pacific	0.9	1.3	5.8	3.6	22.2	7.8	30.2	9.2	47.5	12.1
Europe	50.4	72.7	113.0	70.8	196.0	68.0	218.0	66.9	245.3	62.4
Middle East	0.6	0.9	1.9	1.2	5.8	2.0	9.1	2.8	11.4	2.9
Total	69.3	100.0	159.7	100.0	284.8	100.0	325.7	100.0	393.2	100.0

Source: WTO (1988), p. 24, *Yearbook* (1990).
a number of arrivals in millions
b percentage of total global arrivals in that year

Yugoslavia to have attained the same level. This is somewhat ironic given that the international tourism markets for these countries were very different (Table 1.5): while intra-bloc tourists represented 70.9 per cent of all Bulgarian international tourist nights, they made up only 9.6 per cent of those for Yugoslavia. The intensity rate for Hungary is somewhat lower than for the other two countries, perhaps suggesting that Lake Balaton, the Danube Bend and Budapest are not able to hold tourists for the length of stays which are experienced along the Bulgarian and Yugoslav coasts, thereby revealing landlockedness, and the lack of a sea coast, as a weakness in Hungary's tourism 'holding' appeal.

1.7 Tourism and economic development in a rapidly changing world

Tourism is now arguably the world's largest industry: since 1950 the number of international tourist arrivals has risen from 25 million to over 400 million (Table 1.7, Fig. 1.2), with tourism receipts worldwide at over $200 billion representing nearly 7 per cent of total goods exports, rendering tourism the largest single item of world trade, accounting for 12 per cent of the world's GNP and creating an estimated 100 million jobs worldwide. While most interest and analysis tends to be focused on international tourism, it is estimated that some 90 per cent of total tourism flow is domestic, though difficult to quantify (Tyler, 1989a).

Three major patterns of international tourism flows have been evident, both in relation to generating and receiving countries. First, there continues to be a concentration of tourism activity within the developed countries of Europe and North America. These regions represented 81 per cent of all international arrivals in 1988, albeit a clear reduction in the level of dominance compared to the 93.7 per cent of 1970 and the 96.8 per cent of 1960 (Table 1.8). Hoivik and Heiberg (1980), looking at tourist flows in centre-periphery terms, estimated that about 80 per cent of international tourism took place between centre countries (Europe, North America and Japan), about 5 per cent was between periphery countries, a further 5 per cent from the centre to the periphery and a final 10 per cent in the opposite direction.

Second, in the main regions, the flows are predominantly intra-regional in character such that, for example, European countries constitute the main markets and destinations for other European countries. The European pattern has hitherto been a doubly introspective one in that the western and eastern halves of the continent have been largely mutually exclusive, a pattern modified by unidirectional (core-periphery?) relationships from west to east and from north to south. Indeed, the predominant nature of international tourism flows appears to have been one of comparatively short movement between countries within the same region. The statistical importance of Europe compared to North America (Table 1.8) is partly explained by the fact that in the Old World only short distances of travel are required to cross national boundaries and thereby render tourism definitionally international, whereas in North America one can travel much longer distances and still remain within the same country.

Lastly, superimposed upon these general patterns are more selective longer-haul flows, particularly from the United States, with its large and relatively affluent population of heterogeneous geographical ancestry. It has been projected that long-haul tourism will grow fastest in the mid-1990s, possibly at the expense of travel to neighbouring countries (Edwards, 1985; Frechtling, 1986).

More difficult to discern, largely due to data shortcomings, are the relationships of multiple origins and destinations: circuit tourism is a phenomenon little appreciated in the tourism research literature or discernible from available data.

Several factors point to an imminent boom in tourism growth at a global level:

1. Only some 10 per cent of American citizens currently possess passports.
2. Recognised leisure time is rapidly increasing, and the ideal of six weeks' holiday entitlement for all may not be too far off in much of the developed world.
3. Most Japanese tourism, presenting some of the biggest potential worldwide, is currently male oriented and dominated. This must change soon.
4. Such newly industrialising nations as those of South-East Asia, Mexico and Venezuela stand on the threshold of a significant increase in personal mobility.
5. Last, but by no means least, is the impact wrought by political and economic change in Eastern Europe and the Soviet Union.

1.7.1 European trends

1990 was European Year of Tourism (EYT), the stated aims of which were to boost the industry's dynamism, increase awareness of Europe's tourism potential and bring Europeans closer together. However, while the global industry continued to grow at a steady pace, Europe's share of the market had been subjected to increasing pressure. In 1989, Europe attracted (an unconfirmed) 250 million travellers, representing a notable absolute increase on previous years, but providing less than 63 per cent of the world total, reflecting a continued relative decline of the world's share (Fig. 1.2, Table 1.8).

As the Pacific Rim, Asia and North America had grown in popularity, so Europe had been effectively standing still in percentage terms. The continent needed to protect and enhance its position in the global market, and the 1989 revolutions in Eastern Europe may have provided just the stimulus that was required. Industry observers argue that while at least Poland, Hungary, Czechoslovakia, East Germany and Bulgaria recognise the important role that tourism will hold in rebuilding their economies, there is a challenge to Western countries to join their Central and Eastern European neighbours in a partnership which enables the latter to develop positively, which enlarges the European travel market, and which helps to combat competition from the rest of the world. Joint ventures have begun to provide badly needed tourism infrastructure such as high quality hotels and airport improvements, and more basic elements such as staff training and the extension of credit card acceptance to restaurants, bars and shops (Chapter 4).

1.7.2 Eastern Europe and the Soviet Union

For a 20-year period up to 1988, Eastern Europe and the Soviet Union's overall global share of tourist arrivals had been relatively small but reasonably stable at around 15 per cent of the total. Within Europe, with the continent's global share gradually diminishing, Eastern Europe and the Soviet Union had raised its share of tourism arrivals from a mere 4.1 per cent in 1960 to 18.5 per cent in 1970, to hover in the low 20 per cent range in the 1980s, with a 1988 share of 23.7 per cent. Early indications are that this share may be set to

Table 1.9 Eastern Europe and the Soviet Union with selected Western destinations: international tourist arrivals 1970–1988

	International arrivals (millions)						
	1970	1975	1980	1985	1986	1987	1988
Albania	nd	nd	nd	nd	nd	nd	nd
Bulgaria†	2.5	4.0	5.5	7.3	7.6	7.6	8.3
Czechoslovakia*	3.5	du	5.1	4.9	5.3	6.1	14.0
Former GDR§	nd	1.1	1.5	1.6	2.0	2.1	2.2
Hungary*	4.0	5.0	9.4	9.7	10.6	11.8	10.6
Poland*	1.9	3.6	5.7	2.8	2.5	2.5	2.5
Romania†	2.3	3.2	6.7	4.8	4.5	5.1	5.5
Soviet Union*	2.1	3.7	5.6	4.3	4.3	5.2	6.0
Yugoslavia§	4.7	5.8	6.4	8.4	8.4	8.9	9.0
Austria*	8.9	11.5	13.9	15.2	15.1	15.8	16.6
(FR) Germany*	8.5	8.8	11.1	12.7	12.2	12.8	13.1
Greece*	1.4	3.6	4.8	6.6	7.0	7.6	7.8
Spain†	24.1	19.8	23.4	27.5	29.9	32.9	35.1
Switzerland*	6.8	8.0	8.9	11.9	11.4	11.6	11.7
Turkey*	0.4	1.2	0.9	2.2	2.1	2.5	3.7

Source: WTO *Yearbooks*; UN *Statistical Yearbooks*.

nd no data
du data particularly unreliable due to definitional change
* tourist arrivals at frontiers
† visitor arrivals at frontiers
§ notified arrivals at all registered accommodation

increase significantly as international arrivals from both within the region and from the West are stimulated by political and economic change. However, the patterns within the region are by no means constant (Fig. 1.3, Table 1.9, Chapter 4), and the distribution of tourism receipts (Fig. 1.4, Chapter 3), for example, reveal that while Yugoslavia's arrivals figures are by no means the highest for the region, the fact that it is the one tourist economy which depends upon a predominantly Western and higher spending market, sees its receipts almost equal to those of the rest of the region combined.

Eastern Europe and the Soviet Union, so the conventional wisdom goes, can learn from the West's mistakes. Swift over-development, such as that experienced in Spain and Turkey, places undue pressures on the environment while also creating an image of 'lager loutishness' which drives the real cash-generators away. As regulatory barriers and concrete walls come down across the continent, tourism development is well placed to draw together the key elements of the 'new' Europe.

1.7.3 Eastern Europe and the Soviet Union in the global economy

It has long been argued (for example, Young, 1973, pp. 158–9) that a disadvantage of tourism development is the way in which ownership of land and control of the components of the tourism industry fall increasingly into the

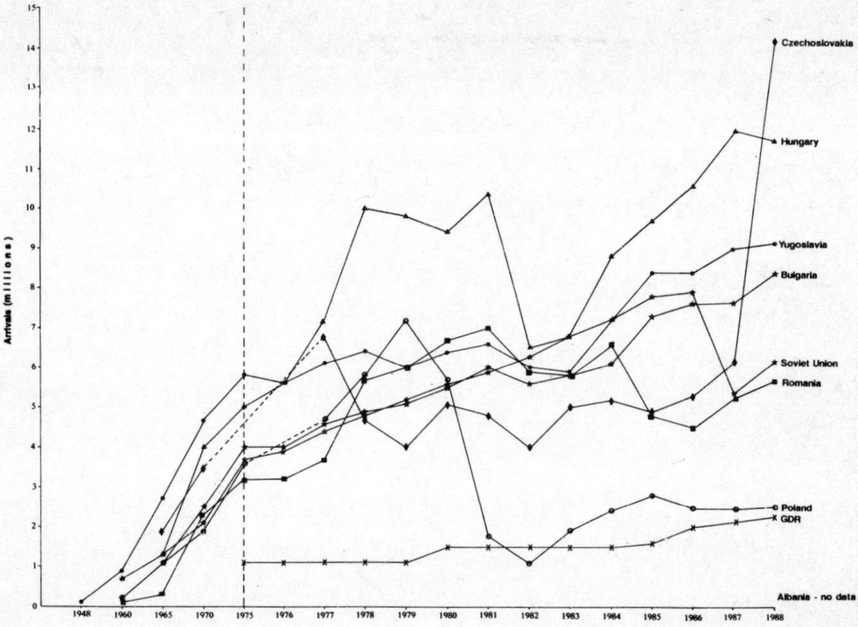

Figure 1.3 Eastern Europe and the Soviet Union: international tourist arrivals 1948–1988

hands of non-residents and of companies based out of the region or overseas. Related to this is the problem of alienation of land through tourist acquisition and foreign settlers. In both cases, the process has barely begun in the societies which have attempted to maintain state control and minimise foreign interests in economic development for much of the previous half century. However, as noted in Chapter 3 below, the role of transnational corporations (TNCs) in tourism-related development processes has received a boost with political and economic change in the region providing for relaxed regulations on foreign participation in, and the privatisation of, indigenous economic enterprises. The economic muscle of TNCs in less-developed societies has witnessed the removal of sovereign control from central, regional and local governments, and it remains to be seen how and when those countries of Eastern Europe now pursuing the full panoply of a market economy are able to cope, not least within the tourist industry, with the inevitably ascendant role of international economic organisations largely outside of their control.

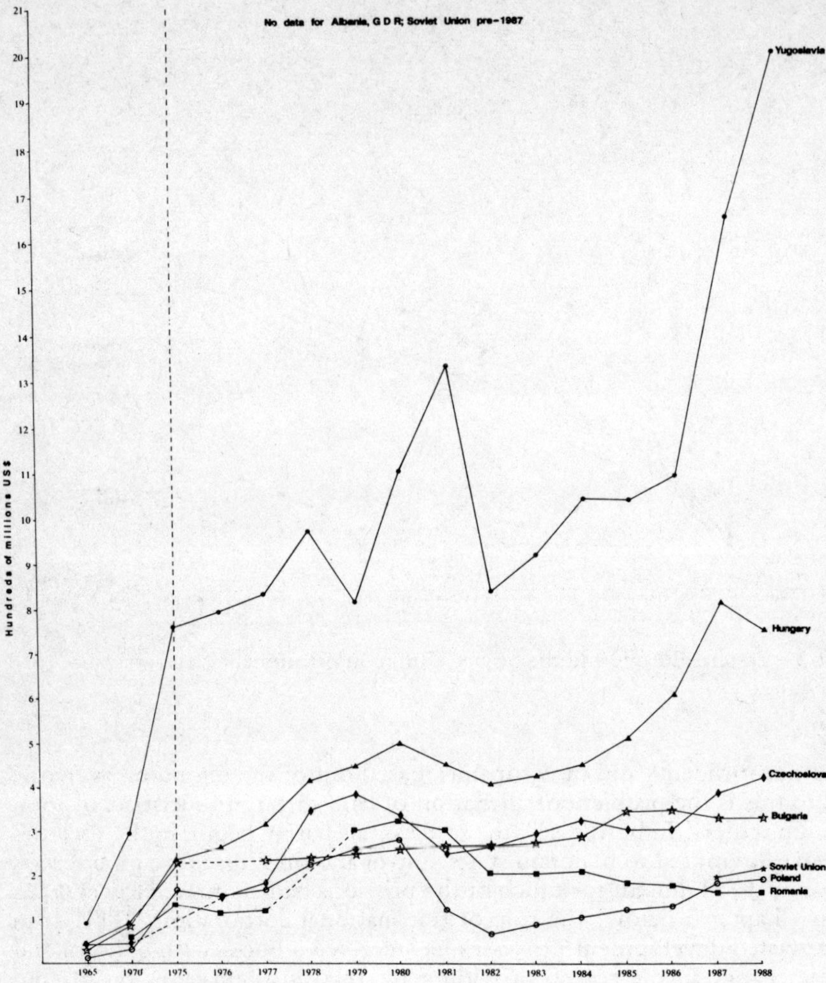

Figure 1.4 Eastern Europe and the Soviet Union: international tourist receipts, 1965–1988

in the post-war period. In the Crimea, pre-revolutionary developments have been elaborated in recent years, and, with less sun but a long pedigree, the East German and Polish Baltic littoral, with its relatively short summer season, caters for a regional and national rather than an international market. Pockets of activity, largely restricted to domestic tourism, can also be found along Albania's Adriatic and Ionian coasts. Additional activities along these belts include selected naturist resorts in Yugoslavia and the application of curative muds along the Black Sea littoral. More recently, the character and slope of beaches has often provided conditions for surfboarding and windsurfing.

Sailing tourism is as yet poorly developed in the region, although it provides a popular and lucrative activity along the Yugoslav Adriatic coast, where the necessary sheltered bays, harbours and purpose-built moorings are available in some abundance (Franzoni *et al* 1990). By 1990, the Yugoslav sailing tourism enterprise ACY together with a number of coastal hotels were administering some 35 marinas with a total of 9,500 mooring berths for yachts, power and sailing boats and an additional 3,500 moorings for wintering purposes. Official estimates have suggested overseas sailing tourists spent about DM100 million in Yugoslavia in 1989, representing a 30 per cent increase over the previous year. In 1988 it was estimated that Yugoslavs owned 12,000 'de luxe' craft, a sevenfold increase on the 1981 figure. The enterprise ACY of Opatija and Makarska Rivijera set up Yugoslavia's first joint-venture tourist company in the Autumn of 1989 with the Swedish yacht club Noble of Gothenburg to build a nautical centre with 320 moorings, a luxury hotel and other facilities. Clearly the potential for such developments elsewhere in the region is substantial.

Ocean cruises may not be immediately associated with the region, but the Soviets and to a lesser extent the Poles, have operated a range of vessels largely for Western hard-currency customers at rates which have usually undercut Western competition. Under the terms of joint-venture legislation, the Soviet Union in mid-1990 set up a $20m Monte Carlo-based project—Prestige Cruises—with an Italian cruise ship operator.

The historic Dalmatian coastal cities of Yugoslavia have long served as stopping-off points for Italian and Greek cruise liners. Ashworth and Tunbridge (1990, p. 165), for example, refer to Dubrovnik as the 'model tourist–historic cruise port', as it has been meticulously restored for a tourist market which is more accessible by sea than by land, and is spatially packaged—a walled city on a peninsula—to fit the time constraints of cruising.

While tourism developments were often initiated during the inter-war period such as the Romanian Black Sea resorts of Mamaia and Eforie as were sea cruises along the Dalmatian coast from Trieste, the opening up of both the Adriatic and Black Sea coasts has been an essentially post-war phenomenon: in the case of the Adriatic this has come about particularly since the building of the Adriatic Highway with World Bank finance in the 1960s, together with improved road and rail access from the Yugoslav interior. On the Black Sea coast Romania initiated new developments between Eforie and Mangalia, while in Bulgaria, from the late 1950s, development included a group of three resorts near Varna, benefiting from the presence of local mineral springs, while in the Burgas area the application of local curative muds became an attraction. Growth also took place around a number of fishing villages and towns, Nesebûr perhaps being the most well known. Post-war growth has often been spectacular: for example, the number of tourist beds available along the

Bulgarian coast increased from fewer than 1,000 in 1950 to a quarter of a million by 1985.

The relatively self-sufficient Bulgarian and Romanian Black Sea coast resorts perhaps best exemplify the type of development designed primarily to exploit the comparative advantages of reliable sunshine, warm summer temperatures and broad sandy beaches which slope gently into a warm sea free from dangerous currents and jellyfish. Such resorts have been offered as hard-currency earning, relatively low-cost holiday centres appealing to sun-hungry northern Europeans caring little about in which country they may be sun-worshipping (Matley 1976, p. 177). An almost inevitable concomitant of such resorts is their relative isolation from the 'real world' of the country in question, a condition which Sampson (1968, pp. 233–4) referred to as the 'ocean liner' effect.

In all areas, however, pollution problems, arising both from the pressure of tourism itself, and from other sources, are posing major environmental challenges to the future growth of this form of tourism development. Beach users are major polluters in themselves, litter being not only unsightly but often dangerous to other users—in the form of broken bottles, cans and the like—and also hazardous to wildlife, particular seabirds, through the thoughtless discarding of polythene bags and other wrappings within which birds can be trapped or suffocated. Oil spills, industrial waste, sewage discharge—not least from coastal resorts themselves—have all reduced the appeal of swimming in sea water, and in some cases have rendered the pursuit potentially harmful to health through the increased possibility of infectious diseases, as well as indirectly via the food chain through infected fish and sea food. Safe recreational fishing is also thereby constrained. The growth of hotels with their own swimming pools and related facilities at least partly reflects this negative reality.

Lakes and rivers not only add to the visual beauty of a region but also offer the possibilities of swimming, sailing, canoeing and fishing, often providing suitable alternative locations to sea coasts, not least for tourists in land-locked countries, or, in the case of the Soviet Union, in the continental interior. Moscow, for example, held its first yachting regatta in May 1990, with 85 craft participating in activities centred on a canal system some 16 km north of the city. The popularity of large bodies of water such as Lake Balaton in Hungary, Bled in Yugoslavia and Bakal in the USSR is notable, although they are vulnerable to substantial tourist and other pressures, rendering some of the environmental consequences noted above. Major commercial arteries such as the Danube, and the Danube–Black Sea Canal present a number of tourism development possibilities as in Hungary's Danube Bend, an area rich in cultural heritage. In 1990, Club Méditerranée signed an agreement with Balkanturist to operate a cruise ship on the Danube from Bulgaria. Yet all too obvious problems arising from water-use conflicts and environmental pressures need to be seriously address.

2.3 The heritage industry

The long and complicated history of the region is well represented in a wide range of 'heritage' attractions, visitors to which are often supplementing other tourist activities rather than visiting them as primary attractions in their own right. However, Sitkina (1985) argued that 70 per cent of tourists visiting the Soviet Union were there for 'cultural' purposes. Certainly, organising evening visits to the opera, ballet, theatre and circus—in addition to such daytime activities as visiting the Kremlin and Hermitage Museums—tends to be an integral part of the Intourist package of services to foreign tourists. Poland has the little-known but highly esteemed 'Warsaw Autumn' contemporary music festival as well as the Chopin piano competition. In Czechoslovakia there is the May Prague spring music festival, from which Dubček's 1968 'socialism with a human face' experiment derived its name.

2.3.1 Sites of cultural history

Such sites provide a useful complement to other tourist activities, helping to diversify itineraries and to spread economic benefits (and environmental impacts) of tourism, and a number of these are discussed in the individual country chapters. More eccentric tourist attractions include the Dracula myth, played up in and around the Transylvanian castle town of Peleş (Romania) (for example, see Senn 1982), the Wieliczka salt mines in southern Poland, known to have been worked for at least 5,500 years, and where 800,000 visitors annually undertake a four-kilometre, two and a half hour subterranean tour. Dating from more recent times is the attractive cultivation of roses between Sofia and Kazanlûk in Bulgaria. Many notable religious buildings act as important complements to other tourist attractions such as the early Croatian churches on offshore islands of Yugoslavia and the Moldavian painted Orthodox churches and monasteries with their exterior frescoes.

2.3.2 Designated areas of cultural history

These are represented at three spatial levels:

1. Whole towns and villages may be protected conservation areas.
2. Particular districts, representing important architectural or archaeological assemblages, may be protected.
3. Individual buildings and artefacts located in areas otherwise less distinguished may be put under care.

All the societies under review possess a wide range of legislative powers with which to enact such protection and conservation. The vigour with which policies of protection and conservation have been pursued will be related partly to:

1. The actual quality and nature of the cultural history.
2. Overall government priorities and thereby the finance made available for such purposes.
3. The flow of overseas funding, for example in Poland from UNESCO and expatriate Poles; in East Berlin from West German sources.
4. The importance attached to such assemblages as symbols and representations of national pride and history.
5. The perceived importance of such areas and buildings for attracting hard-currency-spending visitors.

Slater (1988) points to an anomaly affecting the Germanic Silesian cities inherited by Poland earlier in the century, whereby they appear to have been allowed to decay or have been insensitively reconstructed, in sharp contrast to the sensitive restoration work undertaken in purely Polish settlements such as Old Warsaw and Kraków. In the latter case, the architectural splendour of the former Polish capital has been recognised by UNESCO as being of global importance, with funds provided to restore the old city's physical fabric.

A number of capital cities, most notably Prague and Budapest, have fine assemblages of historic buildings, as do a wide range of centres such as Pliska, the first Bulgarian capital, situated near Shumen, and Dubrovnik on the southern Adriatic. The reconstruction and preservation of total urban assemblages goes back at least to the wartime period when plans were drawn up for the post-war reconstruction of some of the region's finest old urban cores. Rebuilding the war-devastated historic centre of Warsaw acted to emphasise the continuity of Polish nationalism and tended to hold at least as high a priority as 'socialist' construction programmes. Less dramatic policies have followed elsewhere. In Hungary, for example, the centres of 16 towns and five villages have been 'taken into care'. Restoration work in Czechoslovakia shifted in emphasis to systematic programmes for entire town centres, following 1958 legislation laying the basis for the care of historic towns: 35 historic town reservations have been subsequently established (for example, Morris 1973).

Legislation to provide protection for individual listed monuments generally dates back to the 1950s and 1960s, although it has usually required updating and strengthening such as the 1973 Czechoslovak law for the protection of historical objects. In Hungary, monument protection was enshrined in 1949 legislation, but since the Ministry of Building and Construction set up a Monument Protection Board in 1957 and issued building regulations covering monument protection in 1961, progress has been more effective: various palaces of the former Hungarian aristocracy have been restored, as have fortifications at Buda, Eger, Esztergom, Visegrád and other historic centres.

2.3.3 'Ethnic' tourism

Subsumed within the heritage category, 'ethnic' attractions such as folk costume, music, dance, customs and folklore, regional foods, drink, festivals and architecture are variously being maintained, reinvigorated or in some cases patently manufactured or transmogrified (such as Hungarian 'gypsy' music and folklore) for tourist consumption. This process often represents a transfer of rural values and culture to inappropriate urban contexts. Dance groups, choirs and folk ensembles have been maintained by all the countries under review, and in many individual regions, often to very high standards.

Matley (1976, p. 196) also includes within the penumbra of 'ethnic' tourism the return flow of long-term expatriates to their country of origin. Certainly, the large diaspora of Poles, Hungarians, ethnic Germans and even Albanians with strong linguistic, cultural and historic links with their former homelands can been seen as a large captive market with a potential to be exploited. Migrants' cultural associations and societies organise charter flights and sometimes touring itineraries for such return visits. Throughout the post-war period these have provided an important source of foreign currency through gifts to relatives and friends, in addition to the regular sending of remittances. The familiar trade-off, against fears of contagion from these returnees, was particularly problematical in the earlier post-war period.

Recent developments have been encouraging a substantial increase in such visits. For example, early in 1990 three West German travel companies signed contracts with the Lithuanian authorities to organise tours not to the capital Vilnius, but to the seaside resort of Klaipeda, once the Prussian town of Memel. Lithuania's director of tourism was subsequently quoted as enthusing that thousands of Germans whose ancestors came from the area would return for a holiday, with plans to refurbish hotels in the town and local authorities building a German cultural centre and restoring old statues. (Although a short-term constraint which arose at the time was the Kremlin's barring of all foreigners from Lithuania following the republic's declaration of independence.)

Given the reality that Germans provide the most lucrative tourism market, the 'saleability' of the region's Germanic heritage is now gaining considerable impetus with the removal of the old regimes and their often explicitly antagonistic anti-Germanic cultural policies. In this context, Ashworth and Tunbridge (1990, p. 259) raise an interesting question now being addressed in the region:

> In the formerly Germanic world, the relationship between contemporary tourism, historic survival and culturally-compatible reconstruction is very distorted, given the massive war damage but very different economies and political perspectives in West Germany, East Germany and Poland, and the strong survival but again differing perspectives in Switzerland, Austria and Czechoslovakia.

Additionally, the tradition of hospitality prevalent throughout the region could be emphasised in tourism policies. The opening of guest houses, farm houses and other forms of private small-scale accommodation where foreign tourists could stay with a local family and feel that they were living as part of the community and in equilibrium with the local social and cultural environment could be encouraged.

2.3.4 *The role of museums*

As an adjunct to 'living' ethnic presentations and 'working' architectural assemblages, museums have become an important permanent source of national and regional character. With the exception of northern Albania and one or two relatively isolated areas and minority groups, the pace of modernisation and industrialisation has seen the disappearance of many traditional costumes and work methods, requiring a substantial preservation effort, which in a number of cases has come somewhat belatedly. However, many museums dedicated to national cultural heritage in the region do have a long history, often well pre-dating this century. But only in the post-war period, and indeed within the last couple of decades, has the 'heritage' industry been recognised and exploited as a significant hard-currency earner. Large, open-air reconstructions of past ways of life have become popular, with Bucharest's Village Museum, situated in Herastrau Park, to the north of the Romanian capital, being one of the earlier examples. The Hungarians have been developing a similar concept just outside Szentendre, for inclusion in the heavily subscribed Danube Bend excursions from Budapest. The ethnographic museum at Prerov nad Labem in Bohemia, established in 1900, has become an important regional museum with its open-air section inaugurated in 1967. With the rebuilding of the centre of Tirana from the late 1970s, the Albanians established an impressive National History Museum, featuring a folk ensemble motif on its facade on the north side of Skanderbeg Square, while the indoor ethnographic museum was moved from rather cramped quarters to a new exhibition hall.

2.4 Urban tourism

Substantially overlapping with the 'heritage' category, what Matley (1976, p. 192) and others have referred to as 'urban tourism' encompasses a wide range of tourism activities within clearly defined geographical areas (see Ashworth 1989 for a review of the literature), and is receiving increasing attention as a focus of analysis (Ashworth and Tunbridge 1990; Bramham *et al*, 1989).

> It is difficult to itemise all the factors which attract people to certain cities. Apart from the buildings, churches, art galleries, museums, theatres, restaurants, and shops which individually or collectively interest and attract tourists, many cities have an individual character and atmosphere which transcend the mere sum of their buildings and other physical attractions . . . The atmosphere is difficult to define, being a combination of visual impressions based on pleasant or characteristic architecture, attractively laid-out streets or picturesque canals, along with restaurants and cafes serving good food and drink and also the life-style of the inhabitants. [Matley 1976, p. 192]

Not everyone would recognise those last qualities as being characteristic of the attractive atmosphere of the region. However, in recent years, the concept of 'city breaks', encompassing an organised two- to four- or seven-day trip, usually including a weekend, has been extended to the region by Western tour companies, and this form of short-stay Western tourism is likely to receive a substantial boost from the 1989 revolutions. For example, the 1990 'Thomson CityBreaks' holiday brochure featured Budapest, 'an impressive, historic city renowned for the warmth and character of its people' (p. 48); Moscow, 'a breathtaking and unique holiday experience' (p. 58); and Leningrad, which, on a 'twin centre' holiday coupled with Moscow provided 'a fascinating and dramatic contrast between the most famous of Russian cities' (p. 56).

A secondary tourism role of urban centres is simply as a central place and accommodation focus for exploring and visiting adjacent regions or even countries, depending upon transport available and relative accommodation costs between neighbouring regions and countries.

Apart from the world cities of major interest to tourists, there are many smaller cities of historical or cultural attractiveness which may be visited as part of a wider tour of a country or region. For example, Volgograd, Novgorod, Kalinin, Zagorsk, Suzdal, Yaroslavl, Kiev, Lvov, Uzhgorod, Riga, Tallinn, Vilnius, Minsk, Dushanbe, Tashkent, Alma-Ata, Bukhara, Samarkand, Tbilisi and Yerevan are just some of the increasing number of urban centres which have been opened to tourists in the Soviet Union and which are featured by Intourist in their Western package brochures, usually in conjunction with visits to Moscow and/or Leningrad. In Eastern Europe, such cities as Kraków, Bratislava, Dresden and Braşov provide a similar role.

While the urban-based post-war historic representation of these countries, as articulated in 'revolutionary' museums, palaces of culture, heroic statuary and the other baggage of state socialism, will no longer command compulsory visits from school, trade union and cooperativist groups, where they exist at all, a number of interesting artefacts will remain from the state-socialism period as vestiges and symbols of a particular, and not insignificant chapter in each country's development. Some of the more monumental buildings present major challenges and opportunities for imaginative approaches to urban tourism. These include Ceauşescu's monumentalist legacy in Bucharest, and Warsaw's early 1950s' Palace of Culture with its 42 floors and 3,000 rooms, containing 13 conference halls, four theatres, three cinemas, two restaurants, an assortment of museums, galleries and sports and leisure facilities, including a strip bar in the basement, and a post office!

Last, but of increasing importance, is the role of urban-based business and conference tourism (Labasse 1984; Law 1988). Unlike other forms of tourism, business travel tends to be price inelastic and non-seasonal; it usually requires individual arrangements involving relatively high costs, and shorter destination stays than for holiday tourists. As a growing element of travel with the increasing internationalisation of business, segmentation is developing. Three major strands of business tourism can be recognised; (a) regular business travel; (b) travel related to meetings, conventions, congresses and trade fairs; and (c) incentive travel. The latter, a hybrid, in that travel for pleasure is purchased by businesses as a perk for their employees, is yet poorly developed in the region.

However, congress, conference and trade-fair tourism is now growing rapidly. The region has a long history of notable trade fairs with their roots in medieval times. Lasting for several days, many in Western Europe had degenerated into funfairs by the nineteenth century, but they tended to retain their importance in Central and Eastern Europe. The fair at Nizhny Novgorod, for example, one of the major centres of internal commerce and trade with the East, became Russia's largest fair in the nineteenth century (Fitzpatrick 1990). Fairs retained their significance most notably where urban life was least developed, and in the Balkans their number increased significantly during the first half of the nineteenth century, being especially numerous and important in zones of contact between plains and mountains. The decades either side of the turn of the century, however, saw changes in political boundaries; urban growth and railway development breaking down the linkages upon which the Balkan fairs had been based (Pounds 1985, p. 491).

The fairs of Leipzig remain by far the most important of the region. For several centuries the city was close to the eastern frontier of developed, industrialised Europe. Beyond was a region with poorly developed urban and industrial structures. The products of the West passed through the Leipzig Fairs on their way to the markets of the Russian and Ottoman empires, attracting a wide and diverse range of visitors to the fairs. As a showcase for East German industry and agriculture, the biannual post-war Leipzig Trade Fair attracted large numbers of visitors from both East and West. During the spring and autumn sessions, it could be observed that under the old regime,

> The range of goods available in the shops mysteriously increases, while your modest neighbourhood restaurant triples its prices and daringly announces a late-night show . . . private rooms throughout the city and hotel rooms in towns for miles around are pressed into service to supplement the city's own modern hotels accommodating the flood of exhibitors and potential purchasers. From as far away as Poland and Czechoslovakia the coaches roll through the night to set down their passengers for a day at the Fair. [Elkins 1987, p. 208]

Smaller-scale trade fairs in the region have included the Budapest Spring Fair, the 89th of which was held in May 1989 with representation from over a thousand foreign firms, and the Plovdiv Spring Fair, the ninth of which was also held in the same month with representation from some 53 countries.

All of these may pale into insignificance in relation to the planned 1995 Budapest–Vienna World Exhibition. In December 1989 the Bureau of International Exhibitions (BIE) gave the go-ahead for this extravaganza at a time when the Hungarian government, National Assembly and the IMF were involved in complex negotiations over Hungary's substantial budget deficit and enormous foreign debt. The six-month long exhibition, whose theme is to be 'Bridges to the Future', will act as a symbol of new East–West relations and will coincide with the millenial anniversary of the first known reference to Austria, and one year before the 1,100th anniversary of Hungary's founding. It will be the first exhibition with two capitals acting as joint hosts, and made even more unusual by virtue of one of those hosts (currently) being a member of CMEA and the Warsaw Pact and the other a neutral state and a member of the European Free Trade Association (EFTA) (Okolicsanyi 1990). Doubts and voiced opposition to the exhibition have been raised in Hungary both over the country's ability to support the event and its appropriateness for an economy only just emerging from 40 years of state socialism. However, the project's Hungarian supporters, particularly those in the tourism and construction industries, argue that the 1995 World Exhibition would provide a unique opportunity for Hungary substantially to upgrade the capital's transport, communications and tourism infrastructure to world standards. Critics argue that such developments would merely exacerbate the existing socio-economic disparities between Budapest and the rest of the country (for example, see Compton 1987; Dienes 1973; Kóródi 1976).

Hungary's share of the financing of the exhibition could represent the country's largest investment project this century. Given the two-centre nature of the development, its costs would be increased by necessary duplication and additional transport requirements. One fear is that most European Community firms will locate in Vienna, and Budapest will be left with the significantly poorer and less advanced CMEA representatives, thereby evolving a very asymmetrical fair and leaving Budapest with potentially little advantage. Further, 11 of the past 13 world exhibitions—all held in countries with well-developed market economies—have made a financial loss. By the end of 1989 it was being estimated that the cost of the Exhibition to Hungary would be at least \$2 billion, in a country with a GNP of about \$24 billion and a foreign debt of \$20 billion. It is planned that government funding would rise to cover no more than 25 per cent of the total cost, and, as far as possible, overseas funding and sponsorship would be sought.

Most of the countries under review are now placing great emphasis upon business and conference tourism, both because of the hard currency generated and minimum seasonality involved, in addition, of course, to the likely long-term commercial benefits of such activities. Indicative of this orientation, and of the increasing significance of the tourism industry, were two international tourism conferences held in the region in August 1989. That of the International Association of Scientific Experts in Tourism (AIEST), with its theme of spas and health tourism was held in Budapest, with visits to Héviz (Kaspar 1990). The first official meeting of the International Academy for the Study of Tourism (IAST), hosted by the Polish government and the Warsaw Tourism Institute, took place in Warsaw and Zakopane, with an additional visit to Kraków, taking as its theme theoretical approaches to alternative tourism (Eadington and Smith 1990). In the Autumn of 1990 the International Hotel Association held its congress in a newly opened joint Czechoslovak–French hotel development in Prague.

2.5 Spa and health-related tourism

A significant element of the physical environment which has contributed to tourist attraction is the presence of mineralised water, found in springs or tapped by wells. By the seventeenth century there had emerged a widespread belief in the medicinal value of various varieties of mineral waters, either for drinking or for bathing, and spas began to be visited in large numbers for such purposes. The region's spas provided mineral springs and curative treatments for a wide range of ailments. Some became world famous and many attracted a rich and fashionable clientele from abroad, especially during the second half of the nineteenth century. To complement the direct health-giving properties of their physical attributes, spas were usually enhanced by complementary man-made attractions such as parks and gardens, concerts, theatrical performances and other recreation, the quality of which contributed to a spa's popularity.

> The elegance of the 'spa' towns placed them in a different world from that of the new industrial towns. Their neo-baroque architecture, their casinos and salons made them the haunts of the rich and the favoured meeting-places of the pampered politicians of nineteenth-century Europe. [Pounds 1985, p. 126]

Within the Russian Empire, despite the widely acclaimed medicinal value of Caucasian mineral hot springs, many members of the élite sought the social cachet of attending the spas of Central Europe. 'The masses, of course, simply endured circumstances as they found them' (Bater 1989, p. 270).

In the early socialist period, spas were largely set aside for domestic use, falling under state or trade-union auspices. From the late 1950s and 1960s, considerable effort was expended to recapture the hard-currency market and attract relatively wealthy Westerners. Extensive hotel building and other infrastructural improvements have subsequently taken place in a number of such locations.

Many spas have long histories: Sandanski in Bulgaria, the largest spa complex in the Balkans, is claimed to be the birthplace of Spartacus; Băile Herculane in Transylvania was where, according to Roman legend, Hercules cured his wounds inflicted by the Hydra, although the spa became particularly fashionable in the nineteenth century through royal patronage. The curative properties of the waters at Pieŝtany in Slovakia have been in use at least since the medieval period. Under Habsburg patronage, a number of opulent spa houses were constructed in what is now Hungary and Czechoslovakia, where some 50 spas and climatic resorts can be found. These resorts are probably the best known in the region, not least because they have traditionally attracted a large German-speaking clientele. High-quality services were a hallmark of the Czech spas and the Grand Hotel Pupp in Karlovy Vary (Carlsbad) had a world-famous reputation. The isolation of radium from Jachymov pitchblende in 1898 directed attention to the radioactive waters of the town and the world's first radioactive spa was set up in 1906 with the construction of the Radium Palace (now the Marie Curie–Sklodowska sanatorium). State control of the spas was introduced in 1948 when the government became the sole owner of all spas and mineral springs in Czechoslovakia.

With the development of modern methods of medical treatment and a somewhat sporadic faith in the curative powers of mineral waters, spas in many parts of the world appear to have lost their previous popularity. Yet according to the World Health Organisation, a tenth of the world's population suffers from arthritis, and thermalism is increasingly being used to treat it.

In an effort to retain their clientele in the face of loss of popularity elsewhere, diversification of spa activities has taken place alongside upgrading and refurbishment. A number of Czechoslovak spa centres, although some of the best patronised, have been diversifying into activity and sports holidays. International events have been held at Marianské Lázně, for example, including meetings of CMEA commissioners. In Karlovy Vary the development of a new golf course enticed Skanska of Sweden to plan the building of a hotel complex nearby. To ease access, the town authorities have been pressing for improvements at the local airport and have been lobbying West German and Austrian carriers to use the town as a stop-over. Pieŝtany, employing mud baths for the treatment of rheumatism, has a large clientele from the Middle East.

Indeed, recent years have witnessed something of a resurgence of spa centres. With worsening urban living conditions such as atmospheric pollution, noise, unhealthy diets and problems of reintegration into work after illness or accident, classical spas are increasingly fulfilling the function of health centres for both Eastern and Western Europeans (Kaspar 1990). As noted above, spas provided the theme for the 1989 International Association of Scientific Experts in Tourism (AIEST) conference, which was held in Budapest. Indeed, in Hungary, recent hotel projects have been linked with bathing in thermal waters, such as the Saint Margaret's Island development in Budapest and in provincial locations such as Héviz near Lake Balaton. A joint project under United Nations auspices has seen the upgrading of over 30 Hungarian spas in order to increase their capacity.

The mineral water from various spas is bottled in large quantities and widely distributed, with the water of Borsec in Romania having an international reputation and that of Glina in southern Albania having a regional distribution.

In the Soviet Union, the concept of the sanatorium, both for adults and children, grew to become a major element of sponsored domestic tourism. Although numbering perhaps no more than a hundred at the time of the Revolution, by 1939 there were nearly 3,000 with accommodation for almost 340,000. In 1986, the country possessed nearly 16,000 sanatoria and rest homes with beds for about 2.5 million people, at a ratio of about 9:1,000 population (Bater 1989, p. 270).

2.6 Winter sports

Summer sunshine and warm temperatures have long been major components affecting the location of tourist development. But with increasing leisure time and disposable income available in developed Western societies, permitting winter holidays to be taken, cold winter temperatures and appropriate snow cover have also become important factors. Some southern lowland summer resorts keep their accommodation and facilities open for those seeking relief from northern winters and cheaper off-season rates, but it is cold winter temperatures which are significant in the development and location of modern winter tourism. In particular, the growth in popularity of winter sports has been one of the most significant developments of the tourist industry of the last quarter century.

2.6.1 Downhill skiing

As the most popular winter sports activity, downhill skiing has an ancient history as a form of winter transport, but as a sport is relatively recent. While skating is an older sport, the development of artificial indoor ice rinks has made this less popular activity independent of climate. Skiing, even in artificial conditions, is an outdoor sport and normally requires a good snow cover and a mountainous or, at least, hilly terrain—although the last requirement is less necessary for cross-country skiing, which could become particularly popular in Eastern Europe and the Soviet Union. Thus far, however, few skiing resorts have been developed in relatively flat areas. Skiing as a modern mass sport was developed in the Alps, and Alpine-type downhill skiing still tends to provide the model for new developments.

Mountain regions only became popular as areas for recreation and tourism relatively recently. Until the eighteenth century, upland areas tended to induce feelings of fear and danger: they were places to be avoided. Alpine mountain climbing began in the late eighteenth century, but skiing was not introduced into the Alps for another hundred years. Later still, the development of the ski lift in the 1930s led to rapid development of skiing for sport and additionally helped to open up mountain regions to various forms of tourism.

With climatic and topographic differences, conditions for developing winter sports vary considerably between regions. In Eastern Europe, the best conditions for skiing are found in the Carpathians and particularly in the Tatra mountains shared by Poland and Czechoslovakia.

In addition to the appropriate natural conditions of climate, snow and terrain, capital investment must be adequate for centrally heated hotels and apartments, ski lifts, snow ploughs to maintain clear access roads and continuous attention to the ski slopes (Blanchard 1958, p. 202). At some resorts snow-making machines may be employed to supplement snow cover on the slopes or snow may even be imported into the area. *Après-ski* leisure—night clubs, restaurants and bars—are important features of most of the larger resorts. There are, however, two main types of winter sports bases:

1. The village, with a self-contained life and transportation system, which can best be thought of as a 'resort'.
2. The much larger area, with ski-lift stations far apart and linked by public transport which has more of the nature of a 'centre'.

A variant of the latter is the 'created centre', built from scratch on an empty mountain side (Heller 1969, p. 49). The larger centre may appeal to tourists who seek a more sophisticated *après-ski* night life and the smaller resort to those who essentially seek good skiing.

The need, at the planning stage, to anticipate and make ample provision for safety considerations in new mountain centres is a significant factor in their development. Prevention of accidents on the slopes, and the much more serious problem of avalanches, has been highlighted by major tragedies in the Alps, where ski resorts have been overwhelmed by such occurrences.

2.6.2 *Cross-country skiing*

This activity came to Alpine Europe in the early 1970s and would appear to be an ideal recreation form for the newly reformed economies of Eastern Europe to develop as an entrée into the more sophisticated and capital intensive downhill market. Equipment is significantly cheaper than for downhill skiing, it provides good exercise in fresh air and pleasant surroundings, is far less dangerous and as long as snow is present, it can be pursued on almost any type of terrain, including flat country. Cross-country skiing can therefore be carried on in a manner relatively independent of resorts: it requires neither ski lifts nor prepared runs. To date, cross-country skiing has remained a relatively local form of recreation, while the downhill sport is still the major attraction for international tourists.

2.6.3 *Snowmobiling*

By contrast, this activity would seem not to be appropriate for the region, and is currently largely confined to relatively flat areas of northern North America and Scandinavia. Its shortcomings are several:

1. It cannot be undertaken effectively in mountainous areas.
2. It requires considerable mechanical service facilities.
3. Considerable physical and aural environmental impacts are difficult to control.
4. Scant exercise is provided and little skill is required.
5. Large capital outlays on equipment are necessary.

2.6.4 *Heli-skiing*

This pursuit recently arrived in the Soviet Union, although helicopters were grounded in the Caucasus when a serious accident was followed by a fatal one during the 1989–90 season. Fitted with more powerful engines, helicopters were to be used for the 1990–1 season at Gudauri, a one-hotel resort in the Caucasus acting as an Alpine enclave, with facilities recently bought into by an Austrian club holiday operator, some two hours' drive north of Tbilisi. With heli-skiing often banned in Switzerland and Austria for ecological reasons,

Georgia offers a nearer and cheaper alternative to Canada, Kashmir and New Zealand for European practitioners.

2.6.5 *Problems and possibilities*

Post-1989 low-cost winter packages to Romania and Bulgaria have been developed and expanded by Western tour operators. However, political uncertainty, administrative constraints and snow shortages have limited immediate growth. For large companies such as Thomson, whose policy is to abandon resorts with poor snow records, terms of snow guarantees to customers make 'fringe areas' such as Eastern Europe relatively unattractive. Whereas in Western Europe skiers can usually shuttle from low and snowless resorts in main Alpine countries to glacier ski areas or artificial snow, in Eastern Europe and the Pyrenees there are no glacier ski areas, and operators thus face paying out on snow guarantee arrangements unless they move skiers altogether. These conditions are currently a matter of some debate within the industry, and arrangements may vary considerably between operators. Further, the EC proposals to make operators responsible for all aspects of the packages they assemble and sell, partly adopted in Britain by ABTA in November 1990, are likely to further marginalise certain parts of the region with dubious mass-market reputations such as Romania.

The mountains and resorts of the Carpathians, the Tatra, the Harz, the Caucasus and the Crimea offer not only winter sports but also cool respite from the hot dusty summers of the plains below. Now attracting large numbers of Western tourists, winter sports first developed in the region along the south-east German/north Bohemian mountain borderlands, where more than a hundred ski tows and lifts had been developed by the 1970s. Particularly important areas today are the Tatra Mountains on the southern Polish/northern Slovakian border, with more than 300 peaks rising to above 2,500m. Here clear lakes and historic towns have been complemented by modern resort developments. The local claims that High Tatra air is saturated with ozone and volatile oils have seen spa development and particularly the treatment of respiratory diseases. At the Slovakian spa of Smokovec, for example, some 20,000 patients are treated annually (Miškuľová 1989). A wide range of upland areas in the Balkans has recently seen investment being undertaken: Bled, Sarajevo (site of the 1984 Winter Olympics), Ohrid and Plitvice in Yugoslavia, scattered resorts in the Rhodope, Rila, Vitosha and Pirin Mountains of Bulgaria and Carpathian centres such as Braşov, Predeal and Sinaia in Romania. The main Carpathian resort is Poiana Braşov, fully equipped for winter sports but also offering hiking and adventure holidays. Hungary has the beginnings of a winter sports complex around the sanatorium on the Kekes plateau in the Matra Mountains.

Yugoslavia is among seven Alpine countries in the process of producing an Alpine treaty on environmental protection, which will, *inter alia*, help to coordinate tourism policies, particularly the development of ski runs. The International Union for the Conservation of Nature and Natural Resources (IUCN) has identified downhill skiing as the most damaging human activity in the Alpine environment, enumerating some 40,000 ski runs and lifts in the region. It points to off-piste skiers trampling and killing young trees and chalets and restaurants being built at high altitudes damaging soil and forests.

The Union recommends that cross-country skiing and alpine hiking should be promoted on environmental grounds at the expense of downhill skiing (MacKenzie 1989).

Extending the tourist season through a diversification of activities is becoming increasingly important to many upland resorts. Bulgaria's winter resorts, for example, served by Sofia and Plovdiv airports, are around latitude 42° north, yet within three hours' flying time from Britain. At this latitude, the sun is almost 10° higher in the sky than in London. This means longer mid-winter daylight hours and a better chance of getting a sun-tan in March or April. Conversely, at the more southerly latitude, the snow in a typical winter will tend to retreat up the mountains as March and April progress, making high-altitude resorts such as those in the Vitosha Mountains, which have tows to heights exceeding 1,800 metres, a wiser location for late-season skiing than those lower down. Thus Aleka, a small resort in the Vitosha, and Bansko, in the Pirin range, both offer tourist accommodation for winter sports activities, and during summer and autumn they attract visitors coming to appreciate the mountain scenery, its protected fauna and flora, local culture and additionally to take health treatment. While diversification and year-round-activity encouragement are important for income generation, the location of ski slopes and other winter sports activities within a national park can produce fundamental conflicts of interest which may be difficult to overcome.

Yugoslavia's skiing centres are divided between the far northern Alpine resorts of Kranjska Gora, Bled and Bohinj (served by Ljubljana airport) and those near Sarajevo in Bosnia. The skiing here, and at nearby Jahorina, extends above 2,000 metres. Snow can be heavy when depressions forming in the north-western Mediterranean move eastwards. One problem is the local wind, the *Bora*, which occurs when a huge pool of cold air gathers over the interior of Yugoslavia. Only slight encouragement is needed from the pressure pattern to send this cold air cascading as a blustery north-easterly gale through the valleys and gaps in the mountains towards the Adriatic Sea, with potentially dangerous consequences.

2.7 Scenery and landscape for rambling, walking and observation

As noted previously, the landscape or scenery of a region can provide an important attraction for tourists, often in conjunction with other activities: a coastal resort or winter sports centre is enhanced and complemented by attractive countryside nearby. For example, the beauty of the Tatra mountains both enhances the attraction of winter sports resorts, and draws visitors during the summer months for the quieter pleasures of walking amid spectacular scenery. Regions which offer few other attractions can develop a tourist industry virtually on scenery alone. In the case of wilderness areas, for example, the attraction of isolation and solitude paradoxically appeals to many visitors. As noted earlier, water bodies can play an important role in enhancing a landscape. Forest areas also present opportunities for recreation.

Certain particular elements of the natural environment may draw tourists, such as waterfalls, caves and canyons, together with fauna and flora. Examples may include the Plitvice lakes and Postojna caves of northern Yugoslavia. Some may be sufficiently impressive to represent a major attraction in their own right, while others may be visited in the course of a regional tour, particularly if they are located in an area offering complementary attractions.

Many footpaths exist across Eastern Europe which are in regular use by the local population: walking along forest paths, for example, has long been a popular German pastime. These are complemented by an increasing amount of locally available accommodation in family houses as well as more formal chalet and hostel establishments. Much improved tourist information systems, including maps, signposting and locally sensitive literature, is required to attract and stimulate foreign visitors to undertake such informal holidays. However, this is likely to receive a relatively low priority, at least in the short term, since such tourists tend to be relatively low spenders and are therefore not as attractive to bankrupt economies as hard-currency tourists attracted to four- and five-star hotels buying expensive motorised excursions and interacting relatively little with the local population. Such activities are anyway currently impossible in the still closed areas of the Soviet Union, in Albania and, it would seem, in much of Romania at the time of writing.

A 500-kilometre section of the European Wanderway was inaugurated in 1986, extending through Austria into Hungary, running to the northern shore of Lake Balaton (Turnock 1989a, p. 267). In Bohemia, an ancient massif with deep forested valleys and gorges, an extensive area is managed for recreation and tourism, with nature reserves and way-marked trails. In those countries, such as Czechoslovakia, with relatively high living standards, an increased demand for domestic recreation and tourism has seen a high rambling activity rate.

2.8 Wildlife-related recreation

While all countries of the region possess the equivalent of national parks (see Chapter 3), and have designated areas devoted to the protection of fauna and flora, considerable land-use conflicts exist. One of Europe's most important wildlife habitats, the Danube Delta, has not only been under threat from increasing tourism, but owing to disastrous agricultural policies and grandiose development plans, the Ceauşescu regime in Romania had earmarked much of the Delta for agricultural or industrial development (Hall 1988; Turnock 1990a).

2.8.1 Hunting

The association of this recreational activity with the now discredited former communist leaderships, together with increasing environmental awareness, should see it severely constrained in the future. However, as a minority interest, with little scope for further development, hunting has been none the less a highly profitable business: about 7,000 visitors from Western Europe being drawn annually to Hungary alone in the mid-1980s for such purposes. A major 'attraction' has been the ability to shoot species of animals which are no longer present or are rare and protected in Western countries. The Polish government, for example, has permitted hunting of the European bison, which has been deliberately encouraged to breed in a forest preserve in the east of the country after having come close to extinction.

2.8.2 Fishing

This pursuit could offer much potential and be promoted as a means of extending tourist seasons at such locations as Lake Balaton and the Danube Delta. However, degraded ecological conditions in much of the regioin and, in the case of Balaton, coupled with a neglect of fish stocks, mean that much restocking and water quality improvement is required. It is otherwise an essentially local pastime.

2.9 Other sporting events

Horse-riding for pleasure has a long pedigree in both Hungary and northern Yugoslavia, dating from Austro–Hungarian days. In the latter case, a tourism industry has been built up around the Lipica stud farm, famous for its Lipizzaner breed, while in Hungary, 'Huntours', a branch of Ibusz, now offer five varieties of horse-riding tours within the country (Ruler 1989, pp. 221, 227).

The 1984 Winter Olympics at Sarajevo and Moscow's hosting of the 1980 Olympics focused attention on those locations and stimulated substantial infrastructural upgrading, not merely in sport and recreational facilities but also in transport and accommodation. The development of Moscow's Sheremetyevo 2 international airport was undertaken specifically in preparation for the Olympic Games there, the city's hotel accommodation capacity had to be increased by 50 per cent, all main roads into Moscow were widened and resurfaced and customs buildings at all the country's main entry points were rebuilt.

The 1985 construction of a world standard motor-racing circuit at Mogyorod near Budapest saw Hungary hosting its first Formula One event there in the following year. This event is now built into the annual Formula One calendar.

Such major international sports occasions, together with more regular events such as international soccer, athletics, swimming, ice hockey and basketball matches, attract visitors who may spend some extra time and money in the country before or after the events in question. Recent years have seen the growth of a negative side to international sports matches: heightened nationalism and chauvanism, rowdyism, drunkenness, and in extreme cases, mass rioting, resulting in extensive damage to property and human injury. This may clearly detract from the attraction of hosting such events and may exert a negative knock-on effect for other aspects of the tourism industry.

2.10 Artificially created attractions

2.10.1 New values for old?

While such man-made attractions as amusement parks were a common feature of post-war domestic leisure, casinos were a far rarer phenomenon in the region, that at Constanţa on the Romanian Black Sea coast being one of the few to survive through the socialist years. However, values are changing. The recently established casino on the motor vessel *Schonbrunn* moored in the

Danube at Budapest initially excluded the participation of Hungarians. But in April 1990 relaxed Hungarian gaming laws changed this, reportedly stimulating at least one American company into declaring the desire to turn Budapest into the Las Vegas of Eastern Europe. There is, however, regional competition. In 1988, a casino was set up in Karlovy Vary as a joint venture between Casino Austria and the Czechoslovak state enterprise Balnex. It was sufficiently successful for the Austrian company to negotiate further casinos with the Čedok state tourism agency for the Forum and Palace hotels in Prague. An East–West German joint venture has established a casino on the 37th floor of East Berlin's Hotel Stadt Berlin. Eighty per cent of the gross earnings from this venture go to the East Berlin city authorities, and East Germans have been trained to take over from the initial cohort of West German croupiers.

By contrast, there remain the formalised symbols of heroic state socialism such as the Moscow Economic Achievements Exhibition and its smaller equivalents elsewhere in the region, together with more recent manifestations of socialist technology such as the Moscow and East Berlin television towers. These have hitherto acted as essential ideological showpieces for organised tourist group visits, as have the lingering elements of personality cults, from Lenin's embalmed body in Red Square to Enver Hoxha's birthplace in Gjirokastër. Their future roles remain uncertain.

2.10.2 Fiscal considerations

A separate form of artificially induced tourism comes about through differences in national or local laws, taxes, prices and goods availability or in national attitudes and customs. Cross-border shopping forays over the erstwhile 'Iron Curtain', particularly between Hungary and Austria (in both directions) and from Yugoslavia into Trieste, Italy, have been complemented by cross-border excursions, for similar reasons, between the countries of the region (Chapter 4).

A country's artificial level of exchange compared to the main currencies of the tourism-generating countries, can provide an attraction simply in offering low-cost holidays. For example, the 1990/91 'Ski Enterprise' holiday brochure tells us that Romania is 'This season's "in" destination! . . . this is another Eastern bloc country with a very favourable rate of exchange, where paupers can live like Kings' (p. 4); while in Bulgaria, 'British skiers are entitled to a special currency exchange rate . . . last season it was 205 per cent over the official rate—which made Bulgaria the ski bargain of the year!' (p. 20).

Of course, low price levels could reflect low service standards, poor food, unsafe drinking water, a lack of culinary hygiene, dirty bed linen, poor accommodation and the like, which, with associated intestinal disorders and other illnesses could quickly act as a factor of tourist repulsion.

2.11 Religious pilgrimages

While one would not immediately associate such activity with this hitherto officially godless region, its potential would now appear to be considerably enhanced. The three basic spatial flows generally associated with tourism may be observed:

1. Domestic flows, the most famous being Polish Roman Catholics travelling to the site of the Black Madonna at Częstochowa in the south of the country.
2. International flows into the region: while entailing domestic flows also, one of the most interesting recent phenomena has been the now somewhat discredited recurrent apparition of the Virgin in the southern Yugoslav village of Medjugorje after six villagers first claimed to have talked to it on a hill above the village in 1981. This little mountain settlement, which, with a population of no more than 400, once made a meagre living from the vices of tobacco and wine, now hosts over two million Catholics a year, offering thousands of rooms to rent, restaurants and souvenir stalls stacked with religious statuary.

   Special packages have been offered by a niche specialist tour operator in London flying from Heathrow to the pilgrimage site's nearest airport at Mostar. But, as Allcock points out in Chapter 12 in this volume, the Yugoslav authorities' attitude has tended not to encourage such activity.

   While not pilgrimages in the pure sense, tourist visits for purposes of seeing religious buildings, institutions and activities, which perhaps merit inclusion under the 'heritage' category, are now being positively encouraged by a number of the region's tourist authorities. Intourist, for example, now includes 'Religious tours' among its range of special-interest package-holiday itineraries.
3. International flows out of the region: although poorly documented, significant numbers of Moslems from Yugoslavia and the southern Asiatic republics of the Soviet Union are known to undertake pilgrimages to the Islamic holy places in Saudi Arabia and elsewhere. By contrast, the movement of Jews from the region to Israel tends to be dominated by a one-way flow.

2.12 Conclusions

A wide range of tourism activities are available within the region, and opportunities for most major summer and winter pursuits can be found. A great deal of further potential exists, but a number of constraints first need to be overcome. As the old state socialist structures are dismantled and new economic mechanisms are introduced, the region's tourism industry will be increasingly characterised by the penetration of international capital, and both the nature and extent of tourism opportunities will become more dependent upon world market conditions.

3 Eastern Europe and the Soviet Union: overcoming tourism constraints

Derek R. Hall

3.1 Tourism administration: the inherited structure

The organisation of international tourism under state socialism comprised a central ministry or arm of a ministry out of which the role of a national tourism organisation was devolved. Within that tourism organisation, regional and local branches would operate the various tourist services for their area, albeit subordinate to the national planning and organisational framework. Domestic tourism, by contrast, was often a major social or welfare role of trade unions, although other organisations and individual arrangements played an important part.

In some cases, the ministry was not wholly devoted to tourism, but would, for example, be responsible for home trade or for transport, tourism and communications. The Romanian Ministry of Tourism was specifically established in the early 1970s in a conscious effort to increase numbers of both Eastern and Western European tourists, establishing stronger links with, and a greater focus of activity upon, two subordinate organisations, the National Offices of Travel—Carpaţi, based in Braşov to serve Transylvania, and Litoral, in Mamaia, for the Black Sea coastal region. Below these, district divisions operated at a local level. Two other national organisations were also subordinate to the ministry: the Romanian Automobile Club and the Tourist Bureau for Young People (Vuoristo 1981, p. 243). In the case of Poland, the General Committee for Tourism oversaw and encouraged the tourism promotional activities of the Orbis state travel office. In East Germany, a ministry of tourism was only established in the wake of political change in 1989.

In devolved Yugoslavia, although the individual republics and provinces have responsibility for tourism, overall policy is the concern of the Federal Secretariat for the Market and General Economic Affairs, which is assisted by the Tourist Association of Yugoslavia. The Association promotes the country abroad and coordinates the activities of the many local tourist associations and societies.

Generally, the state tourist organisations such as Albturist, Balkanturist (Bulgaria), Čedok (Czechoslovakia) and Ibusz (Hungary) were established (or re-established) after the war along the lines of the Soviet Intourist organisation, itself set up in 1929. This organisation handles both domestic and inbound tourism arrangements. By the mid-1980s it had 28 offices world-wide performing a number of specific functions typical of such organisations:

1. Acting as an agent for the state airline.
2. Owning and managing tourist accommodation and catering arrangements.
3. Controlling tourism surface transport: coaches, car hire and train tickets as necessary.
4. Organising excursions, tickets for entertainment, provision of guides and information services (Boniface and Cooper 1987, p. 12).

Separate organisations for young people have included youth (for example, Sputnik in the Soviet Union) and student travel agencies. They have not always dealt with foreigners; neither have they necessarily only concerned themselves with young people.

Theoretically, those Westerners favouring package-type holidays with little desire to wander or explore further than the most strongly promoted excursion would appear to have been model clients for centralised state socialist tourism organisations. But such organs tended not to be sufficiently sensitive or flexible to respond to the relatively high-quality service demands and changing requirements of Western package tourists. Excessive bureaucracy, inflexibility and standardisation of establishments and services, together with the lack of competition between tourist resorts, organisations and establishments, all militated against improvements in the quality of service.

Piecemeal reforms before 1989 saw some decentralisation of international tourism administration, most notably in Yugoslavia and Hungary, with domestic tourism being influenced by the greater autonomy being given to workplaces, as in the Soviet Union. For Romania, Turnock (1989a, p. 270) argued that further decentralisation of tourism administration from the central ministry to local cooperatives, following experiments carried out in the Iaşi area in the early 1980s, could see agricultural cooperatives taking on responsibility for tourist services and care of historic monuments, thereby putting local knowledge to good use.

The administration of tourism under socialism, following the Intourist model, and, until recently, seen most clearly in the case of Albturist in Albania (Hall 1984b, 1990f) has none the less implicitly acted both to contain and to concentrate tourism—and especially foreign tourism—within very specific spatial parameters. Even before the events of 1989, Turnock (1989a, p. 270) was pointing out that while domestic tourists tended to be relatively more prominent in the smaller centres compared to foreign tourists' concentration, decentralisation could encourage a wider spread of foreign tourism and reduce congestion in the main centres. Upgrading road transport infrastructures and encouraging cooperative and private management of facilities would aid this process, as Hungarian experience in catering, campsites and guest houses had shown. There was scope for developing rural recreation facilities in depopulated mountain villages.

3.2 The impact of economic restructuring

3.2.1 Market orientation

Restructuring towards a market economy now appears to be the major goal of most of the societies under review. Although piecemeal change and internal reorganisation—tinkering with the old system—had been carried on since at least the 1960s, the political upheavals of the late 1980s initiated comprehensive economic change. This appears to have impacted on tourism and tourism-related administrative structures in a number of ways.

3.2.1.1 Privatisation of state assets

A central element of the programme of economic restructuring has been the privatisation of state enterprises. Former ideological dogmas of egalitarianism and full employment—however chimerical (for example, see Winiecki 1988)—are being superseded by economically determined factors of efficiency, competitiveness and profitability as the enterprises of Eastern Europe and the Soviet Union are—at varying speeds—opened up to world market conditions (Sobell 1989). As seen most explicitly in German unification, this process can have a devastating effect in exposing the relative inefficiency and uncompetitive nature of the region's hitherto feather-bedded state-run enterprises. Particularly for those societies with EC membership aspirations, the 1992 EC Single European Market has been a further stimulatory factor to encourage a transformation of their economies into structures comparable to those of Western Europe.

At the time of writing Hungary was in the forefront of the region's privatisation. Within the country's economic restructuring programme, this was impacting upon tourism development. Both MALEV, the state-owned airline, and Ibusz, the state travel agency, were early candidates for privatisation, establishing precedents for other societies.

3.2.1.2 Promoting the development of the private sector

Tourism-related activities are well suited to responding to, and may act as a demonstration effect for, increasing freedoms for the private sector. For example, in 1988 legislation was adopted in Croatia—the republic accounting for some two-thirds of Yugoslavia's tourist trade—to promote the development of the private sector in tourism, whereby Yugoslav citizens would be able to operate travel bureaux, hotels, motels, night clubs and discotheques employing up to ten workers. Such an approach has now spread across much of the region.

3.2.1.3 Adopting self-financing policies

As an extension of the incremental tinkerings with the old state-dominated system, putting enterprises on a self-financing basis has been a tool employed to varying extents over the past two decades. Carried forward to contemporary conditions, it may be seen as one step towards ultimate privatisation and/or full integration into world market conditions. One interesting tourism-related example is the Soviet national airline Aeroflot, which, with no less than 15,000 passenger aircraft, half a million employees, 119 million passengers (1987) and some 70 internationally served airports within the Soviet Union, became self-financing from January 1988. One immediate impact for surprised passengers was the appearance of entrepreneurial inflight 'duty-free' sales on domestic flights, selling children's toys, tights and garish ties, together with the hiring out of hand-held video games. Consequential ill-conceived policies can, however, be counter-productive. In the area of pricing policy, for example, Aeroflot's decision in early 1990 to charge foreigners in hard currency for internal Soviet flights acted as a disincentive to foreign business travel and investment outside of Moscow, as foreign companies would not wish to increase their hard-currency expenditures in the Soviet Union when conversion of locally generated rouble income is virtually impossible. A year earlier, JAT (Yugoslavia) announced that domestic fares for foreigners would be three times higher than those for Yugoslavs—to make up for 1988 losses.

3.2.1.4 Establishing internationally recognised standards

This is being sought in at least two ways. The first entails the admission of the region's organisations to international bodies which promote clear maintenance of standards and quality-control procedures. The second is to allow transnational companies entry into the domestic market to establish their own international standards for emulation by indigenous organisations.

In the first case, at the end of 1989 Aeroflot joined most of the region's other national carriers as a member of the International Air Transport Association (IATA), a condition of which was that international standards would be met on domestic flights. Hungary and Poland became the first East Europeans to join the European Civil Aviation Conference (ECAC) in 1990. This move would help to bring them badly needed expertise to harmonise economic, security and technical policies with the other 23 member states, and to give them an enhanced international potential. Transnational companies are entering domestic tourism markets in a number of ways, most notably in the provision of high-grade hotel accommodation, as seen below.

3.2.1.5 Internal restructuring of enterprises

Again this may be seen as one step towards privatisation and may be accompanied by self-financing mechanisms. For example, territorial branches have been established within Aeroflot as the first step towards becoming independent carriers in their own right.

3.2.1.6 Break-up of monopolies

As one explicit step further on from the above, a group of Aeroflot pilots and engineers have planned a rival airline—ASDA (the Russian acronym for Association of Extra-long Haul Airlines) for long hauls to North America, Australasia and South-East Asia, possibly from 1991. The proposed enterprise has also been interested in diversifying into hotel development and car rental, thus revealing an early example of potential vertical integration within an incipient private-sector Soviet (Russian?) tourist industry.

3.2.2 Impact of CMEA convertible currency accounting from January 1991

One of the most obvious tourist-related impacts of this inevitable development is massive increases in transport fares for citizens of CMEA-member countries travelling through Eastern Europe and the Soviet Union: this will doubtless impose constraints, if only in the short term, on 'intra-bloc' tourism. Early estimates suggested that air fares would rise by 300 per cent and railway fares perhaps tenfold. Travel by road public transport and ship is likely to suffer less impact as fares on these modes are regulated between enterprises rather than under international agreement.

3.2.3 Tourism in an expanded service sector

Table 3.1 indicates the relatively low proportions of employment in the service sector in the region compared to Western Europe. Market orientation and privatisation, the elimination or at least drastic reduction of bureaucratic procedures, Western transnational participation and reactions of citizens to 46 years of pent-up frustrations will see a burgeoning of the service economy within the region. Tourism and recreation services have an important role to play in this process, encompassing as they do a substantial range of directly and indirectly related activities—accommodation, transport, and catering as well as construction and manufacturing.

At the time of writing it was too early to assess the scale and social and economic impact such transformation would have on the region. However, early examples of Western participation in such processes in the Soviet Union (Table 3.2) point to some likely implications for expanding service economies.

3.3 Regulation of travel

3.3.1 Administrative constraints

The numbers, and to a lesser extent nature, of tourist flows can be comprehensively influenced by administrative and bureaucratic controls and impositions. These can cover such areas as visa regulations, currency exchange controls and prescriptions, or at least proscriptions, on tourist movements and activities. In other words, constraints may be imposed before, at and subsequent to the tourist's point of entry. While particularly characteristic of state socialist societies, such constraints have by no means been confined to them. Indeed, such controls existed in Czarist Russia and have continued in a number of the region's countries in their post-socialist transitional forms.

Most of the countries in this volume were subject to such constraints, often severely imposed. As Young pointed out early in the 1970s:

> It is possible to over-plan and to introduce controls which are too rigid, in East Germany one has to pre-book for a visa; and a visa to visit is only issued when a hotel bed has been reserved. The same formalities are necessary if one visits Russia, and the Russians are clearly going to have to decide quite soon how they will control their tourist industry. At the moment they need 20,000 linguists as 'guides' for 2 million tourists, and, by all accounts, a substantial number of night porters and escorts to 'protect the tourist'. With a target of 10 million tourists by 1980, the existing ratios of guides to guests will have to give. [Young, 1973 p. 168]

Table 3.1 Eastern Europe and the Soviet Union with selected Western comparisons: basic employment distribution

	Total workforce (millions)	Major employment categories (1988) Industrial %	Agricultural %	Other %	Employment in category 6 (1985) %
Albania	nd	nd	nd	nd	nd
Bulgaria	4.30	33.0	19.5	47.4	8.5
Czechoslovakia	8.25	36.6	12.1	51.3	11.3
Former GDR	8.94	39.0	10.2	50.8	10.9
Hungary	4.84	33.0	18.4	48.6	10.4
Poland	18.70	26.0	28.2	45.9	8.1
Romania	10.77	33.7	28.5	37.8	5.8
Soviet Union	155.65	24.4	21.7	53.9	7.7
Yugoslavia	9.75	28.7	21.6	49.6	13.7
				Services	
Austria (1987)	3.43	37.7	8.4	53.9	17.7
France (1987)	23.97	31.3	7.3	61.3	14.4
(FR) Germany (1986)	29.23	40.9	5.3	53.7	14.9
Greece (1985)	3.89	28.1	28.5	43.4	15.0
Italy (1987)	23.82	28.2	9.1	62.7	18.7
Spain (1987)	14.31	32.1	16.1	51.8	17.5
Switzerland (1986)	3.24	37.4	6.4	56.2	18.6
Turkey (1985)	18.42	16.8	39.5	44.7	10.1
UK (1986)	27.39	31.1	2.6	66.4	18.2

Source: Bebbington (1990, p. 76); ILO, *Yearbook of Labour Statistics* (1988); United Nations, *Statistical Yearbooks*.

nd no data
Employment category 6: trade, restaurants and hotels

Even before 1989, however, administration of travel was being simplified, especially for Western visitors. Most governments had become sufficiently confident to accept modest contagion and security risks in return for much needed hard-currency inflows. Subsequently, the region's new administrations began to review existing controls, and individual country requirements have been liable to change at short notice (Hall 1990c). For example, in Romania at the time of writing, while visitors' movements were unrestricted, accommodation appeared to be prescribed to that managed by the state or by cooperatives. Since 1975 foreigners had been precluded from staying in private houses, although for a brief time after the December 1989 coup, this position appeared to have been overturned.

3.3.2 Visas

Since the events of 1989, most exit visa requirements have been abolished, and visas for entry to most countries of the region have been easier to acquire,

Table 3.2 Examples of Western participation in the development of recreation and leisure services in the Soviet Union

1.	*Catering*
1a.	McDonald's opened its second restaurant in the region, in Moscow, early in 1990. With Moscow City Council having a 51 per cent share in a venture which had taken 14 years of negotiation, McDonald's established a number of precedents in its first Soviet development. Unable to find guaranteed appropriate quality produce, a $55 million processing plant was built on the outskirts of Moscow with McDonald's staff personally supervising the selection and slaughter of beef; seed potatoes were imported from the Netherlands, with Canadian agronomists supervising their planting; and city authorities reluctantly agreed only to employ temporary staff.
1b.	Baskin-Robbins, the ice cream maker owned by the UK Allied Lyons group, signed a $20 million joint-venture contract in early 1990 to build a production plant with an annual capacity of 8 million tonnes. Muscovites alone consume over 200 tonnes of ice cream daily, and Soviet producers have been unable to meet demand. Baskin-Robbins will initially produce ten different flavours.
1c.	The Finnish company Lihapolar, in a joint venture with the Leningrad authorities, has developed, since 1989, four hamburger kiosks in the city, marketed as Polar Fast Food.
1d.	Pizza Hut, part of the PepsiCo group (which first penetrated the Soviet soft drinks market in 1974), opened its first two Soviet restaurants, built by a UK construction firm, in Moscow during 1990.
2.	*Cinemas* Time Warner and Sovexportfilm agreed in March 1990 to develop two multi-screen cinemas, involving a Western investment of $28 million. In Moscow, a ten-screen cinema seating 4,000 people would be complemented with a nine-screen development seating 3,400 for Leningrad. The Soviet Union claims the world's highest per-capita film attendance. A significant upward readjustment to the existing 24-kopek admission charge would be necessary for these two developments.
3.	*Theme parks* In November 1989 a Soviet delegation was in negotiation with the International Association of Amusement Parks to help provide modern amusement machinery and introduce new ideas into the country's parks. During the Khrushchev era all parks were forced to take down their fences and admit everyone free of charge. As a consequence of underfunding there had been a serious deterioration in Soviet amusement parks' capital equipment. In 1988 they were visited by 1.5 billion people.
4.	*Credit cards* In June 1989 American Express signed its first agreement within the region with the Soviet Bank for Foreign Economic Affairs to make the Amex card available to selected Soviet clients. The range of Western credit cards accepted in the region has been gradually growing.
5.	*Advertising* Since January 1990 the UK advertising poster company Arthur Maiden has been providing poster sites in and around Moscow as part of a 14-year contract with the city authorities. The advertisement hoardings are constructed in Britain and shipped to Leningrad for onward transport. Initially, the poster sites run from Moscow's international airports to the city centre and are essentially aimed at tourists
6.	*Consultancy services* During May 1990 a two-day conference—'Leisure construction and property development in the USSR'—organised by Worldwide Information and the USSR Association of Joint Ventures was held in Moscow.

Sources: Various issues of *Business Eastern Europe*, *EuroBusiness*, *Leisure News*, *Leisure Opportunities*

although, reflecting new market orientations, their cost has often steeply risen as demand has escalated. Several Western authorities have mutually abolished entry visas for the region.

3.3.3 Border-crossing points

As the Single European Market enmeshes Western Europe, so the former Soviet bloc countries of Central Europe, aspiring to EC membership, are modernising their border-crossing facilities to prepare themselves for the indirect impacts of 1992, for future EC accession and, in the shorter term, to integrate local border economies and to ease the movement of both goods and tourist traffic. In early 1990, for example, the task of reorganising Hungary's border-guard service was initiated: 22,000 soldiers were to be replaced by 5,000 professional border guards within five years. A computerisation of border checks was being introduced to all 723 crossing points, for completion in 1992 in readiness for handling the coded EC passport; Hungarian passports would join the system within a few years. The Czechoslovak director of foreign tourism reckoned that computerisation being introduced into that country's border-crossing points would enable arrivals to be processed in less than four minutes each: arguably a delay still far too long by Western standards.

3.3.4 Spatial constraints

Constraints on tourists' movements have operated at three levels:

1. International: through visa and related pre-entry controls.
2. National: through the explicit closure of tracts of a country's territory to foreigners.
3. Local: through verbal or other more explicit indications, precluding movement in areas of economic, political, administrative, military or ethnic sensitivity.

Those at the second and third levels could be reinforced by prescribed accommodation, transport and an omnipresence of official guides, a system which only now persists in Albania, although large tracts of the Soviet Union are still ostensibly closed to foreign tourists. Generally, internal spatial constraints have been swept away, although infrastructural shortcomings in accommodation and transport may still, unwittingly, inhibit tourists' spatial mobility.

3.4 Fiscal constraints

3.4.1 The currency convertibility problem

Until recently, all currencies of the region were inconvertible ('soft'). Theoretically they could not be taken out of, or into, their country of origin, and they were worthless elsewhere. Initially this was to protect these countries' socialist economies, whose structure and function were established differently from capitalist economies and to preclude outside subversive currency speculation. While this situation later highlighted tourism's role as an important hard-currency income earner, it also brought numerous complications in its wake.

In the past, unrealistic exchange rates increased costs and provided a temptation for tourists to deal on the illegal currency black markets. Minimum currency requirements also placed a cost burden on tourists and could be counter-productive by simply turning tourists away. Along with the other two insidious by-products of the currency problem—hard-currency shops and black marketeering—they are now being eliminated through the weight of market forces rather than by administrative instrument. High inflation, resulting from economic restructuring, notably in Yugoslavia up to the end of 1989, and in Poland, have added short-term fiscal complications for tourism processes.

3.4.1.1 Hard-currency shops

In certain state-run establishments, often located in foreign tourist hotels, 'luxury' goods, normally inaccesible to the general public, could be purchased for convertible currency. These were found in all 'socialist' countries. Although criticised for 'ideological subversion: emphasising the desirability of western goods and fostering a petit-bourgeois fetishism' (Turnock 1989a, p. 262), these shops would be patronised not only by foreigners but also by favoured party and government members. Their inherent iniquity in societies supposedly striving for equality of access is being reduced if not entirely removed through increasing degrees of convertibility of the region's currencies, more liberal import regulations and the rise of privately run (competitive) retail outlets.

3.4.1.2 Black markets

As numbers of Western tourists began to grow, compulsory exchange schemes were introduced to counteract the currency black market and to channel hard-currency flows into official coffers. For many tourists, most quality goods suitable for purchase as gifts were available only in hard-currency shops: local currencies were seen to be only good for over-indulging in local beverages and stocking up with inexorable volumes of the works of Marx and Lenin. Yet the currency black market represented the merest tip of an enormous second economy iceberg which underpinned, or at least flourished below, the surface veneer of state socialism. Certainly, one function of the currency black market was to permit the local purchase of luxury goods in hard-currency shops, but more especially it was to provide scarce exchange for those with exist visas to the West.

3.4.1.3 Towards convertibility

As part of a transitional process to bring convertibility to all the region's currencies, a number of countries have sought devaluation as a means of reducing the impact of inflation and undermining the black market. Certainly in response to the first of these factors, and to redress the balance in the country's somewhat distorted economy, a package of measures was introduced into Yugoslavia at the beginning of 1990 which included rendering the dinar convertible. At the same time, the Polish złoty became partially convertible, roughly adopting the domestic black market rate.

The twin processes of increasing liberalisation and movement towards currency convertibility have seen in Eastern Europe and the Soviet Union a growing recognition of the role and stability of the Deutschmark (DM), with a growing number of countries pegging their exchange requirements to DM equivalence. Inconvertibility and its hindrances—not least to the outbound travel aspirations of the citizens of the countries concerned—will remain as long as the region's economies remain inefficient and uncompetitive on world markets.

3.5 Environmental image: the inherited stigma

3.5.1 Sources of environmental pressures

The future growth of tourism could easily be compromised by the substantial environmental degradation to which the region has been subject. The media image of a degraded region has generated negative perceptions which could constrain tourism generation once the post-revolution euphoria has passed. The region's environmental inheritance has been brought about by a number of interrelated factors.

3.5.1.1 The nature of socialist industrialisation

The very nature of socialist economic development, particularly during the Stalinist period, with its emphasis upon rapid economic growth, heavy industry and maximum use of indigenous resources, witnessed massive environmental degradation with high levels of gaseous and solid emissions, particularly in the more developed northern countries, exacerbated by the ubiquitous use of low-grade brown coal to generate electricity (Dienes 1974a, 1974b; Fullenbach 1981; Kramer 1983; Oldberg 1983; Singleton 1987).

3.5.1.2 Bureaucratic inertia

Although environmental legislation dates back to the earliest years of the socialist regimes (and before in many cases), it was largely ineffective. Centrally drafted economic plans would address problems of pollution, but an improvement in environmental conditions did not by itself constitute a plan target. Governments appeared ambivalent in wishing to control excessive degradation, lacking the will to allocate resources to pollution control which might inhibit economic growth or threaten employment levels.

Although severe penalties could normally be imposed on offending enterprises, they usually fell short of curtailing production, and cynical management appeared to be content to pay fines rather than install costly and disruptive anti-pollution apparatus which might jeopardise attaining plan targets. In this way, central government could be seen to be subsidising local authorities by providing continuous pollution fine payments, with the latter becoming economically dependent upon them, and therefore having a vested interest, like the plant managers, in the maintenance of local pollution. Yugoslavia's decentralised system has tended to complicate the central government–local government–enterprise relationship, but the environmental consequences have been much the same (Singleton 1985).

3.5.1.3 Dogma

Atmospheric pollution, brought to Eastern Europe by prevailing winds from the West (Rosencranz 1980; Karrasch 1983), was often cited by the now discredited leaderships to reinforce the old dogma that environmental degradation was a result of capitalist exploitation, and that if environmental problems existed in a socialist society, they must, by definition, have originated in a capitalist one. This attitude merely justified and reinforced bureaucratic inertia.

3.5.1.4 Dependence on 'scientific solutions'

Socialism allied to science was once viewed as a panacea for solving all society's ills. In the case of environmental degradation, appliance of science rather than a socio-economic restructuring of priorities was exemplified by the Prague conference of 1971 which produced a CMEA agreement on scientific and technical cooperation for environmental protection, covering such matters as the rational use of natural resources and the perfection of waste-free technologies. Coordinating centres were set up in Bratislava, Dresden and other cities to little effect. The reliance on nuclear power as a 'scientific solution' to energy problems is perhaps the most outstanding example of this approach.

3.5.1.5 'Modernisation'

Domestic, industrial and district heating systems and motor vehicles have added emissions of carbon monoxide and nitrogen oxides to the already heady atmospheric brew. Although there are as yet fewer vehicles than in Western Europe, there has been only limited interest in fitting anti-pollution devices and many vehicles have been old and poorly maintained. The cessation of two-stroke motor-vehicle engine production and West–East technology transfers will ameliorate individual pollution levels, but the likely rapid increase in higher absolute levels of motor vehicle use will largely cancel out any improvements and will add to the problem of inadequate parking and garaging facilities which already results in the cluttering up of streets and recreational open spaces and increases congestion.

3.5.2 Implications for tourism development

3.5.2.1 Coasts and water bodies

Both the Adriatic and Baltic seas are seriously polluted from the discharge of untreated sewage and of waste dumping from the mainland, harbours and coastal tourist resorts themselves. Regional sewage treatment plants are being developed along the coast, and improvements are also being made along the Vistula valley, but some Baltic beaches—declared part of an 'ecological catastrophe'—will remain closed for some time. On the Black Sea Bulgaria has restricted the growth of industries with pollution hazards throughout a 30-kilometre broad coastal belt, giving priority to service industries. The full onshore environmental impact of offshore hydrocarbon exploration and development is yet to be assessed, however.

3.5.2.2 Urban centres

High atmospheric pollution levels extending from the industrial axis of southern East Germany–Czechoslovakia–south-east Poland encompass major centres of high tourist interest and potential such as Prague and Kraków (Gilewska 1964; Chojnicki 1972; Zwozdziak and Zwozdziak 1985). Deposition figures in excess of 400 tonnes per square kilometre have been reported from Bratislava and Prague (Carter 1985b). Even away from the main industrial areas, atmospheric pollution has attained high levels locally. Research has identified such levels in Hungary's hill zone, in Budapest and in other Hungarian tourist centres (Probald 1974; Katona 1979), in Sofia and the Bulgarian tourist towns of Burgas and Kurdzhali (Tichkov 1974), as well as in a number of tourist centres in Romania and Yugoslavia. Impacts on human health have been substantial: high rates of heart disease, lung cancer and respiratory ailments are common, with localised incidence of malignant tumours such as open cancer of the skin and eyes.

3.5.2.3 The built environment

Historic buildings in some of the most prized urban centres such as Prague, Kraków, Budapest and Dubrovnik have been ravaged by atmospheric pollution from industrial, domestic and traffic sources, often resulting in restoration processes being prolonged and made more costly. An obvious constraint for the tourist is that such buildings may be shrouded in scaffolding and other reconstruction clutter for much longer periods than would be preferred by the local administrative and tourist authorities.

3.5.2.4 Uplands and woodlands

Acid rain damage has been apparent in forests along the whole border region between Czechoslovakia, East Germany and Poland since at least the early 1960s; during the 1970s sulphur dioxide deposits reached 37 tonnes per square kilometre in a number of areas. There has also been concern about the forests on the border of Moravia and Slovakia and those along Czechoslovakia's frontier with West Germany. Other conflicts can be seen in Bulgaria's Pirin Mountains, where a national park is host to the winter sports resort of Bansko, opened in 1981.

3.5.2.5 Water pollution

Excessive pollution, particularly in the north of the region (Zajbert 1975; Turnock 1979, 1982), has meant that pure water transfer systems have had to be developed over increasingly longer distances. At the same time the reduction in forest cover has encouraged rapid run-off and consequently a greater need for artificial water storage to guarantee supplies.

3.5.3 Requirements

While economic restructuring is closing some heavily polluting industrial plant, and considerable Western funding is beginning to assist pollution control, much needs to be done:

1. Substantial investment to be put into separation plants and pollution control equipment.
2. Greater emphasis to be placed on research and monitoring.
3. International environmental action to cope with trans-boundary atmospheric and water-borne pollution, both within the region and from without.
4. The wider and more effective installation of water purification equipment (Turnock 1989b).
5. A substantial change in both bureaucratic and public attitudes.

3.5.4 Responses

1. Pressures during the earlier Solidarność era in Poland (1980–1), through the efforts of its offshoot, the Polish Ecology Club of Kraków, were strong enough to bring about the closure of a limited number of heavily polluting industrial plants. The imposition of martial law in 1981 cut short this process, but it demonstrated what could be done, and this influenced ecological perceptions among Poles and other East Europeans. In Czechoslovakia, the former GDR, Hungary and later Bulgaria, public disquiet over the environment, and green movements—initially clandestine—began to emerge. By the time of the 1989 'revolutions' a number of these movements—such as Bulgaria's EcoGlasnost and Hungary's Danube Circle—were in the forefront of demands for political and economic change (Hall 1989a, 1989b).
2. National environmental programmes were drawn up by a number of countries during the 1980s. Hungary's National Environmental Protection Concept of 1980 was one of the earliest (Probald 1984).
3. Urban green belts and wedges, providing recreational open space and acting as 'lungs' have been incorporated into the plans of such tourist centres as Budapest, Prague and Bratislava, and urban parks have been established on the edges of such Bulgarian cities, as at Stara Zagora.
4. Nature reserves and national parks often date back to the inter-war years, although subsequent industrialisation programmes both shifted priorities away from their enhancement and considerably increased the deleterious effects of atmospheric pollution. The extent of protected areas today varies substantially between countries (Table 3.3), ranging from Romania's 922 square kilometres or 0.4 per cent of the country's total land area to Poland's more then 36,000 square kilometres (11.5 per cent) and the former GDR's 19.1 per cent of total area (20,680 square kilometres). While the extent of these areas is comparable to that of Western countries, and is often greater, stronger protection mechanisms and legal enforcement procedures are required.
5. Scheduled buildings and monuments' legislation generally dates back to the 1950s and 1960s, but it has usually been necessary to follow this up

Table 3.3 Eastern Europe and the Soviet Union: environmentally protected areas

Country	National parks*		Total protected areas	
	Area (sq. km.)	% of total land area	Area (sq. km.)	% of total land area
Albania	nd		nd	
Bulgaria	704	0.6	1,565	1.4
Czechoslovakia	1,727	1.3	19,040	14.9
Former GDR	—	—	20,680	19.1
Hungary	1,418	1.5	5,360	5.1
Poland	1,258	0.4	36,392	11.5
Romania	210	0.1	922	0.4
Soviet Union	5,916	0.03	175,000	0.8
France	10,800	2.0	51,501	9.5
(FR) Germany	340	0.1	18,976	7.6
Spain	1,560	0.3	16,500	3.3
UK	—	—	21,155	5.6

Sources: Cerovsky (1988); Ertz (1979); Foster *et al.* (1984); IUCN (1986, 1987); Paxton (1988)

* as defined by the International Union for the Conservation of Nature (IUCN)

nd no data

with more effective measures like the 1973 Czechoslovak law for the protection of historical objects. This, and wider urban area conservation legislation, requires further strengthening.

3.5.5 Conclusions

Environmental degradation has provided a further psychological and practical obstacle to the development of the region's tourism industry. The conservation task is enormous: for example the total number of scheduled monuments in the region is low by European standards and restoration has proceeded slowly due to shortcomings in funding and political will. The new commercial pressures of tourism may now see renewed vigour in this direction, although paradoxically tourism will also place increasing pressures on the region's natural and man-made environmental attractions.

3.6 The tourism infrastructure

3.6.1 Previous infrastructural constraints

The quality of the region's tourist services has often been low and very variable by accepted Western standards: accommodation, amenities, transport and catering have suffered from decades of neglect in which the economic and ideological cost of upgrading infrastructure to meet the needs of foreigners was considered too high. This has been reinforced by:

3.6.3 Accommodation structure

Hotel-building programmes providing for a reasonable standard of comfort were stimulated by state dominance of all forms of tourist accommodation. Such hotels often acted to enforce segregation between tourists and the local population, a situation reinforced by the exclusivity of highly structured guided tours. In Albania this approach was taken to its extreme by prescribing state hotels for all foreign tourists. In most other societies, however, the common sharing of state, local authority or cooperative-run camp sites permitted an interaction between not only foreigners and native tourists, but also between foreign tourists themselves from the different halves of Europe.

Table 3.6 Eastern Europe and the Soviet Union: numbers of rooms and bed-places in hotels and similar establishments

	1983		1988		1983–8 increase in
Countries	Rooms	Bed-places	Rooms	Bed-places	bed-places (%)
Albania	nd	nd	nd	nd	nd
Bulgaria*	52,813	105,625	53,610‡	111,293	5.4
Czechoslovakia	46,882	95,226	67,815	195,902	105.7
Former GDR	33,827	67,774	nd	216,743	(219.8)
Hungary†	17,824	34,729	32,569	86,807	150.0
Poland	42,992	91,042	nd	576,700	(533.4)
Romania	81,699	164,764	86,510	175,300	6.4
Soviet Union	nd	nd	nd	64,000§	nd
Yugoslavia	137,746	302,573	156,077	358,097	18.4

Source: WTO *Yearbook* (1985, 1990)

* Hotels and motels
† Hotels only
‡ 1985 figure
§ 1986 figure
nd no data

A survey undertaken in the late 1970s revealed that while no transnational hotel groups then operated within socialist countries, of the world's 100 largest hotel chains, 11, with a total of 790 hotels, emanated from those countries. All were state-owned and operating in conjunction with the national tourist agency (Table 3.5).

The role of private accommodation has varied quite considerably in supporting the tourist infrastructure. In Hungary it has become a key element in provision, influenced by the high level of motorised individual tourism to the country from Western Europe, the dispersed nature of attractions around Balaton and along the Danube Bend and not least the country's liberal approach and mobile domestic market. A recent emphasis on the top end of the tourism accommodation market with the building of several four- and five-star hotels with tariffs out of the reach of large numbers of tourists has underlined the necessary role of local provision. Despite the country's substantial housing problems, the renting out of private dwellings for tourist use is extensive: the country's total tourist bedstock is reckoned at about 300,000 of which less than 90,000 was found in registered hotels in 1988 (see Table 3.6). By contrast, private accommodation, as yet, plays no role whatsoever in Albanian tourism, while in Romania a ban was placed on such activity in the 1970s. The different position of Yugoslavia has permitted returning migrant workers to invest in tourism by building large houses with bedrooms which can be rented to tourists. Additional entrepreneurial activities of such groups have included setting up restaurants and taxi services or running a boat on excursions to offshore islands. The tax burden imposed on private establishments by the region's governments—Yugoslavia being no exception—has often been extremely high.

Now most countries of the region are permitting the opening up of the private sector in accommodation and other forms of tourist provision. Poles can take paying guests into their homes, and in Bulgaria privately owned restaurants and hotels are beginning to fill gaps in service provision. Inevitably, such development means a diversion of hard currency away from state coffers, and as long as the old constraints of currency inconvertibility and shortage of consumer goods and services remain, private tourism income will continue to be channelled into, and to fuel, the second economy. Certainly the structural interreliance between the country's booming second economy (Galasi and György, 1985) and international tourist flows has been a significant development feature in Hungary. Inevitably, the extent to which the second economy in tourist services is under-reported contributes towards the relatively poor level of return which the Hungarian national exchequer feels it receives from the country's extensive exposure to international tourism (Böröcz 1990, p. 22).

Table 3.7 Eastern Europe and the Soviet Union: bed-places ratios

Registered bed-places per thousand host population			
Countries	1988	Countries	1988
Albania	nd	Austria	86.0
Bulgaria	12.4	(FR) Germany	18.5
Czechoslovakia	12.5	Greece	39.6
Former GDR	13.1	Italy	29.1
Hungary†	8.2	Spain	27.9
Poland	15.2	Switzerland	41.9
Romania	7.6	UK	14.8
Soviet Union	0.2*		
Yugoslavia	15.2		

Source: Calculations from WTO *Yearbook* (1990)

* 1985 figure

† hotels only

nd no data

Turning to the published data, growth of accommodation provision took place between 1983 and 1988 in all the countries for which comparative data are available (Table 3.6), although discontinuities in the data series for the former GDR and Poland reduce their comparative value. Growth rates varied substantially, from 5–7 per cent for Bulgaria and Romania, revealing stagnation, to the 105.7 per cent for Czechoslovakia and 150 per cent for Hungary. The latter figure, however, is restricted to the hotel sector and is far from a fair reflection of the country's accommodation position. Occupancy rates showed a slight tendency to decrease after 1985 with this expansion, in a range between 50 and 65 per cent by 1987 (for Czechoslovakia, Bulgaria, the Soviet Union and Hungary (rooms only) in ascending order), but with a lower figure for Yugoslavia (43.9 per cent in 1987) emphasising the heightened seasonal nature of tourism in that country particularly along the Adriatic coast (Buckley and Witt 1990, p. 13). Indeed, Yugoslavia's monthly occupation rates for 1988 ranged from a high of 81.1 per cent in August to a December low of 19.3 per cent, representing a lowest:highest ratio of 1:3.19, compared to the Hungarian (1987) figure of 1:2.55 and that for Bulgaria of 1:2.17 (1987) (WTO *Yearbook* 1990). Yugoslavia's high degree of seasonality not only causes large fluctuations in earnings from tourism but also entails substantial social costs in terms of the under-utilisation of productive capacity and local unemployment (UNTC 1982, p. 3).

A more illuminating set of comparative values is perhaps that presenting available bed-places as a ratio of the host population (Table 3.7). These figures reveal both the relatively low level of provision compared to Western Europe—around half the level of Italy and Spain, a third of that of Greece and Switzerland and less than a fifth of the Austrian level—and also the variability within the region, ranging from the reasonably well-provisioned Yugoslavia and Poland (15.2), the moderately-positioned Romania (7.6) and extremely low Soviet (0.2) values. Unfortunately, again the Hungarian data ignore the important private-sector guest house and room rental categories.

Nevertheless, the role of small-scale private accommodation provision, in tandem with other economic reform measures, must be given encouragement to provide services within the largely under-provisioned medium-price range and to inject a greater element of flexibility into the structure of the region's tourist accommodation stock. In 1989 it was estimated that Warsaw was short by 2,000–3,000 beds each night during summer and autumn; Prague had 6,000 beds when 15,000–20,000 were said to be needed for foreign tourists alone, while Budapest was experiencing strain particularly through the rapid growth of business tourism.

3.6.4 Joint ventures in accommodation development

Scope for foreign investment in hotel building and development has seen:

1. The employment of loan capital as a source of constructing tourist facilities such as the $300 million loan agreement between Hungary and Austria for Austrian companies to build hotels in Hungary.
2. Franchise agreements, whereby hotels, restaurants and other service outlets are run by Western chains. In hotel management, for example, the Hyatt, Ramada, Hilton, Penta, Novotel, Forum, Sheraton and Holiday Inn international groups are all represented in the region.

3. The introduction of foreign majority holdings in joint-venture developments such as the development of the Hyatt Regency hotel in Belgrade, completed in 1989, Yugoslavia's first joint venture permitting such a majority foreign holding.

Availability of appropriately trained staff has often proven problematical, although visas for personnel to go to the West for training have now become far easier to acquire (for example, see Ronkainen 1983), and Western staff training and recruiting agencies have been establishing themselves in the region. The import of management training and marketing skills are crucial elements of joint-venture packages, permitting Western partners to retrain workers whose skills have been made obsolete by restructuring.

One of the more striking multi-purpose developments has involved a joint venture between the American Marriott hotel chain, the Austrian construction company Ilban and LOT Polish Air Lines. This saw the opening in October 1989 of a complex which included LOT's new Warsaw air terminal and Marriott's first hotel in Eastern Europe, a 42-storey, five-star enclave, housing a wide range of restaurants and bars, night club and casino, recreation centre with indoor swimming pool, saunas and health club.

Table 3.8 Eastern Europe and the Soviet Union: source countries of hotel development partnerships

Country	Western partner(s)											
	Aus.	Swi.	(FR)G	Den.	Fra.	UK	Jap.	S.Kor.	Swe.	Fin.	USA	It.
Albania												
Bulgaria	★		★		★	★					★	
Czechoslovakia	★				★		★				★	
Former GDR			★				★		★			
Hungary	★	★	★	★	★		★	★	★	★	★	
Poland	★				★	★			★		★	
Romania											★	
Soviet Union	★	★			★		★			★	★	★
Yugoslavia					★	★					★	

Sources: Various issues of *BBC Summaries of World Broadcasts (Eastern Europe)*, *Business Eastern Europe*, *EuroBusiness*

Further notable planned developments include a western German hotel group's intention to construct and manage up to 50 hotels in eastern Germany and an American company's $4–5 million investment in the construction of 20 inn-type hotels in Romania. These developments emphasise the fact that while many joint-venture plans are going forward for hotel building in the region's capital cities, some elements of internal spatial diffusion are taking place. In the Soviet Union, for example, an Austrian group signed a contract in 1989 to construct a 65-house 'Austrian village' in Leninakhan, Armenia, as a winter sports centre, while a French group is helping to develop a four-star hotel in the ancient Uzbeck city of Khiva.

Table 3.8 indicates the span of countries involved in various joint hotel development schemes in the region, although financial, administrative and political constraints on such trends persist:

1. In the former GDR, the state agency overseeing privatisation (Treuhandanstalt) appeared to be favouring fragmentation of enterprise groups, buy-outs and indigenous purchases, intervening to block some West German take-overs, such as a proposed purchase of the GDR's Interhotel group, before it could be broken down into smaller units.
2. Whereas up to early 1990 investors in the Soviet Union were able to raise funds secured on the assets involved in a joint venture, because of the parlous state of the Soviet economy, financial institutions began requiring security from investors, thereby deterring Western companies from forming cooperative ventures. Trusthouse Forte, for example, abandoned plans to develop the Hotel Bucharest in Moscow reportedly because of difficulties in financing the investment.
3. Public debate in Hungary over the fear that state property was being sold off at unrealistically low prices set the context for the country's Supreme Court to declare null and void the establishment of the public limited company, Hungaria Hotels, in which a Swedish consortium was to have had a 50 per cent holding; it ruled that the company should continue to operate wholly as a state-owned enterprise.
4. Debate over the pace and nature of privatisation within Romania's new administration saw the country's newly appointed minister of tourism resigning in February 1990. He particularly opposed the prime minister's proposal to hand over 21 hotels and restaurants owned by the tourism ministry to army management.

3.6.4.1 Accommodation projections

In 1989, the Polish, Czech and Hungarian governments had projected tourism growth over the next five years at around 20 per cent annually. To cope with the increase, Czechoslovakia had planned to double to 12,000 the hotel rooms available in Prague; in Warsaw eight new hotels were in the planning or construction phase. But by the middle of 1990 such plans were already falling far short of projected requirements if the post-revolution growth in tourism to the region was to continue at existing rates (Borrell 1989). Thirty new hotels are being built throughout the Soviet Union, including five in Moscow, to provide 25,000 beds by the end of the century, but this will probably prove to be inadequate. Despite the increasing role of transnational companies and stimulation of small-scale private initiative, the region will continue to experience tourist accommodation shortfalls for the foreseeable future, particularly in the major centres.

3.6.5 Travel agency interests

Rapidly breaking down the monopolistic position of the old state-sponsored travel agencies, a growing number of joint ventures in the field have seen increasing East–West partnerships in travel and tour organisation. Prolific developments took place between the former GDR and the Federal Republic, and will, of course, continue within the unified domestic framework. An early notable development was the partnership between Interflug and Touristik Union International which opened a travel agency in the then GDR early in 1990 to offer travel packages to Spain, Turkey, Tunisia and Singapore. Ibusz, with the Italian Aviatour company, was also quick to open a joint travel agency—Primatours—for holidays from Hungary to Asia. Clearly a major function of such partnerships has been to bring much needed expertise of outbound tourism operations to destinations simply not financially or ideologically within the previous experience of the region's travel companies. Simultaneously, this process is opening up whole new tourism horizons for the region's citizens, or at least those who can afford the prices.

Table 3.9 Eastern Europe and the Soviet Union with selected Western destinations: visitor arrivals by mode of transport, 1988

	Visitor arrivals by mode of transport, 1988 (%)			
Countries	Air	Rail	Road	Sea/river
Albania	nd	nd	nd	nd
Bulgaria	12.2	7.8	79.1	0.9
Czechoslovakia	1.7	24.0	74.1	0.2
Former GDR	3.0	28.8	67.4	0.8
Hungary	3.6	20.5	75.4	0.6
Poland	nd	nd	nd	nd
Romania	5.5	36.2	55.9	2.3
Soviet Union*	95.0	4.0	0.5	0.5
Yugoslavia	5.3	4.2	88.3	2.2
Austria	0.9	5.0	94.1	—
(FR) Germany*	6.6	6.2	83.4	3.7
Greece	nd	nd	nd	nd
Italy	9.1	8.1	80.5	2.2
Spain	31.6	4.7	60.5	3.1
Turkey	50.6	1.6	30.8	17.0

Source: WTO *Yearbook* (1990)

* 1987 figures

3.6.6 Transport and communications upgrading

Both qualitative and capacity problems within the region's transport and communications systems have constrained all forms of tourism, as they have done in many aspects of the economic life of these countries. Table 3.9 indicates that in 1988 road transport was the predominant mode for tourist arrivals in the region, although figures for Yugoslavia and Bulgaria are distorted by high levels of transit traffic, not least of Turkish guest workers travelling to and from West Germany. Romania had a high proportion of arrivals by rail, reflecting its dependence on the rest of Eastern Europe, and, if the figures are to be believed, the overwhelming majority of visitors to the Soviet Union arrived by air, reflecting the substantial distances needed to be covered. All-inclusive tours from Western Europe accounted for many of the air arrivals in Yugoslavia, Bulgaria and Romania, although the overall proportion of arrivals by air was far lower than for Spain and Turkey, the major Western package holidays stereotypes. Clearly substantial potential exists here, if the region's air transport infrastructure can be sufficiently upgraded.

3.6.7 Air transport

In many respects air transport is the key link for future tourism development. CSA (Czechoslovakia), LOT (Poland), MALEV (Hungary) and Interflug (former GDR) have been seen as likely attractive investments for American or Far East carriers looking for a partner to shuttle passengers around Europe, although the four could usefully form an internationally competitive alliance. But all have been flying outdated Soviet aircraft and need substantial investment and innovation. At the same time, improved customer services and staff-training programmes are required, and new routes are essential to extend operations in the region for both tourism and business opportunities. Airports and other ground infrastructures need to be upgraded.

3.6.7.1 An upgrading of aircraft fleets

Even before 1989 a number of Eastern European national airlines were turning to Western aircraft (Table 3.10) and away from the previously subsidised and ageing Soviet makes to improve performance and fuel efficiency and reduce ground staff requirements. Guinness Peat Aviation (GPA)—the Irish organisation which is leasing six Boeing 737s to MALEV—estimate that by the end of the decade some $12–18 billion will need to be spent on upgrading the region's air fleets. Poland's LOT, for example, wants to replace completely its fleet of Soviet-made aircraft by 1997. The recent spate of sales and leasings follows a relaxation in CoCom constraints on high-technology exports to the hitherto Soviet bloc and will intensify competition between European and American planemakers. Even so, given that Soviet engine technology is less advanced than that of the West, sales of Boeings and Airbuses to these fleets have included export controls to prevent engine technology being transferred—contractual obligations require the engines and some of the avionics of these craft to be serviced in the West.

3.6.7.2 Joint ventures in catering, marketing, ticketing and the development of new airlines

The establishment of these has entailed the transfer of computer technology to improve reservations, timetabling and control activities (Table 3.11).

Table 3.10 Eastern Europe and the Soviet Union: developments among the region's airlines

Country	Airline	No. of aircraft	Annual passengers (millions)	Fleet upgrading	Examples of new routes
Albania	—				
Bulgaria	Balkan	48	2.2	—	Sofia – Abu Dhabi – Colombo – Bangkok
Czechoslovakia	CSA	32	1.2	2 218-seat Airbus A310-300s for 1990/1	Prague – Tel Aviv – Mexico City – Hamburg Bratislava – Malta
Former GDR	Interflug	32	1.65	3 Airbus A310-300s, 1989+, the first for a CMEA member country	Dresden – Paris – Hamburg – Cologne
Hungary	Malev	22	1.2	3 737-200s leased from 1988; 3 737-300s from 1991	Budapest – New York
Poland	LOT	29	2.3	3 767s for 1993; 5 more for 1994–6	Warsaw – Sharjah Kraków – Moscow Gdańsk – Moscow
Romania	Tarom	32	nd	3 265-seat Airbus A310-300s for 1992	
Soviet Union	Aeroflot	1,900	132	5 190-seat Airbus A310-300s for 1991/2	Moscow – Tel Aviv – Singapore – Sydney
Yugoslavia	JAT	32	nd	3 MD-11s for 1991/2	Belgrade – Cleveland – Detroit – Pittsburgh

Sources: Various issues of: *BBC Summaries of World Broadcasts (Eastern Europe)*, *Business Eastern Europe*, *EuroBusiness*, *The Economist*

3.6.7.3 New air routes

These are being developed at both international and domestic levels. For example, in 1990, as part of a significant expansion programme by Western airlines following aviation agreements with the region's governments, Alitalia introduced flights to Budapest, Prague and Berlin from Milan and Rome. Some of the region's carriers' share of new routes is shown in Table 3.10. In

Table 3.11 Eastern Europe and the Soviet Union: examples of East–West cooperation in air transport

Lufthansa – Interflug	Joint companies for catering and tourist charter flights (Intercondor), computer software development and a flight simulation centre in Berlin for joint training programmes.
Aeroflot	Joint venture in Istanbul to set up a new airline, Greenair. Cooperation agreement with the Australian travel company Jetset Tours. US Huntsman Chemical Corporation to produce cups and glasses in their own Moscow plant for Aeroflot. Up to $20 million could be invested 1990–5, and several hundred employed to produce a substantial part of Aeroflot in-flight plastics. Air broker and charter flight company Air London, selling Aeroflot's charter seats in the UK. Pan Am exchange of staff for in-service training.
Hungarian Air Service – Ibusz – Austrian Viennair Polsterer Jets	In March 1990 the Danube Air company was formed through a joint venture to develop domestic and international service. This follows a new impetus to re-establish Hungarian domestic flights—largely for tourism purposes—which have not existed since withdrawal in 1969. A weekly service between Budapest and Pecs was inaugurated in August 1990.
Czechoslovak Avov – Air state enterprise and Crossair of Switzerland	In July 1990 the Tatra Air Company was established jointly to link Bratislava with Europe's most important centres: from March 1991 an initial service has operated from Bratislava to Zurich and Munich using 36-seat Saab-340 aircraft. This represents the first regional airline in Eastern Europe and the first rival for Czechoslovak Airlines.
JAT	A joint company was established with the Amadeus global air-ticket reservation system (which will also aid the promotion of the Yugoslav tourist industry abroad).
USSR – USA Civil Aviation Authorities	An airspace agreement was expected to triple traffic between the two countries and to begin direct scheduled flights to such Soviet regional capitals as Riga, Tbilisi and Kiev from the USA.

Sources: Various issues of *BBC Summaries of World Broadcasts (Eastern Europe)*, *Business Eastern Europe*, *EuroBusiness*, *Leisure Opportunities*

addition, the frequencies of established flights have been increased, such as those on JAT's services from Belgrade to New York, Chicago and Los Angeles.

3.6.7.4 Airport upgrading and development

The expansion and improvement of facilities at major airports is being undertaken (Table 3.12), often with Western assistance, to cope with new and likely future demands. The bringing into civil air use of secondary and tertiary level airports and landing strips previously operated by the military emphasises the need to make provincial centres accessible to tourists and business travellers. Four Hungarian provincial airfields were reopened in 1989 for foreign tourist charter flights. This followed Hungary's National Council for Tourism pointing to the growing demand for charter tourist flights, domestic air services, air

Table 3.12 Eastern Europe and the Soviet Union: upgrading of airport infrastructures

Airport expansions and upgradings	
Berlin	Interflug and Lufthansa to build a new airport, construction commencing 1995, probably in the south of the city. Current annual level of passengers through Tegel (W) and Schönefeld (E) is about 12 million: estimates for 2005 suggest 20–30 million.
Budapest	Helicopter terminal to be built. Ferihégy international airport completed in 1988 with Austrian assistance.
Prague	A new terminal is a high priority: by mid-1990 the number of passengers passing through the airport had almost doubled since the 'velvet revolution' of November 1989.
Sofia	Lufthansa and a consortium of west German companies in a joint venture with Balkan Air to build a new airport for a passenger capacity of 5 million by 2010 with expansion to 10 million and above.
Warsaw	May 1990 contract worth DM246m with west German company Hochtief for construction of a new international passenger terminal at Okęcie, a freight depot and a modern catering base for Polish Airlines, to be completed Spring 1992.
Airfields opened to civil use	
Czechoslovakia	Turany airfield in southern Moravia demilitarised.
Hungary	Tokol, near the Danube, 20 km. from Budapest, transferred from military use. Szombathely, a former 'sports' airfield. Balatonkiliti-Siofok, Pécs, Nyiregyhaza, Bekescsaba airfields upgraded and reopened for 1989 tourist season, essentially for foreign tourist charter flights, In 1990 a regular service between Pécs and Budapest introduced.
Poland	Provincial airports seen as having a new future as an air bridge between Scandinavia and southern Europe, providing an opportunity to relieve substantial air traffic congestion over Western Europe.

Source: Various issues of *BBC Summaries of World Broadcasts (Eastern Europe)*, *Business Eastern Europe*

taxis and recreational air services, including sports flying. Eight areas of the country were designated for airport development.

3.6.7.5 Negative effects

However, greater economic accountability within the operating carriers has seen some retrenchment on loss-making routes and airports with the effect of constraining some tourist activities:

1. Interflug cut back on nearly half of its international flights, encompassing most of Eastern Europe, Singapore and Algiers, while doubling inter-German movements.

2. LOT suspended the internal Warsaw–Zielona Gora route in October 1989 because of its unprofitability.
3. In 1988 traffic at Sarajevo Airport declined by 28 per cent, and in 1989 by an estimated fifteen per cent because of reduced flights and destinations by both JAT and Adria Airlines. This placed the airport in a very difficult economic position, with closure a possible option.
4. Ohrid Airport was closed for an indefinite period from November 1989 because of an unsafe runway, reflecting the lack of funds available for its adequate upkeep. Local tourist flows would be particularly adversely affected by this development.

3.6.8 Road services

A substantial amount of road transit traffic has been experienced in the region for at least the past quarter-century. This has been associated with *Gastarbeiter* movement between Western and south-Eastern Europe, and with a growing amount of intra-regional road tourism traffic. Although different problems exist in different parts of the region, the underlying road infrastructure of Eastern Europe and the Soviet Union is now desperately in need of upgrading to meet the new demands of restructured economies, not least in the area of tourism generation. Inadequate lane capacity, poor road surfaces, maintenance and signposting and inadequate roadside services such as petrol filling stations, catering and other retailing outlets all act to constrain growth.

Hungary is perhaps in a better position to cope than many countries in the region, given its level of economic development and entrepreneurial spirit. However, in July 1990, the government announced its intention of developing the country's outdated road system by putting the construction of new motorways in the hands of outside contractors under a system of concessions. Foreign entrepreneurs will build new motorways in exchange for the right to collect tolls and operate the servicing and catering facilities. The total length of the country's public roads is currently 10,000 kilometres, 70 per cent of which is managed by local authorities. Four-lane highways currently make up only 218 kilometres (two per cent) of the total. An additional 500 kilometres of motorway is immediately required to meet current traffic demands. In 30–40 years' time, an additional 1,200–1,500 kilometres will be needed. Plans for 1990 provided for the construction of just 30 kilometres. It was considered essential therefore to involve foreign capital in order to speed construction. For 1990, 12.4 billion forints ($190m) was to be made available for the state road fund, divided between 5.6 billion for new road development and 6.8 billion for maintenance. However, the government estimated that merely to make the long overdue repairs needed for the national road network would cost 160 billion forints ($2,450m), while the additional costs arising from the underdeveloped road system were estimated to be 40 billion forints ($615m) annually.

A similar mid-1990 review of the Czechoslovak federal road system saw the need to extend the existing 540-kilometre network of motorways, begun in 1967, to 1,800 kilometres by the end of the century, with particular emphasis on establishing links with neighbouring countries. Again the state has insufficient funds for such a task and is turning to foreign capital. It was expected that the first tenders would be invited for construction of the motorway link between Plzen and the west German border. The Ministry of Transport estimate for the minimum requirements needed to upgrade the country's transport infrastructure to an acceptable level was almost 136 billion koruna (over $8 billion).

In the Soviet Union, a monumental road building programme was presented to the Russian Federation government in mid-1990 by a Japanese consortium to develop a Trans-Siberian dual carriageway across Russia from Moscow to Vladivostock. This would again be a toll highway, built by a chain of concessionaires.

The IBRD arm of the World Bank has been offering loans for the construction of key sections of the projected Trans-European Highway connecting the Baltic with the Adriatic and the Middle East: for example, a 71-kilometre section from Feketic in Yugoslavia to the Hungarian border at Horgos, is due to be completed in time for the 1995 Vienna/Budapest World Exhibition. Such a spine motorway system would substantially enhance Eastern Europe's road infrastructure and encourage greater movement in and through the region.

3.6.8.1 Motor coach services

New routes are being opened both within the region and from Western Europe such as that between Prague and Vienna which was inaugurated in May 1990, taking five hours and running six times a week, twice weekly extended to Karlovy Vary. This link provides a faster connection between the two capitals than the international rail service. Both Eurolines and Coach Europe, a subsidiary of Britain's second biggest travel operator ILG (International Leisure Group), have extended regular services from the United Kingdom and Western Europe into east Germany, Hungary, Czechoslovakia and Poland. Distances and journey times from the Channel ports to Warsaw and Budapest are now seen as being comparable with those to Barcelona, with the bonus of such attractive *en route* centres as Berlin, Prague and Vienna. The reduction of border formalities is clearly a crucial element in the competitive development of such services.

3.6.9 High-speed railways

Plans eventually to connect Eastern Europe to the expanding Western European high-speed rail network will be dogged again by the enormous costs of upgrading infrastructure. The construction of a high-speed rail link from Paris to Poland via Berlin has been promulgated, but Poland would not be able to carry the financial burden, which would be about $4 billion. A credit offered by the French within the terms of a five-year cooperation agreement would meet only 20 per cent of the project's Polish costs.

3.6.10 Telecommunications

The lack of modern telecommunications systems is arguably the most significant structural deficiency of these countries' economies and of no little importance for establishing an efficient tourism industry. Western technology

Table 3.13 Eastern Europe and the Soviet Union: telecommunications availability 1990/2000

	1990		2000	
	Total phones (millions)	Per 1,000 population	Total phones (millions)	Per 1,000 population
Albania	0.016	5	0.0175	4
Bulgaria	3.0	320	7.8	770
Czechoslovakia	4.0	250	5.2	300
Former GDR	4.0	240	5.5	320
Hungary	1.8	170	2.4	220
Poland	5.0	130	7.6	180
Romania	nd	nd	nd	nd
Soviet Union	36.6	130	70.0	220
Yugoslavia	4.8	200	12.0	450

Sources: Castle (1990, p. 20), from TRC (1990)

which will allow these systems to modernise rapidly is an urgent requirement. A CoCom decision to allow the export of digital telephones to the region stimulated a speeding up of the modernisation process. But although CoCom rules have been relaxed, the United States' Commerce Department refused to allow the telecommunications group US West to build a $500m fibre-optic cable across the Soviet Union because of possible military applications. This would have enabled four times as many calls to be handled than the cables allowed under CoCom limits. Fibre-optics communications will continue to be banned.

In Eastern Europe and the Soviet Union in 1988 there were 56 million telephones, with just 15 per cent of residents having private facilities, compared to West Europe's 208 million (70 per cent), and the United States' 221 million (90 per cent). In Siberia and the Middle Asian regions of the Soviet Union, telephone density is lower than ten per thousand population. The Soviet waiting list for a telephone in 1988 was over 15 million (5.3 per cent of the total population); in Poland the figure had risen to 2.2 million (5.8 per cent) and in Hungary 550,000 (5.2 per cent).

It is estimated (TRC 1990) that Eastern Europe and the Soviet Union will spend $350 billion by the end of the decade on upgrading their telecommunications networks to a level shown in Table 3.13. By the year 2005 the demand for new and replacement telephones will reach 10 million per year. Despite an American ban on participation, a most ambitious scheme is the Japanese-European consortium sponsored $60m 'Central Streke' fibre-optic link from west to east Germany through Poland to Moscow. This could link up to an even more spectacular development in the Soviet Union, a $940m 13,000-kilometre Trans-Soviet fibre-optic link which is to act as the backbone for the regeneration of the Soviet phone system and is due to be completed in 1995. This will form part of a wider world telecommunications network, with a cable running from Japan to Denmark and spurs to Czechoslovakia and Italy.

3.6.11 *Conclusions*

Short-term strategies for increasing international tourist flows include improved marketing and promotion of the attractions of these countries as tourist destinations. Longer-term strategies depend on improvements in the tourist environment, including greater freedom of movement, elimination of currency complications and exchange problems and upgrading the quality of tourist accommodation, catering, entertainment and other amenities, ranging from the availability of petrol to good maps and photographic film (Buckley and Witt 1990, pp. 17–8; Borrell 1989). In particular, transport and communications are likely to be pivotal in connecting the region with the world's business and leisure markets. Growth in business and conference tourism will be particularly stimulated by telecommunications and air transport upgrading. The region's accommodation and catering infrastructures and tourism staff-training programmes may need to keep pace with what could become a rapidly growing phenomenon within a number of countries in the region.

4 Evolutionary pattern of tourism development in Eastern Europe and the Soviet Union

Derek R. Hall

4.1 An evolutionary framework

Several forces have been exerted on the societies of the region to produce varying developmental patterns and processes. These have reflected differences in:

1. Pre-existing levels of economic development.
2. Resource bases.
3. Cultural histories and orientations.
4. Interpretations of 'socialist development': adoption and adaption of ideology to complement or buttress national aspirations.
5. Subsequent attitudes towards, and methods of abandoning, state socialism.

Despite forty years of attempted integration, the region's economies now find themselves confronting varying sets of economic, political and social circumstances. This is no less true for tourism development, for which this chapter proposes a loose evolutionary framework within which to view the systemic characteristics of tourism taken up by these societies within their economic development programmes. While suggesting an evolutionary typology, the framework recognises the differing paths, speeds and attitudes taken towards tourism development and that the 'evolutionary' elements of development have substantially overlapped: the timing and gradients between them have varied both within and between societies.

4.1.1 *Pre-socialism*

Depending on each society's level of economic development and basic societal structure, this period is generally characterised by limited tourism from without, with outbound and to some extent domestic tourism restricted largely to the countries' economic, social and political elites.

4.1.2 *Early socialism*

From the 1920s to the 1950s in the Soviet Union, and the early post-war period in Eastern Europe: this may be termed the 'Stalinist' period in that its basic characteristics and dogmas arose from Stalin's leadership and echoed a number of the dimensions of 'Stalinist' economic policy. This was the era of rapid economic growth based upon heavy industrialisation. Service industry had a minor role, foreigners were regarded with suspicion and centralised state control characterised economic life. Under these circumstances, international tourism was severely constrained: priorities were elsewhere, with economic development on a virtual war footing. The social dimension of state socialism emphasised the well-being of the working population, and to this end enterprise and trade-union-sponsored facilities were developed for domestic, group-orientated tourism and recreation. This 'collective consumption' of tourism and recreation particularly characterised early socialism.

4.1.3 Middle socialism

From the mid-1950s, following the hiatus after Stalin's death in 1953, dogmas began to be relaxed, living standards gradually rose and the need to emphasise, if only for propagandist reasons, international socialism saw a growing development of international tourism within the socialist bloc. Paralleling the growth of international economic aid and cooperation with the CMEA, this phase tended to be characterised by the more developed societies generating most tourist outflows, although the statistics of the period are poorly documented. Yugoslavia largely by-passed this stage, since, having been expelled from the Soviet bloc in 1948, tourism exchanges with the bloc countries were initially embargoed. The Yugoslav economy, having been put in jeopardy by the expulsion, quickly looked westwards, and, from the early 1950s, developed a tourism industry geared to Western markets (Chapter 12). The other exception to this pattern, Albania, enjoyed living standards and an ideological outlook which precluded outbound tourism, although increasing numbers of East Europeans were attracted to the country until Albania's withdrawal from the Soviet bloc in 1961. The overall emphasis of this period, therefore, was the development of intra-bloc international tourism together with the consolidation and expansion of domestic tourism.

4.1.4 Later socialism

Most economies moved to an emphasis on attracting Western tourists to gain hard currency. While some countries were at least developing a Western-orientated industry during the middle-socialism period, albeit often a very limited one, the economic circumstances of the late-1960s and 1970s brought increasing hard-currency debt with varying prospects of repayment to Western financial institutions. The purchase of Western technology with Western loans and credits on the understanding that they could be paid back either in kind or from the profits of selling goods produced by the technology back on to Western markets failed to live up to expectations. As a consequence, most of these countries embarked on programmes of attracting Western tourists. This was despite often inadequate and inappropriate economic, administrative, planning and infrastructural systems, and often with considerable ideological hesitancy towards allowing Westerners access to their territory. Within this context domestic tourism became more sophisticated, with rising levels of car and second-home ownership in the more advanced economies and widening opportunities to organise individualised vacations. Intra-bloc international flows also became more complex, relating not only to recognised tourist areas but also to increasing amounts of 'ethnic tourism', resulting from decreasing constraints on minorities wishing to visit kith and kin located on the other side of international boundaries.

4.1.5 Post-socialism

Still in its early days, post-1989 Eastern Europe and the Soviet Union are experiencing the beginnings of mass-market tourism which could eventually aspire to levels comparable to Western Europe. Restructured, decentralised market economies, joint ventures with trans-national corporations and local entrepreneurial activity will witness both a larger provision for international tourism and a more balanced infrastructural base for its pursuit. At the same time, although initially constrained by currency shortages and economic handicaps, outbound tourism will also take on new dimensions.

4.2 Pre-socialism

Patronised by the ruling and upper classes in the eighteenth and nineteenth centuries, the flourishing development of inland spas and a few coastal watering holes characterised patterns of development in the more advanced, westward-looking societies of the Habsburg, Prussian and to a limited extent Russian empires. By contrast, the lands of the Ottomans, even after Turkish withdrawal, remained hidebound with poorly developed economies, little in the way of entrepreneurial expertise and an image in the West not conducive to attracting formal tourism.

In the case of Poland, for example, the oldest traditions, dating back to the seventeenth century, saw outward travel to those Western European countries with whom Poland had maintained close cultural relations. Initially, young noblemen undertook studies abroad, mainly in Italy. Later, the better-off landed aristocracy and, from the nineteenth century, intellectuals, travelled abroad, especially to France and Italy. Over several centuries the aristocracy travelled to foreign spas for curative purposes. In the nineteenth and twentieth centuries these became more social events.

The second half of the nineteenth century saw domestic tourism developing as two distinct streams of tourist movement for recreation and for cultural purposes, both pursued largely by intellectuals. For Poles, deprived of their statehood until 1918, 'tourism was one of the most important instruments of patriotic upbringing, and it retained this character after independence' (Rogalewski 1980, p. 115).

In Poland, the bourgeoisie comprised the majority of those pursuing recreation at expanding or newly opened holiday resorts. The less prosperous middle class stayed in modest boarding houses and country cottages, often situated in mountain villages. In the inter-war period, summer holiday camps for the children of poor town dwellers were founded, and a limited workers' social movement began providing family holidays.

In contrast to Western Europe, the upheaval of world war—the emergence of new countries and ideologies, only to be followed by economic depression, instability and political extremism—all militated against the growth of a flourishing tourist industry in the region in the first half of the twentieth century. Some limited domestic development during the 1930s, particularly stimulated by hiking and mountaineering associations in Czechoslovakia and Poland was soon undermined by the war years.

In pre-socialist days, therefore, the nature and extent of tourism in any society could be seen as closely reflecting its particular political, economic and social circumstances. This was to change with state socialism, as policies derived from a single source were introduced across the region.

4.3 'Early socialism': 'creative leisure'

In the early development of the then self-styled socialist societies, many aspects of economic, social and political life could be referred to as 'Stalinist' since they revealed patterns and processes of development and attitudes emanating from the nature of the political–economic control exerted by Lenin's successor in the Soviet Union from the 1920s until his death in 1953. As such, the term 'Stalinism' is usually associated with several key developmental elements present in the evolution of a number of state socialist societies. Political scientists might argue that 'Stalinism' as a politico–economic system of control and development attained its apogee in the Soviet Union between 1934 and 1953 and that not all of its essential ingredients were necessarily adopted elsewhere (Lovenduski and Woodall 1987; although see also Smith 1983).

Fundamental to these elements was a centralisation of political and economic control, often to the extent of a focus upon, and a concentration within, the hands of a single individual. Mutually buttressing such a situation was the cult of personality, elevating the individual leader to a level of divine infallibility and ubiquity, such that the Marxian attempt to eliminate formal religion from society was complemented by the substitution of a surrogate demi-god: even to the very last days of the 1980s such a role was abominably pursued by Ceauşescu in Romania. Not necessarily rational methods of internal state control flowed from this seat of infallibility. The 'top-down' nature of decision-making processes inherent within such a system, and its inability to accommodate bottom-up responses, resulted in the diminution of meaningful feed-back, popular participation and policy flexibility. Such leaders, reinforced by their own justified paranoia, became, by definition, cut off from their own citizens and made a grotesque nonsense of the claim of leadership on behalf of the working masses.

Complementing such an approach was the emphasis upon self-sufficiency and boot-strap development—autarky. Heavy industry was seen as providing the only path to establishing the basis for a consolidated socialist state, at the medium-term expense of general living standards. Agriculture was demoted to a role of gaining much needed hard currency through exports and of providing cheap food for the urban proletarian masses manning the heavy industries and defence forces. As a consequence the rural peasantry were poorly remunerated and were dogmatically despised as being backward and reactionary, needing to be transformed by the collectivisation of agriculture and a concomitant industrialisation and urbanisation of the countryside.

The use of ideological rhetoric and symbolism, and the efforts of internal security forces, was employed to exhort unity and cohesion. Where populations were constrained in their mobility and methods of self-expression, manipulated mass mobilisation of workforces was employed to undertake major projects and emergency works, often proclaimed as voluntary effort. To further galvanise internal unity, citizens were repeatedly reminded of the perpetual external threat, were exhorted to continuous vigilance and were generally driven to a state of collective xenophobia as a means of maintaining cohesion.

Under these circumstances, any policy encouraging foreign tourism was at best paradoxical, since:

1. Tourism as a major service industry requires flexibility and the ability to respond to changing consumer demands. Flexibility, market-response and changing fashions were not concepts which sat easily within the Stalinist organisational model.
2. As a service industry, requiring both initial capital and human resources, tourism appeared to be an utterly inessential diversion from the major socio–economic priorities of state socialism.
3. By attracting foreign visitors, tourism was seen to be serving just those people against whom the indigenous society had been galvanised. The delicate supervision of foreign visitors and their interaction with the host population therefore required substantial attention from the state's organs of internal control, both to maintain the validity of the state's xenophobic rhetoric for the host population and for the actual protection of foreign guests.

4.3.1 A socialist tourism model?

Nevertheless, the present writer has previously suggested (for example Hall 1984b, p. 542) that while, not surprisingly, neither the works of Marx nor those of Lenin provided any explicit guidance for a distinctive socialist approach to tourism development, there appeared to be a number of ways in which a socialist development strategy could subordinate international tourism to Stalinist economic priorities:

1. It should provide assistance in the implementation of policies seeking the equal distribution of goods, services and opportunities across the state area.
2. It should be used as a catalyst to improve economic performance and stimulate rapid economic development.
3. Infrastructural improvements and elaborations should follow in its wake to benefit the indigenous population as well as, if not to a greater degree than, foreign tourists.
4. The natural environment should not be adversely effected, and wherever possible, should be positively enhanced by the process of tourism development.

5. The much needed hard currency brought by foreign tourists should be employed for the purchase of essential imports to improve the country's qualitative and quantitative performance.
6. A preclusion, within the tourism process, of alien influences should be secured—whether of an ideological, cultural or economic nature likely to affect those coming into contact with foreign visitors or likely to cause significant economic 'leakages' from the country.
7. International peace and understanding, as defined by the state socialist society itself, should be promoted.
8. Visitors' ideological appreciation should be enhanced by imbuing them with a sense of the superiority of the socialist system in general, and of the host country's own interpretation of socialist development in particular.
9. Tourism should thereby be employed to project a deliberately constructed, self-conscious image of the host country to the outside world.

4.3.2 Creative leisure: sponsored and collective

Tourism and recreation were viewed as essential to the well-being of citizens and to their economically productive capacities. The availability of leisure and tourism was an important component of the cycle of production and reproduction. Being strictly subordinated to political and ideological considerations, however, domestic tourism had a largely organised, group character. Youth tourism was used as an opportunity to create correct attitudes through 'socialist education' (Allcock and Przecławski 1990, p. 5).

The need to concentrate on post-war reconstruction and new political priorities in the Soviet Union in the 1920s to mid-1950s, and in Eastern Europe in the 1940s and 1950s, meant that the role of 'tourism' was restricted to the socio-economic function of improving the health of the new working class as citizens of all socialist societies received the constitutional right of leisure and recreation. National domestic recreational policies were established to secure a system of holidays for working people, especially urban industrial workers. Their major features usually included:

1. Trades-union-run hotels: for example, in post-war Poland the existing stock of boarding-houses was allocated for trade-union use, with administration undertaken through a special enterprise, established in 1948, called the Workers' Holiday Fund. Every person employed in the public sector had the right to a two-week holiday in one of these highly subsidised rest-homes, the cost of transport and accommodation to the individual being minimal. Thus all working people had access to holidays whereas formerly this was only available to economic elites.
2. Individual enterprise- and institution-run holiday homes.
3. Subsidised cooperative holiday homes.
4. A comprehensive network of pioneer and youth holiday camps for urban schoolchildren which were located on coasts, by lakes, in forests and in mountains, often in adapted school buildings. Again, the state took over most of the costs of transport and accommodation.
5. The development of school, institution and social-organisation group excursions to acquaint all members of society with the mother country

and especially with socialist reconstruction and development achievements.

In Hungary in the late 1950s there existed

> . . . a widespread network of holiday resorts. On the recommendation of the trade unions, the workers can enjoy holidays at reduced prices, or, as a special reward, even free. There are special holiday resorts for mothers with small children. Through the nurseries, schools and youth organizations many thousands of children and young people spend their vacation in the summer holiday camps either entirely free or for a very small sum. In 1957, a total of 442,500 men and women enjoyed free holidays or holidays at reduced prices; 170,000 spent their holidays in rest homes maintained by the trade unions and 181,000 in the rest homes of the enterprises and offices. [Halász 1960, p. 225]

Outbound international tourism was now minimal, largely because permission for private travel abroad was rarely granted, little money was available for it and those groups who had enjoyed foreign travel before the war—the aristocracy, bourgeoisie and intelligentsia—had either been eliminated from social life or exterminated during the war.

Soon domestic demand was running well ahead of supply as the rural population began to share urban workers' privileges. Evidence suggests that large families with low incomes, the elderly, and rural peasant households were least well served by this system.

The relative roles of trades unions and employers in the promotion of, and investment in, domestic tourism varied from one country to another. While in Poland enterprises took on the major role for most (collective) domestic requirements, the process still effective in Albania has seen the labour unions taking a predominant position.

Table 4.1 Eastern Europe and the Soviet Union: consumer durables

	Consumer durables per thousand population (1987)					
	Motor cars	Fridges	Washing machines	TV sets	Radios	Telephones
Albania	nd	nd	nd	nd	nd	nd
Bulgaria	127	307	295	314	305	248
Czechoslovakia	182	418	520	445	709	246
Former GDR	206	595	409	476	406	233
Hungary	153	404	349	414	512	152
Poland	74	346	381	390	448	122
Romania	nd	nd	nd	nd	nd	nd
Soviet Union	50	276	205	304	289	124
Yugoslavia	nd	nd	nd	nd	nd	nd

Source: CMEA *Statistical Yearbook* (1988)

From the 1960s, following the consolidation and satisfaction of the earlier needs, in the more advanced countries at least, priorities began to be shifted towards the production of consumer goods, including motor cars, ownership levels of which, however, still remain relatively low (Table 4.1). In some societies rules governing private property ownership also began to be relaxed, encouraging the growth of second- and leisure-home ownership. Pressure for longer holidays and a five-day working week subsequently took place alongside increasing urbanisation and leisure goods availability.

Later developments have seen further trends in domestic tourism:

1. Individuals providing for themselves through the construction of weekend villas, of which there were 300,000 in Hungary by the mid-1980s.
2. Membership of caravan and camping clubs.
3. Cooperative time-share schemes whereby families can buy an interest in blocks of holiday flats with the right to use the accommodation for a specified number of weeks each year.
4. Making individual arrangements for holidays in accommodation through often unofficial intermediate agents.

Now collective institutions are in the process of being privatised in several societies in the region.

4.3.3 Second homes

As a number of the country chapters in this volume point out, second or weekend homes have been a commonplace in the region for some considerable time. In Czechoslovakia a boom in second-home ownership occurred during the 1970s with improved living standards and rising levels of car ownership. Restrictions on foreign travel in the more prosperous countries led many families to invest their resources in a second home.

The growth of second-home ownership presented ethical problems, reflecting disparities of wealth and connections, and often providing a strong contrast with families restricted to a single apartment in squalid and overcrowded conditions. But vested interests in the ruling elite rarely saw the authorities curtailing property rights in such cases. The second home often acted as a safety valve for a family confined to a small rented urban apartment during the week; thus by no means did all second homes involve cases of ownership of two houses (Turnock 1989b). In this way the state was relieved of some of the pressure for greater investment in housing and recreation facilities, and to some extent this could be seen to parallel the selling off of urban apartments which began to gain pace at about the same time. Loans from national savings banks were made available to families to finance the purchase of rural second homes and urban apartments.

Second homes can contribute to village life by providing business for local shops, restaurants and their services. Conversely, high levels of concentration in some settlements combined with intermittent occupancy can have negative impacts on rural society. In the Balaton area of Hungary, for example, the proportion of houses being used as weekend cottages has been more than two-thirds in some locations. For countries such as Bulgaria, additional recreational facilities for city-dwellers could be provided by rebuilding or restoring old and abandoned village houses, which in some regions of the country may account for more than three-quarters of the total stock. In the past, collective farms have also been active in selling or leasing land for second homes, a practice which was seen to help reduce the level of unauthorised and unplanned development (Turnock 1989b). Improvements to farm houses to accommodate tourists is notable in Yugoslavia, where remittances from migrant workers are often invested by their family in tourist services (Barbic 1983;

Carter and French 1975; Lockwood 1973; Matley 1968; Thomas 1
and Vojvoda 1973).

4.3.4 *Current dimensions*

While detailed domestic tourism data are available for only three of the region's countries in international compilations (Table 4.2), a number of observations can be made.

Table 4.2 Eastern Europe and the Soviet Union: domestic tourism arrivals and nights by type of accommodation, 1988

	Type of accommodation: % of total												
	Hotels and similar★		Social tourism estabs†		Private lodgings‡		C & C§		Totals (in millions)				
	a	*b*	*a*	*b*	*a*	*b*	*a*	*b*	*a*	*c*	*b*	*d*	*e*
Albania	nd	nd	nd	nd	nd	nd	nd	nd	nd	nd	nd	nd	nd
Bulgaria	56.7	37.8	22.5	12.5	16.6	43.6	4.2	1.5	7.1	78.9	24.7	0.8	55.4
Czechoslovakia	nd	nd	nd	nd	nd	nd	nd	nd	nd	nd	29.5	nd	71.9
Former GDR	nd	nd	nd	nd	nd	nd	nd	3.3	nd	nd	67.8	nd	nd
Hungary	49.5	24.7	25.2	nd	16.0	66.4	9.3	8.9	3.1	29.2	11.9	0.3	42.9
Poland	nd	nd	nd	nd	nd	nd	nd	nd	nd	nd	nd	nd	nd
Romania	nd	nd	nd	nd	nd	nd	nd	nd	nd	nd	nd	nd	nd
Soviet Union	nd	nd	nd	nd	nd	nd	nd	nd	nd	nd	nd	nd	nd
Yugoslavia	62.4	39.0	14.8	29.7	7.2	16.3	15.6	15.0	12.8	54.9	55.1	0.7	51.3

Source: WTO *Yearbook* (1990); author's calculations

★ hotels, motels, boarding houses and inns
† tourist dormitories, youth hostels, employees' holiday accommodation (and convalescent homes in Yugoslavia)
‡ rented villas and flats
§ camping and caravanning (including mountain shelters, boats, yachts and other 'supplementary' accommodation in Yugoslavia)
a arrivals
b nights
c domestic tourist exposure rate
d domestic tourist intensity rate
e domestic tourist nights as a percentage of all tourist nights
nd no data

1. In terms of domestic nights as a proportion of all tourist nights, the relatively low official figures, ranging from 42.9 to 71.9 per cent would appear grossly to under-represent domestic tourism activity, reflecting the fact that the data only recorded stays in officially recognised accommodation. By definition, much domestic tourism concerns visits to friends and relatives in non-formal accommodation and goes unreported. Comparable domestic nights' figures for Western European countries

range from 86 per cent for West Germany and 74.5 per cent for the United Kingdom, essentially tourist generating countries, down to 37 per cent for Spain and 24–25 per cent for Austria and Greece.

2. In terms of both domestic arrivals and nights, the figures for Hungary are relatively lower than for the other Eastern European societies recorded, suggesting the effects of the combination of a small, landlocked country with relative ease of access to its neighbours and a relatively mobile population.
3. While recorded domestic arrivals at hotels in the region represent between a half and two-thirds of all domestic arrivals, actual nights spent range between only 24 and 40 per cent of the total, reflecting relatively short stays in such accommodation.
4. By comparison, private lodgings, while representing only between 7 and 17 per cent of all recorded domestic arrivals, generate between two and four times as many nights proportionately, although there is an inconsistency in the Hungarian data.
5. Commenting on 1987 data for tourist nights in registered accommodation, the fact that domestic tourism appeared to remain more important than the international dimension suggested to Buckley and Witt (1990) that here were predominantly inward-looking tourism industries not geared to international standards and foreign (that is, Western) tastes, particularly when the bulk of international tourism was indeed from other Eastern European countries (Table 4.3).

4.3.5 Some more equal

While under state socialism the region's working masses enjoyed holiday facilities often unprecedented in their society's history, their leaders' recreational requirements often maintained an uncanny resemblance to those of the previous ruling classes. Hunting expeditions in very private, well-stocked woods and moorlands were particularly notable among the now deeply discredited leaderships of Brezhnev, Ceauşescu, Kadar and Honecker.

The privileged party and bureaucratic elites (*nomenklatura*) also had their coastal retreats. To this day in Albania, large and heavily guarded seaside and lakeside retreats can be found on the outskirts of Durrës, Pogradec, and Vlorë. While in Romania, it could be said that:

> During the summer, *nomenklatura* people are not seen on Bucharest's crowded, sweaty public beaches. They either go to special bathing areas or have weekend villas in Snagov, a resort located 25 miles outside Bucharest. *Nomenklatura* people do not spend their vacations packed like sardines into Soviet-style colonies. They have their own vacation homes. [Pacepa 1989, p. 171]

In some cases such legacies have been remoulded to meet new conditions. On the Bulgarian Black Sea coast, formerly exclusive *nomenklatura* beaches and villas—together with luxurious recreation facilities—have now become exclusive to dollar-paying foreign tourists, while the Bulgarian holiday masses crowd on teeming beaches the wrong side of high wire fences. Club Méditerranée, for example, is transforming the Goldstrand holiday centre near Varna, previously a *nomenklatura* enclave, into a luxury 600-bed resort village, while Maxwell (UK) is converting the former Black Sea government residence at Perla into a conference centre. The opulent Praha Hotel in Prague, once the exclusive preserve of party officials, and Erich Honecker's Baltic island hideaway retreats have also been turned over to tourist use, although in the latter case, to their credit, the East German authorities converted one compound into a 400-bed home for the handicapped.

4.4 'Middle socialism': intra-bloc travel

With pressing political and economic priorities having taken precedence, little international tourism activity took place in the early post-war years. But as the socialist societies became more confident, tourist movements between them began to be generated, albeit at a slow pace. The volume of such movements was usually regulated by bilateral agreement (the CMEA as a supranational institution appears to have had little if any role in this process). Here was an area where economic considerations constrained idealism. In Poland, for example, while there were aspirations in many enterprises to organise foreign excursions, the cost was usually prohibitive. The outgoings for a single two-week holiday on the Black Sea in Bulgaria, Romania or the Soviet Union were equivalent to five to ten two-week holidays on Poland's own Baltic Sea coast (Rogalewski 1980, p. 119). The disparities were too great to permit cuts in domestic tourism spending in favour of foreign holidays; the latter would have appeared elitist. As a consequence, in the case of Poland, the authorities issued a decree prohibiting the financing of outgoing tourism from works' funds, except for so-called 'friendship excursions' to the Soviet Union, and barter holidays, whereby bilateral schemes between enterprises of two countries, not involving foreign exchange, were undertaken, with groups being accommodated in often spartan conditions.

Various other cooperative agreements between socialist countries none the less helped to stimulate intra-bloc tourism. For example, in 1955 the Polish and Czechoslovak authorities adopted a convention allowing nationals of both countries to move about freely within the Tatra mountains using a pass issued by touring offices. This was one of the earliest attempts to develop passport-free foreign travel and carried on a pre-war tradition. In 1960 this convention was extended to the central part of the Sudeten mountains.

Foreign travel became increasingly popular with young people, who had specific organisations acting on their behalf to administer and regulate such tourism: in Poland, for example, 'Juventur' for young working people, 'Almatur' for students and 'Harctur' for girl and boy scouts were granted licences to develop foreign tourism on a barter basis. These could be set alongside such organisations as 'Gromada', serving the rural population, 'Turysta' for urban dwellers and 'Sports-Turism' for sports-fan excursions (Ostrowski, 1986, p. 291).

In a number of cases the 1970s and 1980s saw an easing of administrative constraints on individual travel to other European socialist countries. Böröcz (1990) has argued that within the region exit visa requirements posed more severe limitations on movements than did entry visas. In this way, forced substitution (for more exotic locations) played an important part in intra-bloc movement. Further influencing this development were factors of ethnicity —neighbouring states having cross-border minorities—and the question of individual countries' degree of internal liberalisation. Hungary's liberal and

Westernised image within the Soviet bloc offered an enticing destination for many of the region's citizens.

4.4.1 *Shopping and petty-business tourism*

During these decades a number of bilateral and multilateral problems arose, not least due to 'cross-border raids' whereby excessive purchases of foodstuffs and consumer goods, especially petrol, reflected differing levels of availability, price and currency parities between neighbouring countries. At various times of economic pressure, authorities have sought to restrict such activity usually because of resulting goods shortages within the host country. Tensions have often arisen between neighbours over this issue.

November 1988 saw the Czechoslovak government limiting the amount of goods—including most consumer goods—which foreigners could take out of the country, and instigated comprehensive searches at borders, provoking an official Polish government protest. The Polish, Hungarian and East German governments subsequently retaliated. For the following year, as the political philosophies and realities of the Czechoslovak and Polish governments increasingly diverged, and as more Poles travelled around the region for small-scale business purposes, the Prague authorities waged a propaganda war against itinerant Poles in the country, accusing them of buying up food supplies and creating unsanitary conditions at border posts by exercising their right to leave their own country. Poles appeared to dominate the weekly Ostrava flea market and tended to crowd out cross-border train services. By now, not requiring visas to enter Austria, they were also using Czechoslovakia as a transit route, and inconveniences arising out of increased pressure on customs facilities were occurring on Czechoslovakia's borders with both Poland and Austria.

In September 1989, Czechoslovakia introduced what Hungarians saw as an extremely high petrol coupon price for Hungarian tourists in Czechoslovakia (making petrol about 17 per cent higher than in Hungary) aimed at changing the forint–crown exchange rate. Czechoslovakia claimed the forint was overvalued in relation to the crown, and that Hungarians were buying up relatively cheap Czechoslovak consumer goods and taking them back to Hungary, thereby depriving Czechoslovak citizens of goods rarely in abundant supply.

4.4.2 *Ethnic tourism*

Problems both of constraint and excess have come about in recent years.

In 1985 the Hungarian and Romanian governments signed an agreement for a 10 per cent increase in tourism between their countries for the 1986–90 period. In the previous five-year period the number of Hungarians travelling to Romania had doubled, largely to visit members of the sizeable Hungarian minority in Transylvania. As the internal situation in Romania deteriorated, however, the Hungarian authorities began to complain of the harassment of their nationals by Romanian customs officials, and historically rooted tensions between the two governments were reinforced.

A little further north, 100,000 ethnic Hungarians live just inside the Soviet Union, and from March 1989, Soviet citizens living within 30 kilometres of the border were allowed to travel across to Hungary without either a visa or a letter of invitation (albeit with passports which were only valid in Soviet bloc countries). Four new border posts were opened, but the pre-existing once quiet railway border crossing point of Zahony was overwhelmed with 1.5 million people, 80 per cent of them Soviet citizens (mostly ethnic Hungarian) coming across the border during the first three months of the new freedom. Shopping was the major purpose of the visits, but since the Soviet travel allowance of approximately $10 could buy little of the Hungarian consumer goods cornucopia, wily itinerant Poles set up a consumer goods market and 'informal' currency exchange facilities in a Hungarian field close to the border. Within ten months, 10 million Soviet visitors had crossed the border. 'What the CMEA has been unable to do, ordinary citizens are doing every day: exporting and importing commodities that are scarce due to shortages on both sides' (Okolicsanyi 1989, p. 34).

4.4.3 *Fiscal constraints*

As trends of increasing levels of mobility between the countries of the region have developed, so further problems of currency equilibrium have emerged. In 1989 for example, a number of pre-agreed currency quotas between countries soon became exhausted. By the middle of the year, the 1,200 million forint quota made available by Hungary to the Soviet Union for travel purposes had been spent, as had the 970 million forint quota for Poland. In the latter case, discussions ensued on means of allowing Poles to travel in transit through Hungary if they cashed a minimum amount of hard currency for each day of their presence in the country—a ploy previously only aimed at Western tourists.

4.4.4 *Overall patterns of intra-bloc travel*

Tourists originating in CMEA member countries have normally constituted a significant majority in the others. Inevitably, Yugoslavia has not fitted this pattern, with Western Europe providing the vast majority of tourist arrivals. In recent years increasing rather than decreasing diversity within the European Soviet bloc countries has rendered the generalisation of travel patters hazardous. Different trends appeared to be emerging, at different speeds, in different countries; the subsequent 1989 'revolutions' impacting on some economies much more than on others again set off factors likely to actually increase the pattern of diversity within the region, if only in the short term. Table 4.3 includes data up to 1988 (the last year of the intact Soviet socialist bloc). In indicating the generalised source regions (Soviet Union, Eastern Europe, Western Europe) for tourist arrivals, the table provides several, almost contradictory patterns:

1. The relatively stable and high West European component for Bulgaria, reflecting the large number of Turkish migrant workers passing through the country. Ironically, in the 1990 WTO compendium Turkey is definitionally moved from Europe to Asia, leaving Bulgaria with a 'Western Europe' component of just 9.5 per cent. For consistency, the 1988 Turkish

origin data (41.65 per cent) are included under 'Western Europe' for Bulgaria in Table 4.3. Tourist nights data, by contrast, reveal Bulgaria's to be the economy most dependent on the intra-bloc market, although the data are very limited, with Soviet tourists the most important group (only fourth in terms of arrivals), followed by Poles, Czechoslovaks and East Germans.

Table 4.3 Eastern Europe and the Soviet Union: source regions of international tourists

Country	% of countries' total arrivals											
	1960			1970			1980			1988		
	A	*B*	*C*	*A*	*B*	*C*	*A*	*B*	*C*	*A*	*B*	*C*
Albania		nd			nd			nd			nd	
Bulgaria	9.8	51.1	16.4	6.1	51.7	38.1	6.0	38.4	50.3	5.7	43.1	51.2
Czechoslovakia		nd		1.9	75.0	16.6	4.4	77.3	15.9	2.8	89.6	5.9
Former GDR		nd			nd			nd			nd	
Hungary	7.2	51.2	17.2	3.7	81.4	14.5	4.0	82.9	10.6	5.5	65.2	26.5
Poland	12.4	37.1	14.8	17.8	69.2	8.3	10.1	77.4	9.0	28.1	54.7	12.7
Romania	9.2	69.1	4.9	7.1	76.2	16.0	8.0	77.6	10.0	11.4	79.4	5.7
Soviet Union		nd		nd		nd		nd				
Yugoslavia	0.6	5.5	85.1	1.6	6.6	80.6	3.2	10.2	78.7	3.4	7.3	81.8

Sources: WTO *Yearbooks*; Turnock (1989a) p. 257; UN *Statistical Yearbooks*

A Soviet Union
B Eastern Europe
C Western Europe
nd no data

2. An increasing intra-bloc component for Romania and Czechoslovakia, representing two slightly contrasting trends: in Romania, the absolute decline of Westerners in response to the country's wretched living conditions during the 1980s, while in Czechoslovakia, a reflection of the substantially increased numbers of arrivals from Poland and Hungary added to continuing high numbers of East German arrivals (Tables 4.5, 4.6).
3. A decreasing intra-bloc component for Hungary, revealing gradual absolute declines in arrivals from most other bloc members, and with indications of relative liberalism within the country, increasing numbers of Western arrivals. In terms of tourist nights (Table 4.6), Hungary's Eastern European component revealed a substantial shift between 1987 and 1988, being reduced from 50.80 to 40.55 per cent, with an overall decrease of 28.3 per cent. For example, Polish tourists' nights decreased by 58.5 per cent and those of Bulgarians by 43.7 per cent. By contrast, the share of the rest of Europe increased from 38.79 to 47.77 per cent of international tourist nights in Hungary, with Dutch tourists' nights showing a 61.0 per cent increase and those of the Swiss tourists 46.8 per cent.
4. An increasing Soviet arrivals component in the case of Poland, Romania and Hungary—all countries with a common land border with the Soviet

Union—perhaps reflecting the increasing ability of Soviet citizens to travel outside of their own country. However, such arrivals tended to represent cross-border day trips—'excursionists'—rather than residential stays: Soviet tourist nights in Hungary for example, actually decreased by 22.7 per cent between 1987 and 1988.

Overall, the European market (if one includes the Soviet Union and Turkey) continues to provide the predominant source for the region's tourists (Table 4.4).

Table 4.4 Eastern Europe and the Soviet Union: dependence upon the European market

	Arrivals from European* countries as a % of countries' total arrivals						
Country	1960	1970	1980	1985	1986	1987	1988
Albania	nd	nd	nd	nd	nd	nd	nd
Bulgaria	77.3	95.9	94.7	91.0	94.9	97.1	97.3
Czechoslovakia	nd	93.5	97.6	98.3	98.7	98.7	98.3
Former GDR	nd	nd	nd	nd	nd	nd	nd
Hungary	75.6	99.6	98.5	97.5	98.0	97.7	97.2
Poland	64.3	95.3	96.5	94.7	nd	95.7	94.9
Romania	83.2	99.3	95.6	97.4	97.2	96.5	96.5
Soviet Union	nd	nd	nd	nd	nd	nd	nd
Yugoslavia	91.2	88.8	92.1	94.4	95.5	93.4	92.5

Sources: WTO *Yearbooks*; UN *Statistical Yearbooks*

* includes the Soviet Union and Turkey
nd no data

4.4.5 Intra-bloc tourism generation

Within the region, the strongest tourist-generating countries have been the more developed northern states (Tables 4.5, 4.6, 4.7): the former GDR, generating around 12.5 million recorded frontier arrivals in 1988 (approximately 27 per cent of the 1988 intra-bloc total), recorded the most arrivals for Czechoslovakia and the third highest total for both Hungary and Poland. Poland, generating just over 9 million, provided around 20 per cent of intra-bloc arrivals, the second highest totals for Hungary and Romania and the third highest for Bulgaria and Czechoslovakia. Hungary and Czechoslovakia provided the next two most important sources, with the latter providing the most arrivals in Hungary and the second highest total in Poland. Czechoslovakian sources appeared particularly strongly in the tourist nights data, although these are too limited to be able to draw any conclusions. By contrast, the least-developed members of the region—Romania, Bulgaria and Albania—were weak generating sources (Table 4.7).

Table 4.5 Eastern Europe and the Soviet Union: source countries of intra-regional international arrivals, 1988

	Source countries									
	AL	BG	CS	GDR	HU	PL	RO	SU	YU	Total
To:										
AL	–	nd	nd	nd	nd	nd	nd	nd	nd	nd
			5	**6**	**8**	**3**	**9**	**4**	**2**	
BG†	nd	–	0.43	0.31	0.25	0.92	0.22	0.47	1.45	4.05
			5.13	*3.73*	*2.97*	*11.11*	*2.67*	*5.68*	*17.53*	*48.86*
		7		**1**	**2**	**3**	**9**	**5**	**4**	
CS†	nd	0.47	–	9.40	6.39	4.77	0.19	0.68	0.82	22.72
		1.91		*38.20*	*25.97*	*19.41*	*0.77*	*2.76*	*3.34*	*92.38*
GDR‡	0.003	0.02	0.14	–	0.02	0.57	0.01	0.13	nd	0.38
	0.31	*1.68*	*11.71*		*1.33*	*4.71*	*0.61*	*10.81*		*31.20*
		8	**1**	**3**		**2**	**10**	**7**	**5**	
HU★	nd	0.29	2.24	1.36	–	1.90	0.17	0.58	0.93	7.47
		2.77	*21.16*	*12.90*		*17.98*	*1.57*	*5.47*	*8.78*	*70.65*
		10	**2**	**3**	**4**			**1**	**7**	
PL†	0.04	0.05	1.42	1.08	0.57	–	0.03	1.74	0.19	5.09
	0.68	*0.83*	*22.87*	*17.45*	*9.15*		*0.58*	*28.07*	*3.10*	*82.18*
		3	**6**	**7**	**4**	**2**		**5**	**1**	
RO†	0.001	0.70	0.55	0.33	0.65	0.82	–	0.63	1.33	5.01
	0.01	*12.73*	*9.93*	*5.93*	*11.78*	*14.85*		*11.42*	*24.15*	*90.82*
SU	nd	nd	nd	nd	nd	nd	nd	–	nd	nd
			8		**9**	**10**		**6**		
YU‡	nd	0.02	0.27	nd	0.20	0.16	0.01	0.30	–	0.96
		0.18	*3.01*		*2.22*	*1.82*	*0.09*	*3.35*		*10.69*

Source: WTO *Yearbook* (1990)

AL Albania
BG Bulgaria
CS Czechoslovakia
HU Hungary
PL Poland
RO Romania
SU Soviet Union
YU Yugoslavia

★ tourist arrivals at frontiers
† visitor arrivals at frontiers
‡ tourist arrivals in all accommodation

Bold figures rank order (first ten) in relation to all source countries
Roman figures absolute numbers of arrivals in millions
Italic figures percentage of the country's total arrivals

Table 4.6 Eastern Europe and the Soviet Union: source countries of intra-regional international tourist nights, 1988

	Source countries									
	AL	BG	CS	GDR	HU	PL	RO	SU	YU	Total
To:										
AL	–	nd	nd	nd	nd	nd	nd	nd	nd	nd
BG	nd	–	**3** 3.29 *16.51*	**4** 2.63 *13.18*	**7** 0.52 *2.59*	**2** 3.67 *18.43*	0.06 *0.32*	**1** 3.79 *19.01*	0.16 *0.78*	14.11 *70.84*
CS	nd	nd	–	nd	nd	nd	nd	nd	nd	nd
GDR	nd	nd	nd	–	nd	nd	nd	nd	nd	nd
HU	nd	0.12 *0.76*	**3** 1.43 *8.97*	**2** 2.34 *14.69*	–	**5** 1.13 *7.08*	0.07 *0.42*	**6** 1.08 *6.80*	**10** 0.29 *1.81*	6.45 *40.55*
PL	nd	nd	nd	nd	nd	–	nd	nd	nd	nd
RO	nd	nd	nd	nd	nd	nd	–	nd	nd	nd
SU	nd	nd	nd	nd	nd	nd	nd	–	nd	nd
YU	nd	0.04 *0.07*	**6** 2.44 *4.66*	nd	**10** 0.87 *1.65*	**9** 0.87 *1.66*	0.04 *0.08*	0.81 *1.56*	–	5.01 *9.70*

Source: WTO *Yearbook* (1990)

AL Albania
BG Bulgaria
CS Czechoslovakia
HU Hungary
nd no data
PL Poland
RO Romania
SU Soviet Union
YU Yugoslavia

Bold figures rank order (first ten) in relation to all source countries
Roman figures absolute numbers of tourist nights in millions
Italic figures percentage of the country's total tourist nights

4.5 'Later socialism': hard currency considerations

4.5.1 Constraints on extending international tourism to Westerners

By the 1960s, when the West European package-holiday business was gathering momentum, Eastern Europe was poorly prepared to participate as a host region. Those Western visitors who did arrive tended to be confronted with inconvenience and possibly hostility, in the form of:

1. Complex frontier formalities, often undertaken without a sympathetic approach. For example, as late as 1969 Bulgarian border guards were insisting that bearded men with clean-shaven passport photographs be made to shave before entering the country (writer's first-hand experience!).
2. A limited selection of accommodation, generally sub-standard.
3. Poor roads and motoring services.
4. Limited tourist information such as inadequate maps.

Table 4.7 Eastern Europe and the Soviet Union: generators of intra-bloc tourism, 1988

Country	Arrivals					Nights				
	Numbers (millions)	% of the intra-bloc total	Distribution of rankings 1	2	3	Numbers (millions)	% of the intra-bloc total	Distribution of rankings 1	2	3
Albania	0.04	0.1	–	–	–	nd	nd		nd	
Bulgaria	1.6	3.5	–	–	1	0.2	0.6	–	–	–
Czechoslovakia	5.1	11.2	1	1	–	7.2	28.0	–	–	2
Former GDR	12.5	27.4	1	–	2	5.0	19.4	–	1	–
Hungary	8.1	17.7	–	1	–	1.4	5.4	–	–	–
Poland	9.1	19.9	–	2	2	5.7	22.2	–	1	–
Romania	0.6	1.3	–	–	–	0.2	0.7	–	–	–
Soviet Union	4.5	9.9	1	–	–	5.7	22.2	1	–	–
Yugoslavia	4.7	10.3	1	1	–	0.5	1.8	–	–	–
Total	45.7		6*	6*	6*	25.6		3*	3*	3*

Source: WTO *Yearbook* (1990)

The figures are subject to some error due to:

1. Several stages of 'grossing-up'.
2. The absence of arrivals data for Albania and the Soviet Union.
3. Nights data being limited to those for Bulgaria, Hungary and Yugoslavia.
4. The lack of a separate category in the Yugoslav data for arrivals and nights from former GDR sources.

* The shortfalls in the columns above indicate that additional rankings are contributed by source countries outside of the region (most notably for both arrivals and nights in Yugoslavia)

5. In some cases constraints on geographical movement, a requirement to pre-arrange all aspects of the visit and the necessity for an accompanying official guide throughout the stay.

More specific deterrents have included:

1. The Soviet-led Warsaw Pact intervention in Czechoslovakia in August 1968 following the liberalising 'Prague Spring' of that year which had only a temporary effect on arrivals numbers.
2. The troubled situation in Poland in the early 1980s, with imposition of martial law in 1981 following economic disruption during the Solidarność period.
3. The increasing nastiness of the Ceauşescu regime and the wretched living conditions in Romania—food shortages, poor accommodation and service, early closure of bars and night clubs to save electricity—which saw a downturn in tourism activity throughout much of the 1980s.
4. The Chernobyl nuclear reactor disaster of April 1986.

Although facilities and attitudes had begun to improve, priority had been given to domestic recreational opportunities, and the international dimension continued to be dominated by intra-bloc movements with the exception of Yugoslavia. But as most countries began to shrug off their Stalinist straight-jackets, and individual reinterpretations of state socialism began to take shape, different approaches to the question of tourism development also began to emerge. Yugoslavia's pragmatic attitude had encouraged a rapid growth in tourism by Westerners during the 1950s and 1960s, further stimulated by Western aid and investment in hotel building and road construction along the Adriatic coast (Poulsen 1977; Violich 1972). This decentralised socialist state took the regional lead in both tourist numbers and income generated, to levels comparable with a number of major Western tourist countries, despite various internal upheavals (Chapter 12). Neighbouring Albania, by contrast, pursuing a dogmatic policy of self-reliance, maintained relatively impermeable borders and a highly selective tourism policy limiting arrivals to perhaps no more than 10,000 foreign visitors per annum (Chapter 13). The other countries of the region pursued policies some way between these two extremes.

4.5.2 Emerging patterns of Western tourism

As the international industry developed, tourist flows became notably asymmetrical, in that, intra-bloc tourism aside, the countries of the region generally acted as hosts for, rather than as the source of, international tourists. This reflected two major characteristics of these societies:

1. They enjoyed relatively low levels of economic development and standards of living compared to the major (Western) tourist-originating countries.
2. Their citizens had their movements to 'capitalist' countries severely constrained by administrative and fiscal considerations. While state paranoia over security questions had been rapidly melting away in the face of the substantial inflows of hard currency brought by increasing numbers of Western tourists, these countries had barely begun to provide any form of freedom for their own nationals to travel westwards, Yugoslavia being the exception.

The post-war growth of international tourism across Europe has been superficially viewed in terms of waves flowing from West to East, via regional expansion of tourism in the Mediterranean region. The popularity of 'sun and sea' holidays and the gradual saturation of tourism in other southern European countries directed the tourist wave towards Yugoslavia and later Bulgaria and Romania (Butler 1974, pp. 59–61). In practice, the growth of Romanian and Bulgarian tourism was essentially a response to the growing requirements of Soviet-bloc citizens for warm and sunny seaside holidays. During the 1960s, a period of growth reflected changing official attitudes towards assisting and investing in the tourist industry. The requirement to acquire convertible currency saw development programmes aimed at the West European market. Vuoristo (1981) has argued that declining growth in the 1970s indicated that these countries had achieved maturity in the development of their international tourism. After that time, a rapid expansion took place which, however, did not last more than a few years in most cases.

This pattern of tourism development suggested to Vuoristo parallels with Rostow's model of stages of economic growth in developing countries (Rostow 1973, pp. 86–114): the growth of tourism resembled an S-shaped curve with a stage of 'slow beginning' or 'take-off' being followed by a period of 'strong growth', then of 'declining growth'. This process began at a later date in the socialist bloc than in the West, and as the stage of strong growth was relatively short, so Vuoristo argued, the volume of tourism was therefore not as great as in Western Europe. But the markets of the then two regions of Europe were evolving in different ways. Examining international tourist source patterns from 1960 to 1976, Vuoristo (1981, pp. 241–3) argued that compared to the relatively well-defined and stable catchments of Western tourist economies, the 'take-off' period for the socialist countries was characterised by instability and lack of clarity. For example, from a miniscule proportion in 1961, West Germans made up 35 per cent of all Western tourists in Romania by 1965, and then declined sharply to less than 10 per cent in 1966, maintaining that level to the end of the decade. Such patterns of apparent instability would have at least partly reflected the relatively small numbers of tourists involved, the changing nature of Cold War relations, and the different levels of adoption of Eastern European countries by Western package-tour companies.

Development in the Soviet Union differed again; here the increase in tourist arrivals was slow and even. This huge state only opened gradually to foreign tourists commensurate with infrastructural development, the reduction of security considerations and changes in tourism philosophy.

4.5.3 Western tourism to the region in the last years of state socialism

4.5.3.1 Overall trends

Table 4.3 showed that during the 1980s, under state socialism, the number of Western visitors arriving in Czechoslovakia and Romania actually declined as a proportion of the total number of arrivals. For Czechoslovakia it represented the phenomenon of increasing numbers of East Europeans, particularly East Germans, arriving there, while the Romanian decline reflected the repulsion effect on Westerners of the sad deterioration in living conditions within the country. Bulgaria, Poland and Yugoslavia showed only very small proportional increases, with the data from the first and last of those countries being influenced by transit traffic. Bulgaria suffered from a high level of customer complaints in its ageing sea resorts which led, for example, to Thomson Holidays discontinuing its 1986 Bulgaria programme (Pearlman 1986). Winter sports became a major growth area in Bulgaria, however. Thus by 1988, given the limitations of the data, only Hungary could show a clear proportional increase in Western arrivals, more than doubling the proportion from 10.6 per cent in 1980 to 26.5 per cent in 1988, at the expense of arrivals from Eastern Europe.

As Buckley and Witt (1990, p. 9) have pointed out, it is difficult to assess the changes that have taken place over time in the Soviet Union on account of the major discontinuity which occurred in the data series after 1984. However, a steady growth in visitor arrivals appears to have taken place during the 1980s. Although not revealed in Table 4.3, it would appear that the country's share of Western tourists is relatively large, with Finland being a particularly important source.

Table 4.8 Eastern Europe and the Soviet Union: tourist arrivals from Western countries, 1988

	Arrivals from Western countries									
	Aus.	Fra.	FRG	Gr.	It.	Swe.	Tur.	UK	USA	Total†
Albania	nd	nd	nd	nd	nd	nd	nd	nd	nd	nd
			7	**10**			**1**			
Bulgaria	0.06	0.03	0.28	0.16	0.03	0.03	3.23	0.89	0.02	8.29
	0.67	*0.42*	*3.33*	*1.87*	*0.30*	*0.33*	*38.94*	*1.07*	*0.20*	
	8		**6**		**10**					
Czech.	0.32	0.04	0.65	0.05	0.13	0.05	nd	0.03	nd	24.59
	1.28	*0.16*	*2.63*	*0.21*	*0.51*	*0.18*	*nd*	*0.13*	*nd*	
GDR	nd	nd	nd	nd	nd	nd	nd	nd	nd	nd
	6		**4**		**9**					
Hungary	0.92	0.05	1.13	nd	0.17	nd	nd	0.05	0.11	10.56
	8.70	*0.42*	*10.66*	*nd*	*1.64*	*nd*	*nd*	*0.46*	*1.06*	
		9	**5**						**8**	
Poland	0.05	0.06	0.42	0.01★	0.04	0.06★	nd	0.03	0.06	6.20
	0.80	*0.90*	*6.70*	*0.18*	*0.65*	*1.30*	*nd*	*0.55*	*0.93*	
			8	**10**	**10**		**9**			
Romania	0.02	0.02	0.12	0.03	0.03	0.01	0.05	0.02	0.02	5.51
	0.28	*0.34*	*2.13*	*0.54*	*0.54*	*0.14*	*0.97*	*0.37*	*0.42*	
Soviet Union	nd	0.09	0.24	nd	0.11	nd	nd	0.09	0.15	6.01
	nd	*1.43*	*4.00*	*nd*	*1.85*	*nd*	*nd*	*1.48*	*2.48*	
	3	**5**	**1**		**2**			**4**	**7**	
Yug.	0.80	0.37	2.75	0.16	1.24	0.14	0.09	0.67	0.30	9.02
	8.92	*4.11*	*30.48*	*1.79*	*13.73*	*1.55*	*0.95*	*7.46*	*3.27*	

Source: WTO *Yearbook* (1990)

★ 1987 figures
† all arrivals
nd no data
Bold figures rank order (first ten) in relation to all source countries
Roman figures absolute numbers of arrivals in millions
Italic figures percentage of the country's total arrivals

4.5.3.2 Numbers and sources of Western tourists

Table 4.8 enumerates arrivals from selected Western countries, and Table 4.9 charts nights spent by Western tourists, both for the year 1988. These sets of data reveal:

1. The markedly different tourist markets of Yugoslavia compared with other countries in the region. For example, while in 1988 tourists from bloc countries spent 70.9 per cent of all tourist nights in Bulgaria, the figure for Hungary was 40.6 and for Yugoslavia just 9.6 per cent.
2. Transiting Turks in Bulgaria aside, Western tourist nights tended to gain a higher ranking than for arrivals, suggesting, with longer average stays: (a) the ability of Western tourists to be able to afford both the cost and

Table 4.9 Eastern Europe and the Soviet Union: Western countries' tourist nights, 1988

	Source countries									
	Aus.	Fra.	FRG	Gr.	It.	Swe.	Tur.	UK	USA	Total†
Albania	nd	nd	nd	nd	nd	nd	nd	nd	nd	nd
		10	**5**	**9**		**8**		**6**		
Bulgaria	0.07	0.19	2.05	0.33	0.07	0.43	0.01	1.00	0.03	19.91
	0.34	*0.96*	*10.30*	*1.67*	*0.36*	*2.16*	*0.05*	*4.99*	*0.17*	
Czech.	nd	nd	nd	nd	nd	nd	nd	nd	nd	nd
GDR	nd	nd	nd	nd	nd	nd	nd	nd	nd	nd
	4		**1**		**8**				**9**	
Hungary	1.13	0.16	3.89	nd	0.50	nd	nd	0.17	0.33	15.90
	7.12	*1.02*	*24.44*	*nd*	*3.15*	*nd*	*nd*	*1.06*	*2.07*	
Poland	nd	nd	nd	nd	nd	nd	nd	nd	nd	nd
Romania	nd	nd	nd	nd	nd	nd	nd	nd	nd	nd
Soviet Union	nd	nd	nd	nd	nd	nd	nd	nd	nd	nd
	4	**7**	**1**		**3**			**2**		
Yug.	5.11	1.22	19.79	0.22	5.37	0.83	0.11	5.86	0.72	52.35
	9.76	*2.33*	*37.80*	*0.41*	*10.24*	*1.58*	*0.20*	*11.19*	*1.37*	

Source: WTO *Yearbook* (1990)

† tourist nights
nd no data
Bold figures rank order (first ten) in relation to all source countries
Roman figures absolute numbers of tourist nights in millions
Italic figures percentage of the country's total tourist nights

time to spend longer holidays than their Eastern European counterparts; (b) the more settled nature of Western tourists compared to Eastern Europeans who might be making the most of their exit visas by undertaking circuit tourism, visiting several bloc countries and thereby spending a shorter time in any one. Thus in Hungary, West Germans represented only the fourth largest group of arrivals, but the most important group for tourist nights. Austrians came sixth in importance for arrivals but fourth for nights and Italians ninth for arrivals but eighth for nights. Böröcz (1990) has argued that for Hungary at least, Western tourists tended to stay longer than those from Eastern Europe, probably owing to the greater geographical distance of travel involved. This is not a convincing argument given the contiguity of Austria and the relative proximity of northern Italy and south-eastern parts of the Federal Republic compared to northern Poland, eastern Romania and Bulgaria and much of the Soviet Union. Böröcz (1990) also pointed to the sizeable Hungarian diaspora undertaking family visits (VFR tourism) of somewhat longer duration than other forms of tourism to the country.

3. West Germany clearly provided the most important Western market for all countries of the region for which adequate data are available (that is,

excluding Albania and the Soviet Union), as reflected in both arrivals and nights records. This reflected West Germany's relative affluence, population size and geographical location, past economic and cultural links with the region.

4. Even in competition with Eastern European tourists, West Germans were among the eight most important sources of arrivals for all enumerated countries of the region and the most important source of tourist nights for two of the three countries for which data are available.
5. Overall numbers of other Western tourists were relatively small, with only Italians and Austrians providing a significant regular presence.
6. Of the Western countries not listed, it should be noted that 1988 appears to have been the year that the Dutch discovered Eastern Europe: for tourist nights the country's tourists recorded the highest increases for all three countries for which data are available—Bulgaria (75.2 per cent), Hungary (61.0 per cent) and Yugoslavia (25.6 per cent), ranking them the fifth most important group for Yugoslavia and seventh for Hungary.

4.5.4 Economic impact: tourism receipts

Until the end of the 1980s, the economic impact of international tourism on Eastern Europe and the Soviet Union remained relatively small, certainly by comparison with Western Europe (Table 4.10). A problem for analytical purposes is that the data do not differentiate between hard- and soft-currency earnings from international tourism, a distinction which is particularly critical in the present difficult economic circumstances.

Turkey acted as something of a demonstration effect during the 1980s, revealing a growth of tourism receipts from $327 million in 1980 to $2.35 billion by 1988 (an increase of 620.2 per cent), underlining the substantial and rapid economic impact which could be attained from a relatively low starting point when a new tourism destination is 'discovered', packaged and marketed (Buckley and Witt 1990, p. 10). While receipts declined woefully in Romania (by 45.7 per cent over 1980–8), plummeted in the early 1980s in Poland and then recovered somewhat (31.7 per cent overall decrease 1980–8), they grew in Bulgaria and Czechoslovakia at rates comparable to the major Western tourist economies of Austria, Greece and Switzerland, more rapidly in Hungary (50.6 per cent) and fastest in Yugoslavia (81.5 per cent 1980–8). Indeed, Yugoslavia's total in receipts for 1988 ($2,024 million) was not far short of the figure for the whole of the rest of the region ($2,139 million, without data for Albania and the former GDR). The country's relative dominance appeared to have been diminishing until the 1988 figures were published: the ratio of the country's receipts to those of the next highest country (Hungary) had been reduced from 3.23 in 1975, to 2.21 by 1980, 2.07 in 1985 and 2.02 in 1987. But the 1988 figures, which actually saw a decline in Hungary's income, produced a ratio back up to 2.67.

When turning to the figures for average income per tourist, a number of points emerge from Table 4.10:

1. The difference between Yugoslavia and the other states of the region is again considerable, the 1988 ratio between the Yugoslav average income

Table 4.10 Eastern Europe and the Soviet Union with selected Western destinations: international tourist receipts and average income per tourist, 1975–88

	Receipts (US $ millions)									
	1975		1980		1985		1988		% increase 1980–8	
	a	*b*	*a*	*b*	*a*	*b*	*a*	*b*	*a*	*b*
Albania	nd		nd		nd		nd		nd	
Bulgaria	230	57.5	260	47.3	343	47.0	359	43.3	38.1	− 8.5
Czech.	nd		338	66.3	307	62.7	436	31.1	29.0	−53.1
Former GDR	nd		nd		nd		nd		nd	
Hungary	238	47.6	504	53.6	512	52.8	759	71.6	50.6	33.6
Poland	163	45.3	282	49.5	118	42.1	193	77.2	−31.6	56.0
Romania	132	41.3	324	57.9	182	37.9	176	32.0	−45.7	−44.7
Soviet Union	nd		nd		163	37.9	216	36.0	32.5*	− 5.0*
Yugoslavia	769	132.6	1115	174.2	1061	126.3	2024	224.9	81.5	29.1
Austria	2781	241.0	6442	464.1	5084	334.5	8520	513.3	32.3	10.6
(FR) Germany	2900	329.5	6566	590.5	4748	373.9	8449	645.0	28.7	9.2
Greece	621	173.9	1734	361.3	1428	216.4	2396	307.2	38.2	−15.0
Spain	3404	171.9	6968	297.8	8151	296.4	16686	475.4	139.5	59.6
Switzerland	1606	199.8	3149	355.0	3164	265.9	4240	362.4	34.6	2.1
Turkey	200	166.7	327	375.9	1482	673.6	2355	636.5	620.2	69.3

Source: WTO *Yearbooks*, author's calculations
a Receipts (US $ millions)
b Average income per tourist arrival (US dollars)
nd no data
* 1985–88 figure

figure ($229.4) and the region's next highest, that for Poland ($77.2), being 2.92:1. This represented an increasing gap compared to the 1985 ratio (with Czechoslovakia) of 2.01:1 and that for 1980 (again with Czechoslovakia) of 2.63:1.

2. Languishing with 1988 figures even less than half of those for Poland are Czechoslovakia, Romania and the Soviet Union.
3. Even so, Yugoslavia's level of income per tourist is less than three-quarters that of Greece, less than half that of Spain and little more than a third of that of Turkey, emphasising the relatively low level of per tourist capita receipts in Eastern Europe compared to the major tourist economies of the West.
4. Overall rates of change for the 1980–8 period reveal a number of interesting trends which tend to be reinforced by other data:

    (a) while both Bulgaria and Czechoslovakia increased their receipts over this period (by 38.1 per cent and 29.0 per cent respectively), their average incomes declined: slightly for Bulgaria (8.5 per cent), perhaps reflecting the continuing dependence upon the somewhat economically depressed East European market, but significantly for Czechoslovakia (53.1 per cent), reflecting the substantial increase of

East Europeans in both relative and absolute terms, acting to depress levels of receipts per tourist;

(b) while showing an overall decline in receipts, because of an even faster decline in arrivals, Poland's average receipt level actually rose quite considerably during the period;

(c) Romania's decline in per tourist receipts was roughly commensurate with the country's overall decline in receipts;

(d) while Hungary's receipts increased overall by just over half, the country's per tourist receipts rose by just over a third, reflecting the increasing role of the Western tourist market;

(e) given increasing tourist numbers, Yugoslavia's overall growth in receipts was less spectacular when translated into per tourist receipt terms, with a rate of increase falling a little below that of Hungary and only half that of Poland. But of course, Yugoslavia was already experiencing a much higher level of per tourist spending compared to the rest of the region.

5. Clearly there is a lot of catching up to do in the region, and while not all countries have the natural tourism resources of Yugoslavia, it is perhaps salutary that it is one of the less endowed tourist economies, Poland, which has been able most noticeably to raise its per capita tourist income within just a few years (albeit through a decrease in tourist numbers!), while Romania and Czechoslovakia have regressed, the latter to some extent suffering from its increasing regional popularity.

4.5.4.1 As a proportion of national product

Tourism receipts in the region have remained low, only exceeding 3 per cent in the case of Hungary by 1987, and often much lower (0.3 per cent for Romania and 0.2 per cent for Poland in 1986), although the data are limited, and definitions of national product, especially for comparative purposes are not consistent. These figures compare with over 2 per cent for Turkey (rapidly growing), 4 per cent for Greece, 5 per cent for Spain and 7 per cent for Austria (Buckley and Witt 1990, p. 12).

4.5.4.2 As a proportion of total exports

Tourism receipts are remarkably low by global standards. The WTO (*Yearbook* 1990, p. 18) records that for 1988 tourism receipts represented only 0.94 per cent of the 'European socialist societies' exports (the figures for 1987 and 1986 were 0.99 and 0.92 respectively). By contrast, the figure for 'developed market economies' was 6.99 per cent, while the world average was 6.85 per cent. Buckley and Witt (1990, p. 12) report that Yugoslavia registered a figure of 18.6 per cent in 1986, the only available figure from within the region comparable to those of the major Western tourism economies, but still considerably below that for Spain (25.8 per cent), and somewhat lower than those figures for Greece (20.8 per cent) and Austria (20.1 per cent). No other East European country even approaches Turkey (8.6 per cent), Hungary with 6.5 per cent being the nearest. Figures of between 1 and 5 per cent are the norm for the rest of the region, again underlying the relatively small economic role of tourism, even into the second half of the 1980s.

Concluding from the evidence of visitor arrivals, absolute tourism receipts, tourism receipts as a percentage of national product and as a percentage of total exports, Buckley and Witt (1990, pp. 10–11) argued that in comparison with Western tourist economies, tourism in the region was clearly not attaining its potential. Further, as most international tourists came from other East European countries, hard-currency earnings were relatively low. The more recent data for 1988 would not appear to alter those conclusions significantly, although, as discussed below, major changes to tourist flow patterns and sources have taken place subsequently, with knock-on effects for the industry's relative economic importance.

4.5.5 Impact on domestic tourism

The creation of a tourist industry encompassing both domestic and foreign customers inevitably raised certain tensions of an economic, social and political character. Two problems stood out:

1. How, through segregation and other means, to minimise the demonstration effect of the presence of numbers of (usually richer) foreigners and to preserve ideological discipline among both domestic tourists and those employed in the tourist industry coming into everyday contact with such affluent visitors.
2. The inadequacy of tourism's infrastructure and superstructure (hotels of an appropriate standard, catering, roads etc.), which saw, for example, a direct diversion of resources away from the domestic to the foreign market, with workers' rest centres being adapted for foreign visitors' use, thereby shifting the burden of resource shortage on to the host population (Allcock and Przecławski 1990, p. 5).

4.6 Outbound tourism to the West

4.6.1 Constraints

For both ideological and financial reasons, a range of hurdles and barriers were placed before the citizens of the region constraining their travel outside of their native land and most especially to Western non-socialist countries. The example of Czechoslovakia is not atypical, from which country about 6 million citizens were annually travelling abroad by 1989. All citizens wishing to apply for travel to the West had first to obtain an exit visa from the Ministry of Internal Affairs. Such applicants would have to secure a permit from their place of work, would need to submit their police record with their application and, if male, would need to prove that their military papers would be left in the safe keeping of military officials. In early 1989, these last two requirements were dropped by the Czechoslovak authorities.

A number of recognised methods of travel to the West were available:

1. As part of a group tour, organised by a travel agent. In the Czechoslovak case, Čedok was the largest such agent, organising overseas travel for some 700,000 Czechoslovaks per year by the late 1980s, with programmes available for visits to most European countries, Egypt, India, the United States, Cuba, Brazil and, new for the 1989 season, Thailand. As in other aspects of organised tourism and recreation, a range of associations existed for various 'niche' groups, young people, for those interested in sports and motorists.
2. Self-financed, individual travel which could be facilitied by trade union organisations, enterprises and other places of work such as cooperative farms. Holiday vouchers would be offered at a discount as a reward for those who had gained merit at work.
3. At the invitation of relatives willing to bear the hard-currency costs of the visit. This requirement was actually relaxed by the Prague authorities in July 1989, such that anyone in the West could provide a written invitation, although it had to be officially witnessed and state that the person extending the invitation agreed to pay for all daily and any medical expenses of the guest.

A further hurdle was the question of access to hard currency. For many years this could only be obtained legally in severely limited quantities through state banks. By the mid- to late 1980s these procedures were also being somewhat liberalised. In Czechoslovakia, from 1988 a relative or acquaintance in the West could deposit Western currency—at least $10 worth for each day of the proposed visit—at a state bank, where it would remain until a decision was made on granting the exit visa. From April of that year Czechoslovak citizens were themselves permitted to open hard-currency accounts for the purposes of travel to the West, so long as they could prove that the money was obtained legally.

Leaving one's own country without an exit visa was an offence usually punishable by imprisonment, as was overstaying a visit in the West after the period of the visa had expired.

The officially perceived ideological position of neighbouring countries also constrained travellers' movements even after an exit visa had been granted. Czechoslovaks wanting to take a holiday in Yugoslavia would normally be required to travel the probably longer route via Hungary rather than through capitalist Austria, for which an exit visa would be much more difficult to obtain. Likewise, those wishing to travel to Bulgaria would usually be required to follow a circuitous route through Romania rather than via Yugoslavia, for which an exit visa would again be more difficult in view of that country's (then) relatively liberal attitude (Pehe 1989).

Just as increasingly liberal attitudes were being taken up and attracting Western tourists to earn vital hard currency, so the same liberalism and growing East–West *détente* began to set the scene for increasing numbers of East Europeans to journey to the West and spend the very same hard-won dollars and Deutschmarks. Two responses to stem such leakages could be made by the region's authorities: (a) continue or reimpose restrictions on the ability of citizens to leave the country, and thereby earn the wrath of the post-Helsinki Western world as well as of the region's citizens themselves; and/or (b) as many Western countries had done in times of financial stringency, restrict the amount of hard currency which residents could take out of the country.

4.6.2 *The international context*

The third clause of the Helsinki Final Act (the 1975 Conference on Security and Cooperation in Europe) included a decision to promote free movement and communication of people between all European countries. This would require the reduction of visa and travel document costs for travellers and an easing of all travel for both private individuals and groups.

Nevertheless, for the following decade little progress was achieved, and by the early 1980s, it could still be said that 'practically no tourists come to Western Europe from [the] east while there is some noticeable tourist movement from West to East. The ideological boundary is thus like a semi-permeable membrane: it allows penetration from one side but not from the other' (Vuoristo 1981, p. 241).

4.6.3 *Shopping tourism*

One notable development was the bilateral agreement secured between Hungary and Austria in 1979 to abolish visas. Austrians quickly appreciated that food, drink, fuel and many services were cheaper over the border. They soon came in large numbers to visit hairdressers, dentists and grocers, filling up car petrol tanks and eating out in style before returning home. Not until 1988 did Hungarians gain access to full passports and, theoretically, to unlimited travel opportunities to redress the balance. The first major celebration of this new freedom saw 100,000 going on a shopping spree into Austria, ironically on the national holiday celebrating the 71st anniversary of the Russian Revolution. In total, 3 million Hungarians visited Austria in 1988—mostly such 'excursionists'—compared to a sixth of that total the previous year (albeit still high for East Europeans visiting the West). Still more Austrians—3.8 million—came to Hungary. Hungarians spent $629 million in Western countries in 1988, an increase of no less than 240 per cent over the 1987 figure. In April 1989, over 150,000 Hungarians marked their Liberation Day holiday by again invading Austria, armed with shopping bags, roof racks and trailers. Austrian shopkeepers are thought to have sold $300 million worth of consumer goods in just two days. But such manifestations of liberalism also presented a drain on the Hungarian exchequer, with a significant leakage of much needed hard currency. Within days of the April holiday the Hungarian authorities were forced to tighten a number of customs regulations, not least in summarily halving personal allowances. Hungarians could then only freely change $360 in any three-year period. They could continue to keep dollars earned abroad or 'donated' in hard-currency accounts.

Before the end of 1989, it was clear that for the first time Hungary would experience an overall tourism hard-currency income deficit—$420m as it transpired—such that in November of that year, the hard-currency allowance was reduced further to $300 every four years, available in allocations of only $50 in the first two years. As a consequence of these restrictions and the continued inconvertability of the forint, the currency black market has flourished as never before.

4.6.4 *Ethnic outbound tourism*

Poland has held a particularly distinctive position in relation to outbound tourism in that the Polish diaspora throughout the Western world and beyond placed increasing pressures on requirements for foreign travel. A more liberal attitude towards the issuing of passports in 1956, virtually opened the floodgates for the movement between Poles residing in the country and their relatives living abroad. But with financial pressures and little hard currency in state coffers, permits for Western travel were granted only to those who could provide evidence of an invitation and commitment to cover the cost of their stay abroad. This practice became increasingly common, not just in Poland, and embraced invitations from those other than family members. Air travel was normally undertaken by the home country's national carrier, whereby fares could be covered in the local currency (Rogalewski 1980).

4.6.5 *Tourism of shortage*

Subsequently, other factors came to influence Poles' tourist habits. Gołembski argues that the rapid increase of tourist departures from Poland in the 1984–7 period was unrelated to any improvement in the standard of living, but conversely, to continued economic shortages within the country:

> People travel in order to do business, and this influences in an innovative way the thinking and acting of those who engage in tourism . . . The person who can earn some money abroad, even if this is not much by the standards of the West, and then bring that sum of money into the country, will become a wealthy individual . . . Under conditions of shortage, the prices of goods and labour become incommensurate with their worth in comparison with world prices . . . attempts to make up for shortages through private import and export, as well as by pumping foreign money into the market, become highly profitable. [Gołembski 1990, pp. 57–8]

Ironically for Polish outbound tourism, these developments became especially noticeable just at the time when passport and visa regulations were being further liberalised, and there followed a rapid increase in outbound tourist movements.

> The crowning point of the liberalisation process was the Helsinki conference, where all European countries—the Western European ones in particular—voted for free tourism. The consequences [for Western European countries] of opening the border with those countries struggling against shortages were easy to foresee. Lack of liberalised regulations concerning free employment and free trading were the evidence of Western inconsistency. When reducing passport formalities, the Polish government was well aware of the likely economic consequence of tourism in the form of the increase of foreign currency in bank accounts. Despite its more democratic appearance, there is an air of pimping about this development. People are faced with an alternative—especially those who are young, talented, and possessed with initiative. Either they will leave,

Table 4.11 Eastern Europe and the Soviet Union: tourist arrivals in selected Western countries, 1988

	Arrivals in Western countries								
	Aus.	Fra.	FRG	Gr.	It.	Swe.	Tur.	UK	USA
From:									
Albania	nd	nd	nd	nd	nd	nd	nd	nd	nd
	0.01			0.05			0.01		
Bulgaria	*0.05*	*nd*	*nd*	*0.60*	*nd*	*nd*	*0.21*	*nd*	*nd*
	−10.5			**53.1**			**97.4**		
	0.05		0.06				0.01		0.01
Czechoslovakia	*0.29*	*nd*	*0.45*	*nd*	*nd*	*nd*	*0.19*	*nd*	*0.02*
	31.1		**12.1**				**20.6**		**32.6**
Former GDR	nd	nd	nd	nd	nd	nd	nd	nd	nd
	0.28			0.03			0.06		0.02
Hungary	*1.68*	*nd*	*nd*	*0.38*	*nd*	*nd*	*1.46*	*nd*	*0.05*
	23.7			**50.2**			**117.1**		**26.5**
	0.06		0.13	0.09			0.17		0.05
Poland	*0.34*	*nd*	*0.97*	*1.10*	*nd*	*nd*	*3.98*	*nd*	*0.14*
	190.6		**43.8**	**−7.5**			**197.6**		**0.8**
	0.01			0.01			0.02		0.01
Romania	*0.04*	*nd*	*nd*	*0.12*	*nd*	*nd*	*0.38*	*nd*	*0.01*
	48.3			**56.4**			**18.3**		**17.1**
	0.01		0.04		0.05		0.02		0.03
Soviet Union	*0.08*	*nd*	*0.28*	*nd*	*0.09*	*nd*	*0.52*	*nd*	*0.08*
	37.5		**36.5**		**52.6**		**10.4**		**214.3**
	0.11		0.17	0.39	5.47		0.29	0.03	0.03
Yugoslavia	*0.68*	*nd*	*1.26*	*4.98*	*9.81*	*nd*	*6.96*	*0.18*	*0.08*
	1.9		**4.3**	**−7.5**	**13.1**		**−15.4**	**−38.2**	**8.1**
Arrivals	0.53	0.17	0.37	0.56			0.57	0.26	0.14
from the	*3.19*	*0.45*	*2.99*	*7.19*	*nd*	*nd*	*13.74*	*1.64*	*0.40*
region	**26.2**	**−3.8**	**13.8**	**−1.2**			**21.3**	**1.8**	**27.3**
Total arrivals (millions)	16.37	38.29	13.11	7.78	55.69	nd	4.17	15.80	33.88

Source: WTO *Yearbook* (1990)

nd no data
Roman figures numbers of arrivals (millions)
Italic figures percentage of host country's total arrivals
Bold figures percentage change in numbers 1987–8

earn money (in most cases illegally, and not always in their special skill or profession), and in this way gain the possibility of a good start; or they will stick to the same job in the home country with small prospects of progress. [Gołembski, 1990, pp. 66–7]

But Gołembski confessed that the concealment of this less than flattering form of tourist development has resulted in little being known either about the characteristics of those who travel or about the impact of this 'business

Table 4.12 Eastern Europe and the Soviet Union: tourist nights in Western countries, 1988

	Nights in Western countries								
	Aus.	Fra.	FRG	Gr.	It.	Swe.	Tur.	UK	USA
From:									
Albania	nd	nd	nd	nd	nd	nd	nd	nd	nd
Bulgaria	0.03 *0.03* **−24.3**	*nd*	*nd*	*nd*	*nd*	*nd*	0.01 *0.08* **97.6**	*nd*	*nd*
Czechoslovakia	0.14 *0.15* **35.5**	*nd*	0.15 *0.51* **9.0**	*nd*	*nd*	*nd*	*nd*	*nd*	*nd*
Former GDR	nd	nd	nd	nd	nd	nd	nd	nd	nd
Hungary	0.61 *0.69* **19.9**	*nd*	*nd*	*nd*	*nd*	*nd*	0.08 *0.67* **54.6**	*nd*	*nd*
Poland	0.17 *0.19* **130.0**	*nd*	0.85 *2.83* **33.3**	*nd*	*nd*	*nd*	0.23 *2.00* **89.4**	*nd*	*nd*
Romania	0.02 *0.02* **45.8**	*nd*	*nd*	*nd*	*nd*	*nd*	0.01 *0.08* **−18.6**	*nd*	*nd*
Soviet Union	0.07 *0.08* **64.6**	*nd*	0.13 *0.43* **47.1**	*nd*	0.17 *0.16* **39.5**	*nd*	0.01 *0.10* **77.7**	*nd*	*nd*
Yugoslavia	0.38 *0.43* **3.4**	*nd*	0.42 *1.39* **9.8**	*nd*	0.57 *0.53* **2.8**	*nd*	0.06 *0.50* **−20.8**	*nd*	0.60 *0.34* **−39.9**
Region's tourist nights	1.42 *1.61* **23.5**	3.16 *0.91* **−3.8**	1.56 *5.17* **25.6**	*nd*	*nd*	0.33★ *4.61★* **7.0★**	0.40 *3.44* **33.0**	*nd*	4.80★ *2.77★* **37.1★**
Total nights (millions)	87.58	347.11	30.12	nd	107.03	7.11	11.66	172.90	nd

Source: WTO *Yearbook* (1990)

★ data for 'all Europe' excluding 'Western Europe' (that is, including 'Southern' and 'Northern Europe')

nd no data

Roman figures numbers of arrivals (millions)

Italic figures percentage of host country's total arrivals

Bold figures percentage change in numbers 1987–8

tourism' on the countries which receive such visitors (such as in Berlin and on the Hungarian–Soviet border at Zahony).

4.6.6 *Patterns of travel to the West*

Comprehensive data on outbound travel to the West from the region are not available in a readily digestible form: Tables 4.11 and 4.12 have been compiled from arrivals and tourist nights data from each of the Western countries concerned, as reported to the WTO for 1988. Notable patterns arise out of these data.

4.6.6.1 Significance

East Europeans' overall absolute numbers and proportions of Western countries' inbound tourists remained small, although the data were far from complete. But apart from Turkey, which had managed to attract the Eastern as well as Western tourist market in recent years, no major Western country, for which sufficient data were available, appeared to have had more than about 2.5 per cent of its annual arrivals from the region.

4.6.6.2 Trends

As in earlier tables, there was a clear difference between the patterns of data relating to Yugoslavia and to the other countries of the region: in this instance in terms of the growth of tourism to the West. As both arrivals and nights data show, there was a general and sometimes substantial proportional increase in tourists from the region between 1987 and 1988, reflecting increasing liberal attitudes to exit visa policies coupled with the relatively new and nearby attraction of Turkey—'push' and 'pull' factors. Difficult economic conditions in Yugoslavia, however, saw some modest increases but also some significant decreases in arrivals and nights spent. It should be remembered, however, that in absolute terms the numbers being discussed are still relatively small by Western European standards.

1. Push: the outward movement of Poles increased dramatically in certain directions, although the 190.6 per cent increase in arrivals and 130.0 per cent increase in nights spent in Austria was probably related to the 'economic' aspects of that group's movement patterns, compared to the 197.6 per cent increase of arrivals and 89.4 per cent growth in nights spent in Turkey, more likely a reflection of 'pleasure' tourism. Hungary and the Soviet Union showed a substantial all-round increase in outbound tourism, notably to the United States in the latter instance, although numbers remained relatively small, in this case rising from 9,667 to 30,388.
2. Constraint: ironically, hitherto the country with the most liberal travel policy revealed the greatest constraint on growth, with actual decreases in Yugoslav arrivals in Greece, Turkey and the United Kingdom, and reductions in Yugoslav tourist nights in Turkey and the United States. Arrivals and nights in neighbouring or nearby Western European

countries (Italy, Austria, West Germany) showed modest gains. But overall the impression of constraint is conveyed.

3. Pull: Turkey is revealed as the fastest growing attraction for the region's travellers, with a 1987–8 increase in arrivals of 119.3 per cent and 73.8 per cent in nights spent. Indeed, the only Western source countries to match the high increases in arrivals in Turkey from Poland, Hungary and Bulgaria were Finland (137.6 per cent increase) and Greece (147.6 per cent increase). Austria (35.0 per cent growth in arrivals and 33.1 increase in nights), the United States (33.4 and 37.1 per cent) and West Germany (32.7 and 30.7 per cent) were the other major beneficiaries. Austria's neutrality had aided the mutual abolition of entry visas with most of the region's countries, but the same certainly could not be said of the other two Western countries.

4.6.7 Continuing constraints on outward tourism

Although the situation has been rapidly changing in recent months, a number of administrative constraints still bear down on movement out of and into the region. They are imposed both by East European countries themselves and also by certain Western governments' refusal to abolish visa requirements for visiting East Europeans.

Soviet citizens, for example, wishing to travel abroad still need to pass through a number of hurdles, including acquiring an invitation from someone who will pay the expenses (although now package-tour operators as well as relatives and business contacts can issue the necessary paper), visiting a local visa office to complete paperwork and buying 200 roubles-worth of foreign exchange at the state bank. Previously visas could be arbitrarily refused perhaps because local Communist Party officials had not been notified of such matters as the reason for a divorce, or because all the family wanted to go on holiday together, thereby raising questions of possible defection. Passports were valid for one trip and had to be handed in on return. Most of these restrictions have now been eliminated: it is claimed that visa refusals now amount to just 0.2 per cent. Passports are valid for five years and do not have to be handed in after each trip. At the time of writing, the Supreme Soviet was considering allowing multiple-exit visas (though those who apply for them will still be asking for permission to leave their own country) and the elimination of the need for an invitation.

In the first six months of 1989, 1.7 million Soviet citizens applied for exit visas, nearly as many as travelled abroad for the whole of 1988. That year just over 1 million ventured abroad as tourists and another 800,000 on business. However, 1.8 million represents only 0.5 per cent of the total population. Persisting practical barriers include the fact that new passports cost 200 roubles, which is almost a month's average salary, and while the 200 roubles-worth of hard currency used to be worth $320, after the rouble devaluation of November 1989 it was worth $32. In the summer of 1990 the government stopped providing travellers with up to $200 due to the drain on the country's reserves. None the less, embassies in Moscow have been inundated with visa applications: at the end of 1989 the American embassy was receiving 300 applications a day for tourist visas and more than 250 from people wanting to travel on business. Visas were taking up to a month to be processed. Reflecting basic infrastructural constraints, Aeroflot claimed to have increased the number of its passengers by less than one-fifth during 1989, despite the fact that the number of aspiring travellers had more than doubled. As a result, by the end of that year, the waiting time for a ticket to New York was 13 months.

4.7 Post-socialist transition: multilateral mass tourism?

4.7.1 Change and continuity

Was there ever a true socialist model of tourism development? Will tourism now be the flagship of economic restructuring, the symbol of post-socialist, 'post-industrial' global interdependence? Are we in danger of overestimating the impact of the 1989 revolutions? In most countries of the region, inspired, or in some cases bludgeoned, by *glasnost* and *perestroika*, liberalising tendencies, extending to a relaxation of travel restrictions and other aspects of both inbound and outbound tourism activity, were already becoming apparent in the mid- to late-1980s, even in hard-line Czechoslovakia. Given the apparent minimal change in the essential political substructure of Romania and Bulgaria, together with the uncertainties weighing heavily upon both Yugoslavia and Albania, at the time of writing, the historic differences between the Balkans and Central Europe are reasserting themselves, rendering the concept of 'Eastern Europe' ever more anachronistic.

From the historical viewpoint of mid-1990, there appeared to be a paradox being acted out. The past year had seen enormous changes and uncertainty in the region. The coming year was likely to bring no less uncertainty for just about every country under review. Tourism tends to be sensitive to instability and even minor changes, usually in a negative way. Yet massive increases in international tourism in the region were being recorded in the months prior to this volume's going to press. In discussing global trends in tourism growth, Williams and Shaw (1988, pp. 13–4) recognised three distinctive post-war elements: long-term growth trends, cyclical movements and short-term erratics. In the case of Eastern Europe and the Soviet Union, we may be viewing a convergence of all three elements:

1. An overall increase in growth, which may partly reflect a perceived 'saturation' of tourism in Western Europe, but which also reflects the absolute lower levels of tourism activity in Eastern Europe and the Soviet Union.
2. A shorter-term growth cycle related to the phase of increasing liberalisation instigated in the mid-1980s.
3. The major erratic of the 1989 revolutions, rendering the countries of the region much more 'accessible', both metaphorically and practically, to many Westerners, while at the same time generating a great deal of short-term curiosity value.

Some of these dimensions are neatly encapsulated in a recent tour brochure:

> The whirlwind of change in the Eastern Block . . . has taken everyone's breath away. We must welcome such profound turnabouts as it makes travel there more accessible and increases our understanding of and friendship with the local people . . . we have for some time experienced the growing desire among travellers to visit the new emerging

societies of the Eastern World, and see something of the historic changes for themselves . . . [Explore 1990, *East Europe & Siberia*, p. 3).

How long will the tourism impact of the 'erratic' be maintained, and how far will the local and regional instability constrain longer-term tourism trends?

4.7.2 *Major trends*

The major trends observable at the time of writing could be summarised as:

1. Substantial absolute increases in international tourism, although with considerable variations between countries:
   (a) 'intra-bloc': influenced by continuing business tourism, and, presumably, also statistically biased by the peripatetic movements of East Germans and other 'tourists' immediately prior to the year's revolutions. For example, arrivals in Czechoslovakia for 1989 were, at 28 million, double the figure of the previous year, but included 10.4 million Poles and 8.2 million East Germans.
   (b) from the West: for the first half of 1990 Czechoslovakia recorded 17.5 million arrivals, including a 500 per cent increase in Westerners (4.5 million). In the first five months of the year Yugoslavia recorded receipts of $711 million from tourism, a 48 per cent increase over the same period in the previous year. However, some concern was shown by the fact that pegging a convertible dinar at DM7 had raised prices to West European levels for a generally inferior quality of service. Further, despite increasing numbers, with greater freedom accorded to them, Western tourists are not contributing to national exchequers to the extent that the region's governments would wish. In particular, with a wide availability of private tourist accommodation—much of it unrecorded—and a flourishing currency black market, the Hungarian government estimated that Western tourists were spending three times more than the revenue which reached the state through official tourist channels, thereby reflecting some of the tensions of the transition from a statist to market-orientated society.
2. Notable, but again variable, increases in outbound tourism: most countries have lifted most of their restrictions on outbound travel although currency constraints remain. Romanians, in January 1990 and even Albanians in the following May were theoretically given the freedom to travel abroad, although in the former case hard-currency shortages maintained constraints, and in the latter case upheaval followed when it was clear that the granting of passports was not to be a simple matter. By contrast, Hungary exhibited a net deficit of $420 million in hard-currency tourism receipts for 1989 owing to a substantial increase in outbound shopping tourism (a 53 per cent increase in outbound tourism, with no less than a 158.5 per cent growth in cross-border visits to Austria). For the first half of 1990, however, an 80 per cent increase in arrivals in Hungary had managed to counter-balance the outflow to produce an $80 million surplus.

3. Continuing inter-state squabbles over the adverse impact of cross-border shopping and business 'tourism'. These problems have arisen from two major sources:
   (a) the parity of inconvertible currencies' exchange rates: theoretically, CMEA member countries have bilaterally agreed conversion rates on the basis of comparing the prices of basic consumer goods and services. But, for example, the East Germans in April 1988 and the Czechoslovak authorities in March 1990 came to feel that an unfair rate of exchange had developed between their currencies and the Hungarian forint, with East German and then Czechoslovak goods appearing cheap to Hungarians who were snapping them up to take home. In the latter case, seeking what they considered to be a more equitable exchange rate, the Czechoslovak authorities began to refuse to accept forints from Hungarian tourists.
   (b) the additional impact of declining Soviet oil supplies: this saw the Czechoslovak government introduce petrol coupons for all foreigners from March 1990, partly induced by the additional factor of cross-border purchases. Two types of coupon were introduced for convertible and non-convertible currencies. The mid-1990 Gulf crisis acted to exacerbate this situation. Even the Soviet Union itself in June 1990 introduced petrol coupons for foreigners and demanded hard-currency payment: East Europeans could only pay in their own soft currencies if coupons were purchased (through Intourist) prior to travelling to the Soviet Union.
4. The short-term complicating factor of the transition to German unification. From January 1990 visas and compulsory currency exchanges for West Germans were abolished, and the two German governments established a joint hard-currency fund of DM3 billion from which East Germans could draw DM200 per year to travel to the West. These measures were, of course, superseded by monetary union in July of that year. Immediately after November 1989, West German tour operators began establishing companies across the border in anticipation of new East German joint-venture legislation, to then be followed, just weeks later, by anticipation of unification. At the same time, the travel agency TUI set up Transeuropa (DDR) with Interflug to run joint flights from Berlin–Schönefeld to Mallorca, Monastir, Dalaman and Singapore and from Dresden to Mallorca. Neckerman soon began offering Mediterranean holidays and short breaks to London, Rome and Istanbul. While Spanish tourist officials, attempting to offset a shortfall of tourists from Scandinavia, West Germany and Britain, began offering free sampler holidays to East Germans.

4.8 Conclusions

Although the statistical data are never satisfactory, it is possible to identify certain elements in the evolution of most countries' tourism industries which reflect the development of their political and economic circumstances. The nature of tourist flows would appear to support the notion that in the early years of state-socialist development, domestic tourism—the notion of creative leisure—was the only well-developed characteristic, fitting ideological roles of collective activity and raising the well-being and consciousness of new socialist man. As political leaderships became more confident, as economic development moved away from laying the foundations of a consolidated socialist state and as supranational mechanisms within the Soviet bloc were explored, international intra-bloc tourism, albeit constrained by exit and entry restrictions and financial considerations, began to develop, with the more advanced societies of the north generating a significant proportion of travellers. The subsequent slow-down of economic growth and poor level of technological innovation witnessed ever-widening attempts to ascertain hard currency in order to be able to buy-in Western technology and thereby improve efficiency. In a number of the region's economies one of the means employed to do this was the attracting of Western tourists to resorts and locations not always best equipped to deal with new tourism requirements.

Particularly from the mid-1980s, elements of liberalism and less secretiveness witnessed the irony of increasing numbers of Western tourists arriving in some countries while increasing numbers of the region's citizens were travelling to the West and spending hard-won convertible currency. This began raising a number of philosophical and administrative tensions, most notably seen in Hungary. How far the revolutions of 1989 and their aftermath have unleashed a new intensity and scale of international tourism to, within and from the region remains to be seen. Further, while it was always a hazardous occupation to attempt to generalise about the economic and social development patterns of the Soviet bloc, the increasingly diverse political and economic characteristics of the post-revolution societies of the region render future prediction for the tourism industry across the region as a whole an almost impossible task.

Part two: National studies

5 The Soviet Union

Denis J.B. Shaw

5.1 Introduction

The meaning of the term 'tourism' is no more precise in Russian than it is in most Western languages. On the one hand it can be used to refer to many types of travelling, especially that done for leisure purposes. On the other it can mean a specific type of sporting activity (including hiking, skiing and mountaineering) (Riordan 1977, pp. 3, 187–9) or that species of holidaymaking which involves touring around from one place to another, spending nights in different places. Although the latter definition is that preferred by many Soviet specialists on recreation (for example, Darinskiy 1979, pp. 7–8), the present chapter will use the term in the broader sense accepted by the World Tourism Organisation: 'Tourism denotes the temporary, short-term movement of people to destinations outside the places where they normally live and work and their activities during the stay at these destinations' (Burkart and Medlik 1981, p. v). In this use of the term a distinction is typically made between the tourist and the excursionist, with the former spending at least one night away from home.

Since the establishment of the standard five-day working week in 1968, the ability of Soviet citizens to participate in tourism has considerably increased. In addition to weekends, almost half of the Soviet workforce (excluding the collective farm workers) enjoyed an annual holiday of at least 24 working days in 1987, and more than three-quarters had a minimum of 18 working days. Among industrial workers, only about one-third seem to have spent their summer holiday at home. Sixty-nine million workers and members of their families were accommodated in official rest and holiday facilities in 1988 (a few of these on a daily basis), with 30 million children and teenagers in Pioneer and school camps and other children's facilities (*Narodnoye khozyaystvo* 1989, pp. 60, 73, 238). Moreover, many people found tourist accommodation for themselves. In addition to domestic tourist activity, the Soviet Union has found itself host to growing numbers of foreign visitors, nearly 6 million of whom arrived in 1986. The flow in the opposite direction exceeded 4.5 million (Dolzhenko 1988, pp. 150, 154). Tourism has thus become a significant activity for many Soviet citizens and it may enjoy enhanced prospects as a consequence of policies being pursued under Gorbachev. Yet it also suffers from a number of difficulties and peculiarities which result in part from its uneven development during the pre-revolutionary and early Soviet periods.

5.2 Sources for the study of Soviet tourism

As will become apparent in this chapter, tourism in the Soviet Union is organised and administered by a variety of official bodies and it has never been a priority area for development. For these reasons detailed statistics are not easy to acquire. At a very general level, statistical data are published by the USSR State Statistical Committee in their annual handbook, *The National Economy of the USSR* (*Narodnoye khozyaystvo* 1989). This gives some details on the provision of tourist accommodation by official organisations (though these are not distinguished by type of organisation), their distribution by republic, the number of guests they accommodated, the annual holiday entitlements of industrial and service workers, estimates about how certain categories of employee spend their annual holiday and some other material. Similar data can sometimes be found in republic and local handbooks. Other than these, the best data comes from the various specialised studies undertaken by different individuals or organisations such as the very useful but now sadly dated work of V.I. Azar (Azar 1972) and the research of the Institute of Geography of the USSR Academy of Sciences (Vedenin *et al.* 1976; *Geografiya rekreatsionnykh sistem SSSR* 1980; Preobrazhenskiy, 1986). Several general works dealing with facets of recreation and tourism are referenced at the end of this book. These vary in their approach and academic worth. Many useful articles, sometimes furnished with original statistical material, are to be found in the major Soviet geographical, sociological, economic, planning and architectural journals. These are sometimes translated into English in such journals as *Soviet Geography*, *Soviet Sociology* and *Problems of Economics*. The Soviet press often discusses tourist or recreational problems; major articles are translated and published by *The Current Digest of the Soviet Press*. Finally, the recent period has witnessed the publication of many tourist guide books, handbooks, magazines, itineraries and other materials which can sometimes prove useful for academic study. Detailed maps, however, remain inexplicably classified material.

5.3 The historical and cultural background

In Russia of the pre-revolutionary period the development of tourism was long hindered by the constraints of serfdom, the backward state of the economy and the lamentable condition of transportation. Not until after the Emancipation of the serfs in 1861 did Russia begin to experience her Industrial Revolution and to develop an adequate system of railways. Consequently, before that stage, tourism was largely restricted to small numbers of wealthy nobles, some of whom were influenced by the eighteenth century Enlightenment's fascination with landscape, topography, history and commerce. It was at this time that Russia itself also became an object of curiosity to a small but growing band of foreign travellers, some of whom wrote accounts of their adventures in the little-known Empire. At the end of the seventeenth century, groups of Russians had begun to travel abroad, encouraged by Peter the Great's determination to develop his dominions along Western lines, but such travels were generally undertaken for educational and utilitarian purposes such as study in a foreign university. Not until later in the eighteenth century did the idea that the tour itself might contribute to the individual's enlightenment and enjoyment begin to take hold.

For travellers both foreign and domestic St Petersburg and Moscow long remained the chief objects of interest. But the fascination for art and culture was eventually joined by a concern for health as a stimulus to tourism. Peter the Great himself evinced an interest in spas and encouraged the development of spa settlements at Lipetsk and Martsial'nyye vody in Karelia. Later, at the end of the eighteenth century and in the first third of the nineteenth, spa settlements began to arise at such places as Kislovodsk, Pyatigorsk and Yessentuki, former military strongholds lying close to the mountains of the Caucasus where military operations were still being directed against the mountain peoples. The contemporary fashion for spas also found expression in places like Staraya Russa, situated near the old town of Novgorod. By the time of the Revolution an entire network had developed (*Kurortnyy putevoditel'* 1915), encouraged by the writings of medical men like Ivan Pfeler and F.P. Gaaz. The fashion for sea bathing came rather later and initially concentrated on the southern coast of the Crimea around Yalta. Regular visits from the 1860s by the Imperial family, who established coastal estates at Oreanda, Livadia and Massandra, and the writings of S.P. Botkin helped to popularise the health-giving features of the south coast; the building of a railway in 1873 was followed by the development of private dachas, hotels and sanatoria (Yalta 1910; Vorontsov 1966). Other resorts like Sochi followed suit.

The Emancipation of the Serfs in 1861 left the mass of the population tied by legal restrictions and sheer poverty to their villages, and despite the onset of industrialisation there was little market for mass tourism before 1917. However, in the cities at least, the years before 1917 witnessed the rise of new fashions in recreation and tourism, especially among the educated and prosperous classes. The newly discovered interest in mountaineering, for example, found expression in the Tiflis (1878), the Crimean (1890) and the Russian (1901) Mountaineering Clubs. Cycling was pioneered by various cycling clubs from about 1880 which culminated in the foundation of the Russian Touring Club (1895), eventually renamed the Russian Society of Tourists. By the early years of the new century excursions and tourism were being encouraged by a variety of clubs, organisations and educational bodies (Dolzhenko 1988, pp. 46–60).

Given the aristocratic and bourgeois basis of tourism at the time of the Revolution, it is hardly surprising that the new Bolshevik regime proved determined to change its character radically. Ideologically, the Bolsheviks were committed to the principle that leisure and good health were the right of all working people, part of the new social environment which would allow people to develop all their potentials to the full. The new regime was particularly attracted by the close linkage between tourism and health, and by his decree of March 1919 Lenin nationalised all resorts and spas on Russian territory, declaring that they were henceforth to be used for medical purposes. A second decree of December 1920 nationalised the private homes and palaces on the south coast of the Crimea, including the former Imperial estates, and ordered them to be converted into sanatoria. This health-orientated policy was to be an outstanding feature of the 1920s and 1930s as the number of sanatoria grew from 60 in 1913 with about 3,000 beds to 1,838 in 1939 with just under a quarter of a million beds (*Geografiya rekreatsionnykh sistem SSSR* 1980, p. 29). A new type of institution, the rest home, introduced by a decree of May 1921, was also health-orientated. By 1939 there were 1,270 rest homes with 195,000 beds. A further feature of the new regime was the accent on children's leisure and health. The first Soviet tourist organisation, the Bureau of School Tourism, appeared in 1918. Soon a network of children's Pioneer camps was being organised, of which Artek, opened on the Crimean coast in 1925, was a prototype. General tourism began to receive greater encouragement from the mid-1920s, especially with the setting up of the All-Union Society for Proletarian Tourism and Excursions (OPTE) in 1930. However, with the onset of the five-year plans, tourism was no longer conducted primarily for leisure and health reasons, but other purposes were also espoused with propagandistic, military training and economic aims (Dolzhenko 1988, pp. 80–7).

Table 5.1 Soviet Union: growth of capacity of sanatoria and official recreation facilities, 1940–88

Type of facility	Total number of beds by year ('000)				
	1940	1960	1970	1980	1988
Sanatoria and pensions with medical treatment	240	325	461	551	614
Prophylactic sanatoria	15	43	118	212	295
Rest homes and pensions	195	179	287	380	383
Rest and recreation bases	—	—	288	634	815
Tourist hotels, bases etc.	19	36	157	361	459
Total	469	583	1,311	2,138	2,566

Source: Narodnoye Khozyaystvo SSSR za 1988g, 1989, p. 235

In view of the many problems faced by the Soviet government during the inter-war period, it is surprising that the achievements in the field of tourism were as great as they were. Even so, there is no doubt that tourism development suffered along with other aspects of the consumer sector from the Stalinist emphasis on industrialisation, and the narrow focus on health and production-related facets of tourism permitted many aspects to languish. Moreover, quantitative progress was frequently unmatched by qualitative, and much tourist accommodation was housed in old and sub-standard buildings. A serious setback came from World War II, as a result of which the number of beds in sanatoria was halved and those in rest homes reduced to less than a quarter. The pre-war position was only restored in the mid-1950s. Since then, according to one study, policy has been directed towards: (i) increasing the numbers of tourist accommodation facilities and the numbers of beds overall; (ii) spreading the distribution of tourist accommodation facilities into such underprovided regions as Siberia and the Far East, and increasing the number of tourist routes; (iii) concentrating accommodation into larger and more efficient units and developing the country's principal recreational regions to their full potential; (iv) developing new forms of tourist accommodation and activity to accord with the increasing demands of the most recent period (*Geografiya rekreatsionnykh sistem SSSR* 1980, p. 28). Overall achievements in terms of accommodation can be judged from Table 5.1 where the picture is one of steady rather than spectacular growth. What is not necessarily apparent from such surveys is the fact that, both quantitatively and qualitatively, provision still leaves a lot to be desired.

5.4 Tourism: institutional, administrative and planning framework

5.4.1 Tourism provision

Whereas in Western countries tourist accommodation and other forms of provision are largely developed by the private sector with perhaps a minor supporting role played by the state, in the Soviet Union the state has so far played the dominant role. It is this fact, together with the influence of cultural and historical factors mentioned above, which helps to account for the pattern of tourist provision being somewhat different from that normal in the West.

The pattern of tourist and recreational provision has been described and classified in the book *The Geography of Recreational Systems in the USSR*, published by the Academy of Sciences Institute of Geography in 1980 (*Geografiya rekreatsionnykh sistem SSSR* 1980, pp. 45–63). First in their scheme of classification come sanatoria and pensions with medical treatment which, as noted already, were among the most important forms of tourist accommodation historically. This underlines the long-standing connection between leisure and health which was particularly emphasised in the early Soviet period and which is still apparent today in the continuing popularity of spas (*Nashi zdravnitsy* 1965). Also closely connected to health though not with actual medical treatment are rest homes and pensions, frequently offering a convalescent or recuperative regime to their clients. Then come the various rest and recreation bases which include sports and tourist-recuperative camps, hunting and fishing bases and other facilities. These too are regarded as having a health function and form the basic institutional accommodation for family holidays, hence their rapid recent growth.

The Institute of Geography's scheme regards tourist facilities as a separate category since their function is less health-orientated and more orientated towards the activity of touring. Tourist accommodation facilities include tourist bases, campsites, tourist hotels, shelters and refuges. Like recreation bases, tourist accommodation facilities form a new branch which has grown quite rapidly in the recent past. Also falling under the rubric of tourist facilities come tourist routes (and tours), including those designed for walkers, boaters, skiers, motorists and those travelling by train or ship and the network of excursion bureaux operating in medium-sized and big cities.

Other facilities described in the Institute of Geography's scheme include mountaineering camps, garden cooperatives, summer camps for children of school and pre-school age (including various types of educational, work and recuperative camps and also children's tourist facilities), the network of hotels and facilities serving foreign tourists, international youth facilities, accommodation bureaux in major tourist centres and resorts which advise on private facilities, and national parks.

In general, therefore, Soviet tourism is characterised by an accent on health-seeking (often in a very passive sense) and also by an emphasis on group holidaymaking in camps and similar facilities which may not easily cater to the family. The explanation for this situation lies to some extent in ideology: the long-standing distrust of individualism or privatism and the regard paid to educational aims, especially among children and young people. However, the tendency for holiday facilities to be provided by the enterprise, organisation or ministry for its own employees has probably been a more important factor.

5.4.2 Tourism administration

No one organisation in the Soviet Union administers or coordinates the development of tourist facilities, and in view of the broad scope of the term tourism as used here, this should occasion no surprise. Tourist facilities of many different types are provided by a host of state organisations, enterprises, ministries, local government bodies, collective and state farms, and other institutions. What is unusual from the Western viewpoint is the important coordinating and providing role in domestic tourism played by the All-Union Central Council of Trade Unions (AUCCTU). During the period in which strikes and other forms of industrial action were banned (from the end of the 1920s to the late 1980s) the activities of trade unions were severely restricted and their social-welfare functions became of central importance (Ruble 1981). The provision and planning of leisure and recreation facilities was one of the welfare functions they adopted.

Overall coordination for the planning and development of sanatoria, rest homes, rest and recreation bases and associated facilities is exercised by an arm of the AUCCTU known as the Central Council for the Administration of Health Resorts. This operates by means of republic and local trade-union councils and also through the Ministry of Health. The facilities themselves are provided by ministries, enterprises and other organisations either directly (through their own administrative sub-divisions) or through their trade unions. The Central Council and the Ministry of Health facilitate the training of personnel to run these institutions, and the total number of persons so employed in the late 1970s exceeded half a million. A feature of Soviet welfare provision is the granting to employees of vacations at such institutions often at subsidised rates.

Domestic tourism, in the narrow sense of tourism, is the responsibility for a second arm of the AUCCTU known as the Central Council for Tourism and Excursions. This body dates in effect from 1936 when the AUCCTU took over from the Society for Proletarian Tourism and Excursions (which was liquidated) the chief responsibility for overseeing the development of tourism. Until 1962 this responsibility was exercised in association with the Central Council for Sports' Societies and Organisations, underlining the tendency to regard tourism as a form of sport. In 1962, however, the administration of tourism was revamped, with the Central Council for Tourism (and, from 1969, for Excursions) emerging as the chief coordinating body with subsidiary councils set up in each republic and region. Since that time the Central Council and its subsidiaries have been responsible for a broad range of activities providing tourist accommodation (tourist bases, hotels and so on, much of their finance coming from trade unions), setting up a network of tourist and excursion bureaux in towns and other locations, organising and approving tourist routes and tours, publishing tourism literature of all kinds, overseeing the training of personnel (in universities and other training establishments, including since 1981 the Central Council's own institute), researching tourism and also participating in international contacts and the organisation of foreign tourism. The Central Council has responsibility for overseeing independent tourism: usually group tourist activity organised by tourist clubs rather than directly by the Central Council or its subsidiaries. Thus the Council encourages the formation of tourist clubs in towns and other areas and of tourist sections in places of work. An All-Union Federation of Tourism coordinates the work of tourist clubs of many different types. In the mid-1980s the Central Council of Tourism and Excursions headed a system consisting of nearly 2 thousand enterprises, institutions and organisations employing about 200,000 people.

With the exception of health-orientated tourism (over a quarter of the beds in sanatoria, for example, are for children), children's and young people's tourism has developed separately from that administered by the trade unions. Several different organisations are involved. The Ministry of Education is responsible for school-based tourism through the Central Children's Excursion and Tourism Station which was set up in 1970 with regional stations established somewhat later. The children's Pioneer organisation, the Young Communist League (Komsomol) and other bodies also have important roles. Trade unions, local authorities and other organisations have helped in the formation of a system of work and rest camps, mainly in the countryside. The armed forces have their own tourist organisations, supervised by a section of the Ministry of Defence. Foreign tourism is the responsibility of the Main Administration of Foreign Tourism which became a State Committee in 1983. This form of tourism is discussed in a separate section below.

As with all areas of the Soviet centrally planned economy, the investment that is made in tourism has up to now derived from plans drawn up by the economic planning bureaucracy centred in Moscow. As part of the consumer-service sphere, tourism obtains its funding partly from the sectoral ministries which allocate money to their subsidiary enterprises and partly from the territorial authorities (republics, local authorities). Sanatoria and other health-related institutions, for example, may be built by enterprises using cash from their social-development funds (that is, money derived from profits which may be used to provide facilities for the workers as a form of incentive), by trade unions on their behalf and by the Ministry of Health. Trade unions derive their funds for investment in tourist facilities from enterprise profits, the state welfare budget which they help to administer, from membership dues and other sources. Part of the rationale of the Gorbachev reforms has been to decentralise the economy and to allow more autonomy to enterprises. Thus in the future tourism development should depend to a much greater extent than in the past on investment decisions by individual enterprises and organisations rather than on centrally directed investment. Enterprise-run services, cooperatives and family-owned or even private retail outlets may herald the beginnings of an increased role for the semi- or non-state sector.

Despite the considerable progress that has been made in domestic tourist provision in the Soviet period, that progress has not been rapid enough to cater for an ever burgeoning demand, and tourism has suffered in consequence of recent economic troubles. The entire system of official tourist accommodation can still cater for less than a third of the population. This no doubt helps to explain why many Soviet citizens prefer to take their holidays at home or with friends and relatives; according to official estimates, about two-thirds of industrial employees spend their summer holiday in this way. It also helps to explain the great importance of spontaneous or 'unplanned' tourism, where tourists organise their own trips and seek out their own accommodation independently of official channels. There have been many complaints of the shortage of facilities for tourists and of the poor standards of accommodation and service in rest and recreation bases, for example (Shaw, 1980, pp. 208–10). In other words, as with many other parts of the consumer sector, tourism has suffered from lack of quality control, underinvestment, the woes of the inefficient construction industry and numerous other problems. Of course, exposure to such difficulties will in part depend on the position one occupies in the social and political hierarchy, but the fact is that for many Soviet citizens tourist provision remains far from adequate.

5.5 Geographical aspects of domestic tourism

The impact of tourism across the territory of the Soviet Union obviously varies in accordance with the character of the natural environment and population density. Large parts of the north and east—with sub-arctic characteristics—and the arid lands of Central Asia have low densities of population and have been influenced to only a very modest degree by tourism. Elsewhere, the impact of tourism has been greater but some regions are naturally more popular than others. Moreover, the type of tourism varies from one place to another. One significant factor which limits the spatial impact of tourism in comparison with the West is the low level of car ownership. Soviet citizens are still constrained in their mobility compared to their Western counterparts, and this influences both tourism's distribution and its overall character.

As part of the policy to develop tourism, from the 1960s a number of studies were undertaken to try and assess the tourist potentials of particular areas. These studies varied in character from landscape assessments and surveys of individual environmental factors to attempts to use a multi-factor approach. An example of the latter is to be found in the study by Svatkov and associates (1981). These scholars divided the resources needed by tourists (in the narrow sense of those who tour) into two categories: those resources 'consumed' by tourists as tourists, for example natural resources such as scenic beauty or climatic resources, attractive man-modified landscapes, historical and cultural monuments; and those socio-economic resources needed to support tourism, for example labour supply, energy, financial resources and infrastructure. They then classified the economic regions of the Soviet Union according to their suitability for sightseeing ('cognitive tourism'), health-related tourism and sports-related tourism (mountaineering, hiking, skiing etc.) and also according to their capacity to cope with future increases in tourism. Not surprisingly, in this study and in the closely related one by Putrik and Sveshnikov (1986) the more promising regions for sightseeing and health-related tourism coincide with the better settled and developed parts of the Soviet Union. Those areas which are additionally endowed with scenic or climatic significance (such as the Black Sea and the Baltic coasts or the mountains of the Caucasus and the Urals) or have a rich cultural heritage (such as the old core of Muscovy around Moscow) are assessed as particularly outstanding.

Of greater relevance to an understanding of the present-day geography of tourism in the Soviet Union are studies which focus on the spatial distribution of tourist facilities and on flows of visitors to tourist destinations. This type of approach was adopted by the group from the Academy of Sciences Institute of Geography (*Geografiya rekreatsionnykh sistem SSSR* 1980, pp. 29–63). Their information was gathered in the mid-1970s and is therefore now dated, but the overall patterns are unlikely to have changed greatly in the meantime. The map of the distribution of basic tourist accommodation (see Figure 5.1) suggests a close correspondence with population density, a good deal of the accommodation being situation in the European Soviet Union, especially near major population centres. Areas near warm seas, with pleasant natural environments, mineral springs and medicinal muds are particularly prominent. Outside the European Soviet Union, facilities are sparser and are found near large cities and in areas such as the south-eastern part of West Siberia and the southern parts of East Siberia and the Far East where the natural environment has some particularly attractive features such as lakes and mountain scenery. The map of the distribution of official tourist beds per 1,000 of the local population (see Figure 5.2) shows a high availability of accommodation along the northern littoral of the Black Sea, with slightly lower availability in the neighbouring regions bordering the Sea of Azov, in the North Caucasus and the Caucasus mountains. Elsewhere the distribution tends to correspond to the pattern of population density with little accommodation available in the north, much of the east or in Central Asia. In regions such as Leningrad *oblast'*, the Baltic states, Chelyabinsk *oblast'* in the Urals, the Tatar ASSR and Kuybyshev *oblast'* along the Volga, and the Kirgiz Republic, availability of accommodation is somewhat above average owing to the presence of large industrial agglomerations and an environment conducive to tourism. There is a marked tendency for accommodation to cluster close to sea coasts, lakes, rivers, mountainous districts and other natural attractions.

On the basis of the level of tourist provision, the Institute of Geography group classified the entire territory of the Soviet Union into four zones (Figure 5.3). The first zone, having the highest level of provision, corresponds with the Black Sea littoral, the coast of the Sea of Azov, the North Caucasus, the Transcaucasus and the west coast of the Caspian Sea. This zone contained 12.3 per cent of the Soviet Union's population, but 39.6 per cent of the beds in sanatoria, 34.4 per cent of those in rest homes, 24.1 per cent of those in rest and recreation bases and 38.8 per cent of those in tourist facilities. At the other extreme is the fourth zone, corresponding with north European Soviet Union and most of Siberia and the Far East outside their southernmost regions. This territory contained 2.6 per cent of the national population, only 0.8 per cent of its sanatoria beds, 0.2 per cent of its rest home beds, 0.1 per cent of its beds in rest and recreation bases, but 3.0 per cent of its tourist beds.

A further stage in the regionalisation process was to sub-divide the zones into 19 districts (see Figure 5.2) on the basis of the type of tourism which characterised them and whether they served local or more distant markets. As shown in Table 5.2, the districts vary significantly in the actual composition of their official tourist accommodation. Thus no less than 84.3 per cent of the beds in the North Caucasus were in sanatoria and only 14.0 per cent in tourist facilities. By contrast the nearby Caucasus mountains had 64.9 per cent of their

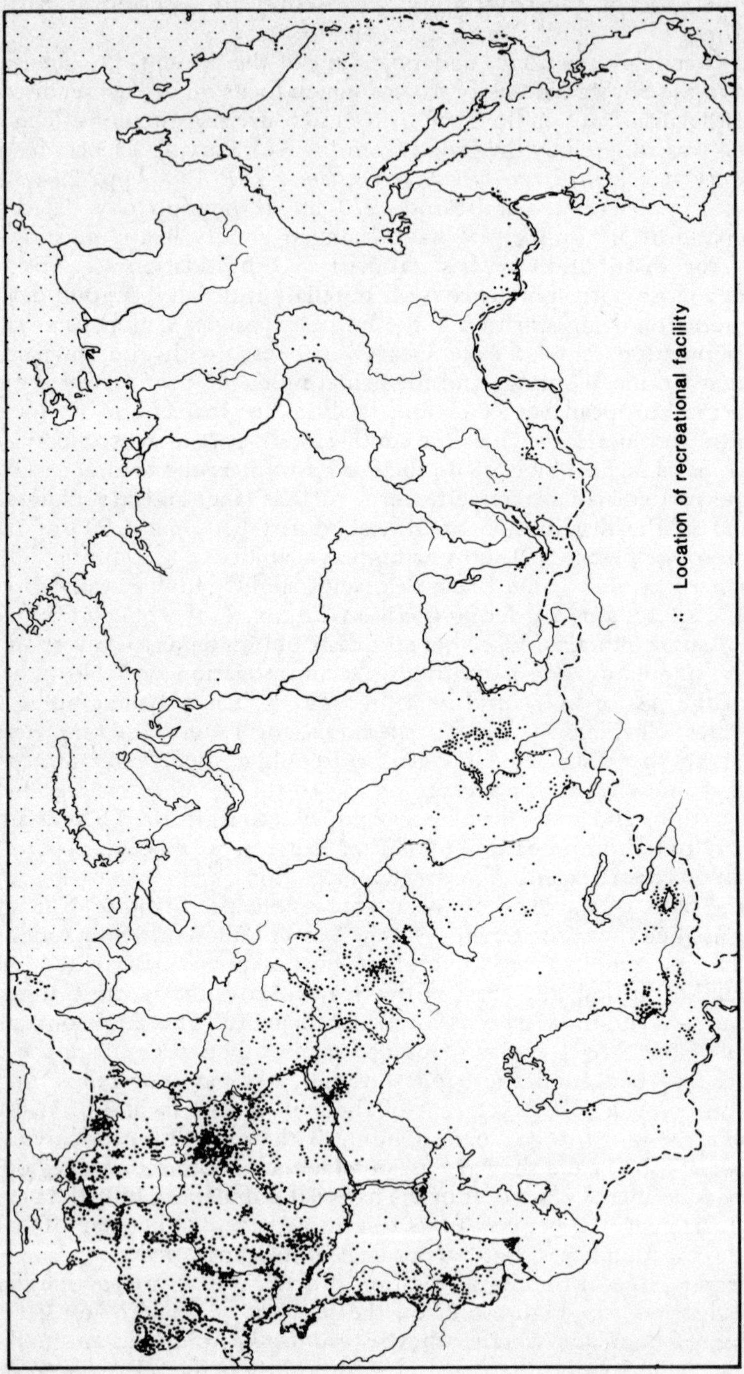

Figure 5.1 Soviet Union: geographical distribution of official recreational accommodation (after *Geografiya rekreatsionnykh sistem SSSR* 1980, Fig. 9, opp. p. 36)

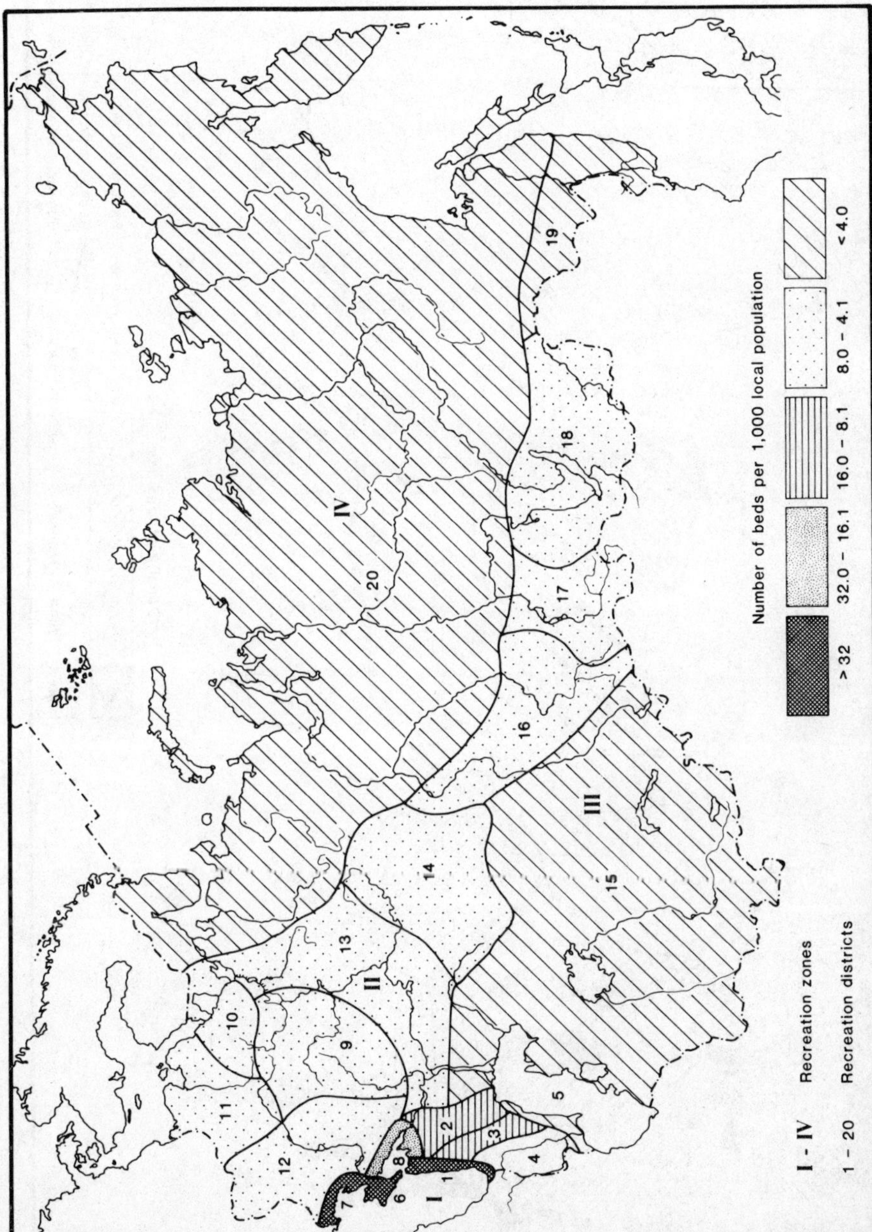

Figure 5.2 Soviet Union: bed spaces in official recreational accommodation per thousand of the local population by recreational zone and district (after *Geografiya rekreatsionnykh sistem SSSR* 1980, Fig. 13, p. 36)

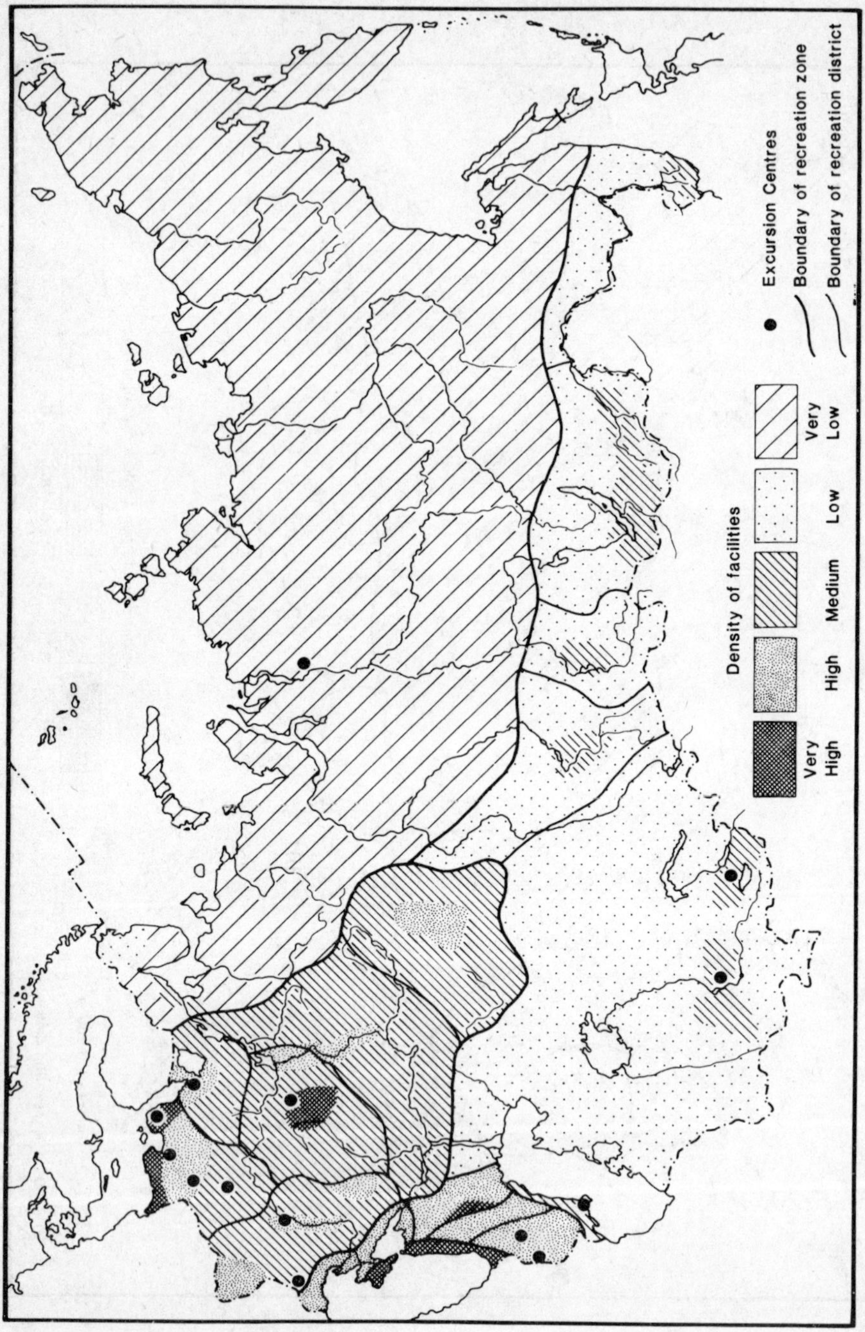

Figure 5.3 Soviet Union: the Academy of Sciences Institute of Geography's scheme of recreational regionalisation (for numbering of zones and districts see Figure 5.2) (after *Geografiya rekreatsionnykh sistem SSSR* 1980, Fig. 14, p. 40)

Table 5.2 Soviet Union: structure of recreational provision in recreational zones and districts in 1976 (%)

Zone and district	Percentage of beds in facilities of different type			
	Sanatoria and pensions with medical treatment	Rest homes and pensions	Rest and recreation bases	Tourist facilities
USSR total	29.6	20.5	24.9	18.1
Zone 1	37.5	22.9	24.9	14.7
1. Caucasus–Black Sea	30.8	35.9	22.7	10.6
2. North Caucasus	84.3	0.6	1.1	14.0
3. Mountain Caucasus	29.4	4.6	1.1	64.9
4. Transcaucasus	50.6	19.3	4.6	25.5
5. Caspian	67.1	19.8	20.0	3.1
6. Crimea	47.7	23.2	21.6	7.5
7. Odessa	22.7	27.6	44.4	5.3
8. Sea of Azov	12.5	20.0	63.0	4.5
Zone 2	26.2	20.8	42.6	10.4
9. Central	28.2	31.4	28.3	12.1
10. North-west	29.8	26.1	27.0	17.1
11. West	27.0	15.5	47.8	9.7
12. Dnepr–Dnestr	26.7	16.0	45.9	11.4
13. Volga	17.9	19.4	55.6	7.1
14. Urals	30.6	18.4	42.2	8.8
Zone 3	37.7	24.4	24.1	13.8
15. Central Asia	41.9	30.9	15.2	12.0
16. Ob–Altay	28.2	19.4	42.6	9.8
17. Yenisey	43.6	18.8	13.1	24.5
18. Lake Baykal	37.2	11.1	32.4	19.3
19. Far East	39.9	16.3	17.2	26.6
Zone 4				
20. North	36.5	7.2	2.5	53.8
Total	29.6	20.5	24.9	18.1

Source: Geografiya rekreatsionnykh sistem SSSR (1980), p. 39

beds in tourist facilities and only 29.4 per cent in sanatoria. This shows that different districts tend to specialise in different types of tourism. An indication of specialisations is given in Table 5.3.

Regional specialisation is in part a reflection of the varying requirements of different types of tourism, and the Institute of Geography group also studied the factors influencing the distribution of each type of facility. Sanatoria, for example, have a tendency to concentrate in zones 1 and 2, particularly south of latitude 52° North. Outside zone 2 (where the Crimean, Caucasus-Black Sea, Odessa and North Caucasus districts are particularly prominent), such southerly districts as Dnepr-Dnestr and parts of Central Asia stand out. The group

Table 5.3 Soviet Union: basic characteristics of recreational districts

District	Basic function	Sphere of influence	Degree of development
1. Caucasus—Black Sea	medical/recuperative	all-union	developed
2. North Caucasus	medical	all-union	partially developed
3. Mountain Caucasus	sports/tourism	all-union	partially developed
4. Transcaucasus	medical/tourism	all-union	partially developed
5. Caspian	medical	local	weakly developed
6. Crimean	medical/recuperative	all-union	developed
7. Odessa	recuperative	serving neighbouring districts	partially developed
8. Sea of Azov	recuperative	serving neighbouring districts	weakly developed
9. Central	excursions/recuperative	all-union/local	developed
10. North-west	recuperative/excursions	local/all-union	partially developed
11. West	excursions/recuperative	serving neighbouring districts/local	partially developed
12. Dnepr–Dnestr	excursions/recuperative	local	partially developed
13. Volga	excursions/recuperative	serving neighbouring districts/local	partially developed
14. Urals	recuperative	local	weakly developed
15. Central Asia	medical/recuperative	local	weakly developed
16. Ob–Altay	recuperative/medical	local	weakly developed
17. Yenisey	recuperative/medical	local	weakly developed
18. Lake Baykal	recuperative/medical	serving neighbouring districts/local	weakly developed
19. Far East	medical/recuperative	local	weakly developed
20. North	medical/tourist	local/all-union	weakly developed

Source: Geografiya rekreatsionnykh sistem SSSR (1980), p. 43

identified two significant factors influencing their distribution: a suitable natural environment (long period of warm weather, the proximity of warm seas, the availability of mineral springs and medicinal muds) and local demand (the presence of a large urbanised population), with the first factor being more important than the second. The distribution of rest homes is somewhat similar, although here the demand factor is rather more important, with a significant proportion of the capacity situated along river banks in zone 2. The Central district around Moscow is particularly well supplied with rest homes (see Figure 5.4). In the case of rest and recreation bases, the demand factor is clearly dominant with two-thirds of the capacity being situated in zone 2 which had 60.1 per cent of the population. Twenty per cent of the capacity is in zone 1, but unlike the case of sanatoria and rest homes, local demand, deriving from the Donbass agglomeration and southern industrial cities, is paramount. The presence of attractive natural features (coasts, rivers, forests) is again important in their location, but since this type of facility is still relatively new they tend to colonise areas not previously secured for sanatoria

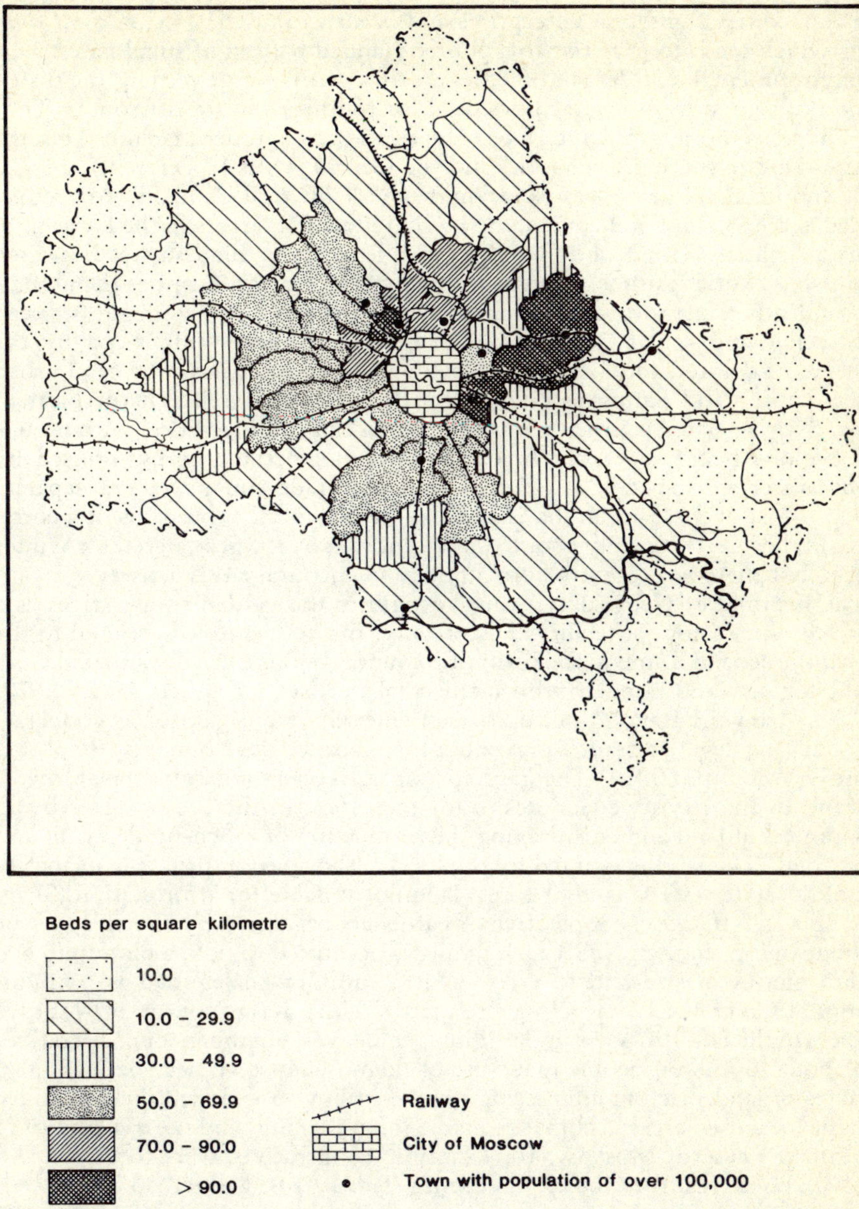

Figure 5.4 Bed spaces in official recreational accommodation per square kilometre of territory by administrative districts of Moscow *oblast'*

and rest homes. Different enterprises and branch ministries secure their own plots which tends to give rise to a poorly planned pattern of small bases.

Environmental and demand factors are also crucial in governing the distribution of tourist facilities (facilities used for touring) and tourist routes. Thus the Caucasus mountains have 15 per cent of all beds in tourist facilities, but the Dnepr–Dnestr (with 12 per cent) and the Centre (with 10 per cent) are also well endowed, largely because of high levels of local demand. Attractive, varied and exotic natural environments are influential factors in the location of tourist facilities. Thus zones 3 and 4, with less favourable climates but often possessing exotic features, contain relatively more tourist facilities than sanatoria and other institutions. In tourism, a distinction must be made between sightseeing and sports-related tourism with the former influenced by the presence of cultural and historical monuments (hence the importance of urban hotels, motels and campsites catering for this group) as well as natural attractions. Sports-related tourism tends to make use of rural facilities, with mountain regions being especially favoured. Mountaineering camps, utilised by mountaineering societies associated with the trade unions, are a separate group. Most of these are in the Caucasus, the rest in the mountains of Central Asia. In the late 1970s only about 10 per cent of the facilities catered for winter sports, but there has recently been a policy to encourage this activity.

The Institute of Geography group recognises the garden cooperatives as a separate type of tourist facility. Historically, the cooperative is related to the dacha, the second home in the form of a country cottage usually situated close to the big city and popular with intellectuals, artists and others (Shaw 1979, p. 130). After the Revolution, dacha settlements were organised as cooperatives but later legal restraints prevented their further development (Preobrazhenskiy 1986, pp. 60 ff.). The garden cooperative was a natural replacement, catering to the city-dwellers' desire for recreation in the countryside, being economical of land and encouraging the production of much-needed fruit and vegetables. The land is granted by the local authorities, in principle primarily out of the state reserve land or forest land not suitable for afforestation (Shaw 1986, pp. 429 ff.), to a cooperative of gardeners organised by an enterprise or its trade union. In the RSFSR each family is permitted to hold a plot up to 600 square metres in size and to erect on it a summer chalet (that is, without heating) of between 12 and 25 square metres with a terrace of up to 10 square metres. In the late 1970s about 3 million people were members of cooperatives and about 10 million people made use of them. They occupied some 180,000 hectares of land. Factors influencing their distribution included the proximity of large urbanised areas, a climate suitable for gardening, and the availability of land (in the case of Moscow, for example, cooperatives were located up to 80–100 kilometres from the city (Vedenin *et al.* 1976)). More than 70 per cent of the members of cooperatives lived in zone 2 (with more than 63 per cent of the urban population), and over 50 per cent lived in the three heavily industrialised and urbanised districts of the Volga, the Centre and the Urals. Close to some big cities, garden cooperatives form a substantial portion of the available accommodation: 49 per cent of that in Moscow *oblast'* in 1981, for example (Preobrazhenskiy 1986, p. 79). They are thus basic to the family holiday.

Since the early 1980s more encouragement has been given to gardening, and recently the number of cooperatives has grown markedly. In 1988, collective gardens occupied 718,000 hectares of land and were held by nearly 11 million families (*Narodnoye khozyaystvo SSSR* 1989, p. 467). A further significant area of land is occupied by collective vegetable allotments. Article 20 of the 1990 land legislation entitles Soviet citizens to receive land plots on the basis of heritable life tenure for the pursuit of personal subsidiary farming, horticulture and dacha construction. Article 21 permits Soviet citizens to receive land plots for market gardening (Fundamentals, 1990, pp. 30–1). Dacha ownerships and forms of gardening and allotment holding may therefore be expected to spread further, perhaps on a more individualistic basis than in the past.

Statistics on 'unplanned' tourism are difficult to acquire and probably no one knows its full extent. Planners estimate that about half a million Muscovites each year rent accommodation in the dacha settlements of Moscow and neighbouring *oblasti*. In addition, many people rent rooms or cottages in agricultural villages, part of whose population has migrated to Moscow or other towns (Preobrazhenskiy 1986, p. 96). Relatively low levels of car ownership and shortages of official accommodation naturally limit people's mobility and the opportunities available for unplanned or spontaneous tourism. Nevertheless, it is a growing phenomenon and its importance is bound to increase with rising car ownership levels and the development of a private or semi-private service sector. In popular resort areas such as the Black Sea coast, enterprising locals have long made money from private rentings (Azar 1972, pp. 42 ff; Shaw 1980, p. 209).

5.6 Land use planning and the environmental impact of tourism

The physical and land-use planning associated with the development of tourist accommodation and tourist resorts is the responsibility of the local authorities (local soviets) acting under the supervision of the State Committee for Architecture and Town Planning. Several institutes attached to the State Committee's system investigate or help design and implement plans for resort areas, and many other institutes are involved (*Geografiya rekreatsionnykh sistem SSSR* 1980, p. 11). The land legislation introduced in 1969 allowed for the designation of a category of resort land with enhanced protection, but this did not usually include land within the boundaries of towns and villages (Shaw 1986, p. 439). The land legislation announced in March 1990 specifies new land conservation measures. Thus a new major land category is designated which is to enjoy enhanced legal protection: land designated for nature conservation, rest and recuperation, recreational, and historical and cultural purposes (article 2). Each of these types of land has tourist significance. Thus nature conservation land includes protected sites, national and dendrological parks, botanical gardens, nature reserves and natural monuments (article 32). In the past there have often been legal and administrative problems regarding the designation and protection of nature reserves and national parks, leading to their infringement by individuals and official organisations (Reymers and Shtil'mark 1978). It may be that the new legislation will ease matters. Article 33 recognises rest and recuperation land as land with natural therapeutic features suitable for the organisation of preventative and therapeutic treatment. Special protection is granted to the land occupied by health resorts. Again, recreational land, which is land suitable for the organisation of mass leisure and tourism, and land with particular historical or cultural significance, is granted special protection under articles 34 and 35. According to article 11, no land having special natural, historical or cultural significance (listed land) may be withdrawn for other uses (Fundamentals 1990).

Land-use planning and nature conservation have tended to suffer in the Soviet Union from the uncertain status of legislative enactments (the lack of an independent judiciary), the weakness of the local soviets and of procedures for implementation and the ease with which powerful vested interests (such as industrial ministries, only very imperfectly controlled by the central planners) have been able to override inconvenient controls. There has been no lack of plans and legislation directly or indirectly fostering tourism. Thus special regional plans have been drawn up and implemented for such important resort areas as the south coast of the Crimea (Pertsik 1973, pp. 11 ff.; Lemeshev and Shcherbina 1986, pp. 116 ff.). In a rather similar way, a whole series of national parks and other types of protected areas have now been designated for tourists in attractive and unspoilt parts of the country (Reymers and Shtil'mark 1978; Lemeshev and Shcherbina 1986, p. 54). However, the official ratification of land use plans may have limited effectiveness (Shaw 1986, pp. 439–41), and tourist areas such as the shores of the Sea of Azov or the west coast of the Caspian Sea suffer from industrial pollution and other hazards.

Of no less concern to the authorities are those problems which arise as a result of the spontaneous development of tourism itself. By comparison with Western countries, the Soviet Union has both advantages and disadvantages in this regard (Shaw 1980). On the one hand, it has an enormous territory and, as noted already, its population is relatively immobile by virtue of low levels of car ownership. On the other hand, there is the ineffectiveness of land-use planning in many areas and low levels of tourist provision. The very spatial immobility of the population leads to considerable pressures on forest parks, national parks, lakes and other water bodies, particularly close to populated areas. Inadequate tourist provision encourages unauthorised camping, the lighting of camp fires, the infringement of laws protecting nature reserves, forests and lakes. Poaching is a common problem in many areas, the result of ineffective controls. Another worry is unauthorised building of dachas, shelters, moorings and other facilities, again the product of inadequate control. Where responsibilities for conservation are diffuse (a common problem owing to administrative complexities and lack of clear lines of authority), controls are likely to be particularly slack. The severe, continental climate of the Soviet Union and the fact that the most favourable climatic conditions are restricted to only a few territories such as the south coast of the Crimea and the west coast of the Transcaucasus means that there is real pressure in those areas to develop ever more accommodation and facilities, possibly to the detriment of the natural environment. Although tourist pressure in mountainous territories such as the Caucasus is as yet much less severe, the authorities are none the less worried about environmental problems there (Putrik and Sveshnikov 1986, pp. 34–5). Finally, insensitive planning or management decisions can add to the difficulties. Tourists are naturally irritated by irrational restrictions; there has been much debate, for example, about allowing access to protected areas. Equally, alarm has been caused in some quarters by plans to give further encouragement to tourism in such environmentally fragile regions as that around Lake Baykal.

Such problems have arisen in the contest of the Soviet Union's centrally planned system. The situation is now changing with new powers being given to the republics and local authorities, greater democratic accountability and moves towards some form of market economy. It remains to be seen whether these developments will make physical planning and conservation easier, or yet more difficult.

5.7 International tourism

5.7.1 Scale

Even before the Revolution Russia was not an easy country to visit. Travellers were amazed by the formalities which had to be completed at the frontier and by the need to keep authorities informed of their whereabouts. In the political circumstances existing after the Revolution, things became no simpler. Nevertheless, the Soviet leaders gradually came to appreciate the advantages of tourism as a means of promoting their ideals and the achievements of the Soviet state, as well as a way of earning hard currency. Numbers of foreign tourists began to rise from the mid-1920s, and in 1929 the tourist agency Intourist was founded to serve them. Altogether in the pre-war period the country was visited by about 100,000 tourists, many of them Communists, trade union or workers' groups whose visits were organised for political purposes. After the war foreign tourism remained at a low ebb until the end of the Stalin period and then began to grow steadily. The number of visitors equalled 486,000 in 1956 and 711,000 in 1960, growing to over 2 million in 1970, over 5 million in 1980 and 6 million by the mid-1980s (Dolzhenko 1988, p. 150). Over 60 per cent of the visitors were from socialist countries. Likewise the number of Soviet citizens travelling abroad has grown from 561,000 in 1956 to over 1.8 million in 1970 and over 4.5 million in 1985.

5.7.2 Constraints

A number of factors have tended to hold back the development of foreign tourism despite the considerable growth. First there has been the long-standing fear and suspicion of foreign influences, particularly manifested in the Stalin era but continuing almost to the present day. Cold War attitudes on both sides have dissuaded many Western visitors from wishing to visit the Soviet Union and prevented the Soviet authorities from allowing their citizens to travel abroad. A lack of hard-currency reserves has also acted as a barrier to foreign travel for Soviet citizens. Coupled with the negative attitudes have been bureaucratic barriers: the difficulties of obtaining visas, artificially inflated costs of foreign travel for Soviet citizens, the need for foreign visitors to the Soviet Union to keep to approved itineraries and to stay only in officially designated accommodation. Large parts of the country have been officially closed to foreigners, including most rural districts. Sometimes this has been because of the underdeveloped nature of the Intourist system, but more commonly because of a wish to keep an eye on foreigners and to prevent them from visiting sites of strategic significance or areas where economic or social conditions are for some reason deemed undesirable. Naturally enough the political and economic barriers to foreign travel have been less serious in the case of socialist countries and the mutual contacts (reinforced by tourist agreements) have been much closer. But even East European travellers found the Soviet Union a more difficult country to visit than most of their socialist neighbours. Under Gorbachev conditions have greatly improved, and more people than ever before are visiting the Soviet Union or travelling from there to foreign destinations.

5.7.3 Tourist destinations and administration

The areas of the country open to foreign tourism have gradually expanded. Before the war, the major tourist destinations were the principal cities of the European part of the country, especially Moscow, Leningrad, Kiev, Odessa, Tbilisi, as well as Yalta, the Black Sea coast of the Caucasus and some other areas. In the late 1960s and early 1970s, five areas were officially recognised for foreign tourism: the Centre (especially designated for cultural tourism and sightseeing), the Black Sea (for recreational tourism), Central Asia (cultural tourism and sightseeing), the Caucasus (sightseeing, health cures and sport) and Siberia (transit by the Trans-Siberian Railway, sightseeing and cultural tourism). Since then the Volga region (Kazan', Ul'yanovsk, Volgograd) and the Baltic states have been added, and others are currently opening up. In 1976 120 cities were open to foreign visitors, 50 per cent of whom visited Moscow, Leningrad and Kiev. There were serious shortages of accommodation in the most popular venues, hence the policy to involve foreign firms in the development of new international hotels in Moscow (Kosmos), Leningrad (Primorskaya) and elsewhere.

Over 70 per cent of the visitors to the Soviet Union have been classified as cultural tourists, travelling to the country to acquaint themselves with cultural, historical and economic achievements. But in addition, some effort has gone into encouraging other forms of tourism: motor tourism, sports-related tourism in the Caucasus and elsewhere, beach and spa tourism, conference tourism (conferences, seminars, exhibitions, fairs) and business tourism (Sitkina 1985). The latter is a major growth area at the present time.

The principal body responsible for foreign tourism in the Soviet Union is the State Committee for Foreign Tourism (originally the Administration for Foreign Tourism, founded in 1964). This body oversees the work of Intourist, the international youth tourist organisation 'Sputnik' (set up in 1958 and running its own network of camps, hotels and other facilities), the international tourist work of the AUCCTU and other activities. In the mid-1980s, the entire system for foreign tourism consisted of over one hundred hotels, motels and camp sites with 55,000 beds and numerous restaurants, cafes, conference halls, swimming pools, clubs, fleets of vehicles and many other facilities. Directly or indirectly the system employed up to 200,000 people.

Foreign tourism obviously makes a contribution to the Soviet Union's hard-currency earnings, but it is difficult to be sure how important this is in view of the lack of official statistics. One estimate is that it generated as much as $500 million per annum during the early and mid-1980s (McIntyre 1987, p. 481). Compared with the total hard-currency earnings from exports in 1986 of $25,000 million, this is not a big sum, but its importance may grow in connection with the new policies now being implemented.

5.8 New developments in tourism

The Gorbachev era, which began in 1985, has been accompanied by a series of wide-ranging economic and political reforms. For the first time since the 1920s people are beginning to speak out, to join pressure groups and to express their viewpoints via a much freer press. In various parts of the Soviet Union, there has been nationalist agitation, strikes and uprisings. Some people have predicted a period of increasing chaos and upheaval. At the time of writing, the Soviet Communist Party has abdicated its claim to a unique political authority although as yet its grip on political power remains firm. There is a strong possibility that a pluralist political system will develop similar to those now appearing in Eastern Europe. Clearly it would be unsafe and unwise to attempt to predict the future. What can be said is that events in Eastern Europe are no sure guide to the future of the Soviet Union, so different are their political and cultural heritages.

As regards tourism, the Gorbachev period has already produced important changes. Soviet citizens are finding travel abroad very much easier than in the past, and private visits have now become possible. The number of exchanges arranged between official organisations in East and West has also grown enormously, while business contacts are burgeoning as a result of reforms in the foreign-trade sector and the proliferation of joint ventures. Financial constraints and the difficulties associated with rouble convertibility are still considerable, however. As regards Western tourism to the Soviet Union, this has expanded as a result of the above factors as well as of a wish to experience the freer atmosphere and excitement of this period. Western visitors now find it easier to arrange visits to friends and to see places formerly closed to them, although there are still many important constraints on movement around the country. However, public disorder associated with nationalist agitation and a rising crime rate could deter visitors. Shortages of foodstuffs and other economic troubles might act as a barrier to tourism development.

Recent and promised economic reforms seem likely to have important implications for the future of tourism. The 1987 Law on the State Enterprise envisaged a dismantling of the centrally planned economy, with state enterprises being required to fulfil state orders as only a portion of their overall activity (and a diminishing one at that) and otherwise being free to participate in what amounts to a market, with incentives payable in the form of bonuses for managers and workers in efficient operations. Potentially more radical is the 1988 Law on Cooperatives which allows not only for the setting up of various types of cooperative which would be independent of the state sector but also for forms of private enterprise through the leasing of state enterprises to employees and the selling of shares to the same. These measures are furthered by the recent land legislation, allowing for permanent tenure by cooperatives and other organisations, and by the new law on property, allowing for various forms of cooperative, social and in effect private ownership (Fundamentals 1990; USSR Law on Ownership 1990). Further laws are promised which, if enacted, would move Soviet society decisively in the direction of the market economy. In the tourist field this may lead not only to more facilities being provided by organisations for their employees but also to the emergence of many more services and facilities catering to the public at large on a commercial basis. In view of the sad neglect of the consumer sector, this would be a welcome development indeed, although at the time of writing progress is delayed by serious economic problems and also political barriers.

The opening of the Soviet economy to the world market is potentially of considerable importance to tourism. Already a number of joint ventures have been negotiated with Western and Japanese firms in the area of tourist development, and others are promised. Current joint ventures include plans to construct a sailing resort at Nakhodka in the Far East, plans for winter-sports centres in the North Caucasus and Kazakhstan, sports and health centres in various locations including Lake Baykal, hotels, restaurants, retail outlets and publishing concerns. Most schemes seem to envisage the earning of hard currency as a principal objective. Also under discussion is the designation of special joint enterprise zones at Novgorod, just south of Leningrad, and other locations. The ancient city of Novgorod was visited by half a million tourists in 1988, but only 50,000 of these were foreigners. The city has great historical and cultural significance and the plan is to develop its international tourist potential in a series of joint ventures with Western firms (*Current Digest of the Soviet Press* 1989, **41**, no. 35, p. 23). Recent reports, however, speak of some degree of local opposition to these ideas.

5.9 Conclusions

Tourism has a long history in the Russian and Soviet context, and because of political, cultural and ideological factors it has some peculiarities of its own. Only relatively recently has it begun to achieve an importance commensurate with that attained in other industrialised economies. But it cannot yet be said to be of great significance to the economy as a whole. As noted above, it contributes only a small proportion to the Soviet Union's foreign-trade earnings, although in an economy traditionally closed to the rest of the world that proportion has a considerable absolute significance. It has also been estimated that about 4 per cent of the Soviet labour force is concerned either directly or indirectly with serving domestic and foreign tourists (*Turizm* 1977, p. 335); this figure may not include people employed to serve sanatoria and similar patients. The consumer sector has long been a relatively low priority in an economic system still geared to industrialisation. As part of that sector, tourism has suffered accordingly.

Things may now be starting to change. The Soviet Union, with its enormous territory and rich variety of cultures, obviously has an enormous potential for tourism, despite the difficult environmental conditions experienced in many areas. Unfortunately, insufficient investment over a lengthy period means an underdeveloped infrastructure with many regions and cities lacking even the bare essentials for tourism and others being extremely overcrowded. The influx of foreign investment capital will undoubtedly help gain some needed ground although it is doubtful whether this will do a great deal to help domestic tourism, at least in the short term. The fate of the latter is much more immediately bound up with that of economic reform and improvements in living standards generally. Unless the deep-rooted problems of the Soviet economy can be tackled, the prospects for domestic tourism remain modest at best.

Given that the Soviet Union's economic difficulties can be ameliorated and that Western investment continues to be made available, the country's considerable experience in the planning and administration of tourism, including the training of specialists, should stand it in good stead. Even then, however, some changes in attitude seem to be called for. First, a more open and less suspicious attitude towards foreigners is needed if travellers are not to feel that much of the country is deliberately being hidden from them. A liberal approach would bring the benefits of tourism to many areas hitherto denied them, especially if it is accompanied by greater encouragement for cooperatives and the private sector. Greater access to the international community would have the advantage of keeping the country up-to-date with changing fashions in tourism, from hotel design to other kinds of provision, and would perhaps help to modify the slightly dated tendency to regard tourism as a form of convalescence or as a medium of instruction and enlightenment. The country has a great deal to gain from allowing its own citizens to travel freely abroad; even if some losses in foreign currency are the consequence, these will surely be more than compensated for by the invaluable experience and the contacts made, with many additional advantages in foreign trade and exchanges of ideas. Finally, there is surely still a need for tourism and other aspects of the consumer sector to be granted full recognition as major contributors to society in their own right, quite as important as industry in the economic and social benefits they convey. One of the ironies of Soviet Marxism is the fact that an ideology which preaches the all-round development of the individual has been so extraordinarily reluctant to embrace the far-sighted policies needed to achieve it.

6 Eastern Germany (the former German Democratic Republic)

Roy E.H. Mellor

6.1 Introduction

Few would have considered the German Democratic Republic (GDR) as one of Europe's 'tourist countries', but it possessed more potential than usually imagined; ironically, that potential is now to be realised within a unified German state. Tourism in the GDR, both domestic and international, had been influenced since 1945 by the geopolitical matrix in Central Europe. The GDR corresponded territorially to the Soviet Occupation Zone and emerged, along with the western Federal Republic, as a sovereign state through the collapse of cooperation between the Soviet Union and the three Western allies. Enmeshed in the tensions of superpower geopolitics, relations between the German states were equally cool and not infrequently antagonistic, yet always avoiding any action which might result in an irreconcilable split. Dismemberment of the Reich territory into two sovereign states and annexation by Poland of the lands east of the Oder–Neisse rivers recast the space relationships of the economic and social fabric around contrasting political philosophies, greatly modifying the pattern of pre-war movement and linkage.

Although bound to the Soviet imperium, the GDR stood somewhat apart from the other satellites. This was occasioned partly by a psycho-political perception of it as a 'conquered' territory, whereas the other satellites had all been 'liberated' by Soviet arms; but also, and more importantly in the long term, by its higher level of economic and infrastructural development. The GDR was usually (if questionably) reckoned to be the world's tenth major industrial power, well ahead of any of its COMECON colleagues except the Soviet Union.

The collapse of the Communist administration in Autumn 1989 left a political and economic vacuum which only began to be filled after the democratic elections of March 1990. One immediate and exceptionally important impact was the liberalisation of movement, allowing free travel between the two German states and the long divided city of Berlin. A Ministry of Tourism was established late in November 1989 to face the challenge of a massive influx of visitors, and the pent-up urge of east German citizens to travel abroad. Its role was to prepare the shift from state-monopoly to a mixed or free enterprise infrastructure, prior to unification with the Federal Republic (Elkins 1990; Hall 1990e).

6.2 Historical development of tourism

The rudiments of tourism and recreational holidays developed as travel was eased by the extension of the railways through the 1860s and spread to a wider public as people began to spend their new wealth in the relative prosperity of the 1870s. Among even the poorer sections of society, new movements, especially those for young people, stimulated hiking and cycling clubs and other outdoor recreation, while the social welfare legislation of the 1880s codified holiday and medical entitlements. Health resorts multiplied and those offering medical treatment became increasingly popular, although some spas of long standing had been visited by the aristocracy even before the eighteenth century. Unlike in Britain spas remained a significant element in medical treatment in Germany. Early this century, several mountain resorts began to build facilities for winter sports. By 1914 a considerable part of the population, especially from the large cities and industrial towns, had become accustomed to a regular holiday, many choosing seaside resorts. But the larger proportion in an essentially continental country went to centres in the uplands and mountains or along the picturesque rivers. When the Age of Wilhelminian Germany closed in 1914, the Reich had a more developed tourist infrastructure than most of Central Europe and certainly all of Eastern Europe.

After 1919, in the Weimar Republic, tourism's fortunes varied with the swings of the German economy. Well into the 1920s international tourism in Central Europe was disrupted by the map of the new 'succession states' and many Germans sought resorts at home. A new stimulus was given to organised recreation such as winter sports, various water sports and even gliding by the National Socialists and their 'Strength through joy' movement, though the facilities offered were perhaps often militarily orientated. Most marked was the expansion of camps and activities for young people offered by the Hitler Youth. The disruption of everyday life following the German collapse in 1945 brought a temporary halt to tourism. Refugees from beyond the new boundaries of Germany as well as evacuees from the heavily damaged towns filled much of the available accommodation, while hotels and hostels as well as complete resorts were commandeered for the use of occupation troops. Several holiday centres themselves had been badly damaged in the fighting. It was not until the early 1950s that both internal and international tourism began to revive, although the latter was delayed for longer in the GDR than in the Federal Republic.

6.3 The major tourist and recreation areas

In the division of Germany, the GDR inherited several significant tourist areas, though none with the international standing of the Rhine and Bavarian Alps in west Germany. The main tourist districts lie in four types of 'landscape': the Baltic coast with sandy beaches, dunes or low cliffs and coastal forest (popular for bathing and water sports); the glacial morainic country of the north and centre with forest, heath and lakes (easy terrain for hiking, cycling or boating); the uplands of the south with extensive forest and many reservoirs (well suited to climbing, hiking, water sports and notably winter sports); and the 'built environment' of historic towns or famous castles and palaces. In addition to the main tourist districts (Figure 6.1), there are around almost every larger town popular local recreation areas.

6.3.1 *Baltic Coast*

The most important tourist area is the Baltic Coast. Good sandy beaches with generally reasonably safe bathing combine with attractive scenery and pleasant air. Along stretches of cliff and dune coast there is also good walking, while coastal lagoons provide some sailing for amateur yachtsmen. Of a total coastline of 1530 kilometres (380 kilometres of 'outer coast' and 1150 kilometres of 'lagoon or Bodden coast'), sandy beaches suitable for bathing extend for 200 kilometres on the outer coast and about 80 kilometres on the Bodden coast. Popular in pre-war times throughout Central Europe, it is reckoned that the Baltic Coast contains around 35 per cent of the total recreational capacity of east Germany and about a third of all long-stay holidays take place here, attracting over 3 million people. To this must also be added some 6–8 million day visitors. The bulk of these visits are in the summer season (May–September), but centres with spa facilities are used throughout the year. Compared to 1937, the number of visitors has increased more than 600 per cent, not surprisingly creating notable infrastructural difficulties. The critical factor at all resorts is the pressure of visitors on the beaches, demanding increasing management to keep them clean and in good physical condition. Effort has been devoted to opening additional centres by building camping sites and holiday homes. Difficulties have been exacerbated by the easier access to the coast with completion of the new trunk railway and motorway from Berlin to Rostock. Liberalised travel could now draw additional large numbers of west Germans and Scandinavians to the coast, intensifying infrastructural problems.

From west to east, the main centres are the long-stay resort of Boltenhagen, the Wohlenberger Wiek and the Insel Poel (weekend and camping visits), Rerik and the largest resort on the coast, Kühlungsborn, while a little inland is the spa of Bad Doberan. Nearby are Heiligendamm and Nienhagen. Some holiday-makers stay in Warnemünde and even Rostock. Day excursions are run from Travemünde (west Germany) by boat to Rostock and Warnemünde. Graal–Müritz is an increasingly popular centre, with considerable potential to expand its functions as a spa, while some 20 kilometres inland Bad Sülze is also a small spa. East of the Recknitz River the coast becomes more indented, with long sandy spits and lagoons, the true Bodden Coast, a landscape of sandy beaches and dunes, scattered heathy woodland and occasional forest. On the long spit of the Fischland–Darss–Zingst lie Dierhagen, Wustrow (an important resort), Ahrenshoop (popular with artists and the higher echelons of government), Born, Wieck, Prerow and Zingst, all long-stay resorts.

The irregularly shaped Island of Rügen is a popular holiday venue, with its many spits and promontories, its numerous inlets and lagoons, sandy beaches and low but prominent cliffs (the Stubbenkammer and Kap Arkona, for example), which complement fine stands of beechwood and meandering streams (renowned for their stork colonies). A group of resorts lies in the south-east around Granitz and Mönchgut, while Vilm, a small island, was until recently a retreat of the higher party ranks.

On the north-east the Jasmund Peninsular with the ferry port of Sassnitz is easily accessible by rail. The Schaabe Isthmus and Wittow Peninsula on the north are a little more remote, with the resorts of Glowe and Juliusruh. Hiddensee Island on the west coast is almost entirely a recreational area. Rügen is essentially a long-stay tourist district.

The most easterly resorts lie around the southern shore of the Greifswalder Bodden and on the long island of Usedom. Resorts on the island are long-stay centres, whereas the Bodden shore is more popular for shorter visits, notably at Lubmin. Usedom's resorts include Karlshagen, Trassenheide, Zinnowitz, Sempin, Koserow, Uckeritz, Bansin, Heringsdorf and Ahlbeck: the last three are the most important. Before 1945 the island was reached by rail and road from its eastern end, but since this passed into Polish hands, access has been made problematic and new links at the western end are urgently required.

6.3.2 Mecklenburg–Brandenburg Lake Plateau

The Mecklenburg–Brandenburg Lake Plateau, primarily significant for domestic visitors, comprises rolling low hills with large forests, patches of heathland and open park-like woodland, but especially several hundred lakes. The sparsely populated countryside has few main centres and accommodation is available chiefly in camp sites, bungalow colonies or private houses. The poor road system makes access in parts difficult, but completion of the Berlin–Hamburg motorway and the new trunk railway to Rostock may encourage more people to sample its good air and tranquil scenery. It is a countryside with appeal to hikers, cyclists and anglers or boatmen. It is little known to foreign visitors and most Germans are long-stay visitors, overwhelmingly between May and October.

A number of areas of both short- and longer-term stays developed earlier this century around Berlin. West of the city are the numerous long ribbon-like lakes and heathland with its thin pine woodland of the Havel valley, for which Potsdam and its many historical associations form the main centre. On the north-east, some 40 kilometres from Berlin, a common destination for short visits, lies rolling morainic country known as the 'Märkische Schweiz', including the spa at Bad Freienwalde. Rather further away but a frequent choice for outings from Berlin is the Spreewald around Lübbenau, with its woodland and network of picturesque small navigable waterways. Berlin itself is not without plentiful recreational opportunities in its woods and lakes.

6.3.3 Southern uplands

The second major tourist area, that of the southern uplands, comprises the Harz, the uplands of Thüringen (including part of the Rhön), the Vogtland–Erzgebirge and related uplands on the Czech–German border. The remains of ancient mountains, these *Mittelgebirge* have many physical traits in common, offering much the same recreational opportunities. They are generally vast uplifted blocks of country, with characteristic broad and often nearly level old erosion surfaces at higher elevations. A few have been markedly tilted, forming huge ridge-like mountainous terrain (the Thüringer Wald, for example), but all have been deeply dissected by rivers. Seen from the lowland,

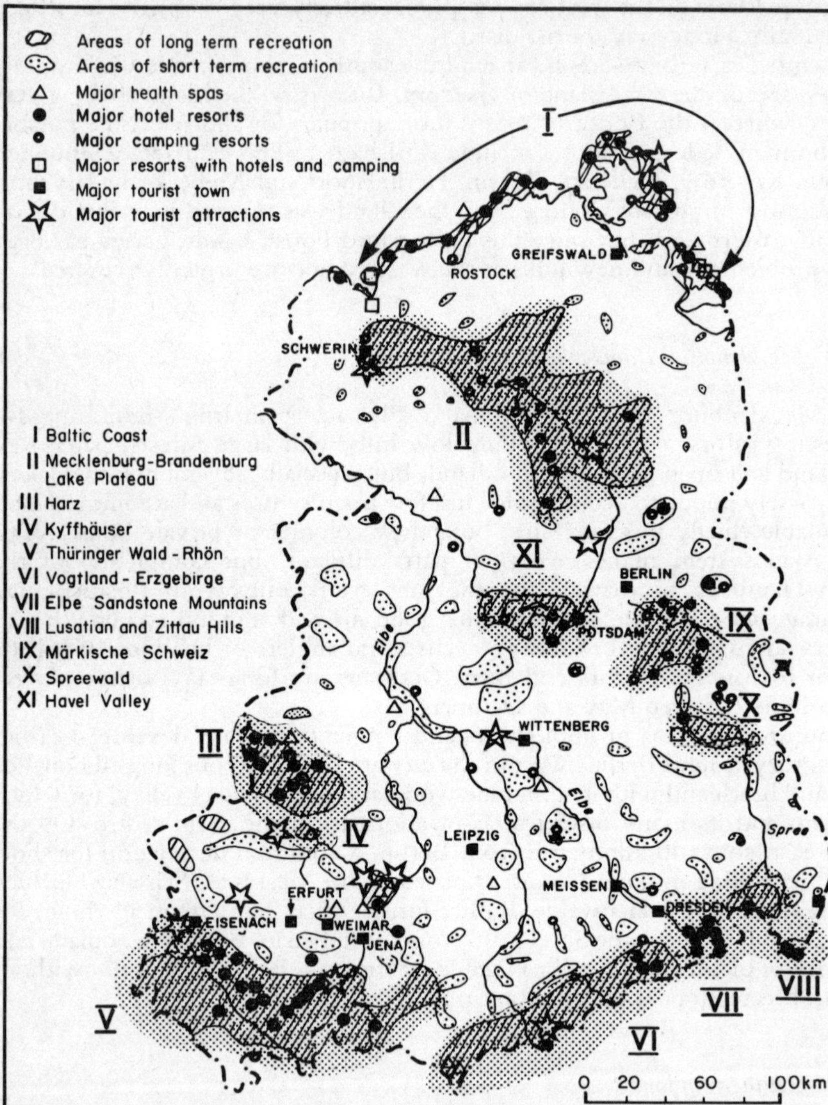

Figure 6.1 Former GDR: main tourist districts

they look like rugged mountains, but from the air or when one climbs to their higher parts, the remarkably level upper surfaces above which rise rounded summits of more resistant rock reveal a quite different aspect. Their raw climate, steep slopes and poor soils mean much of the surface remains sombre coniferous forest, but some of the highest surfaces are bleak and often wet moorland. Nevertheless, these are scenically attractive uplands, valued for their peaceful atmosphere and good air, besides their richness in historical associations and in folklore (the source of many tales codified by the Brothers Grimm last century).

The most northerly upland is the Harz, for over 40 years divided by the inter-German frontier, with the eastern part in the GDR. The impressive landscape, the fine forests, the interesting relics of past mining and metal-working as well as its suitability for winter sports, draw many visitors. The main tourist towns are on the northern slope, like Wernigerode, Blankenburg, Quedlinburg and Harzgerode, but there are also many smaller places offering accommodation. The tourist potential was, however, considerably reduced by the 6-kilometre-wide prohibited zone along the frontier that placed the highest point, the Brocken (1142 metres) and its association with the *Walpurgisnacht* legend, out of bounds to visitors. Before the war these flocked to it by means of a narrow gauge railway to the summit which will now doubtless be reopened. Prior to 1939, the Harz was popular with visitors from the Low Countries who continued to frequent the west German part of the upland. A Harz outlier, the Kyffhäuser ridge to the south, from which superb views can be had, has great scenic beauty, fine beechwoods, notable caves and many local legends. The visitor centres are small villages and spas like Bad Frankenhausen.

The extreme south-west corner of the Republic provides a focus for tourism in the massive dissected ridge-like upland of the Thüringer Wald and its lower foreland and the eastern Rhön hills. Much of the tourist influx is along the crest of the Thüringer Wald, the Rennsteig. This is one of the most heavily forested parts of east Germany, providing hiking and walking as well as excellent scenery and a tranquil atmosphere, while (as in the Harz) the reservoirs in the deeply incised valleys attract many people. The Thüringer Wald has some 14 major resorts, each with over 500 beds, of which Friedrichroda, Tabarz, Finsterbergen and Tambach–Dietharz contain together almost 65 per cent of the total. The main ridge rises to over 900 metres in the Grosse Beerberg and its alignment makes the western face considerably wetter than the sheltered eastern lee, more popular with visitors for its warmer, drier and sunnier summer weather, though the snowier western face offers better winter sports (snow is always reasonably assured above 500 metres and is generally best in February). Plans seek to spread the pressure of tourists from the overcrowded main centres. Major investment is being made in some higher settlements such as Oberhof, lying about 500 metres which have an all-year season. One critical point is the heavy pressure of visitors to the famous Wartburg Castle. The Foreland (with the Werra valley) has two of the most important spas, Bad Salzungen (brine springs) and Bad Liebenstein (for heart ailments).

The Vogtland and Erzgebirge along the Czech border form a significant recreational area, especially for the industrial towns of Saxony. Although a main national tourist district, it also attracts Czechoslovak and Hungarian visitors. The Erzgebirge rises southwards in a broad surface from the Saxon hill country towards the Czech frontier, just south of which it drops steeply onto the broad Eger (Ohře) trough. On the German slope, valleys are incised up to 200-metres deep and the higher surfaces attain 800 metres over considerable parts and even exceed 1,000 metres in places (the highest point in east Germany is the Fichtelberg, 1214 metres): both elevation and intensity of relief decline eastwards. The higher parts all have a fairly certain snow cover in winter. Important centres are Oberwiesenthal, Johanngeorgenstadt, Wildenthal, Jöhstadt and Seiffen, among some 20 main tourist venues. Although the Erzgebirge has a lot of local industry, tourist development has been stimulated in rural districts to offset the poor opportunities for farming. The broken hill country of the Vogtland is easier of access and the many mineral springs (some naturally radio-active) support several spas, with Bad Elster and Radiumbad Brambach (giving radium treatment) of national importance. For a time after the war visitors to the Vogtland were discouraged when uranium mining was at its height around Aue. There are both short and long-stay tourists, while like the Thüringer Wald, effort has been made to separate their different requirements.

The Elbe Sandstone Mountains, one of the most remarkable landscapes in all the German lands, deservedly attract visitors. The scenery of 'Saxon Switzerland' is the prime attraction: the Elbe winds in a deep and often narrow gorge through the bizarre landscape of flat-topped buttes like the Lilienstein (415 metres) and the Königstein (360 metres capped by a fortress) or the Bastei, as well as rock pillars, such as the Schrammsteine and other surprising natural forms. This small district has eight major resorts and two nationally important spas, Bad Schandau and Bad Gottleuba. For about 100 kilometres, from Riesa below Dresden to the Czech frontier at Schmilka above it, the river is navigated by passenger vessels. Visitors come from all over east Germany and it has been popular with tourists from COMECON countries as well as promoted as a holiday venue for people from capitalist countries. Further tourist development faces the dilemma of the pressure of people on an area which is a landscape and nature reserve.

Two minor but popular areas lie east of the Elbe: the Lusatian Hills and the hills around Zittau. The latter, tucked away in a salient between Czech and Polish territory, are focused on Oybin and are particularly busy at weekends, being among the most intensively used areas of the whole southern upland zone.

6.3.4 The built environment

Scattered across the country, both within and outside the main tourist districts, numerous historic towns, castles, palaces and monuments attract large numbers of visitors. Some, like the sites of concentration camps (Sachsenhausen, Ravensbrück), have been used to put across an ideological message. Potsdam is a popular venue, with its historical and architectural attractions, while much has been done to restore Dresden's elegance. The great cathedrals (like Naumburg) are still a draw as are towns associated with famous historical figures such as Weimar (Goethe, Schiller), Eisenach (J.S. Bach), Halle (Handel), Wittenberg (Martin Luther) or even some lesser known places, like Schildau (Gneisenau). A few places retain an attraction for their products (though so far not always easy to obtain), like Meissen for its porcelain,

Lauscha for its glass Christmas decorations, Plauen for lace or even Suhl for its prized hunting weapons. Specialised and traditional products from such towns, if high quality and competitive prices can be sustained, could provide under the new conditions an attraction for visitors from outside east Germany. A very special place is held by Leipzig through its great international commercial fairs held annually in spring and autumn, the most important of such Central European meetings and held almost unbroken since 1165. The fairs attract as many as a million visitors, two-third to the spring event, when the population of Leipzig virtually doubles. Since 1945, the bulk of the visitors have come from COMECON countries, but recent events have seen a massively increased level of participation from Western countries, a trend initiated in the mid-1980s by *glasnost*. During the fairs, direct flights and trains are run to Leipzig from many places throughout Europe.

Capital cities usually attract tourists and East Berlin was no exception, drawing visitors to its historical monuments, museums and cultural activities. As a showpiece of the erstwhile regime and a noted shopping centre in COMECON it was a popular place to visit from within the socialist bloc. By dismantling the 'Wall' and freeing movement in the divided city, great changes may be expected, with effort to 'equalise' standards between the two parts. East Berlin may expect to become the prominent focus for investment, from whatever source, for expansion of the tourist infrastructure. Financial aid from the united Germany will help without doubt to restore further historical sites and to improve the general infrastructure, already begun. Berlin's image in the West will certainly be a critical factor in drawing visitors from Western Europe and North America, while a massive influx of west Germans is assured.

6.4 The role of tourism

Tourism had become increasingly significant (though not a major priority) in the economic geography of the former GDR as the lingering influence of Stalinism faded during the 1960s. As elsewhere in COMECON however, its ideological role aided its winning scarce resources for infrastructural development. Provision of recreational facilities was seen as a means of maintaining a healthy and productive work force, perhaps even in helping to distract popular attention from shortcomings in material conditions, notably scarcity of consumer goods. The considerable emphasis on group recreation and holidays in accommodation provided by the workplace or trade union was designed to build social coherence and an *esprit-de-corps*, besides allowing recreation time to be mixed with political indoctrination. For these reasons, special emphasis was given to holiday and recreational opportunities for young people through camping ventures for the 7–14-year-olds and through this kind of holiday or more formal excursions for older children in the Free German Youth (FDJ) organisation. Under the old regime, well over half the east German population, perhaps as high as three-quarters, made at least one holiday visit each year, usually of the order of 10–14 days. Of these vacationers, well over 80 per cent spent the break inside east Germany (a much higher proportion than their cousins in the Federal Republic). Nevertheless east German citizens have had one of the highest levels of tourism in Europe. Particularly rapid was the growth in weekend trips as public transport improved and car ownership rose, albeit at less than half the west German level, with 42 cars per 100 households compared to 86.

Under the Communist regime, the tourist, hotel, catering and entertainments industries in the former GDR were overwhelmingly a state monopoly. All booking of accommodation and travel was controlled by the Reisebüro DDR (Travel Agency of the GDR), through which all travel companies outside the Republic had to deal. The state Commercial Organisation (HO) ran a wide range of operations, including hotels, restaurants, bars, cafés, nightclubs and the like. The top end of the market was provided by the Vereinigung Interhotel (Interhotel Association) with major hotels and hard-currency Intershops in the main cities, while a few hotels in this category were provided by Mitropa (Railway Catering Services). Some hotel and catering facilities were also provided by the local *Bezirk* administration and even 'individual' (private) enterprise was allowed on a modest scale. For the individual traveller, the limited availability of hotels and restaurants and their usually high cost was a serious disincentive and it was official policy to encourage wherever possible 'group travel', over which rigorous supervision was possible. Radical change is now in train.

The Confederation of Free German Trade Unions (FDGB) has been a major provider of holiday accommodation, owning over 3,600 holiday centres with more than 550,000 beds, supplying in 1987 62.9 million bed-nights. For young people there have been 48 central pioneer camps with 36,500 places, used by 110,721 children in 1987. The FDJ had 269 holiday or recreational centres with 24,717 beds under its control and provided 1.68 million stays overnight in these in 1987. Figures available for the *Bezirk* Rostock (covering the entire Baltic Coast) have been perhaps characteristic of the structure of tourist accommodation. In 1987, 44.1 per cent of holiday-makers were accommodated by the trade-union holiday service; 24.3 per cent went to public camping grounds; a mere 2.3 per cent were found lodgings by the GDR Travel Agency; 3.3 per cent were in private weekend houses and 15.4 per cent were in other accommodation such as privately arranged stays in hotels, inns or private households; while 10.6 per cent were children and young people in specially provided accommodation.

6.5 International tourism

Foreign tourism both by citizens of the former GDR abroad and by foreigners to the GDR was given a boost by the improved diplomatic relations of the early 1970s. The abolition in 1972 of pass and visa restrictions on travel between the GDR and Poland and Czechoslovakia was followed by a rapid rise in the number of visitors. Because of the former GDR's reluctance to provide currency and exit permits for travel outside of the COMECON group, the flow was primarily from the capitalist countries and return visits were few. A unique relationship existed between east Germany and both the Federal Republic and West Berlin. Many people in each territory had relatives and close friends in the other, so that an immense travel potential existed between them. The volume of visits by Germans across the inter-German frontier was always a good barometer of diplomatic and political relations between the two states. Relations between the former GDR and West Berlin had been in part controlled by the Quadri-Partite Agreement of 1974. Between the GDR and the Federal Republic travel regulations were considerably improved by treaty in 1972–3 and by subsequent small but significant improvements. Even so, east Germany was reluctant to allow travel to west Germany by people in the working and military age groups, perhaps from fear of past experiences with defections, so that travel was easiest for older people with compassionate family reasons. Significantly, of visitors from Western countries, around 75–80 per cent were from west Germany.

For east Germans holidaying abroad, a popular area was the Balaton district of Hungary, a country always friendly towards Germans even when their popularity elsewhere was low. The traditional German search for the southern sun drew considerable numbers to another country with friendly relations—Bulgaria—and its Black Sea coast. Large numbers visited Czechoslovakia, the former GDR's nextdoor neighbour, mostly for short stays, but events in the early 1980s in Poland dampened a mounting stream of visitors in that direction. Group travel to the Soviet Union was also common, often seen as a kind of pilgrimage,and there was clearly a strong political dimension in the flow. The main stream of foreign visitors from COMECON has been from Czechoslovakia, the Soviet Union and (apart from its times of troubles) Poland. Nevertheless, foreign visitors from all sources, East or West, have comprised only a small proportion of the total even in the main tourist districts: on the Baltic coast, foreigners have account for only six per cent of all visitors. In the COMECON economies, with their frequent irregular or inadequate availability of consumer goods, visits to other countries have often been stimulated by the hope or knowledge of obtaining articles not available at home. The official GDR view was that visits to COMECON neighbours promoted 'proletarian internationalism and socialist patriotism'.

Visitors from Western countries were perhaps more tolerated than welcomed, bringing with them valuable hard currency. The private traveller had to encash a stipulated minimum sum of foreign exchange for each day's stay: this could be spent in the GDR but any unspent part was not refundable. To tempt visitors, special hotel and shopping facilities (Intershops) were run to offer desirable goods and services, not usually available to local people, in exchange for hard currencies. In recent years much had been done to attract Western visitors by offering thematic holidays with an emphasis, for example, on music or art. A particular 'niche' arose out of the sluggishness of economic development which allowed the survival of several 'vintage' narrow gauge railways, conveniently used to attract railway enthusiasts from the West. Although photographing railways was normally forbidden by the dreaded Stasi security police, the visiting railway buffs were excused the prohibition!

Events in Autumn 1989 lifted the floodgates on 40 years of pent-up wanderlust. Millions of Germans in both states were able to renew family ties and old friendships and to visit, from sheer sentimentality or curiosity, places so long 'out of bounds'. This also applied to many foreigners, drawn by inquisitiveness and the desire for a piece of the Berlin Wall. The surge of people across Berlin as the Wall came down was some indication of what the future would hold. By early 1990, seven rail and 10 road crossings of the Inter-German frontier had already been increased to 75, and in Berlin, 9 crossing points had risen to 35. Within a week of liberalisation, an extra 28 long-distance and 20 local passenger trains across the Inter-German border were being run. Germans could now travel between the two states without visas and other formalities: these facilities were offered to other countries, most of which accepted. To cater for the expected flood of visitors, a massive investment over a wide spectrum will be needed. One area requiring major redevelopment will be the strip of country along both sides of the former inter-German frontier: on the west German side, this had been a 40-kilometre-wide 'development zone' for many years to counter the deadening effect of the sealed border, while on the eastern side, there was a prohibited access zone of some 6-kilometres' width, cleared of all inessential activities and settlement. In this latter belt, some once-thriving tourist centres like Bad Blankenstein on the Saale were completely deprived of their livelihood and declined, and closeness to the frontier debarred visitor access to the Brocken in the Harz.

6.6 Environmental impact of tourism

As the number of tourists increases, so do the detrimental effects of their pressure on the landscape, particularly in fragile environments. There are also conflicting interests and priorities in conservation between tourism and other sectors of the economy. To increase domestic and industrial water supplies, major new reservoirs have been built in upland tourist areas, providing added recreational opportunities but also restricting access to certain areas. The flooding of disused opencast lignite mines has generated much needed recreational provision in the thickly populated Halle–Leipzig area and also in Lusatia. During the 1950s and 1960s the emphasis on industrial production ignored river and air pollution, though both are now being tackled especially as some rivers are a danger to recreational use.

Walking along forest paths is a particularly popular German pastime, easily indulged in east Germany where 27 per cent of the national area is forest (as high as 49 per cent in *Bezirk* Suhl). Coniferous forest predominates and requires careful management to provide open sunlit picnic areas and well-planned forest rides and clearings to open up good vistas. The open beechwood (as in the Harz) is easier to manage for recreational use, but much care is needed with the open pine woodland on the sandy northern soils to prevent serious erosion. Great effort has been made to replant large areas devastated by ruthless clear felling in 1946–7, but recently the attractiveness of forest has been reduced by effects of acid rain. Recreational use of forest is recognised as a management category, including the provision of controlled camping and parking sites.

The popular heathlands across the centre and north require special attention. Their sandy soils and stabilised dunes make them a fragile environment, readily damaged by over-use at a relatively low level of access. Camp sites, parking spaces and picnic sites have been provided to reduce fire risks in this commonly dry landscape. The highest moor and heath surfaces of the uplands, with their low regenerative ability, are especially prone to damage by over-use for such pursuits as winter sports and even by an excessive number of hill walkers. Pictures taken in the 1930s suggest this problem was already present and has simply been exacerbated in recent years.

On the Baltic coast, the rising pressure of more visitors on the beaches demands increased management. With little or no tide to scour them, keeping the beaches clean and attractive is important, but other priorities include preventing dune erosion and damage to the vulnerable low cliffs as people use them.

although these springs were known long before his time. Its reputation is linked to the alkaline properties of the springs, which contain Glauber salts composed of sulphate, carbonate and soda. A short distance from Karlovy Vary lies another old-established watering place, Marianské Lázně (Marienbad), noted since the seventeenth century for its healing properties. While Karlovy Vary is known for its help in chronic liver complaints, stomach diseases and obesity, Marianské Lázně is mainly concerned with the diseases of the digestive system. Another spa, Frantiskovy Lázně, gained a reputation for its springs as early as the sixteenth century when the famous Swiss physician and alchemist Paracelsus (1493–1541) made reference to its waters in 1526. However, it was not until the reign of Emperor Francis II (1792–1835) that a pavilion was built over the spring in 1793 and a plan for the spa drawn up in his honour (Franzensbad). This spa water became noted for aiding diseases of the female organs and in sterility problems. Teplice is the oldest Bohemian spa, with springs known for over 1,200 years; it attracted tourists for its curative properties for rheumatism and arteriosclerosis.

In Moravia, there are fewer famous spas but perhaps the most noted are at Jeseník (neuropsychiatric disorders), and Luhačovice where the curative springs situated to the east of the Moravian Beskidy Mountains possess iodine-rich waters utilized in treating diseases of the upper respiratory tract. In Slovakia, in the Vah valley, the waters of Pieštany Spa are noted for the treatment of rheumatism, arthritis and spinal disorders. Since the early twelfth century, it has enjoyed this curative reputation, although it was known and mentioned in Roman legionary campaigns. In medieval times the sick bathed in pits dug out of the strongly sulphurized mud; today it is one of the country's best equipped spa centres. Sliač, a charming little spa centre situated in the Hron valley (near Banská Bystrica) was first mentioned in 1244; it is noted for the treatment of diseases in the locomotive system, and the spa buildings are surrounded by parks and recreation facilities. Střebské Pleso in the High Tatras is famous for the treatment of respiratory diseases; historically it dates back only to the end of the nineteenth century, when scientific research linked the influence of mountain climates on human health.

These are only a few of the country's many spa facilities; other less internationally well-known spas exist possessing a narrower range of preventative properties, but often appealing to domestic visitors who may prefer smaller and quieter centres, combined with local scenery and recreation.

Such natural conditions are not only favourable for their curative properties but also for scenic tourism; the country is able to offer a wide variety of scenery. The Czechoslovak Tourist Club was initially founded in 1888 during the time of the Austrian Empire. It was devoted to the care of the country's tourist attractions and between the World Wars was the Republic's chief tourist organisation. It consisted of 29 sections, affiliated into 246 local organisations and contained about 45,000 members (Bureš 1929, p. 246). In spite of negative reactions to its development during the Austrian period, the club survived and by the early 1930s had a total of over 500 rest houses, and 28 mountain refuges. The Czechoslovak Tourist Club published its own journal and bulletin, organised lecture tours, excursions, skiing and Alpine sports, exhibitions, and remained the major body for maintaining international tourist links.

A particular aspect of Czechoslovakian recreation was the role played by the 'Sokol' movement; it took its name from the falcon, symbol of heroism and

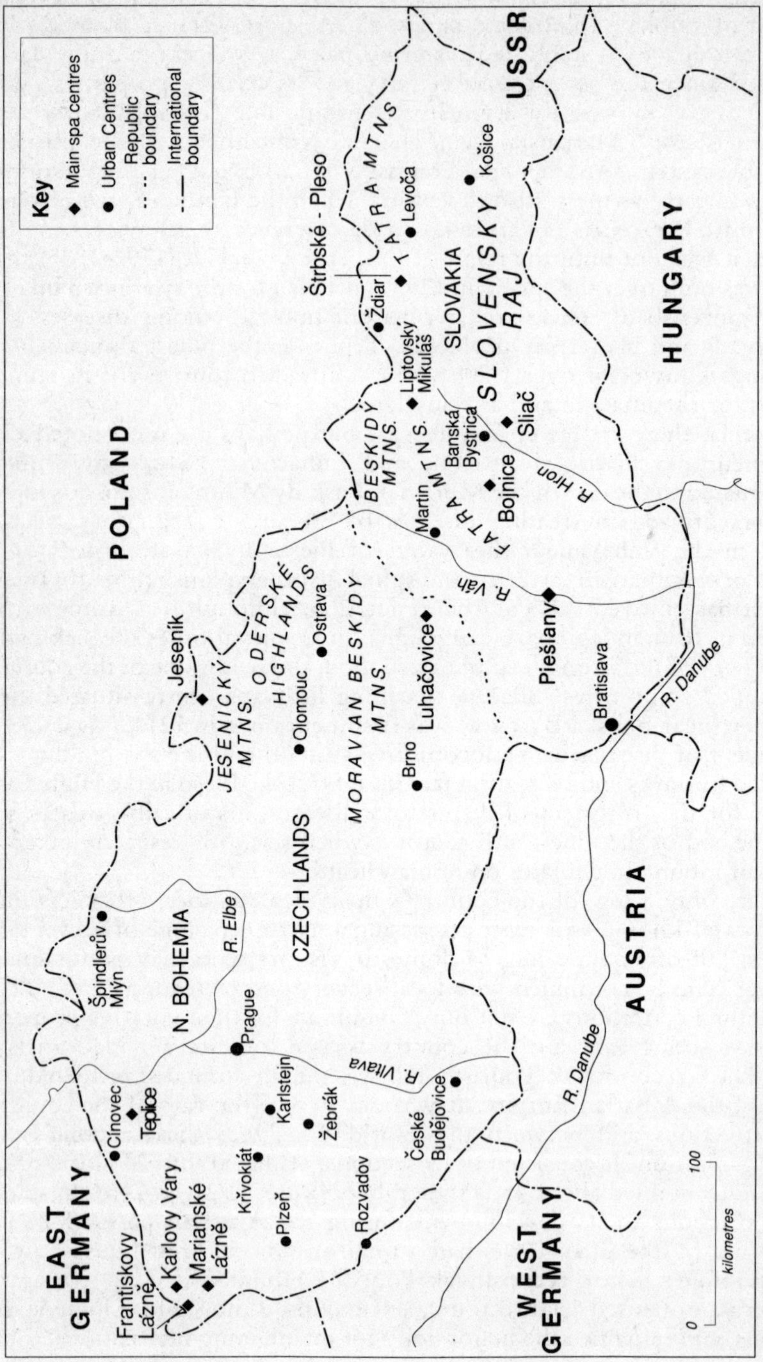

Figure 7.1 Czechoslovakia: tourist attractions

daring. The movement was founded by Miroslav Tyrs (1832–84) in 1882; he placed a great emphasis on the importance of physical culture and training to achieve a harmonious body development (Fisher 1917, p. 55). The idea and achievements of 'Sokol' had an interesting impact on nineteenth-century Czechs and Slovaks after 1918. Sport in Czechoslovakia became more popular after 1918, with the establishment of the new Republic. The Czechoslovak Sports Association (Československá športovní obec) and the All Sports Committee (Všesportovní vybor) provided the main organisation of the country's sporting activity.

After World War II, Czechoslovakia's strategic position in Europe proved a matter of concern both for the Western allies and the Soviet Union. The country emerged territorially, with a similar shape as before, except for the loss of Ruthenia to the Soviet Union, permitting direct Soviet land access to the country. A four-party coalition government ran the country for three years, but in 1948 the Communist Party took control and the Stalinisation of the country inevitably followed. It became a People's Republic, with a Soviet-orientated foreign policy, five-year plans and a programme of agricultural collectivisation and industrial nationalisation. Application of the Soviet model meant tighter and greater centralization of the country and its economic branches, in which tourism was no exception.

Several mass organizations were established such as the Revolutionary Trade Union Movement (ROH), the Czechoslovak Union of Physical Culture, the Czechoslovak Union of Youth and others (Motka 1962, p. 8). During the early 1950s, trade-union-sponsored holiday schemes were a popular form of domestic tourism. This was part of the state's idea of welfare tourism in which the beauty spots, and luxurious spa and summer resorts, which had largely been the exclusive domain of the rich in pre-war days, were now 'in the ownership and service of the working people' (Král 1955, p. 87). A holiday in one of the country's trade-union rest homes was a reward for employment activity; workshop committees and stewards selected those colleagues considered deserving of a holiday by their Works Council. Large factories such as Škoda in Plzeń even had their own particular employees' organisation. The miners had their own spas, reflecting the dangers of their work, as in Bojnice (Slovakia), noted for relief for those suffering from rheumatism and post-traumatic experiences (Veyret 1963, p. 135).

International tourism was organised by Čedok, the national agency. It controlled all first-class hotel accommodation, trains, restaurants and wagon-lits, and also acted as an intermediary for state agencies looking after foreign tourists in Czechoslovakia. Čedok was responsible for accommodation, transport facilities, resort excursions, often using minibuses (Wright 1967, p. 7), and visits to curative spas. It organised individual and group hunting parties and provided hunters with accommodation choices in first-class hotels, mountain huts, hunting lodges or one of the country's numerous chateaux. Foreign tourists who bought one of these established Čedok packages easily obtained an entry visa. Apart from Čedok several specialist travel agencies existed including 'Autoturist' (car travel); 'Balnea' (spas), ČKM (youth travel), 'Rekrea' (group travel, Czech Lands), 'Slovakotherma' (therapeutical sojourns at Slovak spas), 'Slovaktour' (travel exclusively in Slovakia), 'Sport-turist' (contacts with physical-culture organizations) and 'Tatratour' (group travel, Slovakia). Čedok has remained the main state agency for contacting foreign travel agencies world-wide (Anon. 1964, p. 186).

7.3 Statistical sources and problems

The main data are published in the annual statistical yearbook (*Statistická Ročenka ČSSR*) and contain a tourist section from the mid-1960s onwards. The tourist section gives the number of hotel beds available, guests and nights spent by domestic tourists from 1950 onwards at a national level and for the Czech Lands/Slovakia. It also gives the average number of tourist days spent, with a further breakdown which includes domestic tourist visits to spas and military medical institutes, trade union (ROH) and military holiday visits, school recreation and factory visits. Some of this information has not been published since 1971. The type of accommodation available such as hotel category, motels, rented bungalows and autocamping are recorded both at the national and republic levels, together with all the major tourist centres (beds, guests, nights). Since 1965 the number of foreign visitors both from (erstwhile) socialist and non-socialist countries has been published. Tables include average length of stay, and purpose, that is, whether for holiday, official visit, commercial delegations, for health reasons or transit tourist. It should be stressed here that Czechoslovakian statistics include all trips, not only tourists' (počet turistů); it would be more accurate to designate them as 'total foreign visitors'. Details are also given about foreigners visiting Czechoslovakia according to country of origin, through the Čedok and ČKM organizations, although not all foreign tourists use these organizations. Finally data are available on summer and winter camps used by children in the Pioneer organisation, and details of trade-union tourists' activities. These data are sometimes utilised in the monthly journal *Statistické Přehledy*. Tourist studies have also been published on specific topics by the Institute of Tourism; one of the earliest was an analysis of Slovakian tourist statistics for 1947 (Charvat 1948).

7.4 Tourism and economic development

The immediate post-World War II years in Czechoslovakia were characterised by nationalisation and a redistribution of land. The workers' councils acquired an important position in factories, but the economy as a whole was still mixed. Gradually, other forms of ownership disappeared and by 1948 two-thirds of industrial enterprises and half of all commercial exporting companies were state controlled. The setting up of a communist government in 1948 led to closer political and economic links with the Soviet Union under Stalin and greater cooperation with other members of the Eastern bloc. Emphasis was placed on heavy industrial production and a forced process of agricultural collectivisation. Soviet advisers were to be found in all branches of the economy and politics during the period 1949–53, when Czechoslovakia was organised according to a war-footing economy. By 1952 the country faced a monetary crisis with a consequent 80 per cent reduction in the internal value of the Czech 'crown' in June 1953. The state's First Five-Year Plan (1949–53) had effectively moved the country from a liberal to a Soviet-type command economy; investment was now channelled towards heavy industry at the expense of consumer production. The situation in farming and the consumer-goods sector therefore remained critical. In 1954 and 1955 one-year plans sought to restore stability and a more balanced allocation of resources, but the

Second Five-year Plan (1956–60) was similar to its predecessor in giving low priority to consumer needs. The main changes lay in higher investment allocation for the chemical industry, which replaced metallurgy as the first claimant, and in the expanded electricity output. Farming mechanisation was improved, although it remained well below West European levels.

Between 1957 and 1960 a high and generally steady growth rate was maintained with industrial production achieving a claimed 9–10 per cent annual increase. Fixed investment rose even faster and farm output continued its upward trend. Unfortunately, such growth rates could not be sustained; 1961 and 1962 were years of sharp decline. Reforms aimed at greater decentralisation of economic management were introduced in 1958, but only contributed to investment dislocation. The Third Five-year Plan (1961–5) was abandoned in 1963 when it became apparent that results were falling short of planned objectives. Annual plans for 1963, 1964 and 1965 led towards some partial recovery, but it became obvious there was a need for major management and planning reforms. Politics and excessive bureaucracy had undermined the once strong economy.

This in turn led to the emergence of a group of economic reformers bent on making the economy more productive, supported by liberal intellectuals keen on greater freedom and Slovaks aggrieved at domination by the Czech Lands. The outcome in 1968 was eight months of liberalisation finally curtailed by the presence of Warsaw Pact forces in Czechoslovakia and a return to 'normalisation'. The 1970s experienced two distinct periods; up to 1975, emphasis was placed on eradicating all traces of economic and political reform, but then until 1980 some liberalising experiments were allowed, similar to those involving state enterprises in the mid-1960s. The early 1980s were a difficult period economically, particularly for repaying oil debts to the Soviet Union. After negative growth in 1981 and more stagnation in 1982, the following three years displayed some economic growth, with a peak of 3.6 per cent in 1984 of the gross national income. The Eighth Five-year Plan (1986–90) aimed at a similar growth rate, but with the economy forced to curb investments. There were curtailments in construction work and savings required in fuel, energy and raw-material consumption. Efforts were made to improve agriculture and to provide greater production incentives, Western imports were reduced and attempts were made to avoid increased trade deficits with the Soviet Union.

Given this background to economic development planning, how does tourism fit into the overall picture? As already outlined, Czechoslovakia has great tourist potential particularly for Westerners, but until recently the Czechoslovak government was reluctant, often for political reasons, to exploit this situation. For a long time the government had an interest in promoting the tourist industry in order to earn convertible currency, but until the mid-1960s the state authorities were extremely suspicious of foreign, mainly Western contacts. At the beginning of 1964, however, entry visa procedures were simplified and accommodation for foreign visitors was improved. Between January and September 1964, 375,000 foreign tourists visited Czechoslovakia, of whom about one-sixth (63,000) came from Western countries, a significant increase over earlier periods.

Methods of creating tourist and recreation regions were published in the mid-1960s (Kotrba and Přikryl 1964, p. 237). They consisted of assessing five groups of characteristics. The first, and most important group, was related to natural conditions and included the terrain type, height above sea level, climatic average, forested area, water surface and run-off, and degree of pollution. Second, consideration was made of the cultural quality of a region; this was related to the number of spas, their natural therapeutical properties, the presence of architectural monuments especially historic towns, castles and cloisters—and new landscape features such as industrial factories, waterworks and housing estates. The third group of conditions seen as necessary for shaping a tourist region was connected with accommodation facilities and hospitality arrangements and provision of technical sporting facilities such as funicular cable cars, lifts, tow-lines, ski jumps, stadiums and swimming pools.

The fourth group was concerned with communications. The most important factor was transport–tourism links, not only rail and road, but also air and water communications. Research was carried out on tourist transport in relation to capacity, safety, hygienic operation and attractiveness. Finally the fifth group considered by the planners was connected to the natural influences present in each region such as atmospheric and water pollution and the resulting devastation. Natural factors negative for a tourist region included temperature inversion, occurrence of endemic diseases and high occurrence of mosquitoes, ticks and the like. Other factors included the density of industrial enterprises, residential settlements and lack of sufficient recreation facilities, especially around large urban centres.

The official regionalisation of tourism in Czechoslovakia was first proposed in 1962 by the Institute of Regionalisation and Planning in Prague (Kotrba 1968, p. 12), in which 67 tourist centres were delimited. Unfortunately, the terms 'tourism' and 'recreation' were not clearly identified; only recreation regions were delimited, and some significant tourist centres were not included (Mariot 1984, p. 54) such as urban national heritage areas, regions containing important cultural and historical monuments and urban centres like Prague, Brno, Olomouc, and Česke Budejovice—places noted by tourists for holding exhibitions, fairs and congresses. Gradually, between 1978 and 1980 the original tourist regionalisation of Czechoslovakia was updated. This allowed modifications to those tourist areas and centres which had changed over time as a result of development (Mariot 1984, p. 66).

Certainly the 1980s saw a period of improved tourism management in the country. There was some effort to renovate existing hotels and increase their guest capacity, together with plans for the modernisation of the tourist sector up to 1990 (Blaha 1981, p. 52). In 1980 the state tourist enterprise 'Interhotel' demolished 63 hotels containing 1,687 beds and modernised 82 others with a total capacity of 7,588 beds. The plan's priority was to stabilise hotel costs, constructing mainly 'B'-class hotels and utilising light building materials such as wood. This involved making an inventory of 'B'-class hotel construction, structural and material standardisation and improved equipment for cooking and service annexes (such as sculleries, and linen repair facilities). Given the reduction in available investment during the early 1980s, most new 'B'-class hotels were to be constructed by the nearest local building enterprises.

By the mid-1980s tourism had experienced a 40 per cent increase in growth rate over 1970; state spending on tourism increased from 17.4 milliard Czech crowns in 1970 to 39.9 milliard in 1985, equivalent to 15 per cent of the state's business retail figures. The tourist sector in 1985 employed about a quarter of a million people (Blaha, 1986, p. 154). A marginal part of this success was connected with the growth of 'congress tourism', which has become somewhat of a Czechoslovakian speciality. Between 1981 and 1985, 79,000 participants from capitalist countries paid receipts valued at 255.8 million Czech crowns; besides this, spa tourism increasingly attracted Western clientele, especially from Germany and Scandinavia, which together with Arab visitors provided nine per cent of the 11 million days of effective spa health care.

While Czechoslovakia holds many attractions for foreign tourists in terms of artistic and historical monuments, national parks and their scenery and thermal spas, by the mid-1980s tourist facilities still remained limited. In 1981, there were only 200,961 beds to accommodate 17,730,851 visitors, including transit tourists, throughout the year. Industrial investment has remained slow, and tourism still only accounts for about three per cent of all hard-currency earnings. Major changes in Czechoslovakia's tourism occurred in 1988 dictated largely by the urgent need to increase hard-currency revenues: a new programme of hotel construction was launched with Austrian and French participation.

7.5 Domestic tourism and recreation

In Czechoslovakia, the state viewed the main social function of tourism as the 'reproduction of the physical and mental forces of the working population' (Demek and Střída 1971, p. 292). Apart from this central goal, tourism includes the pursuit of sport, cultural and health objectives. During the late 1940s and 1950s increasing numbers of Czechoslovaks enjoyed holidays and recreation facilities, despite a decline in accommodation available, especially privately let rooms. This rise in domestic leisure resulted from a rapid growth of regulated tourism through collective activity provided by trade unions, state industrial enterprises and children's camps. Rest homes belonging to the country's trade unions were located in some of the country's best health and mountain resorts, where workers could spend their holidays in west Bohemian and Slovak Spas, in the Krkonoše and Beskydy Mountains, the Bohemian Forest or the Tatras. Many rest homes were to be found surrounded by woods, on river banks, near fish ponds or lakes and usually in climatically favourable areas. However, the accommodation situation remained critical; between 1955 and 1965 while the number of domestic tourists using trade-union (ROH) facilities increased from 227,000 to 291,000, the number of beds available rose by only 400 (Statistická Ročenka ČSSR 1966, p. 396).

The 1950s were a turbulent time in Czechoslovakia's post-war period. As Horna (1988, p. 84) has noted, it was a time when leisure and free time underwent profound changes: the mass media and the film industry were nationalised, sport was opened up, recreation facilities were established by the trade-union organisations, and training programmes for leisure professionals and practitioners were inaugurated. Organised recreation was perhaps best seen in the 'Sokol' sport and fitness rallies. The eleventh 'Sokol' Rally took place in June–July 1948 with 300,000 participants, trained by some 20,000 voluntary inspectors. The Junior (15–18 years) Rally had 80,000 members taking part (Anon. 1947, p. 82). There was also a sharp rise in trade-union members participating in organized holiday schemes, rising from 4,500 in 1945 to nearly 300,000 in 1953. Summer tourism remained most popular; in 1951 two-thirds of the trade-union participants preferred a summer to a winter holiday; less than 2 per cent pursued a cultural holiday, while a similar percentage were involved in holiday exchanges abroad (Král 1955, p. 93).

It was not until the mid-1960s that there was some decline in this collective type of domestic recreation which in turn signalled the growth of unregulated tourism. Nevertheless, from the late-1960s and the early 1970s socialist ideals predominated in the leisure sphere. Leisure was believed to lead to an 'overall development of personality', which in turn helped the economy and improved the standard of living. This rather simplistic idea that leisure was the panacea to all work process problems was prominent up to the mid-1970s—but is no longer held by contemporary Czech sociologists (Horna 1988, p. 88).

Organised recreation, however, continues to be a part of the national scene. Recreation and active sport are seen as important factors in public health. In 1984 there were over 8,000 physical training and sports clubs in the country, with nearly 2 million members (about one in seven of the population). Of these, nearly two-thirds were adults and the rest adolescents and children. An important part of this regulated recreation was the Spartakiad physical training festivals held every five years and involving thousands of participants (Bauerová 1986, p. 48). For example, the Sixth Spartakiad (Spartacus Games) held in June 1985, saw 175,000 gymnasts from all over the country taking part. This replaced the 'Sokol' spectacular, which, with its pre-war connotations was phased out after 1948, as a result of government legislation standardising sporting activities under the patronage of the country's political party. Unlike the 'Sokol' event, the Spartakiad involved military participation; the whole event was held in the Strahov Stadium in Prague, one of the largest in the world, capable of holding 200,000 spectators (Radio Free Europe 1985, p. 19). Links between recreation and health were also considered important. The country's recreational potential was seen as a significant factor in improving people's health (Hadač and Gottlieb, 1982, p. 120), and state propaganda encouraged its inhabitants to make the most of the various natural facilities available, including rambling, spa visits, scouting, mushroom gathering, camping and use of second homes.

For Czechoslovaks, the second home fits into the strong association the people have with nature and rural life. In 1930 nearly 23,000 second homes existed in the country; between 1945–55, 22,800 were built, and at the end of the next decade they totalled 46,000. By the end of 1980 there were 70,000 second homes in the country. Estimates of actual numbers differ widely: Gardavský maintained that there were 166,000 second homes in the country in 1972, or one for every 28 households (Gardavský 1977b, pp. 64, 71; Herold 1981, p. 52). Perhaps more significant is the difference in figures between the Czech Lands and Slovakia. Population difference for the two republics alone (10.3 and 5.0 million respectively in 1980) provides an insufficient explanation; perhaps more significant are variations in settlement size. In Czechoslovakia demand for second homes is greatest from settlements with 20,000 or more inhabitants; over a third of the population in the Czech Lands live in such centres, but in Slovakia it is only a tenth. Thus differences in the degree of urbanisation between the two republics may also suggest variations in the second-home demand.

In the Czech Lands, the overwhelming importance of Prague (1.2 million population), both industrially and administratively together with high car ownership and easy communication to the surrounding countryside, gave the central Bohemian region an early impetus to second-home ownership (Gardavský 1969, p. 3). In 1971 there were 156,000 second homes in the Czech Lands, of which about a seventh were abandoned rural cottages (Gardavský

1975, p. 124). Research into short-term recreation in northern Bohemia showed greatest popularity for second-home ownership among families with children up to 15 years old (Gardavský 1977a, p. 29; Gardavský and Ryšlavý 1978, p. 43). The 1970s also saw a growth in Moravia in places like the Jeseníky Mountains (Šprincová 1976, p. 70), and around cities like Brno (Výstoupil 1981, p. 78). In Slovakia, there were only 9,844 second homes in 1972, of which a mere 2 per cent were former agricultural cottages (Gardavský 1977b, p. 71). Again it is around the larger urban centres that most second homes are located: Bratislava, Košice, Martin, and Liptovský Mikulás (Mariot 1976, p. 7; Otrubová 1980, p. 133).

It is difficult to identify the actual number of domestic tourists in Czechoslovakia from official statistical sources, as these do not include people who organise their own vacations through friends or private accommodation. Certainly, over half a million children (556,413) visited summer camps arranged through the ROH trade union in 1985 (*Statistická Ročenka ČSSR* 1986, p. 513); a similar number of adults (535,581) spending on average six nights each took advantage of the same organisation's recreation and holiday facilities. In Bohemia, the main attraction areas, apart from the major spa centres, are in the Krkonoše Mountains of north-eastern Bohemia. Places like Špindlerův Mlýn are popular throughout the year (Demek 1975, p. 251; Dohnal and Malá 1964, p. 121), but more generally the Krkonoše area is increasingly popular for winter holidays owing to the varying altitudes, snow cover and forest growth (Sýkora 1976, p. 29). The Krkonoše Mountains are a designated Nature Park area whose forests are unfortunately under threat from pollution. Nevertheless, recreational facilities have already reached the limit planned for the year 2000, and recently a large hotel was built here against opposition from the local population. Areas around major urban centres also prove popular for short-term recreation (Petrůjová 1974, p. 79), especially the region to the south-west of Prague with its medieval castles (Karlštejn, Žebrák, Křivoklát), other national historical monuments and the landscape of the Bohemian karst (Rot 1968, p. 18).

In Moravia, the karst is also a popular recreation area centred around the city of Brno. The demand for recreation, particularly short term, is greatest from the industrial region of northern Moravia around Ostrava. Here people utilise the nearby Beskydy Mountains, Lower Jeseník and Oderské highlands as a means of escape from this industrial agglomeration (Havrlant 1968, p. 144; 1973, p. 64; 1974, p. 20; 1975, p. 50). Slovakia possesses very favourable conditions for tourist development and is popular with domestic tourists not only from its own republic but throughout the country. It contains not only the High and Low Tatras, but also the Small and Large Fatra Mountains and the area of Slovensky raj (Slovakian Paradise).

Interspersed between these mountains, are valleys providing the main communication links and urban centres, many, such as Levoča, having historical significance. There are also designated national parks, as in the High and Low Tatras. There has also been considerable development of short-term recreation around the major cities (Mariot 1971, p.41; Jacková and Herberová 1973, p. 133). Mountain villages, such as Ždiar (Otrubová 1985, p. 70), have seen some growth in their tourist potential, but as in other parts of the High Tatras there is an urgent need for increased accommodation facilities. This will involve greater use of private houses, construction of new hotels and motels which are linked to major skiing areas and the provision of such new infrastructure as ski lifts. Finally, the Slovakian karst has considerable potential for future tourist development (Mariot 1977, p. 222). Most recently there have been calls to develop 'dynamic' tourism (Mišunová 1988, p. 364) in situations whereby areas with several attractions (relief, mineral spas, caves, zoos and botanical gardens) can all be found located along one route or within a locality. Such ideas could well link in to the popular domestic pursuit of camping with many 'autocamps' located at convenient distances on the main highways linking the Czech Lands and Slovakia (Anon. 1983, p. 2).

7.6 International tourism

There is a growing interest from foreign travel agencies in Czechoslovakia and potential exists for this to increase. While, at a global level, tourism accounts for 5 per cent of world trade, in Czechoslovakia it has hitherto only totalled 3.5 per cent of trade with the erstwhile socialist countries and a mere 2 per cent with the West (Anon. 1989a, p. 20). Over 2 million foreign visitors arrived in the country during 1988, but this figure included not only tourist travel proper, but also business trips and arrival of official delegations. In addition, it encompassed tourist traffic in border regions of short duration (at least one day); furthermore, it included foreign visitors only travelling in transit through the country. The actual number of bona fide tourists visiting Czechoslovakia has therefore been substantially lower than that recorded in official statistics, and the number of transit tourists has shown a steady rise since the early 1970s (see Figure 7.2). This also reflects the central position of Czechoslovakia in Europe as a transit area for both Eastern and Western travellers (see Figure 7.3).

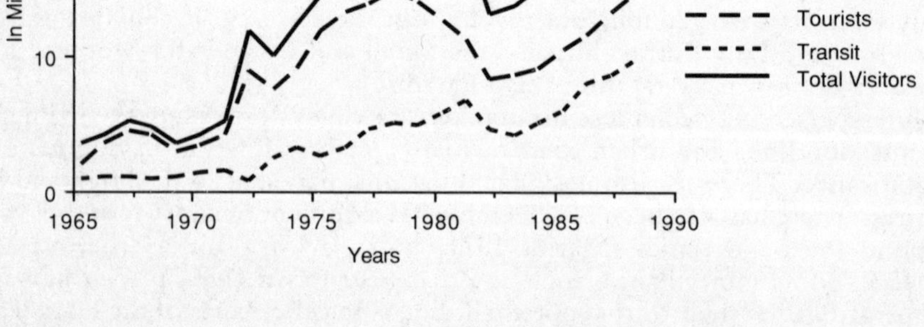

Figure 7.2 Foreign visitors to Czechoslovakia 1965–88

Source: Statistická Ročenka ČSSR83

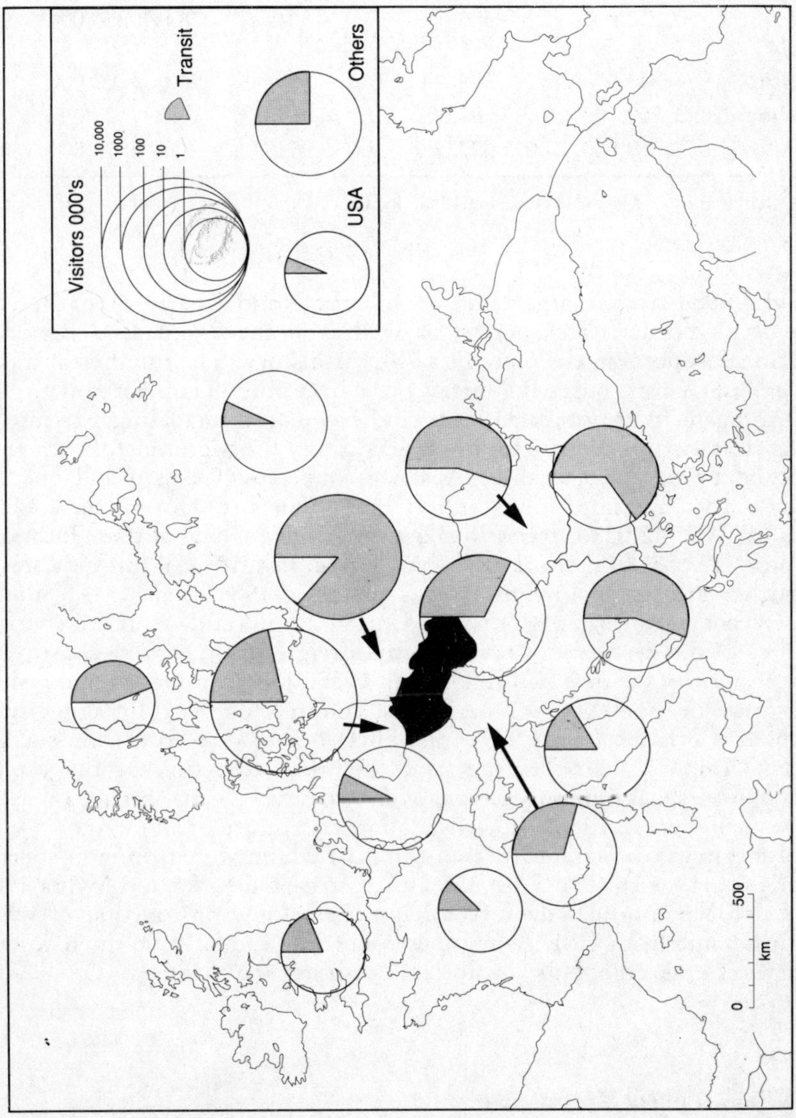

Figure 7.3 Czechoslovakia: foreign visitors, 1988

Source: Statistická Ročenka ČSSR 1989, p. 533

Table 7.1 Number of nights spent by visitors to major tourist centres, 1985

Visitors	Prague	%	West Bohemian spas	%	Krkonoše	%	High Tatras	%
Domestic	842,000	27.5	311,000	44.6	758,000	71.4	686,000	67.5
Foreign of which:	2,217,000	72.5	386,000	55.4	304,000	28.6	330,000	32.5
Socialist	948,000	42.7	299,000	77.5	286,000	94.0	302,000	91.5
Non-Socialist	1,269,000	57.3	87,000	22.5	18,000	6.0	28,000	8.5
Total	3,059,000	100	697,000	100	1,062,000	100	1,016,000	100

Source: Calculated from *Hospodářské noviny* 1986, 36, p. 8

The year 1988 saw the largest number of arrivals and departures registered at the country's border check-points, as well as at the Prague and Bratislava international airports in the republic's 70-year history. The number of travellers in passenger cars, buses and lorries grew by 5 million compared with 1987 to an aggregate figure of 70,931,000, and has placed increasing pressure on customs clearance procedures for foreigners. From the beginning of 1987 entry visas could be obtained at three Austrian, one west German and one east German border crossing points and at Prague airport. During the first six months of 1989, 42,038 Czechoslovakian visas were issued at these locations, two-thirds (27,652) of them at the west German frontier. All this indicates an even further growth in foreign visitors which in 1988 totalled 24.5 million (12.8 per cent more than 1987) who spent 80.2 million days in the country. Some idea of the destinations favoured by foreign visitors to Czechoslovakia may be seen from the data in Table 7.1. In 1985, domestic and foreign visitors spent a total of 26,309,000 nights in the country; of these foreign visitors constituted a quarter (6,744,000), of which 1,964 were from non-socialist countries. Table 7.1 stresses the overwhelming attraction of the capital, Prague, with over 3 million visitors, over two-thirds from abroad, of which well over half were from non-socialist countries. A third of all foreigners spent some nights in the capital, nearly two-thirds of whom were from non-socialist states (64.6 per cent). The West Bohemian spas (Laboutka and Výlita 1983, p. 403) also accommodated more foreign than domestic tourists, of which two-thirds came from CMEA-member countries. Similarly, in the Krkonoše and High Tatras, the bulk of foreign visitors arrived from the CMEA countries.

7.6.1 Tourists from CMEA countries

In 1988, of the 22 million foreign visitors from CMEA countries, 12 million came as bona fide tourists; this compares very favourably with the less than 4 million who arrived in 1971. Greatest growth took place during the late 1970s, but again official statistics can be misleading; the total number of CMEA tourists reached a record level in 1978 (see Figure 7.4), with a corresponding decline the following year, officially explained as due to sanitary/health precautions in the summer of 1979. More precisely however, many of the Hungarian, Polish and East German 'tourists' came for shopping trips to urban centres close to their own border. If these shopping tourists are excluded, a more realistic figure is obtained, showing a net decline in tourist visits; in 1976 these totalled 5.9 million, compared with 3.8 million in 1978 and 3.0 million in 1979 (Blaha 1981, p. 53).

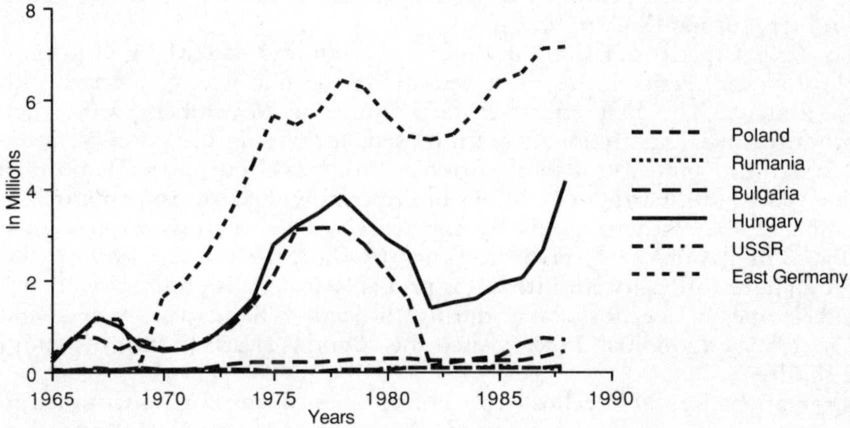

Figure 7.4 Czechoslovakia: tourists from CMEA countries, 1965–88
Source: Statistická Ročenka ČSSR

Even by the mid-1970s there were early signs of change; according to official figures (*Statistické Přehledy*, 1976), in 1975 there was a rise in visitors from the CMEA countries of nearly a fifth over 1974 to a total of nearly 13 million individual trips. While much of this increase was due to trips from Hungary, Poland and East Germany, other CMEA visitors recorded a slight drop (for example, the Soviet Union) or a considerable decline, as in the case of Bulgaria and Romania. In fact, these latter two countries had experienced a steady drop over the preceding five years, from 126,585 and 111,738 respectively in 1971 to 35,670 and 8,087 in 1975 (Radio Free Europe 1976, p. 5). The exceptional rise in tourists from CMEA countries between 1971 (3.7 million) and 1972 (10.4 million) may be attributed to a relaxation in travel restrictions on east Germans by their government in January 1972 (Radio Free Europe 1972, p. 1). The following year, 1973, saw an overall decline in CMEA visitors from 10.4 to 8.5 million owing to an outbreak of foot-and-mouth disease in Hungary and the Slovakian borderland. This led to subsequent Czechoslovakian travel restrictions being imposed during the first half of that year (Radio Free Europe 1973, p. 1). Nevertheless, between 1971 and 1975, 90 per cent of the foreign tourists visiting Czechoslovakia came from the CMEA bloc.

The second half of the 1970s recorded further growth in tourist traffic. Foreign visitors rose by 3.5 million between 1976 and 1977 to a total of 17.3 million individual trips, of which 94.4 per cent were from the CMEA (*Statistické Přehledy* 1977, p. 2). This was mainly attributable to a sharp rise in CMEA visitors, largely from Poland (3.4 to 5.8 million), and more generally from the other Eastern bloc states. For example, both Bulgaria and Romania recorded substantial increases from 35,000 to 79,000 and 8,000 to 32,000 respectively. The continued growth in Polish tourist numbers (Šprincová 1977, p. 110) was somewhat curbed by a new Czechoslovak–Polish tourist agreement in July 1977. This decree imposed financial stringencies on travellers journeying between the two countries, and amounted to a daily minimum and maximum compulsory money exchange rate; this was probably designed to curb smuggling which had been prevalent along the border with its 18 crossing points (Radio Free Europe 1977, p. 9).

The 1980s experienced some decline in the number of CMEA visitors to Czechoslovakia. Perhaps the most sensational decline was connected with Polish tourists. The first effective shock came in November 1980, when reciprocal financial restrictions were imposed, forbidding the purchase more than four times annually of local currencies for travel purposes (Radio Free Europe 1980, p. 9). Further conditions limiting individual tourism appeared in December 1981, with demands by the Czechoslovakian government of a 'verifiable invitation' as a travel necessity (Radio Free Europe 1981, p. 8). Although never officially admitted, it is probably that Polish tourists were not very welcome in Czechoslovakia during the active 'Solidarity' period, and even in 1983, only 85,000 Poles visited the country, nearly a fifth of whom were children.

Deliberations by the Czechoslovak–Polish Commission for Tourism led to the formulation of new guidelines on tourist traffic in August 1984 (Radio Free Europe 1984, p. 8). Under these rules, individual travel was allowed only for family, humane or health purposes; furthermore, new guidelines on group travel stipulated a minimum of 15 tourists, who were obliged to stay for at least three days/two nights per excursion. Similar, but not so dramatic, decline was also experienced by Hungarian visitors who decreased in number from 3.8 to 1.4 million between 1978 and 1982. Some of this may have been related to economic conditions; for example the Hungarian government had imposed strict limits on the volume of goods people could take out of the country. However, there may have been a political motive with the Czechoslovakian government then sensitive to the climate of liberalisation in Hungary (Radio Free Europe 1986, p. 7).

7.6.2 Tourists from the West

Between 1965 and 1988, the number of tourists from Western countries increased from 755,000 to 2,527,000, but the actual percentage declined from 27.32 to 10.31. This was an important factor, as Western tourists are a source of hard-currency earnings. In 1966, most of the Western tourists came from Austria and West Germany and stayed for an average of six days (Král *et al.*, 1968, p. 49); in order to encourage non-CMEA tourists, the government offered a much higher exchange rate for Western tourists.

Figure 7.5 traces the evolution of Western tourists through the 1965–88 period, with West Germans keeping a consistently high profile compared with the Austrians, who have now fallen below the number of Yugoslavs in choosing Czechoslovakia for their holiday. Moreover, in spite of the increase

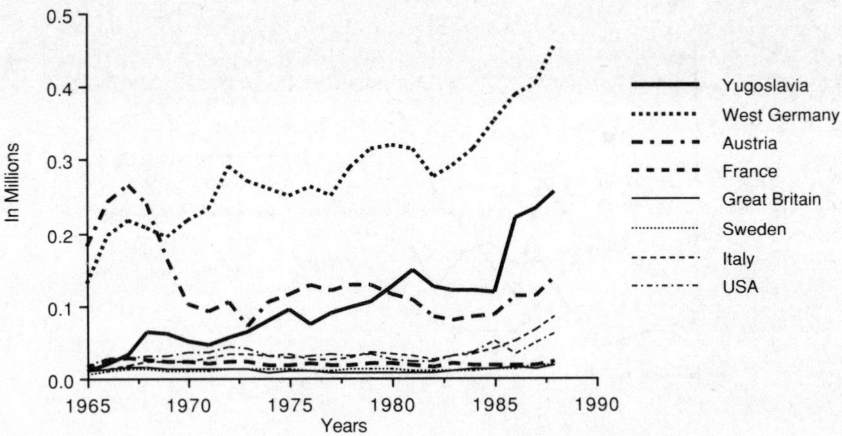

Figure 7.5 Czechoslovakia: tourists from Western countries, 1965–88

Source: Statistická Ročenka ČSSR

in Western tourists the actual average length of stay fell from 6.4 days in 1970 to 5.4 in 1980 (Blaha 1981, p. 53) and to 4.7 in 1988.

During the period 1971 to 1975 the two largest groups of Western tourists came from the neighbouring states of West Germany and Austria. While the number of tourists from West Germany was increasing, their number of Austrian counterparts dropped considerably. One of the major reasons was the foot-and-mouth epidemic of 1973 when tourist traffic between Czechoslovakia and Austria was closed for part of the year. More generally, stagnation in Western tourist traffic during the first half of the 1970s was partly due to increasing hotel and restaurant prices in Czechoslovakia, and partly to a drop in the bonus on official exchange rates from 125 to 75 per cent; furthermore, the tedious entry and visa procedures for Western visitors and their possible refusal for trivial reasons tended to discourage potential Western customers (Radio Free Europe 1976, p. 7). Tourists from Yugoslavia showed a steady increase throughout the 1970s, probably related to *Gastarbeiter* activity in other parts of Western Europe and the possession of hard currency.

The early 1980s experienced some stagnation in Western tourist traffic; this could have been related to an obligatory money exchange for hard-currency visitors. It totalled a 30 DM equivalent per day per person, and 15 DM for children aged between six and fifteen. The Czechoslovakian Čedok tourist organisation recommended that a person purchased the day equivalent sum in voucher form before leaving his destination in order to obtain some price reductions (Tassin 1984, p. 192). However, the late 1980s experienced further growth in numbers of Western tourists.

Finally, in the context of both CMEA and Western tourist traffic, Czechoslovakia appears to be increasingly important as a transit tourist area. The major transit tourists come from the CMEA countries and Yugoslavia (Figure 7.6); curbs on individual stays in Czechoslovakia for Poles had led to their crossing the state in greater numbers for other countries, particularly Austria. Transit passenger numbers of both east Germans and Hungarians had declined until very recently, but Yugoslavs form the largest representation

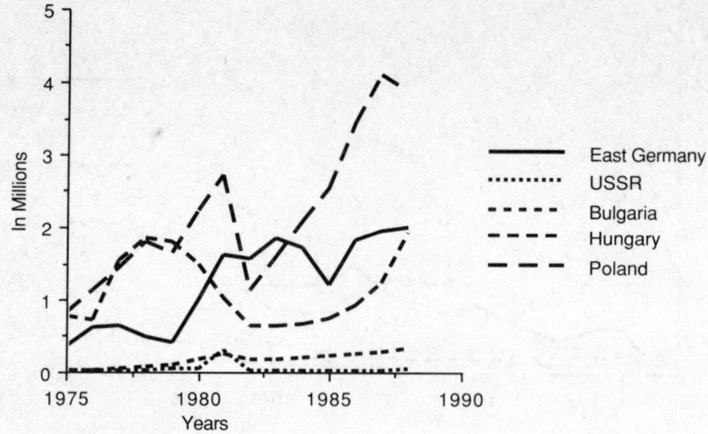

Figure 7.6 Czechoslovakia: major transit visitor countries, 1975–88
Source: Statistická Ročenka ČSSR

from a non-CMEA country to utilise the country's transit facilities. Of the Western countries in 1985, 45 per cent of all Greek tourists were in transit, 41 per cent of the Swedes, 40 per cent of the Danes, and roughly a quarter of the Austrians, Italians and Finns.

7.7 Tourism, *glasnost* and *perestroika*

Up to 1989, Czechoslovakia's government had not been too impressed with the wind of change from the East in the form of *glasnost* and *perestroika*. The government had paid some form of lip service to the idea of *glasnost*, such as the redesignation of 28 October as the country's national holiday and the re-evaluation of literary works by *emigré* Czechoslovakian writers, but these only appeared to be trimmings around the edges. More positive attitudes emerged on the concept of *perestroika* (*Přestavba*); first in January 1987, when principles for the restructuring of the economic mechanism were accepted by the government. These approved some modifications in economic and work legislation and allowed greater freedom for the private sector. They also intended to give more clearly defined rights to state-owned firms and to undertake some restructuring of agriculture. Second, economic reform was to introduce the concept of 'self-management', which in the spring of 1988 saw the election of employees' councils followed by the selection of directors. The third, and probably most important, element concerns the adjustment of prices; this allowed for the recalculation of wholesale prices so that producers received money more in line with production costs and allowed a uniform rate of profit. Subsidies could therefore be eliminated and enterprises could enjoy greater financial independence (EIU 1989, p. 11).

With the establishment of a new democracy, it appears that Czechoslovakian economic reform will continue to follow a cautious route, allowing contemporary conditions to improve. Two new laws would support tourist development: the first in October 1987 agreed to abolish the tourist tax as from

September 1989; second, in April 1988 permission was granted for private citizens to hold a convertible-currency account ($500 minimum–$1,000 maximum) with interest paid at 3 per cent for six and 4 per cent for twelve months. Some of this invested money will be used for tourist development and the buying of goods from abroad.

The other factor which may help Czechoslovakian tourism is the joint venture. This allows for 49 per cent foreign ownership, with profits taxed at 50 per cent, a 25 per cent transfer dividend tax; a Czechoslovakian citizen must be head of the joint venture (Radio Free Europe 1988, p. 25). Foreign partners have been found for building hotel accommodation in Prague, Bratislava and the spa towns of West Bohemia and West Slovakia. An Austrian company (Warimpex) has joined the Czechoslovakian enterprise Balnex to rebuild and construct hotels and restaurants. Austria has also linked the Hotel-Invest AG with Čedok for hotel building and reconstruction. Čedok has concluded an agreement with the French CBC G. Simonet construction company to form the Tourinvest joint venture. Much of this activity is largely concerned with luxury hotel provision to capture the Western hard-currency market.

The Joint Venture Act of 1988 therefore allowed foreign partners from mixed capital companies to participate in Czechoslovakia's tourist development. This will have a spin-off effect on Czechoslovakia's tourist organisations which rose from 12 to 20 in the last two years of the 1980s. A further filip to this trend was the designation of Prague as the congress centre for the Universal Federation of Travel Agents' Association (UFTAA) in October 1989, together with the government's plan to provide the capital, the country's most attractive foreign tourist centre, with 3,500 new hotel beds by 1991 (Anon. 1989a, p. 20).

7.8 Conclusion

This chapter has traced the development of tourism in Czechoslovakia from its early days to the dawning of a new era in 1990. Certainly the country contains both physical and historical potential for tourism through its varied landscapes, spas and medieval cities; much of this was ignored during the late 1940s and early 1950s in the race to build a socialist society with its state control of tourism. Later decades saw a revival of interest in the tourist potential, both for the country's domestic clients through 'welfare' tourism, and in response to the need for hard currency from international Western visitors.

Such demands led to a reappraisal of tourist development. Theoretical research was carried out into the creation of tourist regions, which moved from the planning board to reality, while the 1980s saw efforts to improve the tourist base to include 'congress' tourism and to provide higher-quality spa facilities. Similarly, by the mid-1970s, domestic tourism had shed its emphasis on the collective approach, in favour of a less rigid interpretation of individual holiday travel. Following the country's political changes in 1989 and 1990, there may be less of an emphasis on second-home ownership (previously a popular outlet for non-convertible currency savings) in preference for travel abroad, but the demands for short-term local recreation will probably continue.

International tourism should grow as easier entry facilities evolve. Czechoslovakia may prove an attractive country for Western visitors, while its central position in Europe will ensure increasing popularity for transit passengers. The former high proportion of CMEA tourists will probably decline to be replaced by efforts to attract wealthier tourists from Western Europe, Japan and North America. Much will depend on moves by the new democratic government as to how quickly they adapt to rising potential demand from Western tourists, now willing to consider Czechoslovakia as a possible holiday outlet. Domestic tourism will not develop so rapidly until the country has a more stable economy and a stronger Czechoslovakian currency to allow people to travel abroad. Finally, one may see greater interest in the tourist joint-venture programme in Czechoslovakia which may encourage a marriage between demand for higher Western accommodation standards and the rich variety of physical and historical components that this land-locked European state has to offer.

Note

* The author greatly appreciates the help and advice of Mr. Peter Biely, Deputy Managing Director of Čedok (the Czechoslovakian National Tourist Office) in London, and Miss Louise Saunders from the Cartographic Unit, U.C.L. who prepared the illustrations.

8 Hungary

Paul A. Compton

8.1 Introduction

Hungary is not particularly well placed in competition with neighbouring countries to attract tourists. The country's environmental setting is of limited appeal and there is a manifest absence of a rich, well-preserved historical past. In being land-locked, Hungary, unlike Yugoslavia or Bulgaria, cannot offer the mixture of sun and sea that many tourists now demand. The country does not therefore benefit to any significant extent from the summer package-tour industry of northern and Western Europe. Furthermore, in being situated at the centre of the Carpathian Basin, the topography is dominated by plains and low-lying hills; even the highest points are of comparatively modest elevation. As a result, snow cover is of short duration and there is no winter holiday season to speak of, in marked contrast to Austria, or even Czechoslovakia, Bulgaria or Romania. Nor would people visit Hungary to seek the visible remains of the great periods of European civilisation. Throughout the centuries the land has been fought over time and again and the devastation wrought by the Ottoman Turks, in particular, means that little of historical interest predating the eighteenth century has been preserved. It is true, of course, that Budapest eventually became the twin capital of the Dual Monarchy but that status was achieved late and, while a certain flowering occurred, the city lacks the grandeur of historical Vienna or the charm of old Prague.

8.2 Data sources

Tourist data in Hungary are derived from a process of continuous monitoring. All foreigners arriving on the territory of the Hungarian Republic provide basic personal information plus the reason for travelling to the country. For foreigners from the West, with the exception of Austrians, Finns and Swedes, these data must be furnished as part of the process of obtaining a visa; citizens of countries not requiring visas complete a short questionnaire containing the same information. Both visa papers and questionnaires are collected at points of entry and the information is passed on to the Central Statistical Office. Statistics about Hungarians leaving the country are collected in similar fashion at the point of exit. A second source of information about visitors comes from the compulsory registration of foreigners at their place of stay in Hungary. The foreign citizen must again furnish personal details, but the value of these data lies in the information they provide about the geographical pattern of visiting within the country. Separate registration is obligatory at each place visited, but this can be evaded. That said, no visitor is able to leave the country without registering at least once and the statistics are therefore of acceptable quality and give a representative picture of tourist patterns within the country.

It is the responsibility of the Transport and Trade Statistics Section of the Central Statistical Office to collate and publish statistical data on Hungarian tourism. The coverage of information is comprehensive and is presented annually in the Tourist Yearbook (Yearbook of Tourist Statistics to 1987) under ten main headings: summary date; international visitors; tourist traffic; data on excursionists and foreigners in transit; statistics on hotels and other establishments offering accommodation for payment; organised tourism, that is, group tours; regional statistics relating to Hungary; international payments from tourism; international data, that is, summary tourist statistics for selected countries; appendices, which include exchange rates, statistics on traffic at the various border crossing points and private accommodations. The term 'tourist', 'excursionist' and 'foreigner in transit' have precise meanings in Hungary: a 'tourist' is a foreign visitor who spends at least 24 hours in the country; an 'excursionist' is a foreign visitor who spends less than 24 hours in Hungary; a 'foreigner in transit'; spends less than 24 hours in Hungary and leaves the country at a different place from the point of entry. These definitions are retained in this chapter, except that the term 'day-visitor' is used in preference to 'excursionist'.

8.3 General trends and characteristics

Despite the country's comparative lack of endowments, foreign tourism has expanded in recent decades to become a vital part of the national economy. Indeed, according to the official receipts of exchange, it now accounts for around 2.5 per cent of GDP, although this may well be an understatement as a substantial volume of currency transactions still passes through unauthorised channels. Furthermore, the balance between the income from foreign visitors and the expenditure incurred by Hungarians going abroad became progressively more favourable up to 1987, when income exceeded expenditure more than threefold. Although exchange rates between socialist (rouble-accounting) and non-socialist (dollar-accounting) countries are not easily equated, a rough calculation would indicate that gross earnings from tourism amounted to $830 million in 1987 and exceeded $900 million in 1988. In terms of the absolute value of tourism to the national economy, this places Hungary ahead of Bulgaria, Czechoslovakia and Romania but well behind Austria and Yugoslavia (see Table 8.1).

Although 1988 was an exceedingly good year in terms of the gross tourist income, it was also marked by some relaxation in the currency restrictions for Hungarians travelling to 'non-rouble' countries. In earlier years many of these would have travelled on a letter of invitation and would not have received a hard-currency allowance, but from the beginning of 1988 a hard-currency entitlement was introduced, set initially at $250 per capita for a three-year period. This measure not only generated a 72 per cent growth in the number of Hungarian visitors to Western countries in 1988 compared with 1987 but, more significantly, resulted in a fourfold increase in the outflow of hard

Table 8.1 Gross income from international tourism: Hungary and selected countries (in US $ millions)

Hungary	912	(1988)
Austria	8520	(1988)
Bulgaria	345	(1986)
Czechoslovakia	307	(1986)
Yugoslavia	2024	(1988)
Romania	178	(1986)

Source: Central Statistical Office; extracted from Table 54, 1988 Tourist Yearbook

currency, totalling $644 million in 1988 compared with $186 million in 1987. Since the favourable balance with other socialist countries also deteriorated slightly, the outcome was a reduction in the net income from tourism by more than two-thirds, from $553 million to $169 million, between 1987 and 1988.

Although the figures will not be available until the end of 1990, it is clear that the balance deteriorated still further in the first half of 1989 when expenditure by Hungarians travelling abroad exceeded income generated by visitors to the country by a considerable margin. This further deterioration may be traced back to two decisions taken by the government at the beginning of the year. The first was to abolish exit visas and grant Hungarian citizens freedom of travel; the second was to legalise unauthorised holdings of hard currency and permit individuals to open interest-bearing hard-currency accounts in local banks. The latter measure was designed to mobilise hitherto illegal, and hence unproductive, funds amounting to several billions of US dollars and place them at the disposal of the authorities.

As it happened, the government seems to have mis-timed the sequence of measures implementing the policy. The holding of hard currency was legalised some months before hard-currency accounts became available, but the crucial mistake was to announce well in advance of the event that import taxes would be raised sharply to stem any outflow of funds that might result from these measures. This created a 'window of opportunity' during which the newly legalised holdings could be used to import goods before the increased taxes came into effect. Although the outcome was easily foreseen, it appears to have taken the authorities by surprise. Hungarians, in possession of their unrestricted passports and legalised dollars, schillings and D-Marks, flooded out of the country and beat the tax rise by importing cars, personal computers and other electronic and white goods before the deadline, mainly from Austria. Arguably, a country in economic crisis with one of the highest rates of per capita indebtedness in the world should have channelled these resources into more productive use; with the wisdom of hindsight, it is clear that the mechanics of a basically sensible policy were mishandled by the authorities.

Incidentally, apart from the Hungarians who now have a new car and other consumer 'luxuries', the other beneficiaries in the process have been the Austrian retailers who opened new outlets in the towns and villages close to the border to cater for this 'windfall' business from Hungary, for instance, in Nickelsdorf, Zurndorf, Gattendorf and Parndorf on the main road to Vienna.

The expansion of tourism in Hungary in the last 15 years or so has been achieved in various ways, but an essential ingredient has been the successful selling of Hungary's two outstanding tourist assets—Budapest and Lake

Balaton. Although Budapest is largely a creation of the nineteenth century and is therefore a relatively new city by European standards, it occupies what is arguably the most attractive geographical situation of any European capital. Bisected by the Danube, the picturesque Buda side with its many hills and select residential areas is separated from Pest on the east bank of the river which serves as the commercial and industrial heart of the capital. Like other large continental centres, the city has much to offer in the way of culture and entertainment and is a magnet to the citizens of the neighbouring, former communist, countries for the comparative opulence of its shops and restaurants. Located in western Hungary, Lake Balaton is the largest fresh-water lake in Central Europe. It warms up quickly in summer because of its shallow depth and combines a good climate with attractive environmental surroundings. It has drawn most of its visitors from Czechoslovakia, the former GDR and Poland from among the old socialist countries, and from Austria, west Germany and The Netherlands in the West.

Table 8.2 Foreign visitors to Hungary, 1981–8 ('000s)

	Socialist countries		Non-socialist countries		All countries	
	Visitors	Tourists	Visitors	Tourists	Visitors	Tourists
1981	12,525	9,131	2,316	1,317	14,841	10,450
1982	7,125	4,996	2,707	1,477	9,832	6,473
1983	7,521	5,221	2,942	1,543	10,463	6,764
1984	9,910	6,904	3,519	1,827	13,429	8,731
1985	11,377	7,710	3,749	2,014	15,126	9,724
1986	12,567	8,570	4,079	2,043	16,646	10,613
1987	13,519	9,148	5,434	2,678	18,953	11,826
1988	11,589	7,479	6,376	3,084	17,965	10,562

Source: Central Statistical Office; compiled from data contained in the 1988 Tourist Yearbook

The most notable feature of the Hungarian tourist industry in recent years has, indeed, been the increase in the number of Western visitors, mainly from Europe, which has more than doubled since 1981 (Table 8.2). While this phenomenon cannot be altogether divorced from the perceived attractiveness of Budapest and the Balaton, after all most Western tourism is directed to these two centres, it is mainly to other factors that we must look in order to explain this substantial growth. Part of the reason has been the increasing willingness of *emigrés* to return 'home' regularly, encouraged by the very evident political liberalisation. The recent introduction of direct scheduled flights to the United States and the re-establishment of normal relations with Israel will further assist this process as will the lifting of the prohibition on foreigners buying property in the country.

But of a much greater significance has been the progressive removal of the administrative and financial hindrances that used to deter Western tourism in general, and which has also been an integral part of the wide-ranging liberalisation of Hungarian society and economy. Examples of administrative relaxations have included the simplification of the entry regulations for the citizens of capitalist countries, and visas are now obtainable at all road crossing points and at Budapest Airport. Furthermore, visa requirements have been abolished altogether for the citizens of Austria, Sweden and Finland. At the same time that this process has been going on, tourists from Eastern Europe have been faced with some tightening of controls.

It is on the financial front, however, that the most radical reforms have been implemented. First, the system of compulsory exchange was abolished in the late 1970s. This had specified that before an entry visa could be granted either hotel accommodation had to be pre-paid in convertible currency or a specific amount of hard currency had to be exchanged for each day's stay in the country. It was a system that acted as a substantial deterrent to tourism, although more for the bureaucratic hurdles that had to be scaled than for any financial penalties that might be incurred. Second, the system of multiple exchange rates was replaced by a unified exchange-rate mechanism against Western currencies in 1981. Under the old system different rates of exchange had operated according to the purpose of the transaction and this had meant separate official, commercial and tourist rates. Since the principle determinant of the unified rate was the need to keep inefficient Hungarian industry competitive on the world market, its introduction has created a substantially undervalued forint from the view point of tourism and has made Hungary a very cheap country indeed for visitors from the West. This has arguably been the most important factor bringing about the recent upsurge in Western tourism.

Interestingly, however, and perhaps symptomatic of the general direction in which Hungarian policy has been moving during the 1980s, the growing contacts with the West have been accompanied by a standstill in the number of tourists from Eastern countries: indeed numbers of the latter were almost halved between 1981 and 1982, and it was not until 1987 that the 1981 figure was again exceeded. Hence, the financial changes that have benefited Western visitors have made Hungary a very expensive country for other East Europeans and have therefore tended to discourage tourism from these countries. The background to this is the deep-seated economic crisis that Hungary faces, not least a massive burden of international debt and the attempts that have been made to overcome it. These have involved fiscal reform and the freeing of the price mechanism, but this has generated a high rate of inflation relative to most of Hungary's COMECON partners in Europe who exercised strict control over prices up to the time of the recent political changes. Under market conditions, an equilibrium would be maintained by a downward adjustment in the parity of the Hungarian currency, but within COMECON rates of exchange have traditionally been fixed by intergovernmental agreement and altered only very infrequently if at all. Although this may soon change, the outcome is an overvalued forint and high prices *vis-à-vis* the rest of Eastern Europe.

An allied problem is the lack of currency convertibility within COMECON, which is a further disincentive to the growth of tourism. Balances that Hungary might earn through selling services to tourists from other COMECON countries are not readily expendable and the situation can only be contained by restricting the amounts of currency that COMECON tourists can buy—by both Hungary as the host and also by the countries from which tourists originate. It is limitations of this nature that had much to do with the sharp fall in the number of COMECON visitors to Hungary between 1981 and 1982 as well as with the slowness of the recovery.

In addition, the easing of restrictions on visitors from the West also adversely affected tourism from the then socialist countries through the impact this had on the general climate of opinion in the region. In being tangible evidence of Hungarian liberalisation, these policies were frowned upon by the hard-line regimes in Prague, Bucharest, Sofia and East Berlin and clearly hindered the growth of mutual tourism until the wholesale collapse of those regimes at the end of 1989. Indeed, the deep suspicion of Budapest would appear to have been very well founded; for instance, the removal of the border fence with Austria, and the flood of East German refugees that this triggered off, undermined the Honecker regime in East Berlin, while the actions of the Reverend Lászlo Tökés, a Hungarian Calvinist minister in Timişoara, sparked the Romanian revolution and the overthrow of Ceauşescu.

These developments of the last decade have brought about a fundamental shift in the relative contribution of tourism to the national economy from former socialist *vis-à-vis* non-socialist countries. For instance, whereas in 1975 three-fifths of the gross income from tourism was contributed by the rouble-accounting area, this had dropped to just under one-third of the total by 1987. The trend in net income, that is, after allowing for foreign-currency expenditure on Hungarians travelling abroad, was somewhat less marked but is still in the same general direction. Hence, although comprising little more than a quarter of all foreign visitors to the country, Western tourists, through their substantially greater purchasing power, now account for the bulk of Hungary's earnings from tourism in both gross and net terms. On average they spend four times more per capita than their Eastern counterparts while in Hungary, a ratio that has been remarkably stable over the years. Moreover, they bring in convertible currency that is of immediate economic benefit. Hard economic facts like these go a long way towards explaining the shift in official policy over the years from a distasteful toleration of Western visitors to one of welcome and very active encouragement at present.

Yet regret is still sometimes expressed about the passing of the old system of tighter controls, on the grounds that a 'tourist' forint fixed at a higher rate against Western currencies than is possible with partial convertibility, together with compulsory exchange, would bring greater economic benefits. The crux of the case is that the present system indirectly subsidises the Western tourist at the expense of the Hungarian state because the internal price mechanism is still dependent upon government subventions; in other words, the purchase of goods and services that tourists make while in Hungary are not at true market prices. Indeed, prices may be so far below the world market level as to encourage mass purchases by tourists that disrupt retail trade and cause chronic shortages. (The role of the Austrians in this is detailed elsewhere in this chapter.) What would therefore be seized as an entrepreneurial opportunity in a free-market economy becomes a political embarrassment for the Hungarian government.

Nevertheless, while there is some justification for this argument, it is difficult to see how greater controls could effectively be reintroduced in a limited area of the economy like tourism. The price that would have to be paid, for instance in terms of greater bureaucratic regulation, would be considerable and would fit very uneasily into the liberalising framework now current. Furthermore, it must be kept in mind that Western tourism has only undergone dramatic growth since controls were abolished. Hence, if the growth in the number of Western tourists had continued at the rate recorded between 1975 and 1980, the result would have been a 25–30 per cent shortfall in numbers compared with the actual outcome for 1988. With differences of this magnitude, it is difficult to substantiate any claim that the change to a more liberal regime for Western tourists has been to the disadvantage of the Hungarian economy.

It is still too early to reach any balanced judgement about the impact of the demise of Communism in Eastern Europe on Hungarian tourism. At first sight, one might expect it to bring about some revival in the number of visitors from those countries. But against that all the financial disincentives listed above will remain, at least until the effects of economic reform begin to make a positive impact on the region. Furthermore, liberalisation and the freedom to travel means that East Europeans are no longer locked into a particular set of countries and the West will certainly beckon those who can afford it. Paradoxically, therefore, the liberalisation of Eastern Europe might well lead initially to some decline in the number of visitors to Hungary from these countries.

8.4 Spatial patterns

So far the discussion has concentrated on general trends and has focused on why there are important differences between the characteristics of tourism originating from Eastern as opposed to Western countries. But equally, the more detailed patterns, involving the national origins of tourists and the places they visit within Hungary, are of considerable geographical interest. Broadly speaking, the intensity of international contacts with Hungary exhibits a weak distance-decay relationship. Around half the visitors come from the neighbouring countries of Austria, Czechoslovakia, Romania, the Soviet Union and Yugoslavia and a further 45 per cent from Bulgaria, Italy, Poland, Switzerland, and Germany, that is from those countries which are Hungary's next-door neighbours but one. The only country of any significance outside Europe is the United States (Table 8.3).

That said, there are significant ways in which the spatial pattern differs from a simple distance-decay model. Thus, fewer people visit Hungary from the Soviet Union and Romania than might be otherwise expected. The Romanian figure is particularly low given the large Hungarian minority in Transylvania and the close family ties that still exist with Hungary proper; this may, of course, rapidly change now that the Ceauşescu regime has gone, especially if this also means the abandonment of measures designed to discourage the Hungarian minority from maintaining contact with its cultural homeland. As for Soviet citizens, it is simply the case that they are unable to travel freely abroad, even to other socialist countries, and the overwhelming majority of Soviet tourists come as part of organised tours. Yet even this is now changing, as shown by the sharp increase in the numbers of visitors from the Soviet Union between 1987 and 1988 (Table 8.3). On the other hand, Hungary was more popular with tourists from East Germany and Poland than might be expected on a simple distance basis. Indeed, Poles are reputed to enter the country as much for petty trading—locally called 'Polish markets'—as for bona fide tourism, presumably because of the difficult economic circumstances at home. Hungary was also relatively popular with the West Germans and

Table 8.3 Breakdown of tourists to Hungary by country of origin and of tourists from Hungary by country of destination, based on data for 1987 and 1988 (%)

Neighbouring countries	Foreign tourists in Hungary from:		Hungarian tourists abroad in:	
	1988	1987	1988	1987
Austria	8.7	7.1	10.5	4.5
Czechoslovakia	21.2	27.7	40.3	35.9
Romania	1.6	2.4	13.0	18.4
Soviet Union	5.5	3.9	2.9	2.5
Yugoslavia	8.8	10.0	4.1	6.8
Total	45.8	51.1	70.8	68.2
Next-door neighbours but one				
Bulgaria	2.8	2.8	1.5	5.9
East Germany	12.9	11.9	9.1	9.7
Italy	1.6	1.2	1.3	1.1
Poland	18.0	20.4	10.3	9.3
Switzerland	0.6	0.5	0.2	0.3
West Germany	10.7	8.3	3.2	2.5
Total	46.6	45.1	25.6	28.8
Other countries				
France	0.4	0.4	0.3	0.4
Great Britain	0.5	0.4	0.2	0.2
Netherlands	1.2	0.7	0.1	0.2
United States	1.1	0.9	0.1	0.2
Others	4.4	1.4	2.9	2.0
Total	7.6	3.8	3.6	3.0
Grand total	100.0	100.0	100.0	100.0
N (in '000s)	10,562	11,826	6,754	6,509

Source: Central Statistical Office; compiled from data contained in the 1988 Tourist Yearbook and 1987 Yearbook of Tourist Statistics

Dutch; indeed, as in trade and commerce in general, West Germany was Hungary's most important source of Western tourists.

These patterns form a quite interesting contrast with the destinations of Hungarian tourists abroad (Table 8.3). The most striking point is that proportionately speaking Hungarians were more likely to go to the former socialist countries—typically four-fifths of Hungarian tourists travel to other parts of Eastern Europe compared with the two-thirds of visitors to Hungary who originate from these countries. But despite this, only Bulgaria and Romania received more visitors from Hungary than they send because, in the case of Bulgaria, of the substantial Black Sea package-holiday business (which, incidentally, slumped badly in 1988), and in the case of Romania, the substantial links with Transylvania already referred to. Czechoslovakia and East Germany, but not Poland, were the other places most frequented by

Hungarian tourists. In respect of Western Europe, Austria has been by far the most popular destination, but otherwise the pattern is quite widely dispersed, and Italy, Switzerland, France and Great Britain were relatively more important as destinations than origins. Conversely, West Germany and The Netherlands were relatively more important as origins than destinations.

The distribution of day-visitors, amounting to 3,622,000 individual trips in 1988, is also worthy of comment. Taking the figures for 1987 and 1988 together, just under 75 per cent of the day-trips were made by Austrians, while the bulk of the remainder were visits by Slovaks and Yugoslavs. Day-tripping to Hungary on the part of the Austrians has grown very rapidly—up by over 70 per cent between 1985 and 1988—since the two countries agreed to abolish visa requirements in the early 1980s. The attraction for Austrians has been the availability of cheap goods and services in Hungary and they flood across the border not only from the neighbouring Burgenland but from as far afield as Vienna and Graz. They mostly go on shopping sprees, stripping the shelves in Kőszeg, Szombathely, Sopron and Mosonmagyaróvár, but they also buy more specialised services, like dental treatment, and even hold wedding receptions in Hungary which are far cheaper than in Austria. By contrast, whereas the motive for Austrian day-visitors is essentially economic, Slovak and Yugoslav day-trippers are drawn mainly from those areas of Slovakia and Yugoslavia immediately adjacent to the border where there are substantial Hungarian communities. Similar circumstances exist in the frontier zones with Romania and the Soviet Union and the agreements that have recently been reached to facilitate greater cross-border contact between local populations have already stimulated an increase in day-visitors from both countries.

Table 8.4 The tourist areas of Hungary: distribution of tourist-days, 1988 (%)

	All	International	Domestic
Budapest	29.2	33.6	23.3
Balaton	28.4	38.0	15.6
Mátra-Bükk	5.0	3.2	7.4
Mecsek	3.8	2.9	5.1
Danube Bend	2.9	2.2	3.8
Velence	1.4	1.4	1.4
Other places	29.3	18.7	43.4
Total	100.0	100.0	100.0
N (in '000s)	27,835	15,897	11,938

Source: Central Statistical Office; compiled from data contained in the 1988 Tourist Yearbook

The pattern of tourism by countries of origin, of course, is only part of the picture, and the areas tourists visit when in Hungary are equally worthy of discussion. As already explained, destinations are known with some precision because tourists are required to register at the places visited. However, the simple distribution of destinations can be a misleading index, and a truer picture of the geographical spread of tourism in terms of local importance is gained from the pattern of 'tourist-days' which combines number of visitors with length of stay (Table 8.4). Viewed in this way, it is clear that the patterns of international and domestic tourism differ considerably. International tourism, particularly from the West, is heavily biased in favour of Budapest and Lake Balaton, with Budapest attracting the larger number of foreign visitors but the Balaton recording more tourist-days because the average stay is longer (8.8 days at the Balaton compared with 3.6 days in Budapest in 1988). The Balaton industry is vitally important, accounting for approximately 30 per cent of Hungary's foreign-currency revenue from tourism. Yet at the same time it experiences all the problems associated with extreme summer seasonality, when facilities are simply inadequate to cope with demand. This leads, for example, to high prices and poor service, but more importantly, from the viewpoint of the longer-term health of the lake and its region, to serious environmental deterioration which, if allowed to persist, could destroy the recreational potential of the lake (Bora 1984).

For some time now, eutrophication has been observed in the Kesthely Basin at the western end of the lake. The main cause of this problem is the discharge of agricultural waste and the infiltration of excessive nitrogen and phosphorous from the application of artificial fertilisers on the surrounding arable area. In addition, the growth of tourism has greatly aggravated the problem by stimulating a large-scale, and insufficiently regulated, building programme. The built-up area, comprised of commercial establishments, privately owned summer and week-end homes and buildings owned and maintained by trade unions, enterprises and other institutions for the purpose of organised recreation by members and employees, now extends with few breaks around the whole lake and in many places right up to the water's edge. The problem is that less than a quarter of the homes are connected to the mains sewage network, while a considerable part of the phosphorus originating from individual septic tanks seeps into the lake. In total, communal waste contributes between 15 and 25 per cent of the primary nutrients causing eutrophication.

In recognition of these problems, the lake is now environmentally protected and measures are in train to raise water quality. Among other things the conflicting interests between the tourist industry and agriculture, the main polluter, must still be resolved and this will require substantial and continuing investment in infrastructural improvement. It is quite clear that major macroeconomic inputs are needed to achieve a permanent solution and, in the light of central government financial stringency, this may well involve the principle that the polluter will pay—not only agriculture but also tourists who enjoy the lake's facilities.

Otherwise, the remaining tourist areas of the country are comparatively under-used by international visitors—the Danube Bend north of Budapest, the Mátra-Bükk region comprising the southern-most foothills of the Tatra Carpathians in the north-east, the Mecsek region in the vicinity of Pécs in the south-west, and Lake Velence, a small area of open water lying between Budapest and Székesfehérvár. Together, these areas catered for around one-fifth of domestic tourism in 1988 but managed to attract less than 10 per cent of foreign visitors. Lake Balaton and Budapest, on the other hand, are relatively less important on the domestic scene. However, one must add the caveat that the true domestic picture is somewhat misrepresented by these data to the extent that Hungarians holiday in 'company' and trade-union hotels operated exclusively for the benefit of employees and workers are not included. As a result, the importance of Lake Balaton, in particular, is understated. Moreover, one should add that the lake is a popular location in Hungary for second homes, as indeed is the Danube Bend, which generates further visitor pressure in these areas that is not reflected in official figures.

8.5 Medicinal spas

An aspect of tourism in Hungary, reminiscent of Victorian and Edwardian Britain, is the continued popularity of medicinal spas, made possible by the ubiquitous presence of thermal waters. These derive from the geological structure of the Carpathian Basin (the Basin is still comparatively active tectonically) and high geothermal gradient, which raises water temperatures by 50–70°C for every kilometre of depth. Two sedimentary types are particularly associated with the presence of thermal water; limestones and dolomites of Carboniferous age and the friable sandstones of the more recent Upper Pannonian. Where the limestones and dolomites come to the surface, for instance along the edge of the basin, natural thermal springs occur and these form the basis of the long history of spa culture on the site of present-day Budapest, where it goes back to the Ottoman and Roman times, and also at Héviz, Harkány and Balatonfűred. The Upper Pannonian waters, by contrast, have been extensively tapped by deep drilling in the course of post-war exploration for oil and natural gas, and this activity has led to new spa developments at Hajdúszoboszló and Zalakaros in the last 25 years.

In all, the facilities of 19 medicinal spas are actively marketed for the use of foreigners—nine in Budapest, of which the Gellért, Császár, Lukács and Széchényi Medicinal Baths are the most celebrated, and 10 in the rest of the country (Figure 8.1). The beneficial therapeutic effects are derived from the presence of dissolved minerals—iodine, bromide, sodium, carbonic acid, sulphur and so on—and sometimes the slight radioactivity of the waters (Galla 1989). Impairments to the locomotor organs are particularly responsive to treatment; for instance the National Rheumatological and Physiotherapy Institute in Budapest uses the waters of the Császár Baths. But in addition, Balatonfüred has specialised in the treatment of heart diseases for around 200 years, while Héviz is noted for the treatment of dental disorders, Hajdúszoboszló for diseases of the digestive organs and Harkány for the treatment of gynaecological complaints. Treatment takes place under medical supervision, usually in purpose-built clinics and hospitals attached to the particular spa.

Specific quantitative information about the use of spa facilities is not easily extracted from the statistics. However, the spas of western Hungary have attracted many visitors from Austria and west Germany who 'come for the cure'. Harkány, for instance, received 41,204 foreign guests in its hotels and other commercial accommodation establishments in 1988 and Héviz attracted another 31,500. It is, however, Budapest that offers most to the foreigner in terms of expertise and range of facilities.

Although the medicinal spa business forms a relatively small part of the Hungarian tourist industry, the income earned is none the less considerable because it lies at the high 'value-added' end of the business. Length of stay easily surpasses the national average—visitors are advised that a minimum stay of three weeks is necessary for any lasting benefit—accommodation tends to be in the better hotels and, of course, treatment has to be paid for.

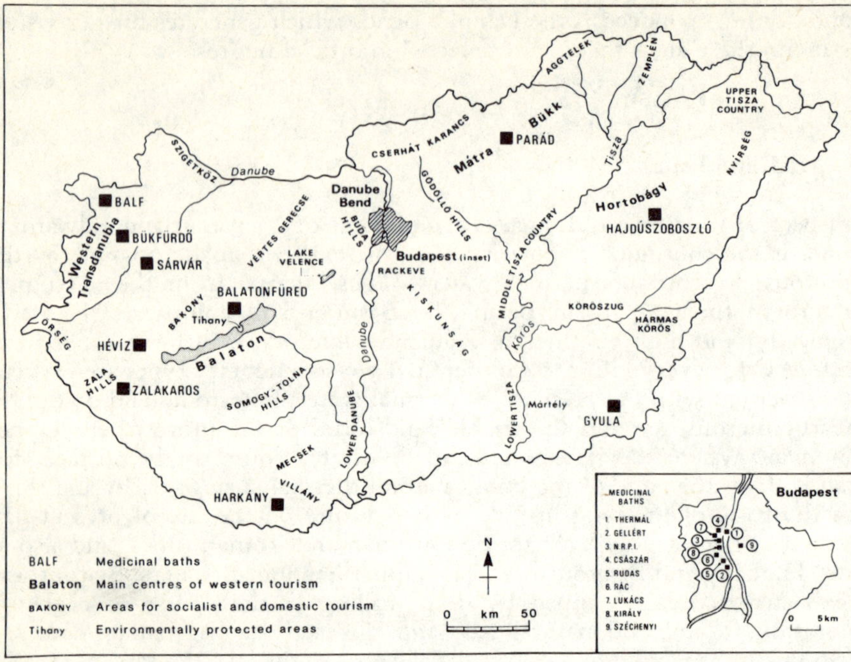

Figure 8.1 Hungary: location of principle tourist centres and regions

8.6 Organisation and infrastructure

With the progress of economic reform, the Hungarian tourist industry has grown into a highly complex, decentralised branch of the national economy involving a multiplicity of enterprises and organisations from hotel and travel companies to county councils and planning bodies. Its regulation, coordination and promotion rests primarily with the Hungarian Tourist Board of the Ministry of Home Trade, which is affiliated to the World Tourism Organisation. But tourism also impinges on the activities of other government ministries, notably the Ministry of the Interior which controls entry to the country, the Ministry of Foreign Affairs which issues visas through its Consular Offices abroad and the Central Statistical Office which collates the statistics about visitors to the country and Hungarian tourists abroad.

The travel business offers a comprehensive service to tourists. In the past, the State Travel Office, IBUSZ, controlled directly by the Ministry of Home Trade up to the end of 1989, held a monopoly position. But economic reform has brought about fundamental change and the business is now competitive and decentralised. The IBUSZ monopoly was broken in the early 1980s with the formation of COOPTOURIST. Now, IBUSZ itself has undergone fundamental re-organisation as part of Hungary's economic liberalisation, and a 40 per cent equity in the company was sold to a consortium headed by Austria's second largest bank, Girozentrale Bank der Oesterrichischen Sparkassen (Dempsey 1989), and was listed on the Vienna and Budapest Stock Exchanges.

The scale of the recent change in the tourist industry is reflected in the multiplicity of different travel agencies that now exist; the state airline, and the rail and long-distance bus companies each have their own travel subsidiaries —MALÉV Air Tours, MÁVTOURS and VOLÁNTOURIST respectively—while the National Savings Bank, in a joint venture with the international group, PENTA, controls OTP–PENTA Tours. Other travel agencies are operated as independent enterprises, some under direct state control, others as cooperatives, for instance, Budapest Tourist, Express and Lokomotiv Tourist, while some small operations are now privately owned. Most county councils also have their own tourist promotion companies, which double-up as travel agencies; for instance, Siótour and Balatontourist serve the Balaton region, Hajdútourist the Hortobágy, and Nyirtourist the far north-east of the country.

The larger concerns operate very much as the big holiday companies in Britain, with package holidays comprising part of their activities. They buy their own hotel accommodation for the season and operate their own charter flights or system of group bookings on scheduled MALÉV services. Not only do they sell holidays in Hungary through their offices and agencies abroad—IBUSZ has branches in most European countries, as well as in the United States, Japan and Australia—but they also organise foreign holidays for the Hungarians. Smaller concerns are in the same package business but operate as intermediaries. Other activities include the renting out of tourist accommodation—much of the private rooming and boarding-house business, for example, passes through their hands—currency exchange, car rentals, the organisation of sightseeing tours and so on.

Some mention of the more significant features of the hotel and restaurant industry is also relevant, given its close links with tourism. Very salient in this respect is the seasonality of Hungarian tourism which creates considerable problems in the provision of accommodation—shortages during the summer season but under-occupancy at other times of the year. Also of considerable importance is the comparative lack of hotels of international standard in Budapest together with good tourist hotels. The former problem is being resolved with the help of Western investment and the Hilton, Atrium-Hyatt, Intercontinental, Forum and Penta chains have all in the last few years opened hotels in the capital. These establishments are owned jointly with the Hungarian state, are managed by Hungarian companies and profits are shared. State and private resources are also being utilised to resolve the shortage of tourist hotels in Budapest. For instance, a subsidiary of the state construction enterprise now operates a small hotel chain and the building of new establishments, *pensio*, with the aid of local private capital is actively encouraged. However, it remains the case that the bulk of commercial tourist accommodation is still in the form of rooms or sometimes complete dwellings that are rented out privately.

The restaurant trade has traditionally been in the hands of companies who either concentrate specifically on catering or are also involved with managing hotels, for instance, the Pannonia and Hungárhotels companies. These are sometimes owned directly by the state through the Ministry of Home Trade, by local councils or by cooperatives. Increasingly, however, the smaller establishments are being transferred to the private sector through competitive leasing based on tenders, while the early 'sell-off' of the larger companies may also be anticipated. Additionally, a wholly private restaurant/catering sector has been allowed to blossom in recent years. This takes many forms, ranging from *lángos* (deep-fried dough) sellers, 'Imbiss-type' buffets serving hot and cold snacks and drinks, through small bars and cafes to high-quality restaurants offering the best in Hungarian cuisine. The private sector is most prominent in the main tourist areas—the Lake Balaton and Danube regions in particular—where it is mainly seasonal, but very good private restaurants are becoming a permanent part of the cityscape of Budapest. In addition, the international fast-food franchises are also beginning to look seriously at Hungary for future expansion. Much to the regret of the admirer of the hamburger *à la Hongroise*, but to the delight of local people, MacDonalds now have an outlet on Vaci utca, in the heart of the city (Hall 1989b).

8.7 Tourism and regional development

Tourism, no less than industry, has formed an integral part of regional development in Hungary (Sándor and Kárbuczky 1989). Its potential for reducing geographical differentials in living standards was specifically identified in a major government statement on regional policy in 1971 (Baráth 1981). This urged more investment in two kinds of area: places likely to be visited by international tourists, not only the recognised tourist venues but also border-crossing points and places along the main tourist routes; and, second, those parts of the country suitable for domestic tourism and general recreational use. But equally, since tourism also creates new tensions in the form of pressure on local services and the environment, it was felt that new investment should go hand in hand with the systematic planning of tourist and recreational areas. Indeed, this had been recognised before the 1971 statement was made, and regional plans for a number of tourist and recreational areas were already in existence by then; for instance, systematic development plans had been formulated for the Balaton region as early as 1958 and for the Danube Bend by 1961.

However, the rational planning of tourism did not go smoothly, and the rigidities of the central planning system meant that essential infrastructural development did not take place. Moreover, the forecasts of tourist numbers, particularly for the Balaton region, were soon overtaken by actual demand. The situation was further aggravated in the late 1960s when a large amount of land surplus to the needs of agriculture was suddenly released on to the market creating an un-anticipated boom in the building of second homes around the lake. The outcome was intolerable pressure on overstretched facilities as well as considerable economic loss.

The first attempt at any comprehensive long-term planning for tourism was undertaken by the Ministry of Home Trade in 1972. This restated the primacy of Budapest, Lake Balaton and the Danube Bend as the country's main tourist areas, but stressed the need to alleviate pressure at Lake Balaton by developing alternative recreational and tourist areas. Later, in 1978, as part of the modifications to the National Settlement Development Plan, 23 recreational areas were outlined, together with the designation of two National Parks (Hortobágy and Kiskunság) and three other areas to be environmentally protected (the Badacsony, the Tihany Peninsula and Mártely) (Figure 8.1).

These measures constituted a significant advance in that they were the first to embody the principle that recreational areas should be given some priority in national development. They were also important to the extent that the 23 areas outlined have formed the basis of the later, more refined work, undertaken by the Scientific and Planning Institute for Urban Construction (VÁTI) and the Research Institute of the Home Trade Ministry (BKI). For instance, in 1979 the BKI suggested that the long-term plan for the regional development of tourism should be based on 24 areas with the objective, among other things, of spreading demand geographically. To this end, it was argued that the tourist potential of second-rank areas should be tapped, taking advantage of the fact that car ownership reduces relative distance and makes distant places more readily accessible. In identifying particular settlements for new tourist developments, it was suggested that account be taken of recreational, sporting and cultural endowments, potential for medicinal spa development, special geographical factors (such as nearness to major border-crossing points), availability of accommodation and the politico-economic significance of places within their region, for example, the county seats of local government should already possess the basic infrastructure to support tourism.

Meanwhile, VÁTI was given the task of formulating a National Plan for Recreational Areas using information stored in the tourist—'T-STAR'—database of the Central Statistical Office. The work was completed in 1982 and 26 areas, covering a quarter of the territory of the country, were identified as suitable for development; around 10 of these were thought to contain some potential for international tourism. In addition, over 600 settlements were earmarked as possible tourist centres of which 567 were in the identified areas. The plan was accepted as a basis for government policy in 1986. Among other things, this sets out the preconditions for recreation and tourism taking into account changing leisure patterns and the physical and economic resource potential of different areas. The principal objectives are to overcome the problems of supply allocation that plague many tourist areas, and which create tensions between local populations and visitors, and also to decentralise tourist activities geographically. The plan defines land utilisation, lists development priorities, sets down capacities and charts the main directions of future development.

In most respects, the National Plan for Recreation Areas makes good sense. It is eminently sensible to reduce the pressure on the Balaton by making other areas of the country more attractive to international visitors—the plan assigns this role to the Danube Bend, the Mátra-Bükk, the Mecsek–Villány region, the Hortobágy, the Lower Danube and the western fringes of Transdanubia adjacent to the Austrian border. But that said, it is clear that the plan has already been overtaken by events. For instance, western Transdanubia can no longer effectively cope with the daily influx of shoppers from Austria which has stretched the local retail network to breaking point. More importantly, however, it may no longer be consistent with the political tone of the country. One may refer, for example, to the curbs placed on public expenditure in response to economic crisis. As a consequence, resources are no longer available from the central exchequer and the ability of local initiatives by themselves to implement the plan proposals must be in doubt. In addition to this and most importantly, the liberalisation of society is being paralleled by a fundamental questioning of the value of the whole planning process. In this climate of opinion, the most likely outcome would seem to be a quiet shelving of the National Plan for Recreation Areas and the assertion of the primacy of market forces as the most efficient way forward.

8.8 Summary and conclusions

In this chapter, the central issues facing tourism in Hungary have been examined. The process of reform has shifted the balance during the 1980s, and visitors from Western countries, although still a minority, now account for around three-quarters of Hungary's income from international tourism. The downgrading of tourism from the countries that comprised Communist Eastern Europe until late 1989 has been deliberate as Hungary has positively sought to attract visitors from the West by relaxing bureaucratic and monetary constraints. Initially, the motive was the country's desperate need for hard currency, but it is now part of the process of political liberalisation and an assertion of Hungary's independence. In addition to the general trends, the chapter has also examined the geographical patterns and organisation of tourism, described the role played by medicinal spas and dealt with tourism as an instrument of regional development.

The speed with which Eastern Europe cast off Marxism–Leninism was breath-taking. The first draft of this chapter was written in Budapest in August 1989, when East Germans were beginning to take advantage of the dismantling of the border fence between Hungary and Austria to escape to the West. At the time, it seemed that the only logical response of the East German authorities to this haemorrhage of population was to restrict the right of its citizens to travel to Hungary and this was confidently awaited. In the event, although restrictions were placed for a short time on travel to Czechoslovakia, the anticipated clamp-down never materialised; instead, it was the Berlin Wall that was dismantled, thereby affording for the first time in almost 30 years freedom of movement between the two Germanies. Likewise, the hard-line Czechoslovak regime had collapsed by December 1989 and its western border with Austria and West Germany was also opened.

Events are still moving very rapidly and, as yet, it is too early to gauge what impact political liberalisation throughout the region is likely to have on Hungarian tourism. One reaction might be to assume that the new opportunities east Germans and Czechoslovaks now have of travelling to the West will lead to some decline in the number of visitors to Hungary from the two areas. Indeed, this is bound to happen if only because east Germans no longer have to meet their west German relatives in some other East European country—Hungary was a popular destination for both east and west Germans for this reason.

But against that, economic imperatives may dictate the continuation of the status quo for some time yet. Socialism has greatly impoverished two generations of East Europeans and until the economic position improves, they will not have the disposable income needed to enjoy the 'expensive' tourist spots of the West. Nor is it likely that the various national treasuries will be willing to disburse scarce convertible currency to support such visits; one presumes that economic reconstruction will have a much greater claim on these resources. The experience of the Hungarians in recent years is probably informative in this respect. Since the late-1970s, Hungarians have been relatively free to travel to the West and this has become an absolute right since new passport laws were implemented on 1 January 1989. However, a hard-currency allowance now reduced to US$50 per person severely constrains this right to travel as does an average monthly wage of around US$120. As a result, the Adriatic Coast and Costa Brava do not constitute the seaside playgrounds for

Hungarians, and this is unlikely to change in the medium term.

The key to any fundamental change in the patterns of Hungarian tourism, and the patterns in the region at large, therefore lies in the economy. This will involve the future shape of COMECON and the degree of association there may be with the European Community. At a more basic level, however, with tourism such a large earner of hard currency for Hungary, one cannot envisage the implementation of policies that might curtail the influx of visitors from the West. On the contrary, every effort is likely to be made to stimulate this further. Furthermore, the progressive liberalisation of the economy, which has meant joint ventures with the West and, before long, will no doubt allow enterprises that are wholly foreign-owned, should serve to lift standards throughout, including the tourist industry. This, in turn, may encourage a shift towards the higher added-value end of the market than has hitherto been possible and a corresponding reduction in cheap room letting and camping.

How such developments might affect tourism between Hungary and her East European neighbours is hard to assess at the moment. In all probability the situation will change little in the next few years owing to inertia. Equally, there could well be some relative revival if the old system of unrealistic fixed-exchange parities is replaced by a more flexible system, as seems likely to happen. Limited convertibility along the lines of the Hungarian model would make earnings in other East European currencies more worth-while economically, and would also resolve the problem of an over-valued Hungarian forint against these currencies. Moreover, Hungary is no longer ideologically out of step with her neighbours, thereby removing another factor which tended to depress tourist interchange during most of the 1980s.

Last, the greatest unknown is the precise long-term shape of the political systems which have replaced Marxism–Leninism and the impact that these will have on the region. There is an assumption in the West that democratic systems of a pluralistic nature will become the norm. It is worth remembering, however, that with the fleeting exception of Czechoslovakia during the inter-war period, the region has no practical experience of Western-type democracy, and that includes Hungary. The inter-war period was one of considerable antagonisms stemming from quarrels over national minorities and the appropriate alignment of frontiers. As the current difficulties in Yugoslavia and the Soviet Union vividly show, these antagonisms still exist and could easily get out of hand. In the case of Hungary, its quarrel with Romania over the Hungarian minority in Transylvania is potentially one of the most bitter. Moreover, relations with Czechoslovakia and Yugoslavia could also easily become strained for the same reason. It goes without saying that the re-emergence of old rivalries would do nothing for the health of tourism in Eastern Europe.

9 Poland

Andrew H. Dawson

9.1 Introduction

This chapter examines the spatial arrangement, regional characteristics, environmental consequences and local–global linkages of tourism in Poland. Initially, the development of the industry and its role in the economy will be outlined.

9.2 The development and role of tourism

The volume and sources of tourism in Poland have changed markedly over time. Before World War II there were only about 2 million tourists in Poland each year, few of whom were from other countries (Berezówski 1978, p. 472). Most town dwellers took their holidays at home, while the peasants—who formed the majority of the population—did not take formal holidays at all. In 1935 about 160,000 tourists were recorded as staying in 13 different parts of the country but chiefly in the Tatry and Western Beskid Mountains of the south, Kraków and the Baltic coast at Gdynia-Sopot; and brief holidays were organised for about 70,000 children. The railways sold 2,045,000 excursion tickets in 1936, of which 1,331,000 were for school or other excursions, mostly lasting only a day, and 573,000 for short holiday trips. Only 141,000 were for longer periods (*Mały Rocznik Statystyczny 1939*, pp. 191, 304).

Since the mid-1950s economic and social change has encouraged tourism. Paid holidays in industry and the service trades, the provision of factory-owned guest houses offering subsidised holidays to their employees, low fares on public transport and the widespread provision of summer holiday camps for children all increased the opportunities for Poles to take their annual holidays in other parts of the country. Moreover, substantial shifts among the population from country to town and from farm work to manufacturing and mining increased the proportion of Poles for whom regular holidays from work were provided. Foreign excursions for groups were also organised to an increasing extent, especially among the countries of Eastern Europe, and some attempts were made to attract tourists from hard-currency countries, especially in the 1960s and 1970s. Official statistics record that in 1978 13 million people were registered as staying in tourist accommodation and hotels in Poland each year and a further 4 million in factory-owned guest houses and

Table 9.1 Polish foreign tourism, 1960–87 (000s)

	1960	1978	1982	1987
Tourists entering Poland from:	184	10,695	1,404	4,776
Czechoslovakia	52	2,171	203	993
East Germany	38	5,752	262	925
Hungary	10	693	40	470
USSR	23	766	465	1,166
Other socialist countries	7	330	46	280
West Germany	11	304	122	380
Other countries	43	679	266	562
Poles travelling abroad to:	216	11,141	995	5,229
Bulgaria	11		178	290
Czechoslovakia	72		78	1,003
East Germany	31		99	1,259
Hungary	13	10,602	225	837
USSR	41		40	456
Other socialist countries	7		58	257
West Germany	7	539	118	475
Other countries	34		199	655

Sources: Rocznik Statystyczny 1967, p. 516, *1980*, p. 452; *Mały Rocznik Statystyczny 1988*, p. 325

that 10,700,000 foreign tourists visited the country, 9,700,000 from other socialist countries and 5,600,000 from the three neighbouring countries of Czechoslovakia, East Germany and the Soviet Union. Similarly, most outside holiday travel by Poles was to Czechoslovakia and East Germany, but Hungary was also important. Outside the socialist bloc, West Germany was both the chief source and destination of tourists (*Rocznik Statystyczny 1987*, p. 506). Table 9.1 indicates that these patterns have been fairly constant during the period since 1960, despite the massive growth of tourism up to a peak in 1978, a fall to 1982 and a modest recovery since then.

9.2.1 Data sources and problems

However, data such as these are not what they seem. Figures for foreign tourists are much inflated by those crossing the country holding transit visas, which allow only a day or two of residence, and the number of foreign tourists who spend longer than this is probably less than half the total. On the other hand, data about domestic tourism almost certainly underestimate the scale of the industry considerably, especially in recent years, for they do not include the large number of unrecorded stays with relatives or in unregistered private bed-and-breakfast accommodation, visits at weekends and holidays to second homes, or local tourism not involving overnight stays. Occasionally, the authorities have published estimates of the total quantity of tourism, such as that 17,500,000 people probably took residential holidays in 1978 while 45,000,000 went on excursions—a figure in line with the fact that 33,577,000 excursion tickets were sold on public bus and coach services in 1980 (*Rocznik Statystyczny 1980*, p. 450, *1987*, p. 348)—and annual estimates are given of expenditure on tourism by households, but even these may be too low. Totals of publicly owned or officially registered accommodation and of its use are given annually for the country as a whole and for each of the 49 voivodships within it, and information is also available about employment and investment in tourist accommodation by the public sector, but, to the extent that these figures omit private, unregistered activity, they are also underestimates.

9.2.2 Tourism administration

Despite the growth in tourism, which has reflected the pattern in developed market economies, the industry in Poland has been organised in a very different manner, and one which has important implications for its spatial arrangement. Much tourism has been centrally planned or controlled. A single state travel agency—Orbis—has hitherto dominated the market, and government, either directly or through schools and factories, has organised most of the group excursions and holidays. Many of these have taken place in scenic or historic areas which might be attractive in any society, but others have visited sights, such as cemeteries or factories, which would be regarded as strange or even repulsive to most Western tourists. Most tourist accommodation is owned by the state, in one form or another. More than half of all bed spaces are in guest houses belonging to factories and other enterprises, trade unions and professional bodies, and a further fifth is accounted for by hotels, guest houses and children's homes. One would expect this pattern to change substantially in the near future. Most of the rest are on camp sites or in private rooms registered with the state for tourist letting. Several hotels have been built since 1970 by foreign companies in conjunction with the tourist authorities but as yet there have not developed competing chains of hotels, leisure centres or other tourist facilities of the sort familiar in market economies, which allow tourists to vote with their feet and to indicate where they would prefer to take their holidays. This situation has also applied to foreign tourism. Shortages of hard currency and also of some of those of the Eastern European countries has meant that for much of the post-war period the scale and direction of foreign tourism has been determined not by the people but by governments. Hitherto, Polish tourists have visited, or at least crossed into East Germany, Hungary and Czechoslovakia briefly, in relatively large numbers, but far fewer have been able to go to the Black Sea resorts or Yugoslavia (Table 9.1).

Polish governments since the 1950s have promoted and developed the tourist industry, both as a necessary source of recreation and relaxation for working people and as a hard-currency earner, but, along with other service industries, it has been considered to be less important than manufacturing and

Table 9.2 Tourism in Poland, 1960–87 (000s)

	1960	1978	1982	1987
Bed spaces (total) in:	147	946	811	857
hotels	25	59	47	53
guest houses	11	31	40	38
children's holiday homes	14	39	41	41
registered private rooms	n/a	118	69	58
factory and trade-union-owned guest houses	76	554	471	502
other	21	145	143	165
Bed-nights (total) in:	9,354	49,659	32,293	37,551
hotels	6,641	14,099	9,312	12,388
guest houses	1,477	5,798	6,145	6,611
children's holiday homes	379	1,499	1,037	1,754
registered private rooms	n/a	20,835	9,547	8,805
other	857	7,428	6,252	7,993

Sources: Rocznik Statystyczny 1967, pp. 426, 514, *1980*, p. 448, *1983*, p. 459, *Mały Rocznik Statystyczny 1988*, pp. 324–5

mining and has not played a major role in the economy. Poles only spent about 1 per cent of their outgoings on holidays and excursions in the mid-1980s (*Rocznik Statystyczny 1987*, pp. 142–3), and, even when transport subsidies and those to factory guest houses are added, the proportion of income devoted to tourism was small. Similarly, only about one per cent of all investment was allocated to the industry (*Rocznik Statystyczny 1987*, pp. 142–3, 188). Nevertheless, the style and number of new, large, private houses offering bed and breakfast in the chief tourist regions of the country, and of modest second homes around all the major cities, would seem to indicate that earnings from the industry, including those that are not declared, may be very considerable in such places. It should also be noted that the contribution of the industry to the economy has been very volatile. Rapid growth in the 1960s and 1970s, especially of foreign tourism, was followed by a sharp decline, again chiefly in foreign tourism (Tables 9.1 and 9.2) at the time of the Solidarity crisis and martial law—a decline which almost certainly contributed to the economic problems of Poland in the 1980s and especially the shortage of hard currency. During the 1960s and early 1970s the country earned a modest surplus from foreign tourism involving hard-currency countries, though it suffered a loss in relation to the other members of the socialist bloc (*Rocznik Statystyczny 1971*, p. 529), and in the 1980s the Polish balance of payments has been in deficit, both in total and in respect of services. However, the use of various currencies—złoty, convertible złoty, convertible rouble and dollar—make any assessment of the exact value of tourism to the Polish economy a matter of guesswork.

9.3 Tourism in the 1980s

9.3.1 The spatial arrangement of tourism in the 1980s

Tourism in any country is the product of the availability of amenities and facilities and of the demand for these. The term 'amenities' is wide. Scenery, climate, historic buildings, famous places, cultural and sporting facilities and accommodation should all be included, but their recognition and use is usually determined by the tourists themselves. However, in the hitherto centrally planned economies of Eastern Europe the opinion of government as to what the foci of tourism should be was of considerable significance not only to the quantity, but also the location, of investment in facilities that cater for tourists.

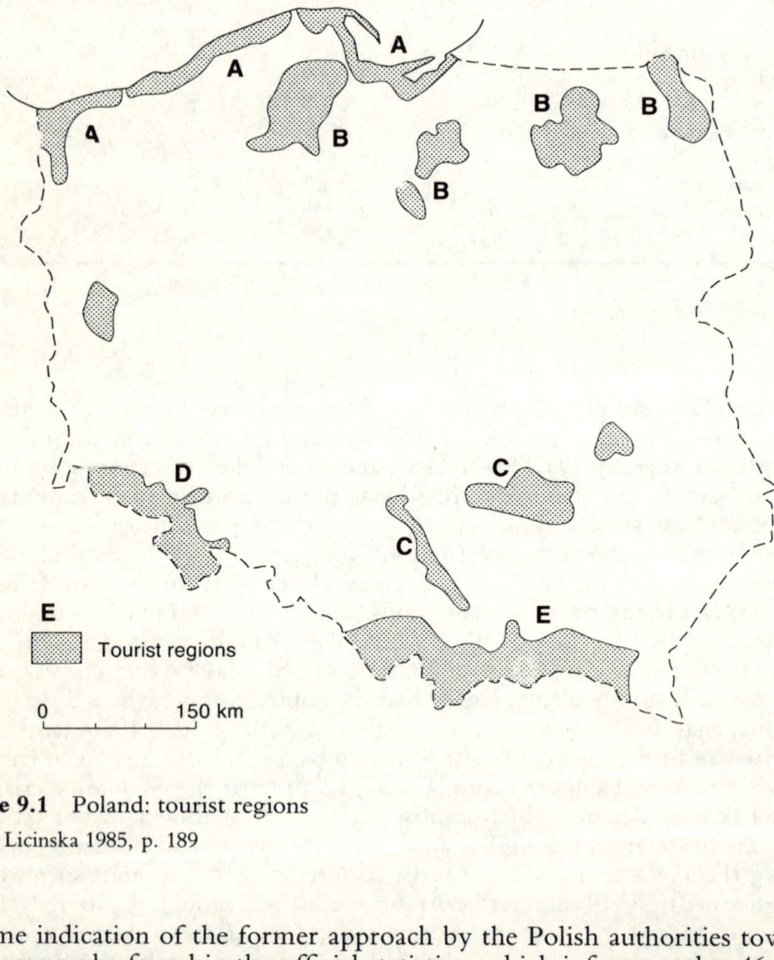

Figure 9.1 Poland: tourist regions
Source: Licinska 1985, p. 189

Some indication of the former approach by the Polish authorities towards tourism may be found in the official statistics, which inform us that 46.5 per cent of the country is 'of tourist value', by which is meant that it contains lakes and coasts, forests and mountains, but that only 3.4 per cent of Poland is of the highest quality, 5.5 per cent of the second quality and the remainder is divided equally between some third and fourth categories (*Rocznik Statystyczny 1987*,

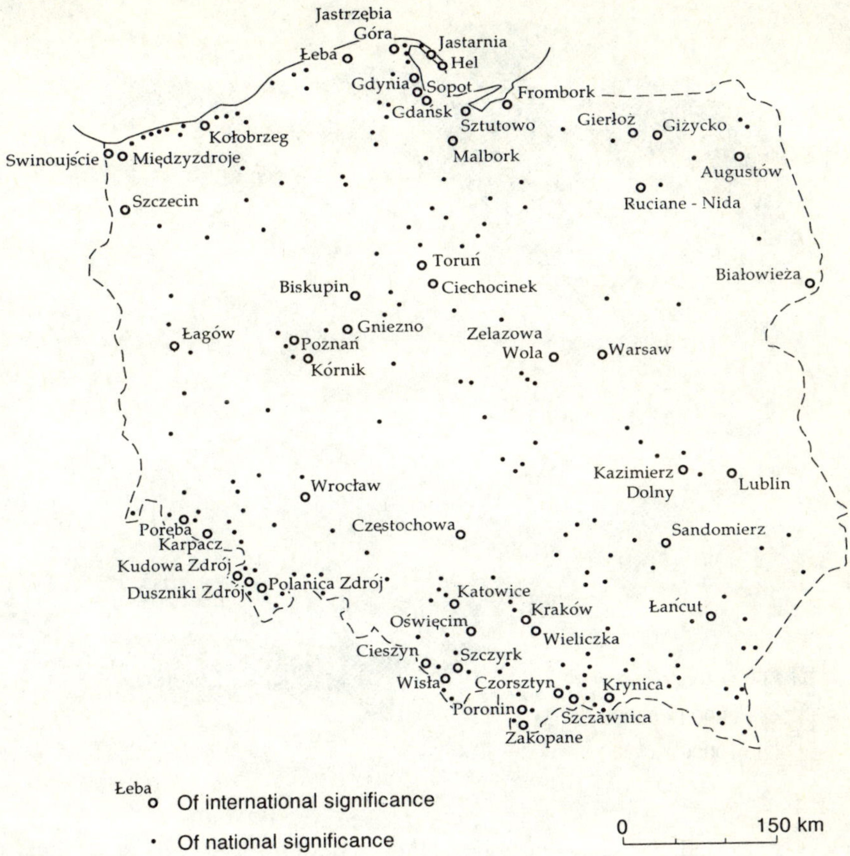

Figure 9.2 Poland: significant tourist sites
Source: Licinska 1985, p. 189

p. 506). This view was echoed in one of the hitherto approved school textbooks on the geography of Poland, which lists 21 tourist regions, covering about a twelfth of the country—an area similar to that of the two highest categories of tourist value—and shows where these areas lie (Licinska 1985, p. 189). Figure 9.1 indicates that they fall into several groups—the Baltic coast (A), an area of sandy beaches and coastal lagoons, the lowland lake districts of northern Poland (B), the upland areas of central Poland (C), and the Sudeten (D) and Carpathian mountains (E) of the south. The textbook also identifies 'significant tourist localities', as distinct from regions, and distinguishes between those of international significance and those of only national importance (Figure 9.2). These designations are a fascinating insight into what those who organised Polish society in the recent past considered that Polish school children should learn to be of value. Historic cities such as Kraków, shrines: to the Christian faith—the Black Madonna at Częstochowa—to national figures—Chopin's house at Żelazowa Wola and shrines to the victims

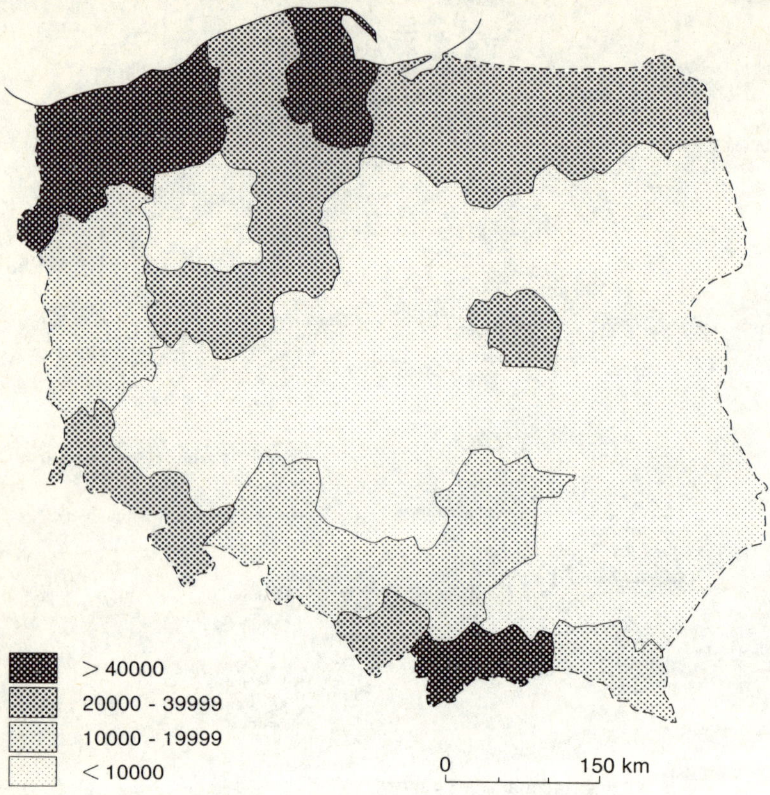

Figure 9.3 Poland: bed spaces for tourists by voivodship, 1985
Source: Rocznik Statystyczny Województw 1986, pp. 327–32

of World War II—the concentration camp at Oswięcim (Auschwitz) are accompanied by the spas of the Sudeten Mountains and skiing resorts of the Carpathians, castles (Malbork) and forest reserves (Białowieza) as well as such unlovely industrial towns as Katowice and Łódź!

Another indicator of the areas which are considered to be attractive to or appropriate for tourism is the provision of accommodation. Figure 9.3 shows that the voivodships with the largest numbers of bed spaces were those along the coast (Gdánsk and Szczecin voivodships) and in the Carpathian Mountains (Nowy Sącz), with other concentrations in the northern lakes (Olsztyn, Suwałki), the Sudeten Mountains (Jelenia Góra, Wałbrzych) and Warsaw. However, there were very few spaces in some of the places indicated by Licinska as being of 'international significance', especially in the industrial areas of central Poland. It may also be noted that the composition of the accommodation varied widely between one part of the country and another, with the guest houses of industrial enterprises largely on the coast and in the Carpathians, chalets chiefly in the lake district, camp sites along the Baltic and private rooms in the Carpathians, Kraków, Poznań and Warsaw. Only children's holiday accommodation and hotels were generally and widely distributed across the country.

The demand for this holiday accommodation shows an even more concentrated spatial arrangement. Four areas accounted for about 70 per cent of all the tourist bed-nights officially recorded in 1983, of which the Baltic coast, with almost a third, was the most important. The Carpathian Mountains accounted for about a fifth and the Sudeten Mountains and Mazurian Lakes for about a twelfth of the total each (*Rocznik Statystyczny 1987*, pp. 327–31). Thus, there are a small number of major tourist areas in Poland, all of which contain significant amenities for tourists and attract large numbers of visitors, but all of which lie on or close to the borders of the country, and distant from such major cities as Warsaw, Łódź and Poznań. Official and popular assessment of the attractiveness of four of these areas—the coast, the Carpathian and Sudeten Mountains and the Mazurian Lakes—would appear to coincide, but elsewhere some discrepancies exist between officially recognised places of tourist significance and the spatial distribution of accommodation and its use. Some of these may arise from the nature of the places. For example, almost all visitors to Chopin's birthplace spend less than a day there, for the house and garden are small and the surrounding countryside dull. Investment in tourist accommodation there might prove mistaken. However, official rhetoric, in the designation of industrial cities as centres of tourism, for example, does not appear to have committed the Polish government to providing extensive facilities in places where the demand for accommodation appears to be limited.

9.3.2 *The regional character of tourism in the 1980s*

Each of the four major spatial concentrations possesses a distinctive physical environment which has shaped the development of tourism within it to a considerable extent.

9.3.2.1 The Baltic Coast

Many kilometres of sandy beaches, backed by dunes, lagoons and low, wooded hills here provide a pleasant environment for seaside, summer holidays. Particularly popular are the relatively sheltered areas of Gdańsk Bay—especially its western side, where Poland's chief seaside resort of Sopot lies—and Szczecin Bay. Between the two, along the exposed and northerly facing coasts, are a string of minor resorts. Further attractions of the area are the historic towns, especially Gdańsk, lying on or close to the coast, Malbork Castle and the low hills and lakes of Pomorze. But it is the coastal nature of the area that is its principal attraction. That coast, and particularly the two bays, are the chief locations for guest house and camping holidays in Poland, providing about 45 per cent of all guest house bed-nights and almost a third of all forms of bed-nights in the country. Most visitors spend at least a week in the area, usually based upon one resort, but the tourist trade is highly seasonal, associated with the June–September period of school and factory holidays, and only a tiny proportion of the accommodation is open throughout the year (*Rocznik Statystyczny Województw 1984*, pp. 327–32).

9.3.2.2 The Western Carpathian Mountains

This region offers the most spectacular scenery and best conditions for winter sports in Poland. The principal scenic area is the Tatry Mountains, which rise to 2,499 metres and are Alpine in topography, offering opportunities for climbing and walking in summer and skiing in winter. These activities and the associated infrastructure of accommodation and cable cars are centred upon Zakopane, which is more obviously a tourist town than perhaps any other in Poland, with a year-round season. Other areas of the Western Carpathians, though not so spectacular, also offer many of the same opportunities to tourists. The Beskid Mountains, to the north of the Tatry, rise to 1,725 metres and are heavily wooded. Two areas within them have been protected as National Parks, and there are many trails for walkers, further skiing facilities and the opportunity to make journeys by raft through the gorge of the Dunajec River on the Czech–Polish frontier. As with Zakopane, the chief resorts, such as Krynica and Szczawnica, began as spas and health centres in the late nineteenth century. The character of the area as a clean and healthy environment has been increasingly valued by Poles as atmospheric and other pollution has grown worse in the urban and industrial areas of the country since World War II. Nowy Sącz voivodship, which includes both the Tatry and high Beskid Mountains, has more beds in sanatoria, more places in year-round guest houses belonging to factories and more registered private rooms for rent than in any of Poland's other 48 voivodships. There has also been much rebuilding and new construction of large private houses in traditional mountain-chalet styles in both the towns and villages of the area since the 1960s, much of which is designed to offer bed-and-breakfast accommodation, to be rented or to be used as second homes by people from all over Poland. The area provides almost a fifth of the bed-nights of the Polish tourist industry and probably depends to a greater degree than any other part of the country upon tourism for its livelihood.

9.3.2.3 The Sudeten Mountains

This area offers a very similar environment to that of the Beskids to tourists. The heavily wooded mountains rising to 1,602 metres and cut by deep valleys are not only scenic but afford opportunities for skiing and walking, while mineral springs have provided the basis for the development of several graciously designed spas dating from the nineteenth century, when the area was part of Germany. Of these, Cieplice Sląskie Zdrój and Kudowa Zdrój are the largest, but several others exist. Many towns also contain historic buildings from late medieval times. The two major concentrations of tourist activity are in the Karkonosze Mountains and around Kłodzko. Much of the tourist accommodation is in the form of guest houses which are open throughout the year, and about a twelfth of all bed-nights in the Polish tourist industry are spent in this region.

9.3.2.4 The Mazurian Lake District

Much of northern Poland is covered by low, morainic hills, often wooded and enclosing many lakes, but nowhere is this description more apt than in the north-east of the country, where two of the largest Polish lakes, each covering more than a hundred square kilometres, are found. These offer substantial opportunities for sailing, swimming and cruising. As on the Baltic coast, much of the accommodation is in the form of camp sites and demands upon it are almost all within the period of June to September. Nevertheless, about 8 per cent of all tourist bed-nights are spent in the region.

All these four regions cover areas that contain within them several resorts, each offering the distinctive range of tourist amenities of the region. However, there are other places which also attract many visitors, not because of their physical environment, but for reasons of history. Two of the most important of these are the cities of Kraków and Warsaw.

9.3.2.5 Kraków

The former capital of Poland is one of the most important architectural monuments in Europe. The medieval castle and cathedral on the Wawel rock overlook the river Vistula and the planned town, laid out after its sacking by the Tartars in 1241. Within the line of the medieval walls—removed in the 1820s and replaced by a boulevard park—lie the great Market Square, with its fourteenth-century Cloth Hall, the buildings of the University, founded in 1364, many medieval and Renaissance churches and eighteenth-century houses. The architectural riches of the Old Town of Kraków are such that it has been recognised by UNESCO as one of the finest monuments to civilisation in the world and has been the subject of an official programme of restoration for many years. Unfortunately, that programme has moved more slowly than has the damage to the stone and metalwork and to the frescoes on the buildings from the very high levels of atmospheric pollution suffered in the city. However, even as late as the 1970s official guidebooks were inviting visitors to inspect, among other sights, the huge Lenin Steel Works and other industrial enterprises which have released huge quantities of dust, sulphur dioxide and other pollutants into the city's atmosphere. Nevertheless, tourists visit the city on day-trips or as part of tours through Poland which also include the Wieliczka salt mine, the Carpathians and the former concentration camp at Oswięcim (Auschwitz). Many come from abroad, and much of the accommodation is in the form of hotels and private rooms. The city of Kraków accounts for about 3 per cent of the tourist bed-nights in the country.

9.3.2.6 Warsaw

In his account of the economic geography of tourism in Poland Berezówski (1978, p. 470) has described the city as 'the great metropolitan tourist region with many unique elements', but this statement may give an inaccurate impression. It is true that the city benefits from being by far the most important entry point to Poland for foreign visitors, as well as being the hub of domestic air and rail services. But apart from a few sights, it can hold little attraction for either foreign or domestic tourists. Popular sights are the medieval Old Town, rebuilt after being destroyed during World War II, some seventeenth- and eighteenth-century churches and palaces and a few places of historic interest close to the city. Official literature also emphasises the city's status as the capital, and approved guidebooks have urged tourists not only to visit the sights mentioned above but also the Unknown Soldier's Grave, the headquarters of the Polish United Workers' Party—a grim office block in the socialist–realist style—and the Soviet military cemetery (Bajcar 1970, pp. 34–6). Hitherto, many officially organised school and factory excursions to Warsaw have included them in their itineraries. The city accounts for about 5 per cent of the tourist industry's bed-nights, but official statistics show that few visitors stay for more than a couple of days, and many foreign tourists combine their visit to the city with a tour of other parts of the country.

9.3.3 The environmental impact of tourism

The picture of tourism in Poland which has been sketched so far indicates that most activity is concentrated in a few, rather small areas of the country. Particular types of scenery attract visitors, and it is in these areas that tourist pressure upon the environment is greatest. These pressures are controlled in the National Parks, channelled by the designation of tourist paths and policed by the many guides belonging to the Polish Tourist Association (PTTK) who lead thousands of excursions every year. However, these excursions only serve about 2 million tourists (*Rocznik Statystyczny 1987*, p. 507), and the majority of those visiting the beaches, forests, lakes and mountains have little or no supervision. In 1966, Rogalewski (p. 20) estimated the total visitor capacity of the chief tourist areas at 5,840,000, of which 2,300,000 were in the mountains, 2,220,000 on the lakes, and only 420,000 on the coast. Greater numbers were considered to be dangerous for the natural environment, but by the 1970s the total number of tourists in the country had reached 17 million, about 5 million of whom were staying on the coast and a similar number in the mountains.

Since that time two major sources of stress have become apparent in the environment of the chief tourist regions. The first of these is from pollutants in the atmosphere and in water which are carried into the regions from elsewhere. Severe atmospheric pollution by industry in Czechoslovakia, southern parts of east Germany and Lower and Upper Silesia in Poland—which surround and lie largely up-wind of the Sudeten and Carpathian Mountains—has been blown into these regions, damaging the forests and historic monuments. Similarly, the Baltic Sea is adversely affected by the industrial wastes that flow into or are dumped in it by the littoral countries, including Poland, which, because of the sea's enclosed nature, disperse only slowly. Moreover, the chief tourist areas of the coast—in Gdańsk and Szczecin Bays—are particularly vulnerable to the wastes flowing down the Vistula and Oder rivers respectively. The second source of stress is direct. Campers, walkers and other visitors all affect the tourist regions they use, and sewage, in particular, poses problems around the heavily used coastal and lake district camp sites, where the sandy sub-soil facilitates the percolation of wastes to the water table.

9.4 The impact of economic and social change

The recent development of tourism is a world-wide phenomenon. Increasing standards of living, more leisure time and falling real costs of transport have facilitated travel and residential holidays. Types of activity, such as skiing and sailing, previously experienced only by the few, have been opened up to the many. Resorts which were formerly inaccessible to all but the wealthy have become popular playgrounds, while new ones have been created to cater for mass tourism. The Polish tourist industry has benefited from these trends, growing rapidly after the mid-1950s until the Solidarity crisis of the early 1980s. It declined sharply, with an 80 per cent fall in the number of foreign visitors, until an upward trend was resumed in the mid-1980s. However, the industry is not well placed to increase its very modest role in the Polish economy, and it seems unlikely that it will be able to develop any special niche which would allow it to increase its share of world tourism or to create new tourist regions within the country in the near future. The attraction of Poland to foreign tourists will remain small when compared with alternative venues. For instance, the Black Sea and Mediterranean will continue to offer better weather than the Baltic, while cities such as Leningrad and London will remain far more interesting than Warsaw. Little attention has been paid to the country by the major Western tourist companies. Underdeveloped facilities, poor standards of service, language and other difficulties will continue to discourage individual tourists. In the mid-1980s Poland was ranked eighteenth out of 21 European countries in terms of the number of foreign tourists it received (*Rocznik Statystyczny 1987*, p. 620), and much of that trade was from the relatively undemanding customers from other Eastern European countries, obliged by currency shortages to stay within the communist bloc. That situation is likely to remain while a radical reform of the industry is undertaken to make it more receptive to the wishes of tourists, especially those from hard-currency countries, and to render it better able to innovate in providing new and imaginative tourist attractions.

However, real economic and social reforms might have very mixed results for the Polish tourist industry. For instance, genuine freedom for privately owned companies to enter the market, or for Polish entrepreneurs to make agreements with foreign operators, or build and run hotels and leisure facilities, unburdened by currency or other restrictions, might lead to rapid improvements in both the quantity and quality of tourist facilities, but probably only in the most attractive and interesting locations, such as the Tatry Mountains and Kraków. Second, any economic regeneration which raised living standards would permit Poles to spend more on holidays, but, if that were to occur together with the removal of currency and passport restrictions, it is not obvious that they would continue to take group holidays in factory guest houses on the Baltic in preference to Western-style packages to Greece, Turkey or Yugoslavia. Moreover, similar reforms in those countries in Eastern Europe which are the chief sources of foreign tourists to Poland might lead to a rapid decline in that sector of the industry as the people of those countries made similar holiday choices. In other words, while a few tourist regions in Poland might undergo yet more development, it is unlikely that this would occur even in all the existing major tourist regions of the country in the absence of any diversification or enhancement of their attractions. To contemplate, for instance, the possibility that Warsaw might become a major convention centre for Europe, or Sopot the equivalent of Atlantic City, is merely to illustrate the scale of the task that would be required to bring Polish tourism into line with that of the developed market economies. Economic growth would also lead to an increase in car ownership. With only about a hundred cars per thousand of the population and poor roads and services for motorists,

Poland lags far behind Western Europe, and the potential for the growth of car-borne tourism is considerable. Any such development would increase the pressure on those areas that lie close to the major cities but are already important resorts, such as the Carpathian and Sudeten Mountains, lying close to the industrial areas of Silesia. It might also encourage the development of tourist facilities in those parts of the country that have been relatively neglected, such as the Eastern Carpathians. All such changes, however, are posited on the assumption that the real wealth of Poles will rise, and it seems that this will be unlikely until well into the 1990s.

9.5 Conclusions

Tourism in Poland grew rapidly between the mid-1950s and 1978, and the pattern of that growth was strongly influenced by the view of Polish governments about the types of recreation that should be available to the people and the countries with which tourist links should be forged. Those views accorded the industry a very minor role in the economy, but official estimates have grossly under-reported the levels of activity and expenditure in its domestic sector, for much small-scale, individual holiday-making has been conducted privately. Nevertheless, the major tourist regions are clearly identifiable, and each has its own distinctive range of activity and seasonal pattern related to its natural environment, but also its own problems of environmental stress. International tourism has been dominated by flows to and from a selection of other Eastern European countries. The downturn in the Polish economy, the Solidarity crisis and martial law of the early 1980s, and the continuing economic weakness of the country during the rest of the decade, have all been reflected in a substantial fall in the number of visitors both within Poland and between Poland and other countries. The upheavals of 1989, with the establishment of a non-Communist government, the collapse of Communist governments in some of the countries with which Poland has had the strongest tourist connections and economic uncertainties throughout Eastern Europe and the Soviet Union, will not only restrict the ability of Poles to take holidays, but will probably reduce once again the number of foreigners visiting Poland. If the new Polish government is able to achieve radical reforms, major changes in the spatial distribution and character of the industry may follow. But many of these will only occur if the reforms lead to a significant increase in the real incomes of the population. If this does occur, many more Poles may take their holidays outside the country, but Poland's attractions may not be sufficient to bring a greatly increased number of foreign visitors to the country. Economic reform and potential change in other East European countries may lead to a sharp decline in group visits from them to Poland. In other words, it is likely that Poland's tourist industry will experience further difficulties in the near future, and it is unlikely that it will ever return to the pattern established between 1955 and 1978.

10 Romania

David Turnock

10.1 Introduction

Romania has considerable potential for tourism with many physical and cultural resources lying close to major sources of demand in a country which is undergoing rapid modernisation. Substantial investments in tourist facilities of an international standard have been complemented by a very positive welcoming attitude on the part of the Romanian people towards both foreign and domestic tourists. But following the onset of a serious economic crisis at the beginning of the 1980s, the official attitude became more ambivalent, with falling standards and heightened state security creating considerable tourist dissatisfaction. Nevertheless, the Ministry of Tourism has enjoyed considerable political influence. The state tourist office has acquired substantial expertise since it was first set up in 1926 (Barbu 1973), and research on tourism has been expedited through contacts with institutes concerned with the social sciences and especially geography (Glavan 1978). Romania has developed a particularly strong interest in the geography of tourism (Turnock 1977) and following some early foundation studies there has been much attention paid to the recognition of tourist regions (Iordan *et al.* 1984; Popovici 1977).

10.2 Resources and development

The resources for tourism in Romania lie fundamentally in favourable climatic and topographical conditions (Ciulache 1979). Although the coastline is short in relation to the size of the country, it comprises a southern section of sandy Black Sea beaches ideal for recreation and a northern deltaic zone (the mouth of the Danube) comprising one of Europe's most distinctive ecosystems. Inland, the Carpathians provide an excellent base for mountain tourism in both summer and winter. The scenery is always attractive, especially in limestone areas (Cocean 1980), but the more heavily glaciated areas are outstanding, while the flora and fauna provide much of interest for the specialist. The lowlands, however, are less exciting, for although treeless steppe is restricted to the south-east, much of the land is at best gently rolling plain and plateau. The divisions are further emphasised when the cultural elements are considered. Although there are a number of historic cities in the lowlands, it is the Carpathian zone, long acknowledged as the cradle of the nation, which is most important for historic monuments and buildings. The force of tradition is frequently expressed in distinctive architecture, costumes and customs (Vladuţiu 1976). Various studies emphasise the value of Carpathian art and legend, particularly church building in wood. Traditional industries and occupations are a long-standing research interest.

The imbalance is likely to increase in future. Romania is well endowed with mineral waters, but while these are by no means restricted to the mountains, the majority of the springs do lie in this area where the first resorts were developed (Cianga 1981). In the lowlands there is a strong accent on intensive farming and some increase in pollution as the completion of the electricity grid draws more industry away from the upland fuel and raw material bases. By contrast, the broad rhythm of economic development in the Carpathians can be more easily reconciled with a strategy of conservation conducive to the development of tourism. Of course there are lowland rural districts which will benefit increasingly from tourism in the future. Facilities will be needed in the vicinity of large towns and cities, especially Bucharest. The same point can be made even more forcefully with regard to the resorts of the Black Sea coast whose visitors may take some interest in nature reserves (like those of the Danube Delta), archaeological monuments (such as the Roman column of Adamclisi) and important economic developments (the Danube–Black Sea Canal, for example, which is ideal for cruising). Away from the Black Sea coast, it is in the Carpathians where the importance of tourism is most evident (Glavan 1978).

10.2.1 *Historical development*

Development of available resources goes back to very early times; the Romans are known to have appreciated the waters of Băile Herculane, Călan and Geoagiu. In modern times it was again the waters that attracted international attention, with their curative value increasingly appreciated in the eighteenth and nineteenth centuries. Austrians patronised Băile Herculane from 1734 (as well as Bazna, Biborţeni, Olăneşti and Tuşnad) while scientific analysis of waters was made by Richard Haquet at Vatra Dornei in 1788 and by Andreas Wolf in the Neamţ area in 1796. In the nineteenth century, Russian soldiers appreciated the waters of Strunga at the start of their Turkish campaign in 1821, while Pucioasa was a popular resort when the Romanian Principalities were under the Russian General Kiselef's military government. Slănic Moldova became known as the 'pearl' of Moldavia after examination of the waters in 1832 (Andrei, 1972) and the lake of Balta Albă near Brăila, featured in French illustrated reviews of the middle years of the century. Meanwhile on the inner side of the mountains, which remained under Habsburg administration until the end of World War I, there were developments at Borsec (patronised by the famous writer Vasile Alecsandri in 1845) and Sovata (inaugurated in 1850). At Tuşnad, mineral springs were allegedly discovered by a hunting party in 1800, giving rise to the sinking of wells and the construction of villas in the 1830s and 1840s.

It was the railway age which transformed the watering places into substantial resorts, such as the cluster of settlements in the Rîmnicu Vîlcea area (Figure 10.1). At Călimăneşti, the cure was first organised under the guidance of Cozia monastery in 1830, and the discovery of further springs at Caciulata brought foreign recognition in 1859 and a stream of distinguished visitors, including Napoleon III. The waters at Govora in the same area were publicised in 1887, and heavy investments were made after 1910 by the Govora-Călimăneşti company at both locations, encompassing hotels, pavilions, villas and sanatoria. By this time Rîmnicu Vîlcea was on a main line railway between Bucharest and Sibiu. Investments were also made at Olăneşti at the turn of the century. However, the history of the resort goes back to the first mention of the waters in 1760, the advertisement of a cure after examination of the waters in 1830, and further promotion by the Bucharest School of Medicine in 1870 (Dogaru 1972). Meanwhile, the first developments were occurring on the Black Sea coast with the first baths at Eforie and Techirghiol in the 1880s. Villas were constructed at the end of the century after the rail link with Bucharest had been completed. The casino at Constanţa was built between 1904 and 1909. Hotels were appearing in the towns, developing out of the traditional caravanning establishments (*hanuri*). In Bucharest, for example, Hanul lui Manuc was built in 1808, becoming the Hotel Dacia in the late nineteenth century before restoration in traditional style in 1971. In the old Moldavian capital of Iaşi the Hotel Traian was built in 1880–2. Gardens (like Cişmigiu in 1850, occupying part of the Dîmboviţa floodplain in Bucharest) and suburban resorts like Lacul Sărat reached by the trams from Brăila in 1898 were also becoming more prominent. Fine scenery was inspiring town dwellers to seek the peace of the wilderness. Organisations were established to promote climbing and to provide simple accommodation. The Transylvanian Alpine Society was formed at Braşov in 1873, and the Transylvanian Carpathian Society emerged at Sibiu in the 1880s. The towering Bucegi Mountains, easily accessible by means of the Bucharest–Braşov railway, witnessed a transformation at Sinaia where patronage by the Romanian monarchy (Peleş Castle 1883) and bourgeoisie brought a measure of urban development, including some industrialisation based on timber resources and hydro-electric power (Ciobanu 1979).

These trends were extended into the inter-war period, especially of note is the International Hotel at Mamaia opened in 1939. But some investment went into locations subsequently lost through the territorial changes of 1940. For example the popular resort of Balcic in southern Dobrogea, annexed by Romania in 1913 passed to Bulgaria, and the therapeutic muds of Cetatea Albă on the coast of Bessarabia, controlled by Romania since 1918 then fell under Soviet control. Moreover, there was a loss of continuity through the war and subsequent revolution, which tended to equate leisure with idleness. The watering places continued to attract heavy patronage but more in connection with the state's health service than international tourism. Railway links were strengthened (for example at Buziaş) and some developmental work was done at Vatra Dornei from 1954. However, an expansion of effort by the Institut de Balneologie has taken place since 1960 with a substantial drilling programme, encompassing a wide range of locations (Stoicescu and Munteanu 1977).

10.2.2 Revival since 1965

The cloistered mentality of the 1950s was not favourable to tourism and the country had virtually nothing to offer when the package-holiday business

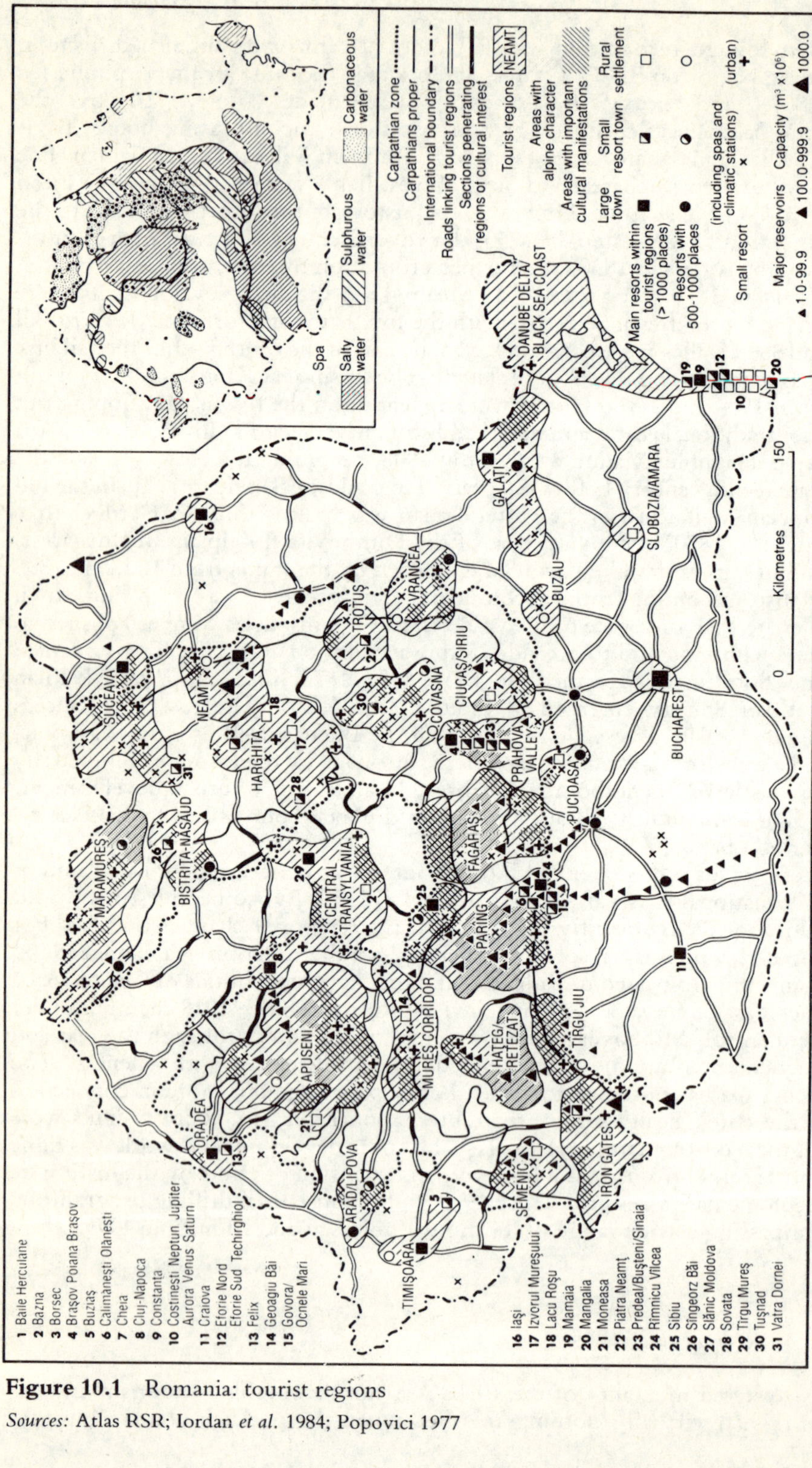

Figure 10.1 Romania: tourist regions

Sources: Atlas RSR; Iordan *et al.* 1984; Popovici 1977

began to gather momentum in the West in the 1960s. But investments made since 1965 have transformed the industry and attracted increasing numbers of domestic and foreign travellers. Using United Nations yearbooks for foreign-visitor statistics and the Romanian *Anuar statistic* for the internal component, it emerges that in 1970 there were 5.2 million Romanian tourists (measured by registrations at hotels, chalets and camp sites) and 2.3 million foreigners (indicated by frontier traffic). In 1985 the figures were 9.8 and 4.8 million respectively. There could of course be considerable double-counting of Romanian tourists where different accommodation was used during a single tour, but against this there is a considerable volume of internal tourism not covered by hotel or related registrations.

Visitors have a wide range of options. Figure 10.1 shows the main tourist zones, simplified from various Romanian sources. Apart from the coastal area, it is evident that there is a strong bias towards the Carpathian zone. Accommodation is available in the long-established watering places as well as the centres for winter sports and in the historic towns on the edge of the mountains. A number of studies have been undertaken on individual regions, for example the Apuseni Mountains (Vlad and Truţi 1984), and research on the tourism potential of various localities continues (Iacob and Ianoş 1987). Numerous artificial lakes (relating to hydro-electric schemes) have enhanced the scenic attractions of Carpathian valleys. Moreover, vehicle access has been improved by the construction of forest roads, reflecting the switch from rail to road transport by the wood-cutting enterprises.

While many developments have occurred in towns, there is also a dispersed rural pattern of chalets and hostels backing up a network of hotels and camp sites. The first *cabane* (chalets or hostels) were constructed at the turn of the century but there are now 55 in the Eastern Carpathians, 110 in the Southern Carpathians (Transylvanian Alps) and 25 in the Western Carpathians. Only six are situated higher than 2,000 metres (all in the Southern Carpathians) but there are 80 between 1,000 and 2,000 metres (54 in the south, 21 in the east and just five in the west). The variations in provision and altitudinal distribution reflect the nature of scenic attractions, with the glaciated country of the Făgăraş, Parîng and Retezat mountains (all part of the South Carpathian group) being particularly compelling (Fratu 1986). Out of a total of 154 glacial lakes there are 29 in the Făgăraş Mountains (at an average height of 2,131 metres), 28 in the Parîng (1,986 metres) and 57 in the Retezat (2,021 metres). Apart from 10 lakes in the Rodna Mountains (Eastern Carpathians) all are situated in the Southern Carpathians. Figure 10.1 also shows the principal road links between the tourist regions and the routes which offer greatest interest from an ethnographic/folkloric point of view. There is indeed considerable scope in most rural localities to examine aspects of culture and natural history thanks to the extensive networks of monuments, museums and nature reserves. Figure 10.2 has been compiled from official lists and guidebooks on the basis of four criteria: accommodation, including camp sites; monuments; museums; and nature reserves. Excluding the 51 rural communes which are recognised resorts, 590 communes (out of a total of 2,654) are represented under at least one heading. This figure then breaks down into 285 Carpathian communes (34.9 per cent of the total) and 372 lowland communes (20.2 per cent). The Carpathian communes are also better endowed as regards the number of attributes for each commune (1.7 times the national average compared with 0.7 for the lowlands).

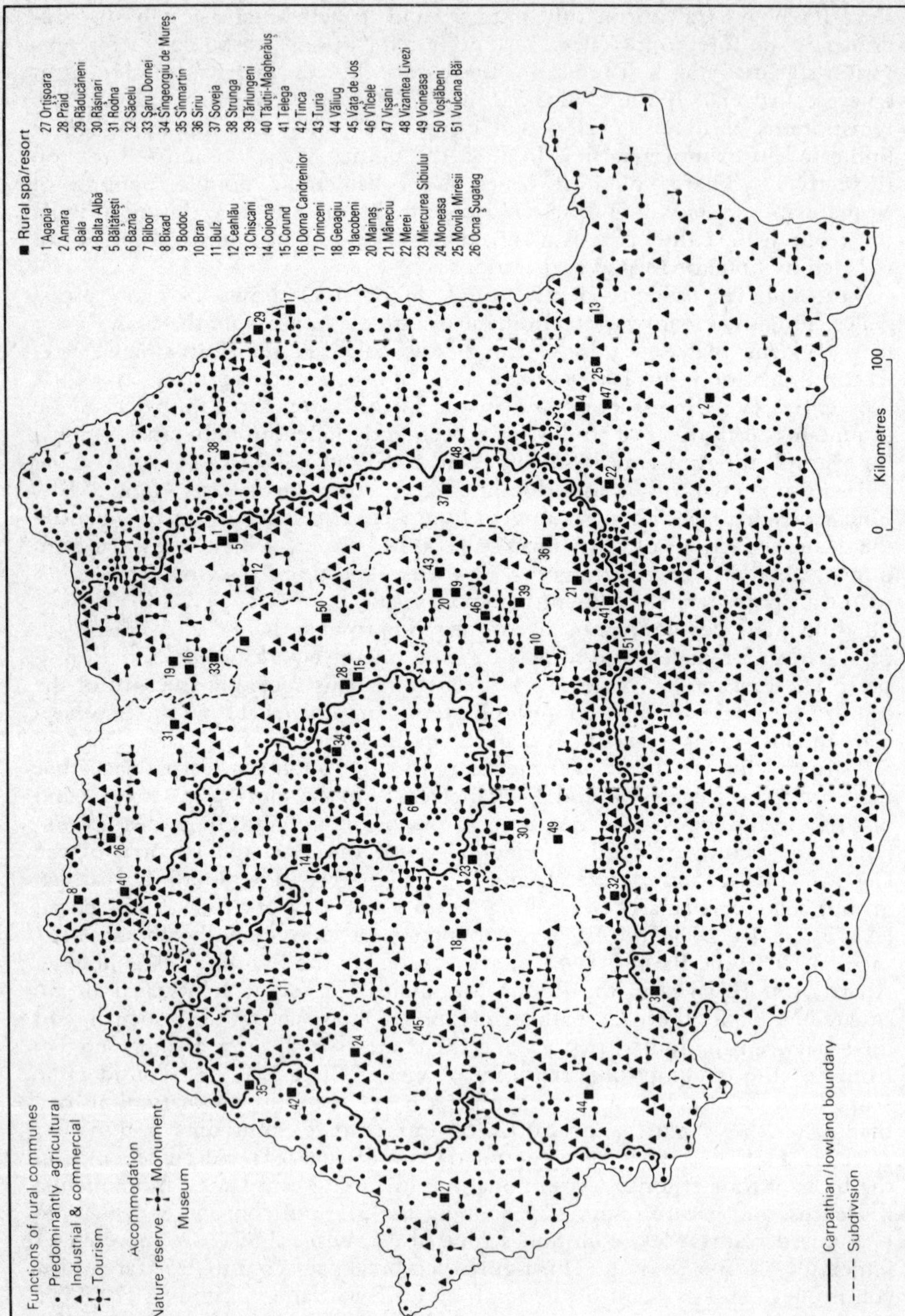

Figure 10.2 Romania: tourist facilities in rural areas

Source: Maciu *et al.* 1986

10.3 Tourism and economic development

In the post-war period there was a transformation both in Romania's economic structure and in the relative importance of the country's urban and rural settlement (Turnock 1986). The communist regime was inclined to see its achievements preconditioned by the revolution of 1948 but it is arguable that the modernisation of the country has been a continuous process over the century since independence in 1878 (Jowitt 1971). Tourism has been featured prominently because of the compelling potential which could feasibly be exploited to meet the growing national and international demand. Yet, despite the undoubted rationality of a programme of development for tourism there was an element of ambivalence and no strong ideological drive. The Communist Party leader (also the state president), who was in power from 1965 to 1989 made no more than the most perfunctory references to tourism in his numerous and lengthy addresses. A major review of his economic conceptions says much about improved living standards and a better environment in the towns and villages, but virtually nothing on tourism apart from a passing mention of the industry as a dynamic component of the national economic complex which can make use of the country's resources (ICCE 1983, p. 289). Even the country's leading ideologists went no further than to mention improving living standards in terms of working conditions, basic requirements for subsistence (housing, food and clothing) and leisure time, the latter 'being one of the particularly important factors for gauging the standard of living' (Trandafir 1972, p. 300). Leisure time was necessary to strengthen links between nature and society and to advance the spiritual as well as the material development of the nation (Trandafir, 1972, pp. 301–2). However it was left to spokesmen of the Ministry of Tourism to spell out these principles in terms of an expanding tourist industry, which was seen by them to be central to a 'multilaterally developed socialist society' (Marinescu 1973; Snak 1973). There is no simple explanation for this official reticence, but it is known that President Ceauşescu was obsessive over the need to maintain manufacturing industry's priority role within the national economy. This was also coupled with a preoccupation with social engineering to create the 'new socialist man', entailing a collective approach to such activities, in contrast to the individualism inherent in most cultural recreation, weekend excursions or occasional vacations. This approach was most dramatically manifested through rural resettlement programmes.

The organisation of tourism after World War II was entrusted to the 'People's Tourism' organisation in 1948 which became the Federation of Tourism and Alpinism two years later. This body was affiliated to the trade-union organisation and to the national committee for physical education and sport. The old national pre-war tourist office became a travel agency within the trade-union organisation. The agency regained its autonomy in 1955 and two years later this Officul Naţional de Turism (ONT) absorbed the state tourist association. In 1971 a new ministry for tourism and sport was created with a number of large subordinate organisations covering the tourist facilities in the major centres of Braşov, Bucharest and the Black Sea coast. This reorganisation followed the first phase of rapid expansion of the tourist industry, which was heavily biased towards certain areas, especially the Black Sea coast, where two-thirds of all 'organised' tourism was focused in 1972. It was also a time when foreign visitors began to increase rapidly: from 500,000 in 1965 to 2.3 million in 1972 in the case of those from Eastern Europe and the Soviet Union, and from 200,000 to 600,000 for those from other countries over the same period. All this marked the start of the 'Ceauşescu Era': while national income increased by 80 per cent between 1965 and 1972 and industrial production by 119 per cent, the growth rates for income generated by internal and international tourist services were 191 and 304 per cent respectively. ONT remains the all-important state organisation for tourism although the Communist youth organisation spawned its own youth travel service in 1968 and there are other specialist organisations concerned with car travel, hunting/fishing and sports in addition to the continuing trade-union travel service.

Table 10.1 Tourist accommodation and usage, Romania, 1970–85

	1970	1975	1980	1985
Number of units				
Hotels/motels	524	721	782	850
Chalets/hostels	358	390	387	427
Villas/pavilions	1316	1503	1561	1505
Total	2198	2614	2730	2783
Numbers of beds ('000s)				
Hotels/motels	84.4	126.4	142.1	155.9
Chalets/hostels	53.7	55.4	66.2	65.9
Villas/pavilions	51.4	59.3	59.1	59.9
Total	189.5	241.0	267.4	281.8
Number of Romanian visitors (millions)				
Hotels/motels	3.73	5.41	7.17	7.56
Chalets/hostels	0.69	1.15	1.37	1.20
Villas/pavilions	0.76	1.04	1.17	1.06
Total	5.19	8.59	9.72	9.82
Romanian visitors per bed				
Hotels/motels	44.1	42.8	50.5	48.5
Chalets/hostels	12.9	20.7	20.7	18.1
Villas/pavilions	14.9	17.5	19.9	17.7
Total	27.4	35.7	36.3	34.9

Source: Anuarul statistic (various)

10.3.1 Tourism data sources and problems

Few statistics are available to show the importance of the tourist industry. Romanian statistical yearbooks do not break down the tertiary sector sufficiently to isolate tourism, let alone consider different categories of employment within the industry. The only figures available for the whole post-war period (1950–85) deal with the numbers accommodated at health resorts. This information (discussed below) is included with other material on public health and deals with Romanian citizens only. There is also information on the number of tourist units, along with the number of beds and the level of usage (Table 10.1), but the earliest figures are for 1970; there is no regional breakdown and foreigners are again excluded. Moreover, the numbers of visitors appear to refer to the number of registrations and could therefore relate to stays of variable length. Hence the calculations of visitors per bed are not valid absolute indicators of occupancy. Regarding employment, the researcher can only rely on miscellaneous statements made in studies of the Romanian economy. It has been suggested that employment in enterprises controlled by the Ministry of Tourism was equal to 0.3 per cent of the wage-earning population in 1965, rising to 0.5 per cent in 1972, and to 0.8 per cent in 1986. In absolute terms this would bring out figures of 21,500, 28,100 and 61,300 respectively. However, if employment in commerce, transport and telecommunications is also considered then the proportion would rise to some 3.5 per cent for 1986 (268,100 people) (Marinescu 1973; Istrate, 1988).

10.3.2 Aspects of planning for tourism

Tourism has stimulated agriculture, especially in the Black Sea zone, and it has also been responsible for major works of planning and construction (Berbecaru 1973). Planning the tourist complex of Mamaia (north of Constanţa) dates back to 1953, and the work of a team of architects under Cezar Lazărescu was extended to the entire length of the Black Sea coast after 1960: the old resorts of Costineşti, Eforie (Carmen Sylva) and Mangalia were enlarged and new complexes emerged at Aurora, Jupiter, Neptun, Olimp and Saturn. Building work has since moved inland from this 'riviera românească', particularly to the Carpathians. Around the city of Braşov, the Institut 'Proiect Braşov' has been responsible for the development of the new resort of Poiana Braşov which, along with older tourist centres in the area such as Buşteni, Predeal and Sinaia, is part of a cluster of places well endowed for tourism in both summer and winter (Ban *et al.* 1973). Planning has also affected other areas, especially since the reorganisation of local government in 1968 and the introduction of local self-financing arrangements which encourage the building of motels and other facilities.

Transport services have increased through the stimulus of tourism. During the summer months there is a heavy internal and international schedule of railway services to the Black Sea coast, while the roads programme has involved not only the improvement of many existing highways but the construction of a motorway which now extends from Piteşti through Bucharest to Constanţa. Following a new road bridge over the Danube at Giurgiu-Vadu Oii (near Hîrşova) on the conventional highway to the coast, there has been the recent completion of a new bridge beside the famous

Saligny railway bridge connecting Feteşti with Cernavodă. This provides a second railway crossing (the old bridge is single track) and a road link for the motorway. A number of new mountain roads have been built, the outstanding example being the Transfăgăraş Highway of 1977, which links Curtea de Argeş and Cumpana in Wallachia with Cîrţişoara in Transylvania via the mountain resorts of Bîlea Lac and Bîlea Cascadă. The list may be extended by consideration of the chair-lifts and cable cars. These are particularly numerous in the Braşov complex, but there is also a cable car between Bîlea Cascadă and Bîlea Lac which is useful in getting to the skiing grounds on the high Făgăraş when the road is closed beyond the resort of Bîlea Cascadă.

10.3.4 Integration with the electrification and woodcutting programmes

A significant aspect of planning for tourism, especially in the Carpathians, has been the liaison with the authorities responsible for electrification and woodcutting (Turnock 1973). Many hydro-electric schemes have been undertaken and these have increased the resources for tourism (Borza 1978). Several reservoirs near major industrial centres (such as Firiza near Baia Mare, Cinciş near Hunedoara and a complex of developments near Resita including Secu, Gozna and Trei Ape reservoirs) have become important for local weekend tourism. Larger schemes linked to the national grid have national and international importance for tourism. The Bicaz project in Moldavia has created an attractive environment for the resort of Durău, while the Argeş scheme has been followed by investment in tourism beside the principal reservoir at Cumpana. More recent projects such as the Iron Gates have been even more closely integrated with tourism from the outset as accommodation for the construction workers has been provided with subsequent refurbishment for tourism in mind.

Forestry has also developed in a manner conducive to the development of tourism. The silvicultural authorities control hunting and fishing, with considerable emphasis on fish farming (Pătrăscoiu 1987). Woodcutting has increased but each woodcutting and transport enterprise must respect the protective function of woodlands in the vicinity of reservoirs (Giurgiu 1980), so that the local environment has usually escaped damage in such cases. However, forest road building to extend woodcutting into areas that were previously ignored, partly because of valley profiles too steep for forest railway construction, has made it easier for tourists to penetrate deep into the mountains by means of vehicular transport. This must be seen in the context of other improvements relating to the national road network. Vehicular routes across the mountains are still limited but they are far more numerous than they were before 1918, when the international boundary followed much of the main watershed (Figure 10.3).

Several strands of tourism and economic development come together very effectively in the Lotru valley (Figure 10.4) where the principal hotel in the resort of Voineasa was initially used as a hostel for construction workers (Ploaie 1983). Further accommodation is now being built around the principal lake of Vidra. Circulation in the area is facilitated by a road system which has been much improved through the strategic need for access to the watersheds and also through the woodcutters' desire for penetration along the main valleys (where previously railways and funiculars were only occasionally

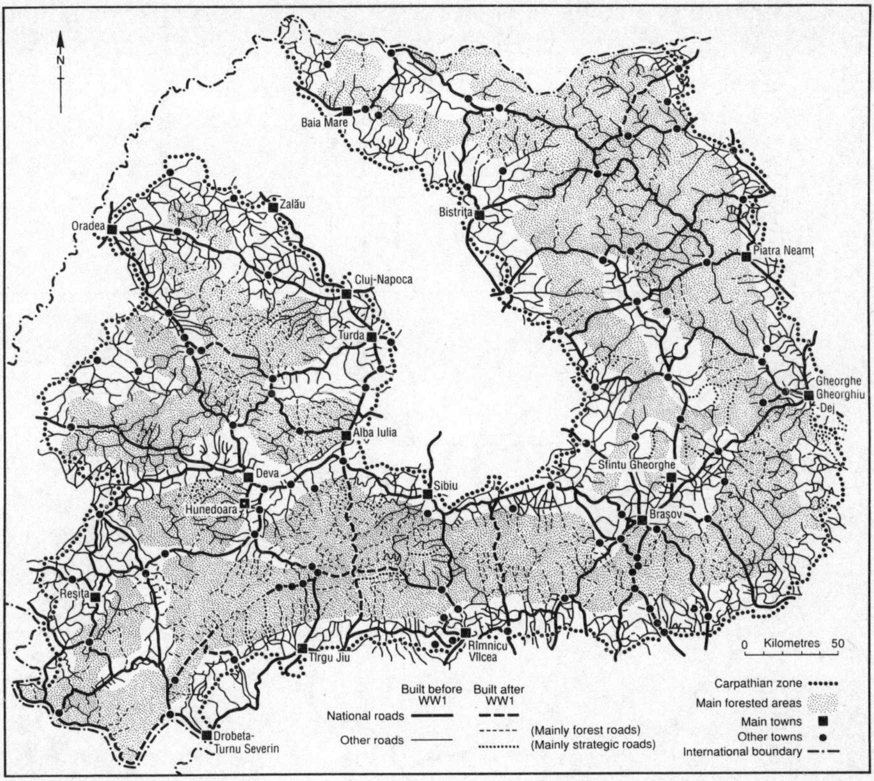

Figure 10.3 Romania: development of the Carpathian road network
Sources: Atlas RSR: Dragomir *et al.* 1981; Oancea *et al.* 1987: fieldwork

provided). Cultural resources have been harnessed (Filip 1981), and a conservation programme is needed to ensure that the various interests can co-exist harmoniously. Considerable effort goes into monitoring the situation, and nature reserves have been set up in particularly sensitive areas. This is part of a nationwide programme. The first reserves, such as Domogled near Băile Herculane (1931), Zimbru near Arad (1938) and Beuşniţa Forest (1943) have been supplemented by some 250 other places of botanical and geological interest. Much woodland is to be regenerated and the Retezat National Park (Figure 10.1) will be joined by others (Bănărescu *et al.* 1980).

10.3.5 Settlement planning (sistematizare)

It was intended that the number of towns would increase by some 500 by the turn of the century, and the tourist industry has been regarded as a significant factor in assessing the potential of existing villages for promotion to urban status (Turnock 1990b). Voineasa in the Lotru valley is one of the candidates and Ocna Sugatag in Maramureş is another outstanding case where the closure of a salt mine in 1950 was followed by the opening of a spa and climatic station

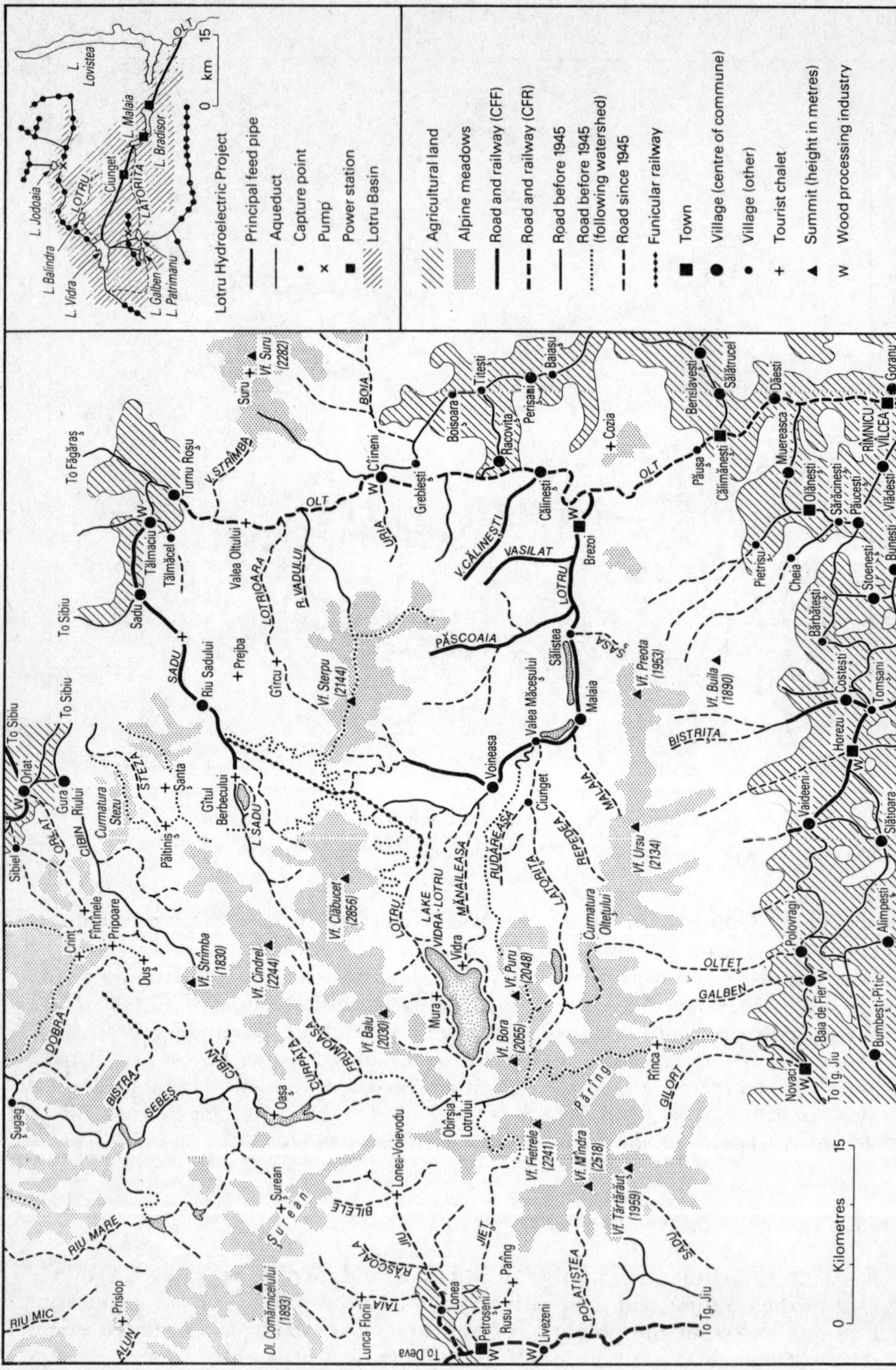

Figure 10.4 Romania: development of communications in the Lotru Valley

Sources: Ploaie, 1983; topographical maps; fieldwork

in 1976 with expansion of facilities to cater for a thousand visitors. On the other hand, there is reluctance to encourage a further decentralisation of tourism to reach all rural areas. It has been suggested (Institut de Géografie 1974) that in declining rural settlements in selected parts of the Carpathians the population might be encouraged to offer goods and services to visitors. This 'resort village' concept has been advocated for the Apuseni Mountains (Păcurar 1987), but the idea seems to have been resisted by the old regime, ever wary of economic and political liberalisation.

10.4 Domestic tourism

The statistical basis for assessing domestic tourism is inadequate, but figures of 1.24 million visits in 1965 and 12.00 million in 1987 show both the scale of the activity and the strongly upward trend. It is most unlikely that these figures are derived from registrations for accommodation since the returns published in the statistical yearbooks between 1970 and 1985 show the number of overnights related to domestic tourism rising from 5.19 to 9.82 million. These figures can then be broken down into different categories of accommodation (see Table 10.1). Since there is also information on capacities, calculations for level of usage can be made (although the international component cannot be taken into account). In the case of villas and chalets it is quite common to find a link with a particular industrial enterprise. Thus the engineering and metallurgical enterprises at Reşiţa have holiday accommodation in a rest house at Crivaia on the Gozna reservoir while the steel works of Oţelul Roşu owns a villa at Poiana Mărului.

Table 10.2 Romanian nationals at health resorts

Year	Numbers visiting ('000s)			
	Holiday only	Water treatment	Total	Persons per 1,000 population
1950	125.8	75.4	201.2	12.7
1955	146.4	162.3	308.7	17.7
1960	230.5	226.4	456.9	24.8
1965	318.2	310.8	629.0	33.1
1970	561.8	366.7	928.5	45.8
1975	972.9	580.9	1,553.8	73.1
1980	1,463.6	801.6	2,265.2	102.0
1985	1,931.0	693.4	2,624.4	115.4

Source: Anuarul statistic (various)

Statistics on the patronage of health resorts (see Table 10.2) extend back to 1950 and show a growth from just 125,800 in that year to 1.93 million in 1985. When the numbers are related to population growth a near tenfold increase emerges: from 12.7 visits per thousand to 115.4. Many of the resorts remain small but there is great potential for expansion (Teodoreanu 1981). It is not possible to discriminate between individual family travel and group travel although the latter is almost certainly the more important in connection with the published figures. It is appreciated that travel can have the desirable effect of stimulating pride in national achievement. Members of Romanian youth organisations have been expected to attend summer camps which often involve travel to school-dormitory accommodation in some distant part of the country. Meanwhile, there has been a good deal of individual initiative with respect to visits to relatives in the countryside. Second home ownership is low even though the law against ownership of more than one property can be by-passed by having dwellings placed in the names of different members of the family. Day-excursions constitute another important activity which has grown with increasing levels of car ownership and road modernisation. However the petrol shortage (along with the law permitting the use of private cars on alternate Sundays only) imposes a constraint. Facilities on the urban-rural fringes are, however, improving (Stoica 1986).

10.5 International tourism

Since 1958 Romania has been a member of the International Union of State Tourist Organisations and ONT is affiliated to international organisations for travel agencies and the planning of tourism. It is accepted that the growth of international tourism requires a conducive 'atmosphere' involving not only peaceful conditions but minimum travel formalities. Great progress was made during the late 1960s and 1970s and the number of visitors increased rapidly, particularly travellers from the socialist countries.

Information on the number of foreign visitors to Romania given in United Nations' yearbooks goes back to 1959 when 67,000 arrivals were recorded. Over the next five years (1960–4) the average was 150,000 (an annual increase of 37.6 per cent on 1959). The late 1960s (1965–9) showed an annual average growth of 107.7 per cent over 1964 with an average of 1.14 million visitors. Comparable figures for 1970–4 were 21.6 per cent (3.02 million), followed by 11.6 per cent (4.36 million) for 1975–9 and 1.8 per cent (6.41 million) for 1980–4. However, the pattern of annual increases was broken by a slight recession in the mid-1970s (3.80 million in 1974 falling to 3.20 in 1976) and by much sharper declines in the 1980s. After a record year in 1981 (7 million) there was a slump to 5.94 in 1982 and to 5.80 in 1983. Then a revival to 6.58 in 1984 was followed by falls to 4.77 in 1985 and to 4.53 in 1986 (the latest figures available at the time of writing). In economic terms, the industry generated $303 million in 1981, but contributed only $178 million in 1986.

Foreign tourists tend to be concentrated in relatively few areas (Swizewski and Oancea 1978b), where services have deteriorated considerably. The United Nations' statistics are inadequate for detailed analysis, but it is evident that between 1980 and 1981 visitors from Western Europe declined by 15.5 per cent while arrivals from socialist countries increased by 8.2 per cent, providing an increase in business overall. However, between 1981 and 1985 there was a decline in both categories (24.3 per cent for Western Europe and 32.5 for Eastern Europe and the Soviet Union). In the case of Western Europe the decline was relatively small for Benelux countries (11.2 per cent), France (16.7) and West Germany (17.4) but heavier for Italy (30.2), Austria (39.2), Scandinavia (42.0), the United Kingdom (42.3) and Greece (50.6).

10.5.1 Eastern Europe and the Soviet Union

The attractiveness of the beaches has drawn many travellers from Czechoslovakia, the former GDR and Poland, while Hungarians visit Romania to see relatives in Transylvania. There was a rapid growth in interest by Czechoslovaks after 1968, since Romania declined to support the Warsaw Pact intervention against the 'Prague Spring' reform movement. But this factor is no longer relevant, and a deterioration in Romanian tourist services has had a discouraging effect. In 1979 Romanian authorities suddenly decided to insist that all foreigners should pay for petrol in hard currency and many East Europeans were stranded until their governments made emergency arrangements. Nevertheless, the tourist exchange patterns have been heavily imbalanced. Passport and foreign currency regulations have made it very difficult for Romanians to travel to any foreign country, although Eastern European countries have dominated the limited foreign programme hitherto operated by ONT for Romanian citizens.

10.5.2 Other countries

There is no doubt that travellers from non-CMEA countries are welcomed for economic reasons. In 1973 the earnings from foreign tourism were stated to be equivalent to 4 per cent of the value of exports, but were double that figure in the case of non-CMEA countries. Earnings from tourism in these markets were greater than the value of exports of machinery or chemicals. Investment in new tourist facilities was therefore considered very good business, and it was argued that the costs could be recouped within 12 years (Gavrilescu 1973). Unfortunately, the austerity policy of the 1980s prevented services adequately meeting the needs of Western visitors, and some disenchantment arose on the part of package-tour operators who found the Romanians unresponsive to their many complaints. Sensitivity over questions of sovereignty further constrained cooperation arrangements which would have brought foreign investment in new tourist projects. The fear of dependency was plainly significant and probably helps to account for the ambivalent attitude to international tourism in general.

10.6 A concluding view

The current reform era in Eastern Europe initially saw Romania firmly out of step with much of the rest of the region. The country's regime claimed to have pioneered a socialist economic strategy to meet all current needs and rejected advice to the contrary as unacceptable interference in the country's domestic affairs. International tourism remained sluggish with little immediate prospect of any renaissance. Romania's share of Eastern Europe's international tourism fell from 9.8 per cent in 1983 to 5.9 in 1986. For a number of years, a minimum daily currency exchange had been compulsory, and the choice of accommodation was restricted to premises under state or cooperative management. Austerity brought energy conservation and the demise of late-night entertainments. The dogmatic emphasis on radical schemes of town planning—redeveloping inner-city districts and reorganising rural settlement along the lines of semi-communal living in apartment blocks in key villages—robbed the country of many of its historic buildings and traditional landscapes. Growing international concern over these policies, triggered in part by alarm over the treatment of the Hungarian minority in Transylvania in 1988, meant closer security surveillance of foreign visitors and rumours about the possibility of restricting travel to designated tourist regions. It was widely appreciated that morale in the industry was low but tourism was only one aspect of a much wider malaise.

The Romanian tourist industry is a large one although its growth, like its present geography, has been uneven. Despite thoroughly inadequate statistical coverage, there are indications of considerable importance as regards employment, patronage and international economic exchanges, to say nothing of the ideological/educative importance of the domestic sector of the business. There is undoubted potential for further growth and a clear economic case for expansion of the industry can be made, with good prospects of a revival over the longer term. The Ministry of Tourism has acquired considerable expertise, and innovative projects continue to attract investment (such as the establishment of a sanatorium in an old salt mine at Tîrgu Ocna). Moreover, the industry is large enough for continuity of employment to be an important political issue. Tourism is one of a small number of influences working to restrain excessive development and extend the environmental protection strategy which has been much discussed over the last two decades. Despite certain aberrations, such as deforestation in the Carpathians (only recently brought under control), and land reclamation in the Danube Delta (where the Roşca-Letea area has attracted the attention of UNESCO as a 'reserve of the biosphere'), there does not appear to be genuine concern. The recreational atmosphere of the Black Sea coast may have been compromised by heavy industry in Constanţa/Năvodari and Mangalia, but a threat to the beaches from chemical waste dumped at Sulina has been alleviated. Above all there are the human resources comprising the Romanian population (and especially the rural population) which have hitherto been undervalued by a security-conscious regime hostile to private enterprise, but who must now be drawn into what Istrate (1988, p. 28) has described as the revitalising of Romanian tourism.

There are obvious difficulties with any assessment made during a period of sweeping reform in Eastern Europe. The persistence of a Stalinist regime to the very end of the 1980s clearly worked to the disadvantage of Romanian tourism since foreign visitors were discouraged by heightened security. Ironically, this particularly affected visitors from other, more 'liberal' East European countries who hardly relished a return to the cloistered conditions from which their countries had escaped. However, Romanian participation in the prevailing trend towards liberalisation will be beneficial in removing the constraints which have recently upset foreign visitors and in directing both capital and enterprise to meet the rising demand. Domestic tourism is in a quite different situation, involving as it does the vast majority of Romanian families who have no option but to take their vacation inside the country.

Growth is conditional on greater prosperity which will only be achieved slowly even now that radical restructuring of the economy can be contemplated. Indeed in the short term political change could depress domestic tourism through a surge of interest in foreign travel (if only to neighbouring countries) that the removal of travel restrictions might stimulate.

Ironically, in the first months of The Front for National Salvation, despite the lifting of the ban on privately accommodating foreigners, overseas visitors were being restricted to a handful of tourist centres, with stronger spatial constraints being imposed than in the days of Ceauşescu. In February 1990 the Minister of Tourism resigned following the requirement to hand over 20 tourist hotels to the army. With May 1990's somewhat dubious national elections confirming the Salvation Front's ruling position, the immediate future for the Romanian tourist industry remained, at the time of writing, very uncertain.

11 Bulgaria

Frank W. Carter

11.1 Introduction

Nature and history have helped to make Bulgaria a country well suited for tourism. Today, one of the country's most cosseted industries as a major hard-currency earner, tourism attracts visitors from Western Europe, North America and the Middle East. Bulgaria is also one of the main destinations for tourists from Eastern Europe and the Soviet Union. The country enjoys a wide variety of resources for tourist development (Figure 11.1) and is located on one of the shortest routes from Europe to the Middle East. Bulgaria's relief is extremely varied, ranging from the Black Sea coast to the Rila–Rhodope massif which in places is over 2,000 metres high. About 40 per cent of the country consists of plateaux and hilly areas, and a further 30 per cent forms the lowland plains, while 28 per cent may be designated as mountainous. Throughout the country the climate is temperate and agreeable with an average annual temperature of 12° centigrade. Historically, Bulgaria is rich; treasures dating back to the Thracian period have been unearthed, while evidence of Roman and later occupations abound. A wealth of ancient cultural monuments exist, often tucked away in remote parts of the country; old villages, monasteries, oriental architecture and objects of natural beauty can all be found by tourists wishing to extend their knowledge and experience of this part of Europe. The beaches of the Black Sea coast provide ample opportunity for their less adventurous, sun-loving counterparts.

11.2 Tourism in historical perspective

Growing interest in tourism first appeared towards the end of the nineteenth century with the founding of the Bulgarian Hiker's Society in 1895. Its activity mainly concentrated on mountain tourism and the provision of facilities (such as rest huts) for visitors to the higher parts of the country. The early part of this century experienced the development of spa tourism, in places noted for their curative qualities since medieval times. Mineral spas were modernised and balneo–medicinal centres were established in places like Bankija (near Sofia), Kustendil, Vorshets, Kostenets, Momin Prochod, Hisarija, and Velingrad. Similarly, mountain resorts were located in Borovets, Pamporovo and Undola in the Rhodope Mountains, Karandila and Daulite near Sliven. Here the first holiday rest centres were built, and there soon followed the organisation of summer camps for children (colonies) in mountain and coastal villages. Several monasteries such as Rila, Bachkovo, Trojanski and St. Konstantin near Varna rented out rooms to visitors in the summer months.

The inter-war period saw the beginning of recreational tourism along the Black Sea coast with visitors not only from Bulgaria, but also from Poland and Czechoslovakia. This activity was concentrated mainly in Varna and Nesebûr. During the 1930s this coastline attracted about 15,000 tourists annually, laying the foundations and helping to establish an infrastructure for the later post-war boom. The pre-war period also saw an increasing interest in the preservation of nature for recreation purposes with the founding in 1928 of the Council for the Protection of the Countryside by the Bulgarian botanist Stefan Petkov (Carter 1978, p. 69). This led to the establishment in 1931 of the Vitosha National Park on the outskirts of the capital city which remains today a very popular short-term recreation area. Finally, in 1937 the Bulgarian government decided to establish a private travel agency called 'Balkan', but tourism remained a very underdeveloped part of the economy with a few tourist societies and sports clubs; trade unions possessed about 15 rest houses and sanatoria on the Black Sea littoral (Vielzeuf 1971, p. 32).

After World War II there came a turning point in the growth of tourism with the enactment of a new law by the government, awarding all Bulgarians the right to fourteen days' holiday each year with an additional day for every two years of employment. Even so, this was only a beginning for the tourist movement in Bulgaria, for there were still insufficient hotels and similar establishments to accommodate any large-scale growth. There was a move to encourage foreign companies to refurbish some of the older hotels and adapt them for future needs. This programme was cut short with the establishment of a new Communist government in Bulgaria in 1948.

Clause 76 of the new Bulgarian constitution gave every citizen the right to a holiday, a reduction in the working day, annual paid leave and the creation of a large resource of holiday homes. In certain areas, buildings were nationalised and placed at the convenience of trade-union employees; workers could live here for two weeks contributing only about a quarter to the costs, the rest being subsidised by the state. In 1948 the state tourist organisation 'Balkanturist' was established, based on the Soviet 'Intourist' model (later to be called the State Committee for Tourism—DKT), which began to invest in a tourist infrastructure for Sofia, most large cities and on the Black Sea coast with the construction of the Druzhba complex near Varna. In 1952, the country had a total of only 116,000 (implicitly domestic) tourists. However times were changing with the death of Stalin and the de-Stalinisation process of the early 1950s. Even so, in 1955 fewer than 3,000 foreign visitors entered the country, yet the government realised that here was a potential source for foreign currency, particularly from West European nations.

In February 1956 the Bulgarian Communist Party officially announced its de-Stalinisation programme. This provided the necessary lever for the development of tourism both at a domestic and international level, although it would take time to create the right conditions for intensive growth. The period 1956–73 can be designated as the first major post-war phase of tourist development. In 1963, the old 'Balkanturist' state agency was superseded by a new General Tourist Agency whose president held ministerial rank; three years later this was transformed into a Committee for Tourism which answered directly to the Council of Ministers. It was an inter-ministerial organisation with responsibility for the planning, financial provision and promotion

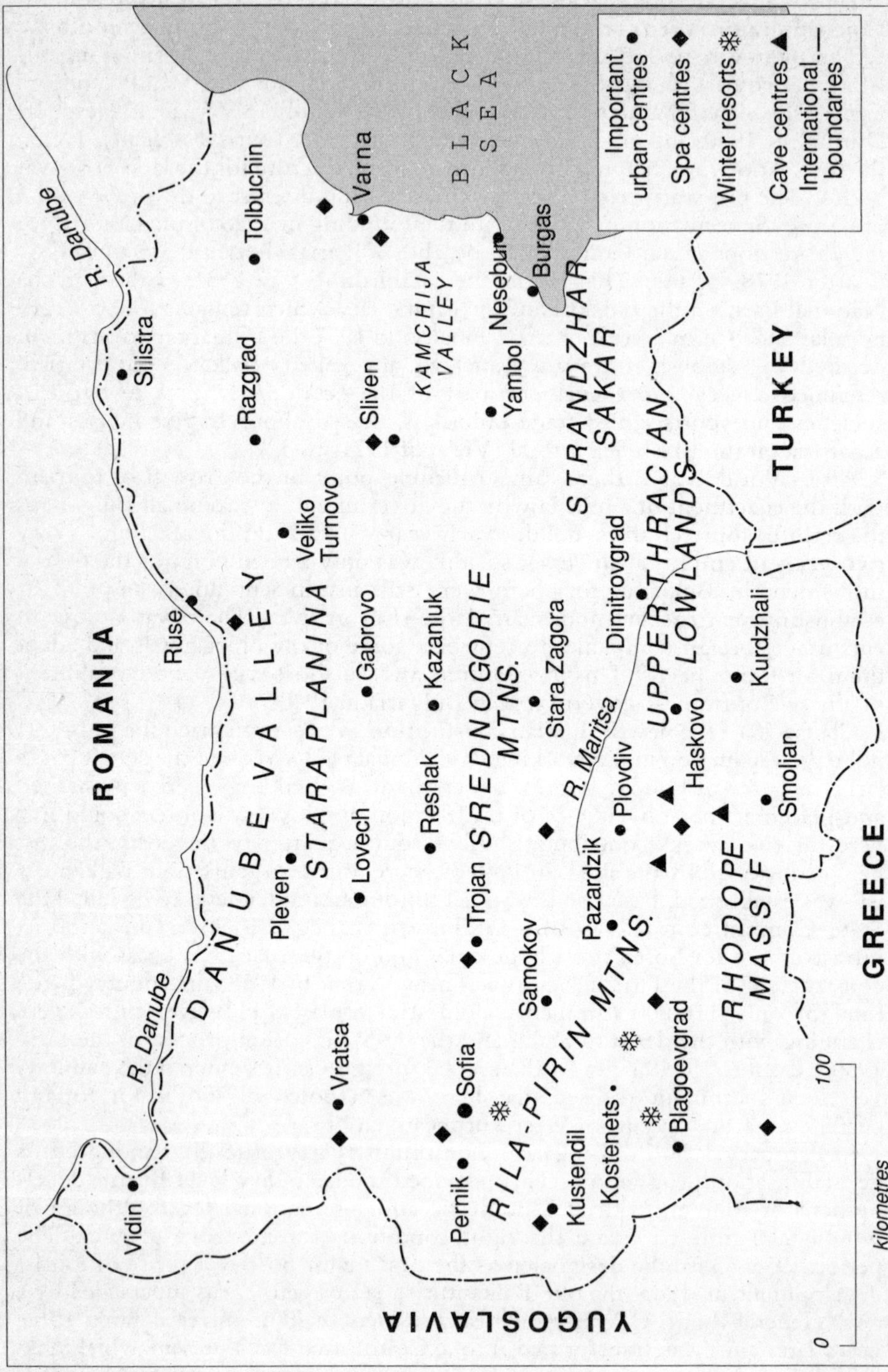

Figure 11.1 Bulgaria: major tourism areas

of large-scale tourism and was in charge of all state tourist enterprises, district administration and large national associations such as trade unions, youth organisations, cooperatives, tourist unions and motoring associations. Several ministries were involved and they coordinated their efforts when applying for financial support from the national budget (Poncet 1976, p. 155). The Committee for Tourism controlled several state enterprises; for example, Balkanturist was responsible solely for international tourism, Turist dealt with hotels and restaurants, Rodindturist (established in 1962) organised travel arrangements, Hemus looked after individual tourist needs and Balkanship, founded in 1966, had three tourist boats at its disposal.

Other organisational changes were introduced to encourage tourist development. These included simpler entry formalities for foreign visitors, easier currency regulations (since 1964), and, after 1967, no visas were needed by foreign nationals staying in the country for between 24 hours and two months. In the same year Bulgaria, along with Yugoslavia and Turkey, signed a declaration in Ankara for the creation of the Balkans into a 'communal tourist zone'. Finally, Bulgaria made agreements with certain West European tourist groups, such as Club Mediterranée, 'Touropa' and 'Club 33', allotting them places and facilities at tourist resorts, especially on the Black Sea coast. In spite of these obvious attempts to attract foreign tourists and develop the industry, tourism was only allocated 1–1.5 per cent of the funds from the national budget during this period.

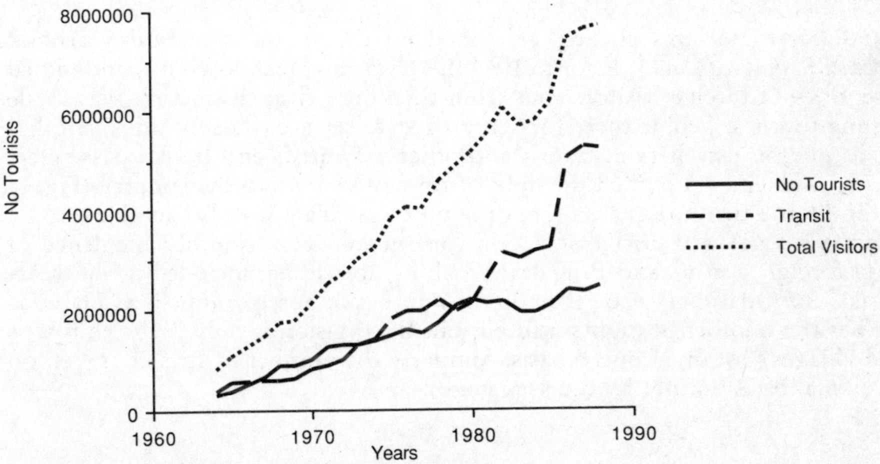

Figure 11.2 Foreign visitors to Bulgaria, 1964–88

Source: Statisticheski Godishnik

The second post-war phase of Bulgaria's tourist development dates from 1974–80. This was a period of mixed fortunes on the international front as a result of the 1973 oil crisis. Even so, a fifth of Bulgaria's foreign-exchange earnings from non-CMEA countries came from tourism in 1974–5. Furthermore, in 1973 the XI Party Congress decided on the intensive development of industry. The government's Committee for Tourism was reorganised with a brief to reconstruct and modernise its industry. The coastal tourist season was to be extended and there was to be greater investment in mountain and spa tourist centres. Similarly, tourist itineraries were to be extended and specialist tours developed. In turn this would create demand for better services, improved transport facilities, selling of souvenirs and provision of sports facilities. Reorganisation of the industry continued, and in 1977 a new State Committee for Tourism was announced with responsibility for carrying out state policy, management and all economic activity connected with international and domestic tourism and recreation.

Much of this effort was made to attract foreign tourists, whose number had steadily risen from 291,000 in 1964 to a peak of 2,457,280 in 1988 (Figure 11.2). In 1980 an Association for Economic Tourism and Recreation of the Working People was established as a voluntary public economic union to support the industry in general and the State Committee for Tourism in particular. The early 1980s experienced a decline in foreign tourists after the hiatus of 1981 and led to yet further reorganisation; in October 1983 a Bulgarian Association for Tourism and Recreation (BATR) was established which replaced both the 1980 association and the State Committee for Tourism. The new organisation combined both roles and was a 'public–state agency' being given economic plan targets to distribute among the various organisations it supervised. Its long-term success has yet to be seen but by 1985 there was a distinct increase in tourists.

11.3 Data sources and problems

Data sources for this chapter are based on the annual statistical yearbook (*Statisticheski Godishnik*). Prior to 1964 there was no breakdown into individual categories of foreign visitors, but from then on a clear distinction was made among tourists, people there for work or state service, those visiting families etc as guests, travellers in transit and others. Tourists and transit passengers have consistently provided the bulk of foreign visitors to the country (Figure 11.2). Domestic tourists are more difficult to calculate as only members of the country's various tourist associations are given. The monthly incidence of both foreign visitors and Bulgarians visiting abroad are included in the yearbooks. Information is also given on the number of hotels and beds available as well as the number of nights utilised, but the division is only between towns and villages, not on a tourist basis. Similarly the number of spas are given on an annual basis but not by tourist category.

11.4 Tourism and economic development planning

At the end of World War II, Bulgaria was a less-developed Balkan state with 6 million inhabitants. Over four-fifths of the active population was employed in agriculture, with less than a tenth in industry. Tourism hardly existed, with a mere 15,000 participants utilising hotels built during the inter-war period by governments dependent on German and Czech capital investments. Apart from these luxury hotels no others existed, for unlike Central Europe pre-war Bulgaria had no substantial middle class to increase demand. Even by 1956 only one hotel existed on the Black Sea coast, at Varna. Post-war reconstruction was gradually to change this situation with an emphasis, particularly after 1948, on industrial development. Socialist planning gave priority to full employment and industrial diversification, which in turn led to rapid population growth (7.6 million in 1956) and rural-to-urban migration. By 1956 one in three Bulgarians was an urban dweller; by 1968 this figure had reached nearly one half of all inhabitants, with Sofia now a city of a million, while Plovdiv and Varna had over 200,000 inhabitants and Ruse and Burgas more than 100,000. Greater prosperity ensued with car ownership rising from annual sales of 3,000 in 1960 to 9,000 in 1965 and 21,000 in 1968 (Bachvarov 1984, p. 3).

Prior to 1956 and the de-Stalinisation process, tourism had been largely a domestic affair. Its development was largely associated with the post-1948 socialist revolution which provided new social conditions and rapid urbanisation. It was mainly 'welfare-orientated' tourism for purposes of rest, health, spa treatment, annual holidays and camping, and week-end tourism, especially generated from the rapidly growing cities to accessible upland areas. Ideologically, it was encouraged by the socialist government for, as Marx pointed out, leisure time is as important as labour time in contributing to the common good (Marx and Engels 1964, p. 265). While domestic tourism is widely dispersed throughout the country, foreign tourism has been growing since 1956 but largely in connection with the Black Sea coast and the capital, Sofia.

A critical stage in tourist development came with the 1969 decision of the Politburo to develop sport and tourism. This gave a new impetus and direction to the organisation of Bulgarian tourism. The gates were opened for the growth of mass tourism. A further boost to development came with the reorganisation and creation of the Committee on Recreation and Tourism (KOT) in April 1973. According to the Sixth Five-year Plan (1971–5), the task assigned to tourism was

> that international tourism will be developed, that we will raise the level of service and effectiveness, that we will increase the length of the holiday season by means of developing winter tourism and utilizing mineral spa and maritime resorts, that we will intensify the use of hydropathic (balneotherapy) sanatoria treatment, that we will develop and varify services in the tourist regions such as special attention being given to sections on trade and transport facilities for tourists. [Dinev *et al.*, 1973, p. 76]

Such state objectives were to act as a trigger for economic development. Communications were a critical factor in tourist growth. By the late 1960s, only a fifth of Bulgaria's 30,000 kilometre road network was hard surfaced, including the major international route from Yugoslavia via Sofia to the Black Sea coast and Istanbul. Similarly, rail connections needed improving: less than a fifth of the 3,898-kilometre rail system was electrified and a third was still dependent on steam traction. Average speeds were slow at around 60 kilometres per hour, and the journey from Sofia to Varna took seven hours, a discouraging factor for international tourism. Air transport was better developed, with links from Sofia to all major European capitals, but a flight from, for example, London to Varna still took nearly four hours. Subsequently, much investment has been directed towards improved communications and by the mid-1980s all main tourist centres were easily accessible (Carter 1990c).

Tourist accommodation facilities were also greatly improved. During the mid-1950s construction began on the Black Sea tourist resorts of Druzhba and Zlatni Pyassatsi, followed in 1958 by Slunchev Bryag and Albena. Similarly, new large hotels were built in some of the major urban centres such as Sofia,

Plovdiv, Turnovo and Pleven. In 1956 only 14,000 beds were available in the country's hotels, but by 1965 these had more than trebled in number to 47,000, and in 1978 there were 75,000 beds in 361 Balkanturist hotels. The building of camp sites, begun in 1962, also developed rapidly from 45 sites (28,000 beds) in 1968, to 67 (over 65,000 beds) at the disposal of campers in 1978. By the end of the 1970s there were a further 140,000 beds available for foreign tourists in private lodgings, which had been first made available in 1966 (Bokov 1981, p. 452).

Part of the planning process also led to the creation of tourist regions. These may be defined as based on the unity of a territorial recreational system and its natural, socio-demographic and economic surroundings. These were meant to ensure the effective functioning of the system within a relatively compact territory which contains recreational specialisation (Bachvarov and Apostolov 1982, p. 23). Seven basic tourist regions were delineated—the Danube basin, the Stara Planina mountains, the Intermontane–Srednagora region, the Rila–Pirin mountains, the Rhodope Mountains, the Vitosha–Osogovski region, and the Black Sea coastal region. The delineation of each region is based on a number of criteria. These include natural conditions and aesthetic values such as scenic beauty, historical architecture, and objects of cultural importance; the role of transport facilities and amount of fixed capital. The regions also have to be flexible to change, as tourist numbers vary, while time has to be allowed for the organisation of labour and capital needs and the overcoming of economic inertia. They also need to be adaptable to rapid spatial expansion in response to the growth of transport facilities and supply of tourist material such as souvenirs. Finally, there must be some adaption to the seasonal variations in demand and the economic consequences of such change. Tourist regions were therefore delineated according to projections of tourist movement and the degree to which resources could be utilized. Within the tourist regions several levels exist including micro and macro regions, sub-regions, nuclei and specific tourist objects, all related to the economic infrastructure of the region as a whole (Bachvarov 1970, pp. 345–7; Dinev 1974, p. 121, Dinev 1982, pp. 132–3).

By the early 1980s, capital investment was largely devoted to adapting part of the seasonal tourist facilities for all-year exploitation. This involved enlarging some hotels with additional storeys, adapting some hotel rooms for families with children, altering some hotels to cater for medical tourism and enlarging or providing hotels with sports and entertainment facilities. Further, capital was allocated for improving restaurant amenities, roadside service stations for transit tourists, equipping tourist centres with a greater variety of shopping centres, constructing halls for congress tourism and improving the effectiveness of private lodgings. Finally, new restaurant and fast-food outlets were built, and the up-grading of many hotels to at least the international three-star standard was undertaken.

Tourism has also stimulated the growth of the economic and social infrastructure. The industry now employs 1.25 per cent (around 50,000) of the country's labour force during the active tourist season from May to September, much of it concentrated along the Black Sea coast. This area contains nearly two-thirds of the country's beds allocated to hotels and camping sites, and employs 6–8 per cent of the active population (Naidenova 1989, p. 3). Tourism has also influenced the development of the food and delicatessen industry, especially through market gardening, fruit growing, viticulture and livestock production, as well as employment in local transport services. A fifth of Bulgaria's viticulture is concentrated along the Black Sea coast, centred around Varna and Burgas (Bachvarov 1984, p. 8). Similarly, fruit production is important here, especially in the Kamchijska valley, noted for its apples, peaches and apricots, and centred around Burgas. Tourism has also stimulated vegetable production with large areas around Sofia, Plovdiv, Pazardzhik, Burgas, Varna, Pleven and Blagoevgrad. Between 1965 and 1986 the souvenir industry has experienced a thirtyfold increase with production focused on eight centres, two-thirds of the output being sold in tourist markets. Light industry has also benefited from tourism with 4–6 per cent of total production supplying tourism, especially in the furniture, textile and glass-manufacturing branches. Tourist centres also demand large amounts of supplies from the food–delicatessen industry; between 1970–86 such supplies to the Black Sea tourist region have increased threefold.

11.5 Domestic tourism and recreation

Tourism and recreation for Bulgaria's own population offers two basic choices. There is the so-called 'welfare orientated social tourism', organised through a person's workplace, trade union or education centre, and the commercial tourism which is also open to foreign visitors. The most important organisation for social tourism is the Bulgarian Trade Union, whose membership has grown considerably in recent years. For example, in 1960 there were 404 local tourist associations with nearly half a million members; by 1973 both these figures had doubled and in 1985 there existed over a thousand associations with more than two and a half million members. These associations are complemented by the other major form of social tourism organised by the Bulgarian Tourist Union, youth movements and sports organisations. They have under their control a large number of rest houses, and camp sites which are either free (financed by trade unions) or based on very low costs for participants. There are also chalets owned by state enterprises for their workers, which can also be used by tourist association members. In 1981 about 4 million people took advantage of this form of tourism (Bachvarov and Apostolov 1982, p. 75) but there has also been a growth in other forms of tourist associations, such as the Bulgarian Automobile Union or the Hunting and Fishing Union.

The social composition of the tourist association membership has varied in recent years. In 1960, blue-collar workers formed 28 per cent of the membership, but dropped to 26 per cent a decade later, only to rise to 35 per cent by 1985: the proportion of white-collar workers dropped from 28 per cent to 19 per cent between 1960–70, and in 1985 remained at 17 per cent. The number of members from the professional group (scientists, doctors etc.) has remained fairly consistent at around 40 per cent over the whole period. Similarly, the proportion of female members has continued at around 43 per cent, while students form about five per cent of the membership. Figures for other Bulgarian tourists are difficult to ascertain as some utilise the commercial tourists facilities, but by far the largest number find lodgings with parents, friends or in private accommodation.

Bulgaria's domestic tourist and recreation flows reveal five basic patterns (Stankov *et al.*, 1985 p. 132). The first and probably the most significant is from the large urban centres to the Black Sea coastal resorts, especially to places like Slunchev Bryag and Nesebur (Vasiliev 1984, p. 128). The second major stream attracts people from all over Bulgaria to visit the medicinal spa resorts, particularly those in the central and western parts of the country. These include such places as Hisarija, Bankija, Vorshets, Sandanski, Narechen, Velingrad, Kustendil, Pavel banja, Slivenski banja, Albena and Golden Sands. Some of the spas have received special attention. For example, the tourist complex of Shipkovski mineral baths, situated in the Trojan district, has been in constant use since 1941 with over a daily thousand visitors at present. The baths are categorised as part of the calcium–magnesium–sulphate water group and are particularly suitable for sufferers of gastric, liver and colitis complaints as well as kidney stones. Around the baths the government has invested in seven rest centres capable of accommodating 2,600 people (Shipkovenski 1986, p. 14). Similarly, spa treatment facilities are now available throughout the year at Zlatni Pyassatsi on the Black Sea coast and are recommended for patients with nervous, respiratory and cardiovascular complaints.

The third group is attracted to the various objects and places of historical and cultural interest, usually in the form of specialist itinerary tours organised from large and medium-sized urban centres (Dinev 1978, p. 166). The fourth main pattern consists of tours around the periphery of large urban centres; Sofia and a number of other significant-sized towns contain clearly designated tourist zones around them which prove attractive for short-term recreation. People situated in less attractive urban centres such as Ruse, Pleven, Vidin or Blagoevgrad utilise regular transport links to villages in the Danube Plain and Upper Thracian Lowlands (Vodenska 1984, p. 117). Finally, domestic tourists are attracted to the mountain areas of the country, especially places in the Rila, Pirin and Stara planina mountains (Barbier 1984, p. 377; Slavkova 1983, p. 39). The Rhodope Mountains (Penkov 1987, p. 2), Sofia's own Vitosha mountain and the Sushtinska Middle Forest Mountains to the east of the capital are also popular. This tourist movement contains both short- and long-term recreation, with Bulgarians attracted by the sporting, hiking, caving and other opportunities offered by these mountainous areas, mainly located in the south-west and central parts of the country. Many such areas are close to neighbouring large towns and encourage urban periphery short-term travel. In summary, these five major flow patterns reveal the dispersed character of domestic tourism. Travel to the Black Sea coast and peripheral tourist zones around large urban centres is the easiest to organise independently by Bulgarian nationals.

The other main form of recreation is connected with second homes. Since the mid-1960s, ownership of 'weekend' houses has played an increasing role in the development of the country's landscape. Precise details of their number remain unclear, as questions asked in the 1985 population census on second-home ownership have not yet been published. Laws controlling the construction of second homes have existed in Bulgaria since the early 1970s and a study from the end of that decade has given some idea of their spatial distribution (Grigorov 1980, p. 15). As expected, approved zones for second home construction were greatest around the capital, Sofia, and the adjoining administrative region of Slivnitsa. These were followed by Burgas on the Black Sea coast and Silistra in the Danube valley. To a lesser extent the coastal regions of Varna and Tolbuhin, and the inland areas of Veliko Turnovo, Lovech, Blagoevgrad and Pazardzhik, have proved popular regions for second-home ownership. This is not the full picture, however, as many second homes have been built without state permission, often on arable land, private plots, or auxiliary farms attached to non-agricultural enterprises (Carter 1990c). There has also been some government encouragement for people willing to convert houses in abandoned villages for recreation purposes, especially in the backward Strandzha–Sakar administrative region of south-east Bulgaria, and in parts of the country's more mountainous areas.

11.6 International tourism

Bulgaria's international tourism began to develop seriously in the late 1960s when the State Tourist Board offered holidays to foreigners which combined a week's minibus tour of the country and a week in Istanbul. As an alternative, foreign tourists could spend up to a week relaxing on the Black Sea coast at the region's best hotels and beaches, or in the capital, Sofia (Eperon 1969, p. 2; Bachvarov 1970, p. 338). Attempts to attract foreign tourists date from a decade earlier for, 'It may be said that the 'fifties of our century marked the beginning of international tourism in Bulgaria and the 'sixties and the 'seventies—its accelerated development' (Petrov 1981, p. 150). British tourist publications also noted this growth in the early 1960s (Pritchett 1960, p. 108). By the end of that decade, German geographical literature had noted this development (Constantini 1969, p. 255) and its potential for foreign tourists through careful planning and management (Losanoff 1968, p. 125).

The number of foreign visitors increased dramatically between 1964 and 1985 (Figure 11.2). In 1964 official statistics first differentiated transit and tourist figures; the decade 1966–72 saw more tourists visiting the country than transit passengers, but the latter exceeded the former during much of the seventies largely because of the numbers of Turkish 'Gastarbeiters' travelling to and from their homeland to Germany and other parts of north-west Europe. In 1979 equal numbers of tourists and transit passengers were recorded, but since then the latter have again increased considerably. The year 1964 also saw the withdrawal of Bulgarian visa requirements for visitors from other socialist countries; those from capitalist countries could obtain them at the frontier. In consequence, the number of foreign visitors increased dramatically; in 1960 they totalled less than a quarter of a million, but five years later had reached one million; by 1970 the figure was two and a half million, in 1981 six million, and in 1988 there were over seven and a half million foreign visitors.

Within the European member countries of the CMEA, Bulgaria and Romania offer some of the best opportunities for seaside and sunshine (Bachvarov 1975, p. 7). Figure 11.3 traces the growth in popularity of Bulgaria for CMEA tourists between 1964 and 1987, with Czechoslovakia and Poland the leading tourist source nations, a trend set prior to World War II. Czechoslovakian tourists revealed a remarkable rise in numbers in the late-1960s, coinciding with the events of the Prague Spring and its aftermath; by 1987 they were the second largest group with over 354,000 visitors—a fifth (21.12 per cent) of all CMEA tourists. Numbers of Polish tourists to Bulgaria showed a dramatic rise during the affluent years of the 1970s, but declined during the troubled early 1980s, rising again by 1987 to over a quarter (29.82 per cent) of the CMEA tourist total. Tourism patterns of the other four European CMEA

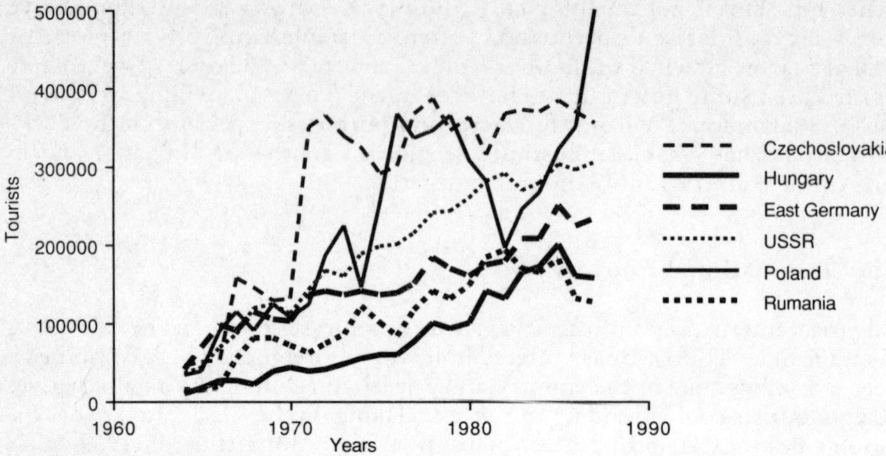

Figure 11.3 Bulgaria: tourists from CMEA countries, 1964–87
Source: Statisticheski Godishnik

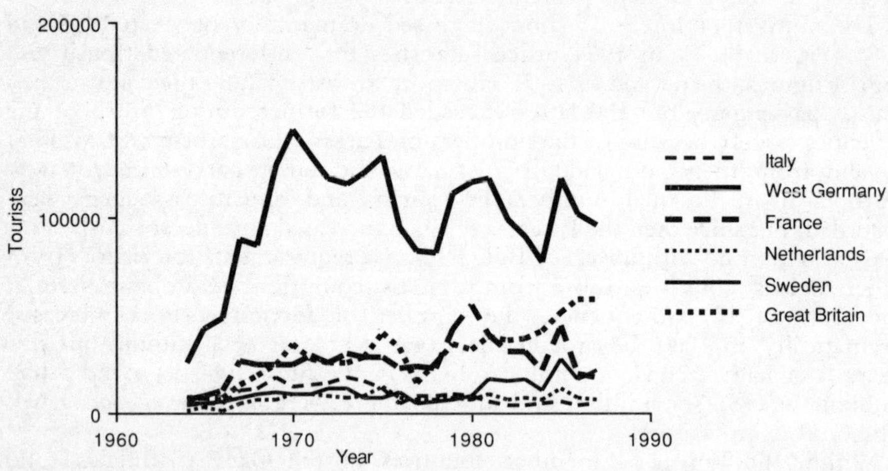

Figure 11.4 Bulgaria: major West European tourists, 1964–87
Source: Statisticheski Godishnik

states—the Soviet Union, the former GDR, Hungary and Romania—portray a more even growth, with the latter experiencing some decline in recent years. The length of stay in Bulgaria reveals a different pattern, with Soviet citizens remaining on average 11 nights, east Germans and Poles eight nights and Czechs and Hungarians seven nights; Romanians on average stay only one or less suggesting short-term cross-border visits to relatives or excursions.

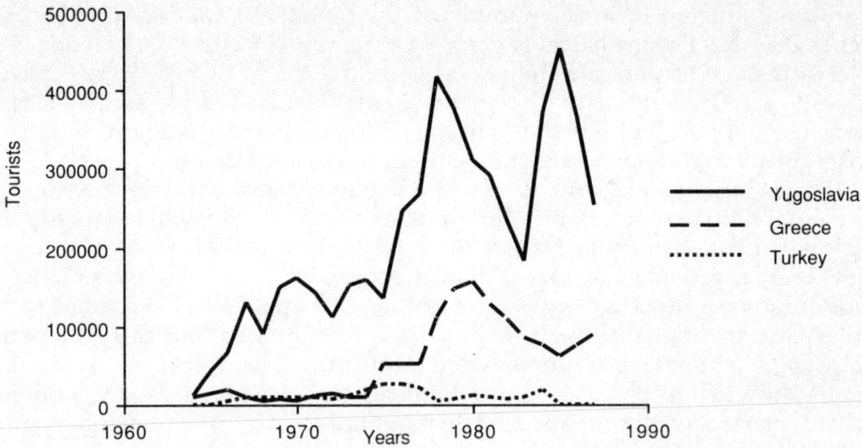

Figure 11.5 Bulgaria: tourists from neighbouring Balkan states, 1964–87
Source: Statisticheski Godishnik

Bulgaria also provides an attractive holiday centre for visitors from the West, particularly for those from north-west Europe and from neighbouring Balkan states (Figures 11.4, 11.5). Tourists from these countries are especially welcome, as they are a source of hard-currency earnings for Bulgaria. The largest number of visitors, however, arrive from neighbouring Yugoslavia (over a quarter of a million) providing more than 40 per cent of non-CMEA tourists. Many Yugoslavs travel to Bulgaria to meet relatives, or to visit Sofia and its vicinity as well as going to some medicinal and spa centres (Bachvarov 1979, p. 113). The Black Sea coast is less attractive to them, as Yugoslavs have their own Adriatic coastal region. Over a fifth of Yugoslavia's overall total cross Bulgaria in transit *en route* to Turkey. More important for the Bulgarian economy have been visitors from West Germany and Great Britain. The early popularity of Bulgaria from around 1970 for west Germans has somewhat waned, but with 267,000 tourists in 1988 they still represented about a fifth of all tourists from the West. Numerically, Greece with 150,000 tourists in 1987 was second in importance to West Germany as a source, a decreasing trend in numbers having been reversed from 1986.

Of the other West European nations, Great Britain, with 87,000 tourists in 1988 and an estimated 100,000 in 1989, has shown increasing interest in Bulgaria in recent years. A Bulgarian study showed that between 1970 and 1981 the number of British tourists to Bulgaria rose by 15 per cent, of which over a third were categorised as from the working class, followed by pensioners and those in the 'freer' professions (Rakadzhiyska and Radilov 1984, p. 150). In fact, the growth of international tourism and increasing numbers to Bulgaria from EC countries has prompted the analysis of various problems associated with hard-currency earnings and exchange rates. This is related to Bulgaria's own prohibitive currency exchange system, and ways are being studied to adjust the tourist earnings' balance between Bulgaria and the EC. Price comparisons between basic goods are being made, while exchange rates and seasonal differences in the number of EC tourists to Bulgaria have been under evaluation. From a hard-currency viewpoint, the length of stay made by EC tourists is critical for the Bulgarian economy; the most nights have been recorded by west Germans with an average of 12, followed by Swedes (11), Britons (10), French and Dutch (eight each). In comparison, the few Turkish tourists spend on average less than one night in the country.

Bulgaria's international tourists reveal a strong seasonal component. About half the foreign tourists arrive during the months of July and August, a situation that has changed little since the 1960s (Vielzeuf 1971, p. 49–50). June and September provide a further fifth of the tourist sojourns, but over the last decade these two months have seen a decline in popularity. November and February are traditionally the least popular tourist months but this situation may change with the growth of winter tourism. The means of travel to Bulgaria shows an overwhelming predominance of car and coach, accounting for three-quarters of all tourists; a further eighth arrive by train, a tenth by air and less than 1 per cent by boat (Stankov *et al.*, 1985 p. 136).

The main destinations for foreign tourists are the Black Sea coast and the capital Sofia, again a phenomenon little altered since the early 1970s (Poncet 1976, p. 162). In fact, four-fifths of all foreign tourists stay at Black Sea coastal resorts (Bachvarov and Apostolov 1982, p. 68). The more adventurous tourists embark on coach tours from the Black Sea resorts inland, high preference being given to visiting the capital (Sofia), Veliki Turnovo, Plovdiv, Kazanluk, Pleven, Ruse and the mountain resorts of Borovec, Pamporovo and Stoletov Peak. Short-term tourist movement is most popular among visitors from Yugoslavia, Romania and Greece who usually tour areas adjacent to their own frontier. Winter tourism is also a growing attraction for foreign visitors. The largest mountain resorts are located in the Rila–Rhodope Mountains and Mount Vitosha. Here summers are cool (20–25° centigrade), but the winters are mild and winds relatively gentle. Snow cover is plentiful and is present for up to 180 days annually. These areas offer ideal conditions for winter tourism and sports; leading centres are Pamporovo (1,620 metres) and Borovets (1,300 metres). Similarly, Mount Vitosha's surrounding area has excellent skiing and tobogganing facilities and snow can remain in parts up to the end of May. Sofia is only half an hour's drive away (Carter 1990c).

Specialist tourism is another attraction for foreign visitors. International health tourism is one of the most promising and effective ways of utilising the hydrothermal resources of Bulgaria. This is particularly so for the thermo-mineral waters in the tourist recreation zones along the Black Sea coast, in the Rila–Rhodope mountain massif and in the Stara Planina Mountains. These areas contain some of the best-quality water in the Balkan peninsula, along with spas noted for the curative properties of their mud. Much of this potential has yet to be realised; the provision of top-quality technical equipment, health centres containing international comfort standards and qualified staff are still needed (Sterev 1985, p. 30). Another possible attraction for foreign tourists is visiting caves. The country has over 2,000 of these, and eight of the largest have been adapted for tourist visits with lighting and improved access.

In the Rhodope foothills at Chepelare, a speleological museum has been established which attracts increasing numbers of international visitors. Furthermore, the caves and gorges in the Trigrad and Kritchin regions have considerable tourist potential, as do other karstic areas of the country (Tassin 1985, p. 30; Nicod 1982, p. 227). Potentially, therefore, Bulgaria has much to offer the foreign tourist, with a range of attractions capable of satisfying a large variety of tastes (Kilian 1985, p. 101).

11.7 The impact of *glasnost* and *perestroika*

The radical and massive changes taking place in the Soviet Union have created a period of uncertainty in Bulgaria. Admittedly, Bulgaria has experienced upheavals before, especially after the 1956 April plenum which led to an intensive and ambitious modernisation programme pulling the country's economic base away from agriculture towards industrialisation. The gates were opened for the economic reforms of the 1960s (Lampe 1986, p. 199), but these were never coupled with genuine liberalisation. While *perestroika* is intended to revitalise the individual and involve him/her fully in public life, *glasnost* is, and will continue to be, essential in this process.

The emphasis of *perestroika* is on improved management. It is true that the Bulgarian tourist industry went through a difficult period, particularly after the Chernobyl accident, when tourists stayed away from Bulgaria and other parts of Eastern Europe. Furthermore, the main aim of restructuring the country's tourist agencies was to improve efficiency and foreign-currency income. In the early 1980s both tourist and recreation agencies were lagging behind the growing demands of domestic and foreign tourism in the country. Recreation facilities were not fully utilised, or were constantly in need of maintenance, while sightseeing tours, mountain trips and medicinal/spa facilities were poorly developed.

The situation has now greatly improved. The latest tourist idea is to encourage theme tours specialising in a particular aspect of Bulgarian life: these include monasteries, ornithology, botany, historic cities etc. and hope to attract a different type of clientele from those only wanting sun, sand and sea.

The Bulgarian Association for Tourism and Recreation (BATR) was established in October 1983 with the task of improving these shortcomings. It has been partially successful, helped by the investment of the equivalent of 3–4 million dollars annually in publicity and marketing in an industry which employs more than 50,000 people. The publicity seems to have worked, with tourists once more visiting Bulgaria in considerable numbers. In 1987, 3.8 million tourists from the West and a similar number from the socialist countries spent their holidays in Bulgaria. Hard-currency earnings increased by a fifth. The greatest attractions are the skiing resorts at Mount Vitosha, Borovets and Pamporovo, followed by the resorts along the Black Sea coast. Further, recent legislation allows private individuals in Bulgaria to establish their own small restaurants, giving tourists an alternative to hotel meals. Bulgarian families are now allowed to rent out rooms to foreign tourists, while state-run hotels are looking to Western chains such as Sheraton to invest in Bulgaria through joint ventures or on a management contract system (Dempsey 1988, p. 18). Such changes could eventually lead to greater liberalisation in the tourist industry, with closer contacts being encouraged with West European companies in the hope of boosting Bulgaria's hard-currency earnings.

In 1987 the XIII Congress of the Bulgarian Communist Party at its July Plenum and the National Party Conference in 1988 called for reconstruction of the economy and territorial organization (Geneshki 1989, p. 5). This led to the reduction of the country's 30 provinces (*okruzi*) to nine, which it was hoped would make economic planning more rational, and help stimulate development of the technical and social infrastructure (Naidenova 1989, p. 5). Attention is also being drawn to the need for closer synchronisation between what tourists want and what the industry can supply (Khristova 1988, p. 114). A better contractual system for international tourism in Bulgaria, particularly for tourist service contracts, is also needed (Rachev 1988, p. 131). Finally, increasing attention is being paid to the nature of international business tourism and the way this should be encouraged by Bulgaria's tourist industry (Bonev and Trifokova 1988, pp. 84–6).

11.8 Conclusions

The foregoing pages have attempted to assess the role of tourism in Bulgaria since World War II. That it is an important sector of the Bulgarian economy is in no doubt, although in recent years it is true that the Bulgarian tourist industry has been through a difficult time. Investment strategy now favours greater emphasis on light industry and more effort placed on the consumer sector. Given the changing political climate of the country, there is a transition from the previous command to a market system. More private initiative will be forthcoming in the tourist industry with attempts to attract more Western visitors and to cater for their needs, although initially these changes have taken place within the framework of the existing cumbersome administrative system.

The tourist industry, if properly developed, can enhance the development of many regions within the country. Improved transportation and better hotel accommodation could benefit both the economic and spatial structure of the industry. Clearly there are problems in this transformation, particularly in hotel management. Older hotels must be refurbished up to standards demanded by Western tourists to compete with the newer hotels attracting hard-currency customers. Hotel staff have to be given more incentives to maintain quality services which are efficient and quick. Hotel managers need to be aware of the norms expected by foreign, especially Western tourists. This can be improved by attracting foreign hotel chains to invest in the industry and employing local labour through joint-venture schemes.

Tourists will also demand improved conditions in the social, cultural and environmental sphere. Greater care and investment will be needed for the country's rich cultural heritage: easier access to religious centres; restoration of earlier architectural styles, albeit some of a foreign (Ottoman) culture; and less emphasis given to monuments extolling the glories of socialist realism. The negative aspects of post-war investment in heavy industry will have to be tempered through improved environmental quality. Pollution of varied kinds from large enterprises around the capital and other large cities directly conflicts with tourist demands for environmental quality which the fledgling Ecoglasnost movement may tackle.

Tourism is seen as one of the major earners of hard currency and everything is now being done to give financial priority to future tourist projects. The industry can help greatly in resolving the country's present hard-currency debt, providing the right formula can be found for attracting Western tourists in ever-increasing numbers. Present changes throughout Eastern Europe will undoubtedly be felt in Bulgaria's tourist industry. Many tourists who previously avoided the country for political reasons will now consider visiting Bulgaria. For Bulgarians wishing to travel abroad the situation is more difficult. For some time exit visas have been easily obtained, but financial stringencies have limited their use. Each Bulgarian visiting abroad, unless in an official capacity, has been allowed to take only $20 out of the country, a very restrictive factor. Given an improved internal economic situation and better balance of payments, this allowance may be increased or removed entirely.

Note

* The author greatly appreciates the help and advice of Mr Angel Angelor (Bulgarian National Tourist office in London) and Miss Louise Saunders from the Cartographic Unit UCL, who prepared the illustrations.

12 Yugoslavia

John B. Allcock

12.1 Introduction

Within the development of the institutional structure of the tourism industry is mirrored the growth of Yugoslavia's distinctive variant of socialism. The study of tourism provides an excellent case study both of those features of the Yugoslav system which are idiosyncratic and those which indicate characteristics more generally typical of the erstwhile centrally planned economies of Eastern Europe. First, a brief historical account of the development of Yugoslavia's tourist industry will be undertaken, concentrating particularly on the field of policy-making. This chronological account relies on a number of sources (Kobašić 1980, 1987; Cicvarić 1980; Unković 1981).

12.2 Statistical data sources and problems

One relatively unusual feature of the Yugoslav tourist industry, which possibly has its roots both in its long history and in the characteristics of post-war socialism, is the relatively easy availability of statistical information. The Turistički Savez Jugoslavije (Tourist Association of Yugoslavia) located in Belgrade is the source of an irregular series of studies of particular aspects of the trade. Much more useful on a regular basis are the publications of the Savezni Zavod za Statistiku (Federal Bureau of Statistics). Their monthly bulletin *Indeks* carries rather raw data, usually relating to the period up to about four months prior to publication. The annual *Statistički Godišnjak* (Statistical Yearbook—also available in English and French) carried much fuller data, together with breakdowns for each republic and the major cities. Each of the republics also produces its own yearbook, providing data down to the level of each municipality.

These data, while extremely useful, have two principal limitations. They do not always answer questions which may be of interest to social scientists. There are also some serious inaccuracies and inconsistencies. Definitions of what constitutes a 'tourist' in the context of Yugoslav statistics are, to say the least, loose. Virtually any foreigner visiting the country for any purpose will appear in the tourism statistics, and figures for domestic tourists seem to omit entirely the users of week-end cottages. Data relating to seasonal fluctuations in employment are badly out of phase with the actual seasonal rhythm of tourism flows. Information relating to the activity of the private sector is subject to very large errors, largely as a result of the failure to report activity to the local authorities. For these reasons, the data should be treated with some caution, although they do permit very extensive and intensive study of tourism in Yugoslavia.

12.3 Tourism policy: an historical survey

12.3.1 Tourism in pre-war Yugoslavia

International tourism is not an entirely post-war feature of the Yugoslav economy. Its emergence, at least in those parts of the country formerly included within the Austro-Hungarian Empire, closely parallels that of other important European tourist centres. A number of spas (such as Lipik or Pakrac) were founded in the late-eighteenth century, and resorts such as Opatija (Abbazzia) emerged in the Istrian peninsula during the middle of the nineteenth. These served a largely aristocratic clientele, and they reflected the current ideologies of health, offering a variety of 'cures' (Allcock and Counihan 1989). Travel by steamer became possible along the Adriatic coast in the later 1840s, and the Julian Alps and Istria were made accessible by rail from Vienna during the last quarter of the century. Both of these developments stimulated the spread of tourism. By the end of the century the entry of a growing bourgeoisie into the market gave a further impetus to this process. Especially important in this respect was the occupation and subsequent annexation of Bosnia and Hercegovina by Austria. Several venerable hotels dating from this period still make their contribution to Yugoslavia's tourist industry—the Grand Hotel 'Imperial' in Dubrovnik, for example, which opened in 1897.

The industry continued to grow in importance after World War I, particularly when the economy of the newly created Yugoslav state, seriously shaken by the years of depression, found a welcome source of foreign-exchange earnings in international tourism. In spite of this, both the Austro-Hungarian government before unification, and the Serb-dominated Yugoslav government after unification, tended to adopt a strongly 'continental' view of the national economic interest, and gave little positive encouragement to the development of tourism, centred as it was principally along the Adriatic coast (Ensminger 1978).

By the outbreak of World War II, therefore, Yugoslavia had already established a tourism industry and had determined the most important features of its physiognomy. It served a relatively wealthy custom, drawn largely from the economically and politically more powerful states to the north. The development of facilities had taken place principally along the Adriatic littoral, and in large measure this had come about because of the active intervention of capital from outside the region. In 1938 Yugoslavia provided more than one and a half million overnight stays for foreign visitors—or about 29 per cent of its total tourist trade.

12.3.2 The era of trade-union tourism

When the Yugoslav state was reconstituted after the war, tourism was given a very different direction. The over-riding aim of the new regime with respect

Table 12.1 Changing patterns of patronage for different types of Yugoslav resort, 1953–88 (%★)

Type of resort	1953†	1958	1963	1968	1973	1978	1983	1989‡
All tourists								
Capitals of republics & APs.	. . .	24	23	25	22	19	21	16
Spas	8	6	5	5	5	5	5	5
Coastal	17	25	33	35	40	40	40	49
Mountain	7	9	9	8	8	9	9	9
Other	68	35	31	28	25	20	26	22
Foreign tourists								
Capitals	. . .	15	31	29	25	25	23	13
Spas	1	1	1	2	2	1	2	2
Coastal	45	74	51	53	57	58	60	64
Mountain	7	5	—	—	—	—	—	7
Other	47	5	16	16	16	16	15	14
Domestic tourists								
Capitals	. . .	23	22	26	25	20	23	18
Spas	9	7	7	7	7	7	7	8
Coastal	15	21	25	23	27	31	30	35
Mountain	7	10	9	9	10	11	9	10
Other	69	39	36	35	31	31	31	26

Sources: Statistički Godišnjak for relevant years; Yugoslav National Tourist Office

★ Figures do not always total 100 because of rounding
† For 1953 data for regional capitals were included under 'other'
‡ Jan.—Sept. only
– fewer than 0.5%
AP autonomous provinces

to the economy was rapid industrialisation and, within the rigid framework of centralised economic planning established by the Communist government, no independent role was envisaged for tourism. The socialist order dictated a turning away from those activities which could be said to have served the needs principally of foreigners of the leisure class. But there was nevertheless a need to reward the achievements of labour and provide for the rest and recuperation of those by whose efforts the foundations of a new society were being laid. Tourism was no longer a privilege, but a constituent part of the process of socialist reconstruction.

Under the new conditions, international tourism was allowed to wither, and such resources as could be spared were devoted to the development of holiday centres of a hostel type for workers and the youth, for the provision of travel grants and for subsidies to appropriate catering organisation (Zečević 1973). The new spirit is vividly conveyed in the renaming of Dubrovnik's former luxury hotels: the 'Exelsior' became the 'Dubrovnik', the 'Argentina' became the 'Beograd', and the 'Imperial' became the 'Moskva'. Elite tourism became mass tourism—but not in the sense of modern commercial mass tourism.

Vukičević has coined the useful phrase 'trade-union tourism' to describe this phenomenon, which has also been described by Hall and others as 'social tourism' (Vukičević 1978; Hall 1984b).

A particular point to note in connection with this phase is that the spas, mountain, and other inland resorts experienced a period of favour, enjoying the advantages of proximity to the larger urban centres, in competition with the seaside resorts which were later to dominate the picture. Indeed, until the early 1960s the republican capitals rivalled the coastal resorts as centres of tourism attraction. Figures are not available for the years immediately after the war, but as late as 1953 the littoral was receiving only 17 per cent of all visitors (Table 12.1) and providing 32 per cent of their overnight accommodation. In keeping with the centralised planning which prevailed throughout the economy at this time, tourism and catering were under the control of offices located in the federal Ministry of Commerce and Supply in Belgrade. The single state travel agency Putnik supervised the travel arrangements of this almost entirely domestic tourist flow.

By 1953 foreign guests, at around 245,000 per annum, had still not surpassed the total for 1938, and their overnight stays amounted to only 55 per cent of the 1938 figure (Table 12.2).

12.3.3 The creation of 'self-management'

The year 1952 represents a turning point in the development of Yugoslav tourism. The conflict between the Yugoslavs and the Soviet Union resulting in the expulsion of Yugoslavia from the Cominform in 1948, and the resulting economic blocade of the country by its former allies and trading partners, would have been a serious enough shock. They came together with other events which imposed radical economic and political changes (for example, see Singleton and Carter 1982; Lydall 1984).

Although enormous strides were made towards 'accelerated industrialisation' under the First Five-year Plan, its extremely overambitious character, the lack of experience of the Yugoslav regime, and the excessive rigidity of its organisation resulted in great economic difficulties. These were exacerbated by the agricultural situation. Largely as a consequence of the slights on the genuinely socialist character of its development flung at Yugoslavia during the dispute, the leadership embarked upon an attempt to match 'accelerated industrialisation' with the 'accelerated collectivisation' of agriculture. Poorly and hastily planned, incompetently executed and hampered by two years of serious drought, the programme collapsed after 1951. The destruction of the country's framework of external economic relations thus coincided with the collapse of one of the major props of its domestic economic strategy. The escape from this predicament was sought by means of three interrelated sets of reforms: a reorientation of the country's trading policy; an enactment of the political changes which came to be known as 'self-management'; and the first moves towards 'market socialism'. These general developments can be seen to have had a profound impact on the growth of tourism.

There is no evidence that in the search for alternative trading partners and new sources of external income tourism played a very significant role at this time. It is more likely that the devaluation of the dinar in 1952 to one-sixth

Table 12.2 The growth of foreign tourism in Yugoslavia, 1938–88 ('000s)

	Tourists			Overnight stays		
Year	Total	Foreign	Foreign (%)	Total	Foreign	(%)
1938	939	276	29	5,479	1,562	29
1950	2,361	41	2	8,819	179	2
1953	3,179	245	8	9,140	855	9
1956	3,281	394	12	10,740	1,333	12
1959	4,563	835	18	19,795	3,433	17
1962	5,249	1,242	24	22,983	5,270	23
1965	7,942	2,658	33	32,651	11,240	34
1968	9,864	3,887	39	38,300	17,210	45
1971	12,719	5,239	41	54,791	25,849	45
1974	14,425	5,458	38	64,999	29,727	46
1977	16,587	5,621	34	73,488	29,026	39
1980	18,089	6,410	35	87,106	36,978	42
1983	18,790	5,947	32	90,649	35,355	39
1986	22,176	8,464	38	111,134	51,400	46
1989*	17,481	7,779	45	91,427	46,022	50

Sources: Statistički Godišnjak for relevant years; 1989, Yugoslav National Tourist Office
* Figures for Jan–Sept only

of its former level—intended simply to make Yugoslav exports more competitive in general—had the unintended consequence of also making the country more attractive as a tourist destination. The only measure which may be construed as directed toward a stimulation of foreign tourism was the liberalisation of passport regulations (Dubey 1975, p. 32; Radišić 1981, p. 77).

In many respects the most dramatic consequences of the break with the Soviet bloc were political rather than economic. In particular, the task of authenticating the socialist credentials of the regime fell to the newly created 'workers' collectives'. Experimentally introduced in 1949 in a number of large enterprises, these were elevated the following year to the status of centrepiece of the Yugoslav system. Initially the terms of reference of the new 'workers' councils' placed them emphatically within the framework of the state economic plan and subordinated them clearly to the enterprise directors. The new system of 'workers' self-management' rapidly came to have a central and novel significance, especially when taken in conjunction with the reform of local government.

Paralleling the process of economic decentralisation was an equally important process of political decentralisation. Although during the wartime struggle the Communists had relied heavily on local 'Peoples' Committees' to provide a framework of government in areas under their control,. after the cessation of hostilities local government reverted to being a network of agencies of central state and party organs. A 'General Law on Peoples' Committees' introduced in 1952, however, established these as the chief units of government throughout the country. Both of these new developments were consolidated in a new Constitutional Law enacted the following year.

Although in many respects the new system might be said to have been intended to solve acute problems of legitimation following the break with the Cominform, there is little doubt that there were wider practical consequences. There was a thoroughgoing devolution of authority to both commune (*opština*) and enterprise; moreover, these two institutions were made mutually dependent.

Under these circumstances the apparatus of central planning of the Soviet variety, adopted after the war, was rendered increasingly inappropriate. The First Five-year Plan was followed in 1951 by an *ad hoc* one-year plan and a redrawing of the planning law. The former Federal Planning Commission was replaced by a smaller Institute; the new philosophy of 'social' planning adopted a more indicative approach to the determination of 'basic proportions'; the direct regulation of production was replaced by measures such as price and fiscal controls and the regulation of investment. Under the new order a far greater part was played in economic policy by the banks—especially by newly established investment, foreign trade and agricultural banks. The centrepiece of this financial system was the General Investment Fund, which became the principal agency through which the federal government was able to allocate resources.

The new system of allocation, laid down in a law of 1953, initially operated through the device of *auction*.

> When an auction is announced, those who are interested are invited to submit their applications. Such applications must state the purpose for which the loan is asked, the amount of the loan, the amount needed in foreign currency, the rate of interest the enterprise is willing to pay, the expected time for completion of the project, the amount of circulating capital as a percentage of total capital required for the project and a fully elaborated investment policy. [Pejović 1966, p. 15]

Although under this system investment was generally allocated to the highest bidder, political considerations continued to play some part in the decision-making process.

The impact of these institutional changes was reflected in changes in the pattern of investment. Whereas in 1953 only a trivial proportion of investment in fixed assets came from sources other than the federal government, by 1960 this had fallen to around 60 per cent, with nearly 30 per cent coming from local (communal and district) sources (Zečević 1973, pp. 191–8). As the reorganisation of the banking system got under way the role of the state in investment continued to decline, so that by 1964 the banks were providing roughly a third of all investment in fixed assets. These developments have been identified subsequently as the movement by Yugoslavia towards 'market socialism'.

The significance of the above-mentioned developments for the tourism industry in Yugoslavia was substantial. The industry now competed with other sectors of the economy entirely on a 'sink or swim' basis. In many respects tourism emerged from the competition badly. The radical fragmentation of economic and political decision-making capacity to enterprise and commune level led to acute spatial disparities in terms of the effort which was put into the development of tourism, depending upon the relative strength of commitment to tourism held by local elites. This tendency was strengthened after 1954 by the creation of 'Chambers of Trade', which although established at federal and republican levels, worked most effectively at the communal level. The role of these institutions has been seriously underestimated by observers of the Yugoslav economy (however, see Dirlam and Plummer 1973, pp. 83–6). Membership of the chambers was made compulsory after 1958.

This tendency to localise the sphere of effective action was heightened by successive recastings of the federal policy-making structure for the industry, and it was not until 1953 that the formation of the Tourist Association of Yugoslavia gave a reasonably stable state-wide framework for tourism (Ensminger 1978, pp. 29–30).

The mid-1950s were thus a difficult time for tourism. The break with the Cominform cut off Yugoslavia from some of its major customers (particularly Czechs and Hungarians), and this trade was only slowly replaced by tourists from western countries, especially from West Germany, Austria, Italy and the United Kingdom. Under the impact of reduced subsidies the domestic market stagnated. The majority of investment was devoted to the renovation and updating of existing capacities, and the number of hotels actually declined during this period. The acute fragmentation of the industry under the system of 'self-management', whereby every hotel or even local office of a travel agency became an independent operating unit, posed a number of serious problems, above all in the area of marketing.

Table 12.3 Yugoslav investment in selected sectors, 1965–86
(Gross fixed investment in millions of dinars at current prices)

Year	Total	Agriculture and forestry		Industry		Catering and tourism	
			%		%		%
1965	20,378	1,924	8	6,708	41	1,155	5
1968	34,370	1,991	6	10,131	29	2,526	7
1971	64,651	4,722	7	21,000	32	6,985	11
1974	117,400	11,087	9	38,588	33	7,218	6
1977	268,000	20,800	8	98,000	37	15,900	6
1980	545,600	36,700	7	199,600	37	32,200	6
1983	1,029,500	106,200	10	376,300	37	49,600	5
1986	5,047,000	411,600	8	1,889,700	37	317,600	6

Sources: OECD, 1972 (p. 58), 1985 (p. 65) and 1987/8 (p. 101)

Towards the end of the decade, however, things began to improve. The auction system for investment was abandoned and replaced by a select commission, which scrutinised bids for development loans. A new five-year plan introduced in 1957 acknowledged the importance of international tourism, and loans were made available at preferential rates (Zečević 1973, pp. 172–80). After 1960 there was a steady rise in the volume of investment in the sector (Table 12.3), and over the decade 1953–62 this was reflected in a quickening response from the foreign market. Whereas the total numbers of tourists registered increased by only about 40 per cent in this period (overnight stays more than doubled), there was a fivefold increase in the number of foreign holidaymakers, and a sixfold increase in the number of nights they spent in

Yugoslav accommodation. Even so, the domestic market still accounted for more than 75 per cent of the trade.

12.3.4 The years of crisis and reform

By the end of the 1950s economic reform was needed badly in Yugoslavia. The realignment of economic interest after the break with the Cominform had taken place behind high protective barriers which were inconsistent with the development of longer-term links with the non-communist states. The country had relied heavily upon aid rather than trade to see it over the crisis, and exports declined as a percentage of the value of imports from 97 per cent in 1954, to 62 per cent in 1961. The real extent of formerly disguised unemployment could no longer be overlooked, as thousands of Yugoslav workers left (at first often illegally) to find work abroad. A process of adjustment was begun in 1961—the year in which, according to Horvat (1976, p. 21) 'everything went wrong'. The five-year plan was suspended after only one year of operation, and a wide-ranging programme of reforms was commissioned. Multiple exchange rates were abolished, and Yugoslavia became an associate member of GATT. In 1965 a package of more than 30 laws was passed which covered, *inter alia*, exchange control, taxation and the banking structure.

Two features of the reform process are of special significance for the development of international tourism. The outstanding change wrought in this period was an effective regionalisation of the Yugoslav economy. The ultra-fragmentation of the early years of self-management was replaced by an emphasis on the role of the republics as the units of economic coordination. The concern with foreign-exchange earnings, and the reform of the foreign-currency regime, created conditions which strongly favoured tourism enterprises. Republican governments emerged as highly active agents in the creation of tourism development policy, acting through the newly regionalised banking structure and typically in association with both local government and the consortia of firms which grew up within the sector.

These processes were especially significant in the Republic of Croatia, which occupied by far the greater part of Yugoslavia's Adriatic coast. The republic not only possessed some of the country's most obvious opportunities for tourism development but was also faced in a particularly acute form with the problem of economic emigration. Tourism seemed to offer an economic magnet which might serve to counter this tendency. It is during this period that a number of Croatian academics emerged as outspoken and active advocates of tourism as a component of development policy and were highly successful in their mission.

The years of crisis saw a remarkable change in the performance of Yugoslavia's tourist trade, and were of prime importance in laying the foundation for the following decade of expansion and the specific forms which this took. Two additional events which were to play a central role in the growth of tourism merit attention here. Between 1961 and 1965 the Adriatic highway was completed, running from Rijeka in the north to Petrovac in Montenegro. Built with Western advice and money, the road was not intended to serve exclusively the needs of tourism but also to help to integrate this otherwise isolated and economically backward area more fully into a wider transport network. Clearly, however, this resource was of substantial importance for the tourist trade, particularly since the majority of holidaymakers from abroad arrived in Yugoslavia by road (Allcock 1983).

A measure of the seriousness with which the potential of tourism was regarded at this time can be seen in the invitation extended to the United Nations to become involved in the planning of Yugoslavia's tourism development. This involvement took two forms. A consultancy mission was organised, which reported in June 1965 (Savezni Komitet za Turizam, 1965), reviewing a wide range of issues relating to the industry, including its organisation, the standard and range of services offered and the implications of tourism development for urban and transport planning. Partly arising from this investigation, an extremely ambitious project was mounted, also in association with the UN, to prepare a comprehensive spatial plan for the whole of the Adriatic coastal region. This was undertaken in association with consultancy companies from Poland and Italy, and its report was presented in 1968 (Ujedinjenje Nacije 1968). The oddity about these exercises is that they postdated many of the most important decisions and developments connected with the creation of Yugoslavia's tourism industry.

12.3.5 The tourist boom

Stimulated by the need to obtain convertible foreign currency, government bodies and business enterprises at all levels began during the late 1960s to pursue the expansion of foreign tourism. 'Market socialism' has frequently been taken rather uncritically as a description of the Yugoslav economic system, particularly after the economic reform of the 1960s. The history of the expansion of tourism in this period indicates quite clearly, however, that the unquestioning use of this concept as a tool of analysis has to be challenged. Perhaps a somewhat greater regard was paid than had previously been the case to the rationality of economic decisions in the area, but we are far from a situation in which calculations of an economic rate of return on investment were the principal factor governing decisions about the composition, purpose and location of capital.

The General Investment Fund was abolished as a planning instrument in 1963, and many aspects of its role were taken over by the territorial banks. The Federation did retain responsibility for the administration of a fund for the support of the underdeveloped areas, but the coastal zone was excluded from the remit of this body. Although tourism was declared to be a federal development priority, the direction of investment into the sector fell largely to other mechanisms, particularly the foreign-currency regime and the banks.

The new Law on Foreign Currency Trading enacted in 1966 introduced into economic policy a new and controversial device—the retention quota. According to this measure, enterprises which exported goods and services had the right to retain for their own use a proportion of the foreign exchange created by the transaction. For the majority of exporters this was fixed at 7 per cent, although for selected sectors there were premium rates: for tourism in general, 20 per cent but for travel agencies the quote was even higher (Bičanić 1973, p. 127). Foreign-currency holdings of this kind were extremely useful as a lever for obtaining favourable credit arrangements with the banks, which in any case were enabled by legislation to provide a variety of incentives to firms wishing to invest in the tourist industry. So attractive did the expansion of tourism become during the late 1960s that, running counter to federal attempts to direct funds into the underdeveloped regions of the country, banks from Macedonia were investing their own resources in Croatian tourism projects (Lyall 1968).

There is some evidence to suggest that the enthusiasm of the state at various levels, for tourism, ran ahead of the actual take-up of the benefits offered. Certainly, when in July 1967 a legal framework was introduced whereby foreign enterprises could invest directly in Yugoslavia in association with a Yugoslav partner, the response in the tourism sector was disappointing, and the preferred route for foreign capital into tourist development remained via Yugoslav banks raising loans abroad. The new five-year plan ushered in, in 1966, anticipated a total investment in tourism of 7 billion dinars, whereas the actual sum committed was 4.7 billion. Although the years 1970–1 did see tourism receiving record levels of investment, measured as a percentage of gross domestic investment this was only 67 per cent of the plan target. The same plan projected a growth of accommodation to 244,000 beds by 1971: the number attained (if measured in terms of 'basic accommodation') was 213,393, or 141,884 if hotels alone are considered (Kobašić 1987, pp. 20–1, which gives figures different from those available in official sources).

The period after 1965 was one of unparalleled growth for the tourism industry in Yugoslavia. By 1974 more than 5 million foreign tourists were spending nearly 30 million nights in Yugoslav accommodation. They earned for the country a net income in convertible currency of around $644 million, which for the first time took earnings from travel into second place in Yugoslavia's league table of invisible earnings, behind remittances from Yugoslav workers abroad (Table 12.5).

Without detracting from that achievement, however, it is necessary to recognise that in this period also emerged some of the most significant problems for tourism which have continued to pose difficulties ever since. The role of the federal government in the main was to create a general climate of support for the growth of tourism. In this process the abolition of tourist visas during the United Nations' 'International Tourist Year' of 1967 played an important part. The federation also took responsibility for the various stimulative fiscal and investment measures mentioned above. There was, however, little effective regulation or even monitoring of the ways in which these various measures were utilised.

Excessive attention was paid to the volume of investment, without due consideration being given to its effectiveness. In part this was owing to the prevailing economic theory of the time, but in large measure it is a reflection of the competition between local and regional elites, for whom the grandeur of a development project appears to have been more important than its economic rationality. Planning for tourism was also seriously unbalanced in that effort was directed disproportionately to the creation of accommodation, without paying appropriate attention to other essentials in the sector. Two specific deficiencies have been criticised repeatedly by Yugoslav commentators. There has been a constant shortage of trained staff in the sector, particularly in the area of senior management. Marketing has also lagged far behind. Although Yugotours was founded in 1960 precisely to coordinate the marketing of Yugoslav tourism abroad, the expansion and refinement of services has constantly trailed behind need. The industry has tended to be oriented towards

Table 12.4 Growth and changing composition of the capacity of accommodation in the Yugoslav tourist industry, 1965–86

Year	N %	Total capacity	'Basic accommodation'	*Of which hotels*	'Complementary accommodation'	*Total capacity in private sector*
1965	N	385,409	94,692	*60,832*	290,717	*144,609*
	%	100	25	*16*	75	*38*
1968	N	450,960	132,432	*90,144*	318,528	*182,395*
	%	100	29	*20*	71	*40*
1971	N	770,628	213,393	*141,884*	557,235	*219,891*
	%	100	28	*18*	72	*29*
1974	N	673,993	226,736	*164,256*	447,257	*265,317*
	%	100	34	*24*	66	*38*
1977	N	717,791	253,632	*183,893*	464,159	*285,689*
	%	100	35	*26*	65	*40*
1980	N	1,060,803	269,627	*197,438*	791,176	*309,334*
	%	100	25	*19*	75	*29*
1983	N	1,196,229	299,061	*221,694*	897,169	*358,709*
	%	100	25	*19*	75	*30*
1986	N	1,321,901	337,994	*249,309*	983,907	*419,229*
	%	100	26	*19*	74	*32*
1989	N	1,401,070	362,252	*262,445*	1,038,818	*454,963*
	%	100	26	*19*	74	*32*

Sources: Statistički Godišnjak for relevant years; 1989, Yugoslav National Tourist Office

the 'reception' of guests rather than their 'acquisition' (Marković *et al.* 1980, pp. 13–4).

The lack of balance in the development of Yugoslav tourism is further illustrated by the highly skewed pattern of size in tourism and catering organisations. Most business organisations in the sector are quite large. This is not due principally, in the opinion of this author, to a kind of cultural hangover from the past, as Sallnow (1985) has argued. Much more significant have been two other factors. The system of self-management itself tends to place a premium on size because of the way in which it requires enterprises to shoulder the burden of administering aspects of the fiscal, political and social security systems to an extent which would be impossible in a small outfit. Thus, in spite of a succession of campaigns to stimulate small businesses, beginning at the time of the economic reform, success in this direction has remained limited. Furthermore, the system of dispensing grants, bonuses and other incentives to economic development tended to place the initiative in the hands of existing enterprises—the principle of 'to him who hath'.

12.3.6 The years of stagnation

The process of regionalisation which dominated Yugoslav economic and political life following the economic reform of 1965 brought its own contradictions. Increasingly the federation was eased into the position of simply

Table 12.5 The role of tourism in Yugoslavia's balance of payments, 1965–86 (figures in millions of US$)

Year	Trade balance			Services and transfers (net)						
	Exports (fob)	Imports (cif)	Balance	All services	Foreign travel	Workers' remittances	Transport	(5) as % of (4)	(6) as % of (4)	(7) as % of (4)
	(1)	(2)	(3)	(4)	(5)	(6)	(7)	(8)*	(9)*	(10)*
1965	1,094	1,289	−195	235	63	59	118	27	25	50
1968	1,265	1,797	−532	415	136	149	144	33	36	35
1971	1,814	3,253	−1,439	1,110	175	695	244	16	63	22
1974	3,805	7,520	−3,715	2,532	644	1,379	396	25	54	16
1977	5,254	9,634	−4,380	2,798	750	1,427	568	27	51	20
1980	8,978	15,064	−6,086	3,795	1,515	1,539	832	40	41	22
1983	9,914	12,154	−2,240	2,514	862	1,167	795	34	46	32
1986	11,084	13,096	−2,012	3,112	1,105	1,636	1,749	36	53	56

Sources: OECD, 1972 (p. 68), 1985 (p. 74) and 1987/8 (p. 110)

* The figures in these columns total more than 100% because they are percentages of the net balance of services and transfers, not income only; throughout this period there was a recurring substantial loss on the investment account

holding the coats in a succession of bouts of confrontation between republican interests (Burg 1983). The most dramatic of these confrontations took place in 1970–1, when a growing popular movement demanding increasing autonomy for the Republic of Croatia was only suppressed by President Tito with great difficulty, narrowly falling short of serious physical conflict. Tourism policy featured prominently in this particular struggle and in particular the role of the 'retention quotas' for foreign-currency earnings.

As Yugoslavia's most successful earner of foreign exchange through tourism, the Croats resented the quotas, even though tourism continued to carry entitlement to privileged quota status. Their anger was aroused by the yet higher proportion of such earnings which was siphoned off for what were represented as either unworthy or wasteful projects such as excessive spending on the support of the federal apparatus in Belgrade or the subsidisation of inefficient heavy industry in the underdeveloped republics. Notwithstanding the fact that tourism was buttressed hugely by a range of credit support and other schemes, financed from federal resources but enjoyed disproportionately by Croatia, the retention quotas were represented by Croat politicians at the time as a variety of robbery disguised as privilege.

The earlier reform programme had not solved the problems to which it had been directed; indeed during this period Yugoslavia embarked in earnest upon a programme of extensive external borrowing in order to mask what were important structural deficiencies, and which was later to be its undoing. The need for further profound change was underlined in 1973, when Yugoslavia fell victim to the international 'oil shock'. In spite of continuing deference to the idea of 'market socialism', economic life remained dominated by political agents. Not surprisingly, their response was not to withdraw from the scene but to identify the solution to problems in political terms. In 1974, therefore, the Yugoslavs were presented with their fourth post-war constitution, and two years later (probably more significantly) with the remodelling of the self-management system through the new Law on Associated Labour (usually known by its acronym, ZUR).

A detailed account of the Constitution and ZUR is not required here, but the arrangements they instituted complemented each other in important respects. At the political level, an inverted hierarchy of 'delegations' ascended from the neighbourhood to the federation. In the economy each work organisation was reconstituted as a 'basic organisation of associated labour' large enterprises were divided into 'complex' organisations (typically referred to by the acronyms OOUR and SOUR). Coordination between units, either for the provision of collective services or the realisation of common projects, was to be achieved by means of a series of 'social compacts' or administered through 'self-managing communities of interest'.

In many ways, therefore, Yugoslavia found itself during the 1970s undergoing a return to the fragmentation which had characterised the formative period of self-management of the 1950s. This cumbersome system, which many have held to account in large measure for the current economic crisis of the country, did nothing to further the development of the tourism industry. In many cases it imposed absurd costs, in that a travel agency, with branches scattered throughout Yugoslavia, might be constituted as an OOUR, requiring regular and extensive travel on the part of branch representatives to take part in the consultation processes normal to the self-management system. A unified approach to marketing, already noted as a long-standing weakness of the Yugoslav tourism industry, was at first further inhibited, although moves were later made to compensate for this through the combination of enterprises on a SOUR basis and through the more effective action of local and regional chambers of trade. The situation was not improved by organisational changes which took place in the administration of tourism at a federal level. In keeping with the wider reform of both economic structure and the constitution, mentioned above, the Federal Committee for Tourism was abolished, and coordinating responsibility for the sector absorbed within the Federal Secretariat for Commerce and General Economic Affairs. In effect, from the federal point of view this constituted a downgrading of tourism. It was not until 1982 that this was rectified through the creation of the Coordinating Board for Tourism, charged with the task of introducing a degree of complementarity between the activities of the six republics and two autonomous provinces of the federation (Kobašić 1987, p. 40).

The new five-year 'social plan' inaugurated in 1976 continued to give a prominent place in its stated goals to the development of tourism, as the capacity of the industry to earn convertible foreign currency came explicitly to be recognised in government circles. Various stimulative financial measures remained in the government repertoire of indicative planning tools. The period was nevertheless one of stagnation for tourism. The creation of new accommodation continued (although below plan targets), but results were very uneven. The escalation of transport costs occasioned by the oil crisis was clearly a contributory factor to this; but internal factors remained more significant.

A feature of note in the expansion of tourism during this period is the growth in the private sector. Although broadly committed to a system of 'social ownership' in the economy, the right of individuals to own the means of production and to employ others (within strictly defined limits) is enshrined in the Yugoslav constitution. With specific reference to tourism, this had been confirmed and subject to detailed regulation under legislation enacted in 1965 which included recognition of the right to receive paying guests in private homes. Even so, the situation of the individual entrepreneur has always been problematic in Yugoslavia, and little systematic research has been carried out on the private sector (however, see Singleton and Carter 1982). The actual situation has varied enormously between localities, depending upon the attitude and actions of local political elites. The uneven operation of the fiscal system, in its bearings upon the self-employed, has always been highly controversial. In spite of these deterrent features, the 1970s saw a steady expansion of the private sector, especially in the coastal area, where not only accommodation but also catering and a variety of ancillary services for tourism grew up on the basis of private initiative. These activities were particularly successful in attracting the savings of Yugoslav workers who had spent time working abroad; and as Yugoslavia's economic situation has continued to deteriorate, access to the hard-currency earnings which tourism offers has grown in importance, providing a vital second income for many families and as security against inflation.

There is no way of assessing accurately the size of the private contribution to Yugoslavia's tourist economy. Official figures for this period accounted for nearly a third of the total accommodation available to the individual sector, absorbing about 15 per cent of the overnight stays by foreign holidaymakers. The incentives to underestimation or downright concealment of income from this source are considerable, however, and undoubtedly its true significance is much greater, even though it is impossible to say by exactly what order of magnitude (Allcock 1990).

12.3.7 The 'showdown'

This account of Yugoslavia in the post-war years have attempted to indicate that the country's tourism industry needs to be understood within the context of a wider institutional framework of economics and politics, and that at both levels there have been continuing structural problems of a deep-seated character. The year 1983 may be taken, however, as a kind of watershed, not in the sense that the nature of the problems changed in any significant way, but because the conflict over their possible resolution moved on to a different plane. (There remains considerable room for argument over the timing of the onset of the current Yugoslav crisis (but see Lydall 1989).) In that year the International Monetary Fund was invited to provide assistance, and this involved discussion of the possible need to reschedule at least a part of Yugoslavia's substantial external debt.

Because of the acute degree of fragmentation of the Yugoslav economy, the first problem facing the federal government was to discover just what was the size of this sum. Regional banks had been contracting loans for various purposes on their own account with no reference to any central financial authority. (At this stage the National Bank of Yugoslavia had few of the functions which are normally associated with institutions described as 'national banks'.) To the extent that the size of this problem was known, it had remained a state secret. Release of the information was necessitated by the fact that the Federal Assembly had to debate and approve the package of measures demanded by the IMF. The discovery that the country's total hard-currency indebtedness amounted to about $20 billion (or nearly $1,000 per capita) was a profound shock, being, after Poland, the second highest level of foreign indebtedness in Eastern Europe.

The IMF proposals having been adopted (after acrimonious debate), the government set about the task of drawing up a long-term programme for economic 'stabilisation', which has involved an extensive and complex series of institutional reforms. These have in many ways flown in the face of rooted ideological stances (a considerable liberalisation of the position of the private sector) and entrenched political interest (the reassertion of federal financial control in the banking system). The movement towards reform has been fraught with the most serious conflict, to the extent that in December 1988 the federal Prime Minister Branko Mikulić was forced to resign because of his failure to secure assent to his proposed budget. (This was the first such resignation in Yugoslavia's post-war history.) The package of reforms, which were still undergoing discussion and implementation at the time of writing, is far-reaching indeed, envisaging not only the reconstruction of the banking system, the foreign-exchange regime, the law relating to the economic participation of foreign enterprises and the law relating to private enterprise, but also the complete reconstruction of ZUR.

The circumstances in which Yugoslavia has undertaken these changes have posed their own problems. Not only was the country faced with the consequences of the 'second oil shock' of 1979 but also the general world depression of 1979–84. Delay in the reassertion of proper central control over economic policy had allowed the rate of inflation to climb to around 2,000 per cent per annum by the end of 1989. At the same time, the obvious and considerable internal economic stress of these developments has been reflected in heightened internal political tensions. The most dangerous of these has been the conflict over the constitutional status of the republic of Serbia, which resulted in the re-establishment of republican (Serb) hegemony over the predominantly Albanophone and Muslim Autonomous Province of Kosovo during 1989. In fact, inter-republican rivalries have reached such a peak of intensity in recent years as to spell the effective demise of the League of Communists of Yugoslavia as a unified political force, and have led some commentators (external and internal) to predict the disintegration of the country.

In spite of these difficulties, the reform programme has not been without its successes. Prime Minister Ante Marković has managed to see the most vital of his reforms on to the statute book—even if these have yet to be validated in practice. The hard-currency foreign debt was reduced to $17 billion by the end of 1989, and there was a trade surplus in convertible currency of around $2.5 billion in the previous year. With the other states of Eastern Europe, especially the Soviet Union, Yugoslavia also has a regular, massive trade surplus.

In January 1990, the Marković government announced that the dinar was to be made fully convertible, tied initially to the Deutschmark. Although the effects of this programme of reforms have yet to be fully assessed, their initial impact has been remarkable. At least in the short term, inflation has been eliminated. It is feared, however, that a direct consequence of these changes in the financial regime will be a rise in the relative price of the Yugoslav tourist product. Under these circumstances, it is plain that attention to the quality of what is offered will be of vital importance. Thus economic changes have underlined very forcibly the need of the industry to attend to issues such as marketing and the environment.

As in the former period of crisis in the 1960s, tourism has come to be recognised as having an important part to play in the attainment of economic stability. The new medium-term 'social plan' of 1981 had already identified tourism as an important sector, hoping to achieve around 64 million overnight stays by foreign tourists by the end of the plan-period in 1985. The economic potential of tourism was also emphasised in a memorandum submitted to the Krajger Commission (on economic stabilisation) by a team of eminent Yugoslav social scientists in 1982 (Vidaković 1982). Under the newly introduced regulations governing joint investment projects with foreign countries, tourism enterprises have not been slow to respond to the opportunity. At least two republican consortia (from Croatia and Montenegro) prepared publicity material which was being used to secure interest in new tourism projects on the part of foreign investors during 1989, covering in all 142 separate projects. (Croatian Chamber of Commerce 1989; Chamber of Economy of Montenegro, 1989).

Yugoslavia's awareness of the vital importance of tourism to its future economic well-being is illustrated also in the fact that Yugoslav experts and officials have been among the most active in the discussions surrounding problems relating to the control of marine pollution in the Mediterranean basin, and in the Adriatic in particular.

It is too early to assess their actual significance yet, but clearly the recently introduced changes in the laws relating to private enterprise and foreign investment, and the projected reform of the taxation system (especially as this impinges on the situation of smaller enterprises), have been designed with their relevance to the tourism sector in mind.

12.4 Patterns of change

Although the growth of Yugoslavia's tourist trade has been remarkable over the post-war period, that process has been by no means an even one. The patterns of change which can be documented bear the marks of the movements of policy outlined above.

Bearing in mind the strength of the industry in the pre-war period, its post-war recovery was slowed by the adhesion of the government to a policy of socialist reconstruction which subordinated tourism to the needs of industrial development and encouraged 'trade-union tourism'. Since the mid-1950s there has been a move towards a commitment to the expansion of foreign tourism. This observation must be qualified in two respects. The strength of that commitment has varied considerably, depending upon the political saliency of Yugoslavia's need to obtain hard foreign currency. The expansion of tourism has been repeatedly hampered by the distraction of internal economic and constitutional reform of one kind or another. Consequently, there have been periods of impressive growth associated with the economic reform of 1965 and with the post-1983 drive to 'stabilisation'. The years following the introduction of self-management in the 1950s and the politicisation of the economy under the ZUR after 1976, however, were both characterised by stagnation.

The political dimension of Yugoslavia's post-war development is also reflected in the distinctive regional pattern of growth. Yugoslavia possesses a great wealth of potential resources for tourism—in addition to its better-known coastal area, there is the historical legacy of its ancient cities, cultural monuments and health resorts, and inland areas of scenic beauty, particularly of the 'lakes and mountains' category. These hold out the possibility, in theory, of creating an industry with a wide geographical spread, and of offsetting to some extent excessive seasonality. These possibilities have only been realised to a limited extent in practice, however, as over the years since the war the measure of regional concentration of the trade has, if anything, increased, and a seasonal dispersion of visitors has hardly been achieved at all. Roughly a third of all tourists, and more than a half of their overnight stays, are accommodated during the two months of the peak season—July and August. The spas and other health resorts declined somewhat after the period of 'trade-union tourism', although they have held their share of around 5 per cent of the market since the 1960s. Mountain resorts have also only succeeded in sustaining their modest 8 or 9 per cent of volume. For both of these categories, domestic visitors provide a disproportionate amount of their custom.

At one level the rigidity of these patterns can be seen as the result of unadventurous marketing. Spas, for example, have only been featured in the Yugotours brochure since the late 1980s. Here again, however, it makes sense to read these developments in policy terms. The fact that types of resort other than the coastal have not been marketed more vigorously has to do in part directly with the failure to modernise their facilities to a standard which is

Table 12.6 Yugoslavia's principal resorts, by type and rank order*

Type of resort†	Resort	Rank order
Capital cities	Belgrade	=1
	Zagreb	3
	Ljubljana	6
	Sarajevo	12
	Skopje	14
	Novi Sad	=25
Spas	Vrnjačka Banja	=8
	Soko Banja	17
	Ilidža	=29
Coastal	Dubrovnik	=1
	Budva	4
	Herceg Novi	5
	Crikvenica	=8
	Split	10
	Makarska	11
	Šibenik	13
	Selce	16
	Baška	20
	Novi Vinodolski	21
	Hrvar	=22
	Malinska	=22
	Rab	=25
	Korčula	=27
	Krk	=27
	Orebić	28
Lakes and mountains	Ohrid	7
	Bled	15
	Zlatibor	18
	Kranjska Gora	19
	Plitvice	24
	Bohinj	=29

Source: Jugoslavia, 1989, pp. 345–6

* The items are arranged in rank order according to a score which combines both numbers of tourists and the number of their overnight stays at each resort

† 'Resorts' are those places officially classified as 'tourist destinations' in Yugoslav official statistics

acceptable to the foreign visitor. The direction of investment has been, as previously argued, a rather haphazard affair, in which the development of resources has largely been left to regional (republican) or local authorities. The concentration of Yugoslavia's principal resorts on the Adriatic reflects in part, therefore, the more sustained commitment of Croatian interests at all levels to the creation of a tourist industry (see Figure 12.1 and Table 12.6). Similarly, the emergence of Ohrid to the rank of seventh in the country's tourist destinations reflects the determination of the Macedonian republic to gain a slice of the tourist cake. Both Zagreb and Sarajevo have benefited enormously from the injection of funds into the area to support international sporting

Figure 12.1 Yugoslavia's principal tourist resorts

fixtures (the University Games and the Winter Olympic Games respectively), and Belgrade was recently given a very expensive face-lift to prepare it as the destination for the Ninth Summit Conference of the Non-Aligned Movement. The current attempts to market Serbia's monasteries and other ancient cultural monuments can also be seen as flowing from the upsurge of Serbian nationalism.

On the negative side of the balance, clearly the political context of tourism has seriously limited some aspects of its development. Most notably, the place of pilgrimage at Medjugorje, in Hercegovina—known throughout the Roman Catholic community world-wide—has at best been tolerated by the authorities. The village does not figure in the list of 'resorts' in Yugoslav official statistics—and visitors are largely reported in the form of figures for places such as Dubrovnik, through which many arrivals come by air. The place is only sign-posted at the local level, making it quite difficult to find for the traveller who is not a member of an organised pilgrimage group.

Of more general significance has been the combination of neglect and discouragement suffered by the private sector until recently. While contributing a significant proportion of the fund of accommodation available, political conditions have generally confined private entrepreneurial activity to the offering of lodging in private homes and the operation of small businesses such as restaurants and taxi hire. The impact of political attitudes in this respect has varied considerably between regions and even localities. While plentifully available along the coast, the free availability of private rooms inland is largely confined to areas such as the Plitvice lakes, Postojna caves and the various skiing centres.

12.5 Tourism and the environment

In common with the other countries of Central and Eastern Europe, Yugoslavia has also experienced a number of conflicts over environmental issues in relation to tourism, although on the whole these have been less severe than in other places. The principal occasion for these has been the inadvisable location of industrial plant, often for political reasons, in the early post-war years, when the current dogma of development stressed the primacy of heavy industry. The results of some of these decisions have ranged from the unsightly presence of industrial dirt in or adjacent to tourist centres (the steel works in Jesenice, on the edge of the Julian Alps), through vigorous local controversy (the chemical pollution of the coastal waters near Split) to near catastrophe (the narrow aversion of the complete death of the river Tara, in Montenegro, by effluent from a lead smelter). Little is available in English on these issues (although see Coley 1985), and Yugoslav tourism experts remain silent. In some cases, by way of contrast, local interests have acted strenuously in order to try to limit any environmental damage which might be occasioned by the growth of tourism. The development of Ohrid, in Macedonia, as a resort is a case in point. (Even here, it remains to be seen whether the laudable ambitions of the civic authorities have been realised in practice.)

One factor which has made life easier for the Yugoslavs in this respect has been the fact that the country's principal zone of tourist development has been the Adriatic coast, which at the end of the last war was an economic backwater, in which tourism has been allowed to develop without substantial competition from other economic sectors.

On the other hand, Yugoslavia's highly decentralised system of self-management has made for difficulties in the identification of responsibility for the control of environmental problems. Also the relatively under-developed nature of the country's administrative structure has meant that the enforcement of the law relating to a number of planning matters has lagged seriously behind the real growth of the problem. There has been particular difficulty with the 'wild' construction of housing in and around tourist centres. The fragmented and clientilistic nature of political structures has also enabled local cliques of political and economic grandees to force through projects which have been, to say the least, questionable on environmental grounds.

12.6 Tourism and socialism

The Yugoslav achievement has been considerable (Allcock 1986). With an annual inflow of more than 9 million foreign guests, representing about 4 per cent of total European turnover (and a domestic trade in excess of 13 million tourists in 1988) the country undoubtedly has achieved a pre-eminence as an international tourist destination among the states of Eastern Europe (Buckley and Witt 1990). The Yugoslavs clearly place the greatest hopes in its future, as official projects envisage 2.2 million beds by the year 2000, earning revenues of some $6.8 billion. But in the extremely uncertain political climate of Eastern Europe at the start of the 1990s, few would wish to hazard a prediction of their likely success.

Yugoslavs (and academic experts on Yugoslavia) are fond of emphasising the differences which set the country off from the rest of Eastern Europe. Some, indeed, contend that Yugoslavia is not 'Eastern European' at all. Discussion of this point could easily degenerate into the blatantly ideological posturing which currently surrounds the attempt of Hungarians to assert the specifically Central European character of their culture. On the other hand, there is a serious issue to be examined here, in that the Yugoslavs have not abandoned claims to have developed a form of socialist system, and the experience of their tourist industry illustrates well several problems which apparently do recur in all forms of socialism. The distinctive features of the Yugoslav experience are not trivial, but they do mask deeper continuities with that of their neighbours with hitherto more obviously conventional economies of the centrally planned type. There are four aspects of the Yugoslav development of tourism which do stand out as special.

12.6.1 *Distinctive features of the Yugoslav experience*

Yugoslavia has a relatively long experience of international tourism which undoubtedly gives a variety and depth to the range of tourist facilities which it has to offer. Experience does count at a number of different levels, and one of the greatest assets which Yugoslavia possesses in this respect is the institutionalisation of traditions of service of a reasonably sophisticated kind which have led to relatively high standards of satisfaction among foreign guests. This gives a degree of stability to the industry which is not enjoyed in those countries whose tourist industry simply has been built upon price advantage or the operation of limitations on the freedom of travel.

Although Yugoslavia entered the post-war period committed to the kind of 'trade-union' or 'social' tourism which has been typical of the other states of the region, it was forced quite early to abandon this under the impact of external events. Yugoslavia very soon developed a genuine openness to travel. There have never been anything resembling 'ghetto' settlements for foreign tourists, even though differential rates and currency provisions have been employed at certain times. This development has been fostered very largely by economic motives, and the tourist industry can be seen to exemplify in many respects Yugoslavia's 'market socialism'.

Probably the aspect of the Yugoslav system which has attracted the greatest attention from foreign commentators in the past has been its 'self-managing socialism'. The most significant feature of this in many respects, as illustrated in this chapter, is the fact that the 'system', since 1953, has passed through a complex series of major revisions: in 1963–5, 1974–6 and again in the current period. These changes have not been purely cosmetic but have entailed significant shifts of emphasis between local (communal or enterprise), regional (republican) and federal levels of responsibility. The abandonment of the Stalinist model of central planning has meant for Yugoslavia, therefore, a constant process of adjustment in the entire nature of social and economic policy-making. In many ways this process has been very disruptive for Yugoslavia's tourist industry.

Finally, one of the benefits of this process has been that where local and regional elites have been able to see economic advantages in tourism, they have been able, within the system, to capitalise upon them. The constant 'failure' of Yugoslavia's tourism trade to realise the succession of planning targets should not be taken as negating this point. There is no independent measure of the rationality of these targets. Regionalism is seen typically by political scientists looking at Yugoslavia as a source of 'problems'. While there is a great deal of truth in that, the relative independence of regional centres of power has also been on occasions a distinctive strength, and this is illustrated well in the development of tourism, especially in Croatia.

12.6.2 *Common features of the Yugoslav experience*

Five features of the development of tourism in Yugoslavia, on the other hand, bear close resemblance to the situation in other Eastern European countries and suggest that there is merit in treating the countries together.

Although much has been made of the way in which Yugoslavia has attempted to introduce 'market socialism' well in advance of any of the other countries of Eastern Europe, the extent of its real achievements in this direction can be exaggerated. The tourism and catering sector has been the recipient of a wide range of political measures which have interfered substantially with the market for the factors of production: controlled interest rates for loans; 'retention quotas' and other aspects of exchange control; legislative limitations on the development of the private sector; and many others. Yugoslav social scientists currently appear to have reached a broad consensus with respect to the character of the present crisis of their country in that they emphasise the continuing importance of various forms of political control over economic processes. Any close study of the development of tourism in Yugoslavia will reveal the limited extent to which 'market socialism' has been realised in practice.

Three aspects of the continuing influence of state-socialist approaches to economic problems are illustrated in Yugoslav tourism. First of all, one encounters here, as elsewhere, the tendency of central planners in socialist systems to think in terms of the expansion of aggregate 'production' targets without giving adequate attention to questions of the integration of services, the standards achieved and the need to market the product properly.

This is closely related in practice to the indifference or even hostility to the private sector. In common with other Eastern European countries, Yugoslavia has had a persistent difficulty in developing small businesses, largely a result of the limitations placed on the freedom of the individual entrepreneur. Whereas individuals have made a very significant contribution to tourism in the offer of accommodation and in catering, Yugoslavs themselves within the industry have repeatedly stressed the under-utilisation of potential here. Certainly Yugoslavia has been ahead of its colleague-states in this respect, but the difference is one of degree rather than kind.

The most prominent similarity between the Yugoslav experience and that of other centrally planned economies has been the almost obsessive concern of those involved in tourism with its potential to earn convertible foreign currency. Early in the post-war period, Yugoslavs came to appreciate the significance of tourism in this respect and this is an aspect of tourism policy which predominates in Eastern European thinking about tourism more generally. The fact is that tourism has become important everywhere in the region as a means of obtaining the supply of hard currency which is necessary to offset other aspects of the economic weakness of the system of socialist planning. Without the combination of earnings from its workers abroad and its foreign tourist trade, the Yugoslav economy would have been long ago in even more desperate straits than it is now.

Finally, at the time of writing the whole of Eastern Europe is enduring acute political and economic turmoil. Whereas in many respects these developments are accompanied by a great sense of hope and excitement both within and without the region, we are standing on the threshold of a period of change the dimensions of which cannot yet be fully grasped. Yugoslavia is no exception to this. To the country's generally acknowledged economic difficulties must be added the burden of inter-ethnic conflict. Tourism is notoriously sensitive to political disorder. Tourists like to feel safe. Essential as it is to the economic stability of Yugoslavia, its tourist trade could readily be endangered by any serious deterioration in the conditions of internal order. In that respect also, therefore, Yugoslavia can be seen to be sharing a common destiny with the rest of Eastern Europe.

13 Albania

Derek R. Hall

13.1 Introduction

Flanked by the tourist economies of Greece and Yugoslavia, yet physically enclosed by high fringing mountains, and ideologically detached, Albania's fascinating blend of natural and cultural elements presents the potential for one of the finest holiday environments in Europe. However, the very features which make it so attractive, coupled to the country's economic and political circumstances, have conspired to confound any significant exploitation of this potential.

The smallest of the states reviewed in this volume, with a population of 3.3 million, Albania is no larger than Wales or Sardinia or the American state of Maryland, measuring some 340 kilometres north–south and 150 kilometres east–west at its widest point. The 472-kilometre coastline borders the Adriatic and Ionian seas and is characterised by sandy beaches, rocky promontories and sheltered harbours. The climate reflects both Mediterranean and continental influences with hot dry summers and changeable, often wet weather in late autumn and winter. About 70 per cent of the country's territory lies above 300 metres and 30 per cent is above one thousand metres. Albania's mountains are the southern continuation of the Dinaric Alpine range: young folded uplands aligned south-east to north-west and dissected by anticlinal domes and tectonic basins. These mountains act as a barrier between the Mediterranean climate of the coastal plain and continental conditions further inland. Annual precipitation in the mountains rises to over 2,000 millimetres: snow cover extends from early winter to late spring.

Successively colonised by Greeks, Romans, Huns and Visigoths, Albania then succumbed to Turkish invasion in the fifteenth century and was nominally removed from Europe for almost half a millenium: the Turkish influence on language, culture and religion remains. In the late nineteenth century, Albanian nationalist movements began to echo developments elsewhere in Central and Eastern Europe: notional independence from the waning Ottoman Empire was gained just prior to the First World War. During the inter-war Zog regime Albanian interests were increasingly subordinated to Italian economic aspirations, which culminated in military occupation of Albania in 1939. The Italians were briefly followed by the Germans before the establishment in 1944 of a socialist republic.

This new republic narrowly escaped absorption into post-war Yugoslavia when the latter was expelled by Stalin from the Soviet bloc in 1948. This secured the position of Albania's communist leader Enver Hoxha, who was then able to purge all potential internal opposition as being pro-Yugoslav. Hoxha's reverence of Stalin was life-long, and relations were broken with the Soviet Union in 1961 and with China in 1978 when he considered those countries to have reneged on Stalinist principles. Following Hoxha's death in 1985 the country's leadership continued to denounce developments in the rest of Eastern Europe, equating *perestroika* with a restoration of capitalism (Pellumbi 1988; Zanga 1989b, 1989c). In contrast to this rhetoric, the Ninth Plenum of the Central Committee in January 1990 unveiled a range of economic, political and social readjustments, evidently designed to defuse the growing unrest fuelled by events elsewhere in Eastern Europe.

Albania's near-obsession with cultural and economic independence had hitherto been rooted in an historical context: much was made by the country's leadership of the Albanian's pride in self-reliance (for example Gurashi and Ziri 1982). In 1976 this stance was institutionalised by Article 28 of the new constitution, which precluded the taking on of external loans or credits. While this position projected a steadfast image to the outside world, it also presented a considerable stumbling block to economic development and to relations with other members of the 'common European home'. As this volume was going to press, this policy was clearly undergoing reassessment, and major implications for tourism development appeared inevitable.

13.2 Historical aspects of tourism and recreation

Economic and social retardation under the Ottoman Empire and the area's isolation from Western Europe resulted in little tourism development before the 1920s. By the middle of that decade, Etherton and Allen (1928, p. 195) could report on an interview with the then President Zog in which

> . . . he discussed affairs in Albania, the improvements he wants to carry out to attract the tourist, and the ups and downs in his country, all of which must be attended to before Albania can be converted into another of Europe's playgrounds as he plans to do . . . he was a strong believer in road development. He asked our opinion of the hotels, and when we told him that the country must equip itself with better ones, decided to inspect them and endeavour to provide amenities for tourists.

Yet in the late 1920s and through the 1930s, facilities for travellers were minimal, and leisure facilities for the domestic population, apart from the small political and social elite, were virtually nil. A limited number of hotels gradually developed in the major towns, largely for business travellers. The picture of other types of accommodation is sketchy. Albanians were renowned as ready hosts for any stranger, as famous earlier travellers in the country such as Edward Lear (1851; Hyman 1988) and Edith Durham (1909) have testified. By the inter-war period this hospitality was exemplified by the Bektashi Islamic sect, whose monastery near Krujë became a well-known source of accommodation for Western travellers (McCulloch 1936, pp. 170–1; Hamsher 1937, pp. 88–90; Matthews 1937, pp. 71–84). Later foreign implants, in addition to Italian hoteliers, included the Albanian–American Institute, near Kavajë. This was an agricultural school operated by the Near East Foundation, much frequented by foreign travellers (McCulloch 1936, pp. 164–6; Hamsher

1937, p. 92). Modern tourism in inter-war Albania is certainly poorly documented, although Diack and Mackenzie (1935, p. 188) noted some development at what is now the country's main tourist centre at Durrës Beach.

Access to the country was variable. McCulloch (1936, p. 135) could report an over-night boat service from Bari, on the Italian coast, and the availability of chartering small motor boats across the Ionian Sea between Sarandë and Corfu. Lyall (1930, pp. 148–9) had earlier travelled by Lake Shkodër steamer from the Yugoslav village of Rjeka via Virpazar to Shiroka, the southern lakeside village which acted as the outport for Shkodër when the water level was too low to travel further. Today Shiroka is favoured by Albanian day-trippers from Shkodër, and Lezhë. In the mid-1930s, one could fly from Thessalonika to Tirana, a comfortable two-hour journey in an Italian plane, or even travel on the twice weekly Italian flight to Shkodër. By 1939, a thrice-weekly service connected Tirana with Rome, Thessalonika, Sofia and Bucharest. With internal civil aviation centred on Tirana, a daily flight linked the capital with Shkodër. Podgorica (Titograd) and Cetinje in Montenegro. Further connections were provided to Durrës, Vlorë, Gjirokastër, Korçë and Kukës. A total of five airfields and nine landing grounds plus three seaplane alighting areas were recorded for the country (Mason *et al.* 1945, pp. 339–40). Today only Rinas airport, north of Tirana, is used for regular commercial purposes.

Road access into Albania was northwards from Ioannina, or south or westwards from Yugoslavia by one of several routes. The most infamous of these was at Han i Hotit, in the extreme north of country, used today by travellers entering from Titograd. Today the foreign tourists' inaugural trudge across the hundred metres of no-man's land laden with luggage and foreboding, towards an armed border guard, has become firmly entrenched in the pantheon of European travel-writers' clichés (for example Newby 1985, pp. 111–12). Lyall (1930, p. 167) could write of the spot in the late 1920s:

> Soon we came to an extraordinary country, where great grey rocks stood up like statues out of the scrub-oak, anything up to twenty feet high. A perfect place for an ambush . . . we crossed a stream; on the opposite hill a stone marked the actual frontier . . . Next we had to cross a river flanked by a broad, reedy swamp, over which ran a crazy wooden bridge about a quarter of a mile in length . . . It was, I think, the worst bridge I have ever seen . . .

Thus the nature of pre-war access to and travel within Albania, coupled with generally impoverished economic conditions and potentially unstable political circumstances, constrained any significant tourism development.

During the Italian occupation, the then opulent Dajti Hotel was built in Tirana, and remains today as the capital's hotel for businessmen and diplomats, contrasting with the much brasher and more recent 14-storey Hotel Tirana and its package tourists.

In 1956 a state tourism organisation, Albturist, was established with Soviet assistance, following the Intourist model. An international tourist industry based largely on visitors from the socialist world was developing but was cut short by the Sino–Soviet rupture and the end of Soviet influence in 1961. Albania's tourism potential had been recognised by Czechs and Russians in the 1950s (Albturist 1969; Ward 1983), both groups taking a particular interest in the 'riviera' coast between Vlorë and Sarandë. The Czechs had hoped to develop Dhërmi on the Ionian coast as a holiday complex for their own workers. To the north, Soviet aid had helped to establish the five-hotel complex at Durrës Beach, which today remains the largest concentration of international-standard tourist accommodation in the country. Khrushchev is said to have looked upon Albania as the potential Mediterranean playground for the rest of the Soviet bloc. 'Khrushchev came here and had a look. "Don't spoil the landscape with industries", he said, "Let's have a socialist division of labour. We'll industrialise ourselves, and you can grow lemons. Then we'll come here to you to swim". But then our government said, "Comrade Khrushchev, we've no intention of becoming a spa for Soviet functionaries. We've in mind to follow Comrade Stalin's advice and industrialise our country."' [Myrdal and Kessle 1978, p. 14] However, the Soviet opinion persists: 'The stable warm dry weather, the sandy beaches, the abundance of fruits, the existence of picturesque mountain localities and spas near the sea create favourable prerequisites for the development of recreational facilities and tourism' (Alisov *et al.* 1985, p. 234). Yet it was Albania's strategic position—the only Soviet-bloc state having direct access to the Mediterranean after Yugoslavia's expulsion from the bloc in 1948—which the Soviets most valued.

Table 13.1 Albania: international standard hotels

Period of building	No. of hotels	Approx. no. of beds	Locations
Pre-1953	1	150	Tirana
1953–62	7	1,630	Durrës, Fier, Gjirokastër
1963–72	1	100	Berat
1973–82	11	1,500	Elbasan, Korçë, Krujë, Kukës, Lezhë, Përmet, Peshkopi, Pogradec, Sarandë, Shkodër, Tirana
1983–8	0	—	—
1989+	3	300	Ardenicë, Berat, Vlorë

Sources: Albturist (various); author's field observations (1974–90)

With deteriorating Sino–Albanian relations in the early 1970s, a hotel-building programme commensurate with an expansionist foreign-tourism policy was inaugurated, such that between 1973 and 1982 11 hotels were built, providing approximately 1,500 beds—almost doubling Albanian international standard accommodation capacity (Table 13.1).

At existing tourist locations, this programme permitted older, poorly equipped hotels to be devoted purely to internal use and aided the gradual opening up of new tourist routes and venues. The new hotels at Kukës and Peshkopi, and at Përmet, helped to upgrade infrastructure in the country's mountainous north-east and south-east respectively and to facilitate the gradual opening of those regions for tourism purposes. Facilities and resting places on existing tourist itineraries could also be elaborated, as at Berat fortress, Drilon, Fier, Këlcyrë, Ksamil, Vlorë and Uji i Ftohtë. This latter consolidation

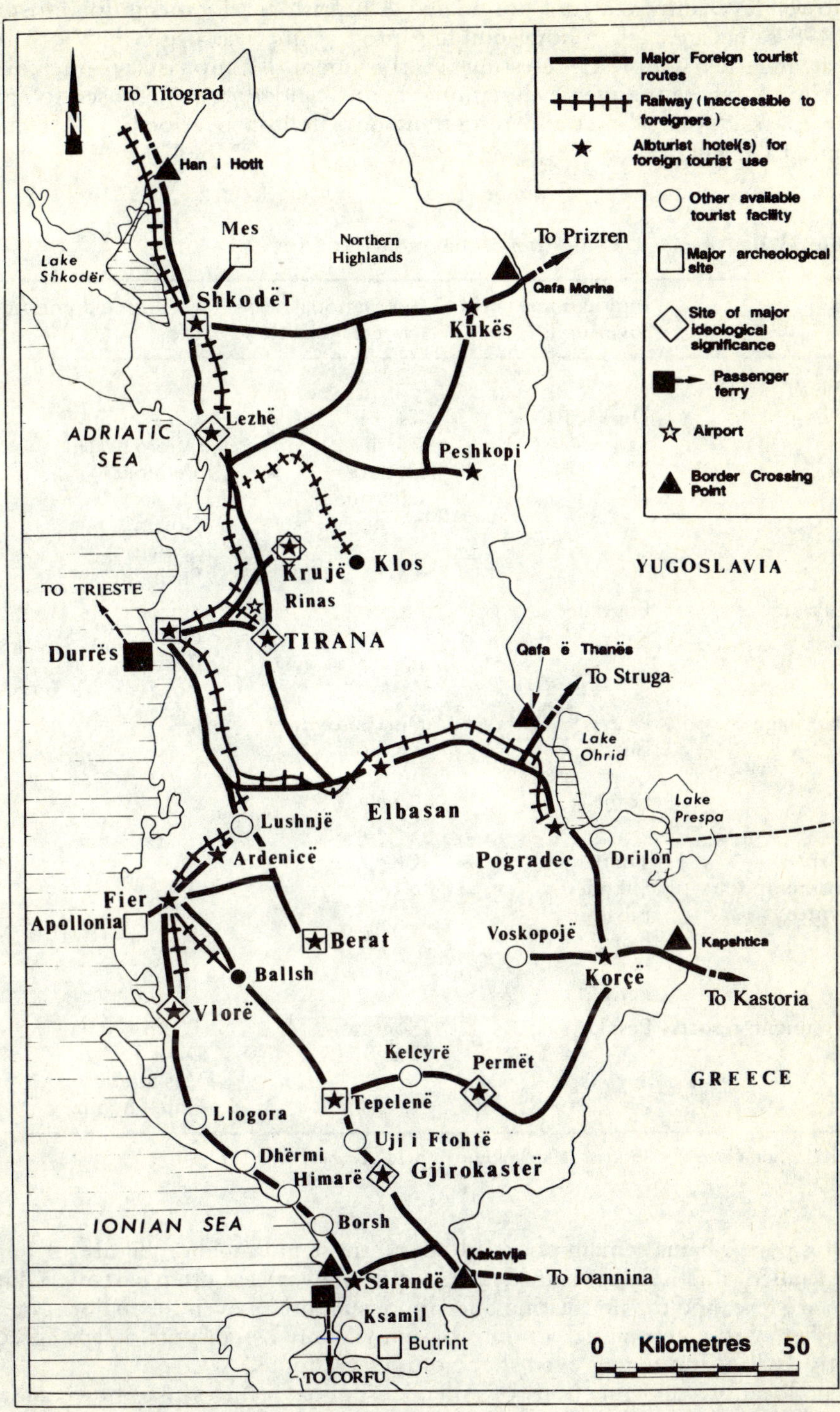

Figure 13.1 Albania: tourist centres and routes

of lower-level infrastructure dominated Albturist developments for most of the 1980s, before again a hotel-building programme was begun in Vlorë and Berat, together with the interesting refurbishment of a monastery—including the church where the medieval national hero Skanderbeg is supposed to have been married—as a hotel and restaurant on a hilltop overlooking Ardenicë (Table 13.1, Fig. 13.1).

Table 13.2 Albania: classification of main tourist centres

Use	International stays (overnight)	International stops (*en route* facilities)	Exclusive domestic use
Typology			
1. Coasts	Durrës Beach Sarandë	Ksamil Borsh Himarë Dhermi	Uji i Ftohtë (Vlorë beach) Velipojë Divjaka Golem Seman Shëngjin
2. Lakesides	Pogradec Kukës	Drilon	Shiroka Lura Razma Boga
3. 'Heritage' sites	Krujë Berat Gjirokastër Lezhë	Durrës town Apollonia Butrint Tepelenë Rozafat	
4. Urban 'contemporary' centres	Tirana Shkodër Elbasan Korçë Fier Përmët	Kavajë	
5. Mountain resorts	Peshkopi	Llogora Këlcyrë	Theth Dajti Voskopojë Qafë Shtama

Sources: Anon (1989c); Albturist (1969); author's field observations (1974–90)

Roads in Albania remain poor. Although those indicated on Figure 13.1 are all metalled, maintenance is inadequate, carriageways are often narrow, white lines are few, and the undulating and sinuous nature of even the major routes, together with a substantial amount of animal-drawn transport, keeps speeds relatively low and render even short journeys arduous.

The locations and functions of Albanian holiday centres may be classified into five main types, which in their turn can be further defined according to their degree of international or domestic tourism exclusivity (Table 13.2).

13.3 Tourism administration

The country's tourist organisation, Albturist, represents the state monopoly machinery covering all tourist activities—accommodation, catering, transport, foreign exchange shopping, guides, and contacts with foreign travel organisations. Usually no more than a handful of tourist companies, and often far fewer, represent each interested (and acceptable) foreign country from which tourists are recruited for 'package' holidays. Friendship groups and other ideologically committed associations also despatch delegations. The organisation is responsible to Albania's Ministry of Internal trade, with a Directorate based in Tirana and branches located in 14 other tourist centres. It is responsible for both foreign and internal tourists, although as noted below, the latter's vacational requirements are usually dealt with through their trade-union organisation or on an individual basis.

Albturist is organised into seven departments, covering relations with foreign countries, hotels, catering, planning, transport and hard-currency shops. The most recently established department, that for publicity and propaganda, reflects a sea change in attitudes towards tourism stimulation. Within the department concerned with relations with foreign countries, there are five sections, representing the major foreign-language groups of visitors to the country.

13.4 Access to the country

At the time of writing, six airlines (Interflug, MALEV, TAROM, Olympic, Swissair and Air France) operated a total of nine round trips into Albania every week; a regular flight from Sofia was planned by Balkan Air. The country's first post-war international ferry service, between Durrës and Trieste, was inaugurated in 1984, but while claiming to accommodate passengers, it functions essentially as mail and freight transport (Hall 1987a). Two years later the long-awaited through railway line from Durrës to Titograd was inaugurated (Hall 1985a, 1985b, 1987a, 1990b), but this has been dogged by poor inter-state relations. Although used only for goods transport, there have recently been suggestions that international through passenger services could be introduced on the line.

In May 1989, a passenger ferry was inaugurated between Corfu and the southern Albanian resort town of Sarandë, largely for the purpose of day excursions to Albania, at a frequency of two sailings per week during the summer months. This venture was being operated by Corfiote entrepreneurs and had survived to a second season. Re-introducing the concept of 'day-trippers' into Albania, albeit within the constraints of a strict Albturist regulation, this development represented the first link between Albania and the nearby Greek island for 40 years. Tourist entry from Greece is otherwise limited to one land route and a weekly air service from Ioannina. Few other regular land connections exist: a reintroduced series of day-visits from Dubrovnik to Durrës and Tirana via the northern border crossing point of Han i Hotit, and, from January 1990, a regular coach service between Korçë and Istanbul.

13.5 Domestic tourism

Albanians have long flocked to the coast in summer, the range of coastal resorts available for domestic tourism being far wider than that offered to foreigners (Figures 13.1, 13.2, Table 13.2), not least because of infrastructural constraints.

The greatest concentration of both international and domestic tourism accommodation and activities is focused in and around Durrës Beach. Here, working people from all over the country come to the country's most extensive beach and stay in a wide range of accommodation, comprising hotels, villas, and a pyramidal five-storey apartment block, as well as stable-like terraced huts both on and off the beach. Shops, kiosks, a post office, cinema, circus site and other facilities are ranged along the main road which backs onto the beach area. To the south of the international hotel complex are villas and gardens, high-walled and armed-guarded, presumably for higher party and government members, also adjacent to the beach. South beyond these are further public beaches.

Next in importance is the major city, port and holiday centre of Vlorë. It is here that the Adriatic Sea ends and the bluer Ionian begins, and with several sandy bays the coast extends south to Sarandë, where the tourist hotel used by foreign tour groups is also a favourite for Albanian honeymooners. Facing the island of Corfu and enjoying spectacular sunsets, the town is claimed to receive a daily average of eight hours' sunshine. A beach-side trade-union hotel complex was opened here in the late 1980s. As Gardiner (1976 p. 57) observed:

> Sarandë marks the southern limit of Bregdeti, 'the coast', the red riviera . . . I would nominate it for the title of the most beautiful sixty miles of Mediterranean shore. That it is also the least developed goes without saying. Cruise passengers in the Adriatic see this shoreline through binoculars, but they don't see the half of it—not the frying-pan-shaped inlets,the lake-isles of Porto Palermo, the turquoise gulfs near Dhërmi and Borsh, the rivers of olives and avalanches of orange and mandarin bushes which flow down from the heights of Llogora . . . a littoral made for tourism, a littoral where hardly a tourist has ventured if you except the young Albanians who caper in the sea in the vicinity of a State holiday home.

Inland, the country's lakes and mountains are currently exploited almost exclusively for domestic use. Albania shares three major lakes with its neighbours, and of these Shkodër and Ohrid are by far the most significant, with Pogradec on the western shore of the latter the most important resort, with the best lake beach facilities. Here as elsewhere water sports, particularly those employing motorised craft, have tended to be inhibited, both by the economic situation and by the tight control on population movement in border areas.

In the alpine north-east mountains foreign tourists are limited to stop-overs in the towns of Kukës and Peshkopi. Still relatively inaccessible to large vehicles, the health resort and walking centre of Theth is possibly the best known in the region. From here, peaks of up to 2,600 metres are accessible. Close by are the lake resorts of Lura, Razma and Boga, in the heart of the Albanian Alps. Domestic facilities also exist in mountain resorts located close to the capital, particularly on the Dajti mountain, at Qafë Shtama, in the centre of the country, and in the south-east at Korçë and Voskopojë, the latter being a popular centre for children.

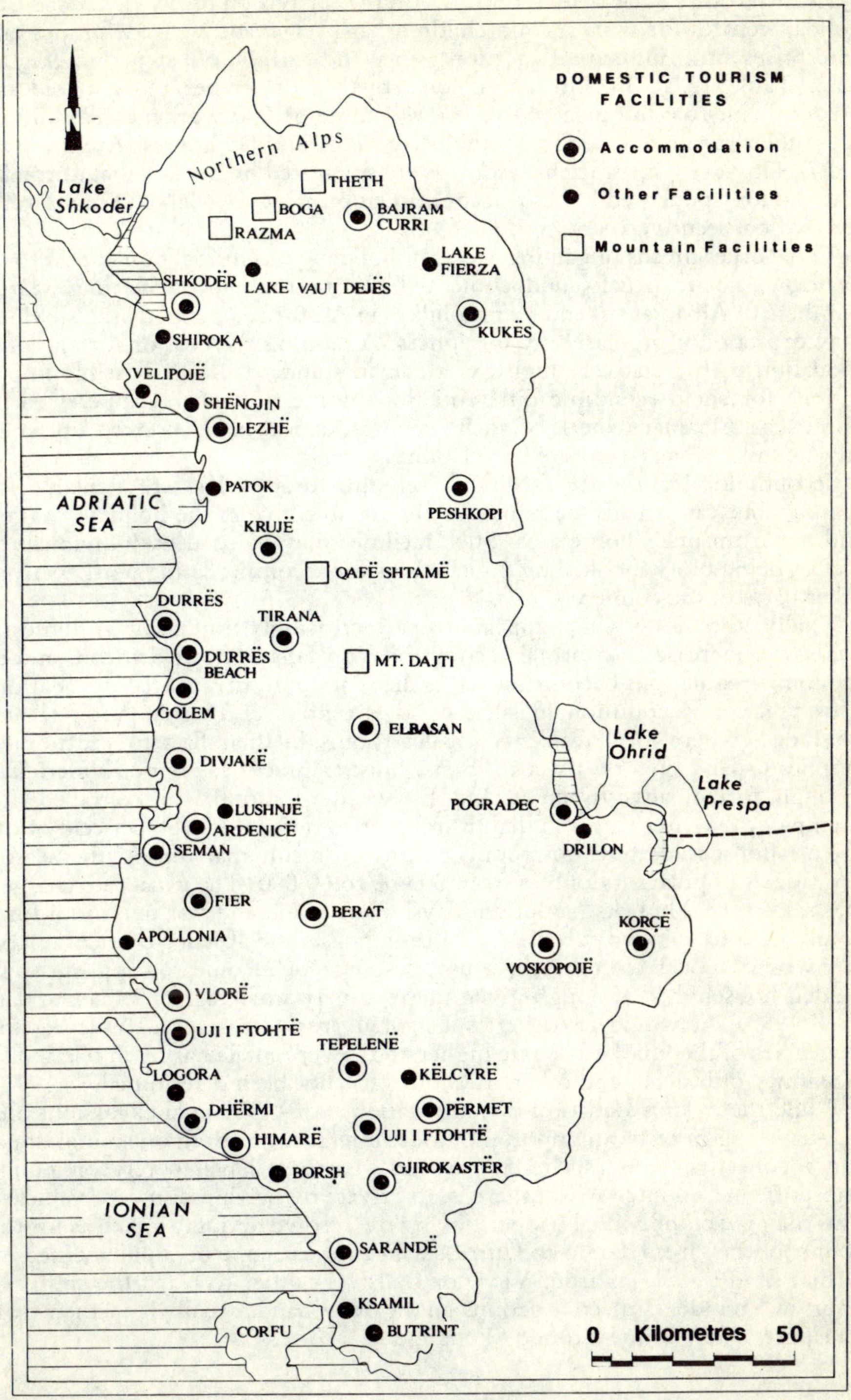

Figure 13.2 Albania: distribution of known domestic tourism facilities

As in all other societies within this volume, provision of heavily subsidised holiday centres for workers and children has been made by trade unions and enterprises in a number of locations since the early socialist period (Figure 13.2, Table 13.2). In Albania, it appears that the trades unions hold the predominant role in this activity. In 1989 some 61,000 workers and children spent their summer vacations in the network of holiday homes (Anon 1989c, p. 27). However, insufficient resources are suggested by the fact that normally trade-union sponsored holiday accommodation is not available to any family for two consecutive years.

Three other means of gaining access to holiday accommodation appear to be available, albeit virtually undocumented. At the top end of the range, large numbers of Albanians spend their holidays in Albturist-operated hotels, which may or may not be shared by foreigners. Assuming the cost of such accommodation to be relatively high by Albanian standards, with possible implications for socio-economic differentiation, domestic demand appears to be unmet, as Albanians speak of such accommodation being booked up far in advance and of very restricted availability.

Second, local authority facilities, including beach huts, are available for renting, but can usually be booked only via an office in the holiday location and not from one's home area. Such facilities may be used by individuals as well as being block-booked by trade unions for accommodating workers from other parts of the country.

Finally, the mode which appears to be increasingly important as domestic recreation increases, as formal accommodation fails to meet demand, and as economic regulations become looser, is the renting of private accommodation. This practice is common in such holiday centres as Durrës, Sarandë and Pogradec, where local residents sub-let rooms in their flats to vacationing families usually on a two-weekly basis. Such transactions are not undertaken through formal advertisement, but by word of mouth. In Pogradec, for example, the writer was told that in summer something like 80 per cent of the town's households hire out rooms, with the result that during the season Pogradec's population doubles from 30,000 to 60,000. The usual rate charged was said to be 200 Leks (about ten days' average income) for one room for a family of four for two weeks. As Albania boasts the absence of income tax, this would appear to represent a useful source of income for appropriately located households, although given the relatively small size of Albanian flats (Hall 1990a), it would also exert substantial pressure of space. Whether the exigencies of the 'market' dictate higher and lower rental charges in relation to proximity of beaches and other attractions has not been determined.

While there is no statistical documentation, non-residential excursions and day-trips appear to be an important mode of recreation. Both on an individual and a collective basis, such activities do of course have to rely on public transport, in a country where there is no private ownership of motor vehicles. This may entail individual trippers taking overcrowded trains—such as for the hour's journey from Tirana to Durrës, which may need to be supplemented by further road travel—as from Vlorë or Ballsh, in order to reach the southern resort of Sarandë. Collective groups on the other hand, usually have their own transport, albeit a time-expired Skoda bus.

13.6 International tourism

13.6.1 Balancing the tourism trade-off

The pursuit of foreign tourism by a developing country can have considerable social, economic and political consequences. For hitherto enclosed and strongly ideological societies such as Albania, fears of alien influences and 'contagion' contracted by host populations who come into direct contact with tourists can be substantial. Tourism planners have therefore attempted to maximise the economic benefits to be derived from the industry while minimising its potentially adverse social and environmental impact.

Albania has made considerable efforts to maintain this balance with a 'prescriptive' approach to tourism development. This has included the following key policy characteristics:

1. The group visa system, which has required potential visitors to subscribe to a group tour at least two months before the planned visit, and has acted to screen out those considered to be undesirable.
2. Up to the early 1980s the country rigidly adhered to the notion that tourists should conform to a particular dress sense. Albania's points of entry thus had resident barbers and tailors whose role was to 'advise' new arrivals on Albanian notions of sartorial appropriateness.
3. Much Western literature is still proscribed, particularly if of a political, religious or vaguely titillating nature.
4. Foreign tourists have been required to enter the country and move around within it as a permanent, coherent group of usually a minimum of 15 members. Such groups' conspicuousness has contributed to the ease of their 'policing'. Contact with the local population has been kept to a minimum, although an increasing degree of personal contact between foreign tourist and native Albanians has been possible since the mid-1980s.
5. Itineraries, official guides, transport and accommodation are all prescribed, being provided specifically and exclusively by Albturist. Visitors in groups stay in Albturist hotels, on a full-board basis: the opportunity for foreigners to stay in the homes of ordinary Albanians remains nil. This is particularly ironic in view of the well-known traditional Albanian hospitality shown towards guests. Most Albturist hotels appear to be patronised by Albanians, but foreigners tend to be segregated—often none too successfully—in separate dining rooms and hotel floors.

The use of public transport was, until, recently, implicitly proscribed for foreigners unless accompanied by an Albturist official. Local buses may now be used, but even Tirana is of a sufficiently limited scale to permit the traveller to explore most of the city on foot. The expanding railway system (Hall 1984a, 1987a, 1990b) is both slow and 'off-limits'. There is a limited scope for taxi travel in the capital, and some bicycle hire facilities, but no car hire or out-of-town independent travel: outer-urban road checks preclude even the consideration of such activities at present. Private ownership of motor vehicles by Albanians is prohibited, but hitching lifts in collectively owned lorries and other vehicles appears to be an important, if informal, domestic mode of transport, particularly in the countryside.

13.6.2 The heritage factor

Entailing pre-historic, classical, medieval and recent historical assemblages and artefacts, a range of 'heritage' experiences is available to both international and domestic tourists. This is institutionalised by the designation of Berat and Gjirokastër as 'museum cities', of Krujë as a 'hero city', and of 'museum zones' covering sections of cities such as Durrës and Shkodër. Such important archaeological sites as Apollonia and Butrint, which feature on most foreign tourist itineraries, are safeguarded by the state, and as yet have not been burdened with tourist-related commercial developments.

By 1989, Albania was the only remaining country in Europe where laudatory works on Stalin were available over the counter in tourist hotels. These volumes have now been removed and replaced by hard-currency consumer goods. From 1973 until the mid-1980s, Shkodër's atheist museum—just around the corner from the former Roman Catholic cathedral—was often included in tourist itineraries, but after Hoxha's death, a loosening of attitudes towards religion was revealed. Not only was Shkodër's infamous tourist attraction closed, but museums dedicated in a positive way to religious artefacts were opened. That in Korçë, the 'Museum of Medieval Art', has, as its focal point, a superb walnut iconostasis. The eighteenth-century former Orthodox cathedral of shën-Mëri within the castle of Berat, is now a museum dedicated to the sixteenth-century icon painter Onufri, who helped establish a Berat 'school' of iconography. The museum even has its own illustrated foreign-language guide book (Nallbani 1989). Any visit to such museums is, however, still prefaced/justified by quotations from Enver Hoxha emphasising the need to treasure and learn from past Albanian material culture. Onufri, for example, is linked with the 'anti-Ottoman resistance of the Albanian people' (Nallbani 1989, p. 3). Religious artefacts, including reproductions of twelfth-, fourteenth-, and sixteenth-century icons, have also appeared on foreign tourist postcards produced under the auspices of Albturist.

13.7 Tourism and economic development

Until recently, the Albanian authorities had failed to publish any hard data on tourism flows, financing, economic consequences of tourism development, related employment or social impacts. Indeed, apart from very brief and superficial reviews (Mandi 1980; Anon, 1982a, 1988a, 1989c), one guide book long out of print (Albturist 1969) and a handful of hotel pamphlets, virtually no information on the Albanian tourist industry was made publically available. At least up to the 1989 edition (KPS 1989), the activity had never featured in the country's annual statistical handbooks, and, with just one or two notable exceptions, had been ignored in political leaders' speeches and writings. Albturist's role up to the end of the 1980s had tended to be passive rather than active, responding to requests from foreign countries to send tourists, rather than explicitly promoting Albania abroad for tourism purposes. Even overall tourist numbers had been uncertain. For the 1976–80 period the present author had estimated an annual average of no more than 2,500 (Hall 1984b, p. 549). During the 1980s, numbers were clearly increasing. However, other observers, equally unsure, suggested that Albania 'accepts no more than 6,000 tourists a year' (Thomson 1988, p. F1), or that 'last year a mere 7,500 foreign tourists were admitted to the land' (Ascherson 1988, p. 9). When pressed by the present writer in 1988, the head of the English section of Albturist would only admit to 'roughly 10,000', from more than 20 countries in Europe and Latin America.

With the establishment of a Promotion Department within Albturist, a more pro-active role began to be pursued: towards the end of 1989 a promotional pamphlet (Albturist 1989) and tourist map (Albturist, nd) were produced, some postcards and hotel pamphlets were updated and improved and a colour documentary film *Tourist Spots in Albania* was shown at the First International Festival of Films on Tourism held at Gudalajara, Mexico. Further, in February 1990, the daily *Zeri i Popullit* published the first-ever Albanian tourism statistics. In 1989, 14,435 tourists were admitted to the country, including 3,830 Greeks and 633 Yugoslavs. In addition, 744 Greeks entered purely for the purpose of visiting relatives, while 643 Albanians travelled to Greece for the same purpose. Ninety-four Albanians travelled to Yugoslavia, although much was made of the fact that a further 610 had their applications for visas rejected by the Belgrade authorities. In all, some 1,400 Albanians were said to have travelled abroad during 1989 (about 0.04 per cent of the total population).

While the standard English-language literature on Albania's social and economic development processes is somewhat variable in quality (for example Pano 1968; Marmullaku 1975; Logoreci 1977; Prifti 1978, 1979; Pollo and Puto 1981; Biberaj 1990), any on its tourism dimension is largely non-existent. Albania has been notably missing from general analyses of East European tourism (for example Cambau 1976; Pearce 1981, 1987b; Robinson 1976) although Boniface and Cooper (1987, p. 121) managed to devote one paragraph to the country. Indeed, among the varied literature on the role of tourism within the development processes of socialist societies (for example, Shivji 1975; Poncet 1976; Turnock 1977; Allcock and Przecławski 1990), it would appear that only the present author's contribution (Hall 1984b, 1984c, 1990f), reference to those contributions (Turnock 1989a, pp. 259–60) and a response (Romsa 1984) have sought such a discussion in relation to Albania.

With the loss of client, if not dependency relationships with the Soviet Union and China, tourism could have been employed as one means of attempting to overcome an economic introspection reinforced by the country's 'puritanical' 1976 constitution. The cycle which impacted on Eastern Europe in the early 1960s (lack of foreign exchange—inability to purchase new technology—low quality production—inability to sell exports—consequent lack of foreign currency) largely characterised Albania for a decade and a half up to the end of the 1980s (Hall 1984c, p. 609, 1990f, pp. 39–40), and the limited nature of tourism pursued was certainly inadequate to help clear any hard-currency bottlenecks.

In many ways, the organisation of tourism has been restricted by, and subordinated to, strategic considerations. The continued sensitivity of border areas—arguably some of the most beautiful parts of the country—restricts movement on land, while offshore, at the coastal resorts of Sarandë and Durrës Beach, and on Lakes Ohrid and Shkodër (both shared with Yugoslavia) active patrol vessels serve to remind potential long-distance swimmers of patriotic obligations. The mid-1970s, with the Sino–Albanian *entente* in retreat, saw defensive pill-boxes emplaced in most parts of the country, not least along the coastal beaches, and for a time, tourist resorts were completely closed to allow the defences to be installed.

13.8 Changing circumstances

At the time of writing, the whole future of tourism and economic development in Albania appeared to be in the melting pot. Although the country was pursuing a gradual and arguably measured approach to social and economic change in the years following the death of Enver Hoxha, increasing internal and external pressures coincided with dramatic change elsewhere in Eastern Europe to render the turn of the decade a watershed for Albanian development processes.

13.8.1 Gradual change 1985–9

From the mid-1980s, signs of a slackening of the Stalinist straightjacket began to reveal themselves in growing pragmatism in political and economic affairs (no doubt reflecting the fortunes of an internal power struggle), coupled with mounting internal and external pressures for change.

After Hoxha's death in 1985 there was a noticeable increase in effort to improve Albania's foreign relations and international image: diplomatic relations were established with West Germany in 1987, and trade between the two countries dramatically improved. Bonn went on to provide Albania with DM20 million to cover financial and technical cooperation for 1989 and 1990.

In 1987 Albania and Greece terminated the theoretical state of war which had existed between them since 1940. In the following year they signed an agreement on cross-border trade and travel covering their difficult 250-kilometre land frontier and the narrow channel between Corfu and the Albanian coast. One consequence of that agreement was the inauguration of the ferry between Corfu and Sarandë noted above. The number of Greek visitors to Albania increased substantially in the late 1980s: 1,265 in 1985, 4,673 in 1986 and over 6,000 in 1987 (Anon 1988b, presumably quoting Greek sources), although official Albanian figures for 1989 list 3,830 Greek tourists and just 744 Greeks entering to visit relatives.

In 1988, the decentralisation of foreign-trade activities was undertaken with the establishment of seven district-based enterprises aimed at promoting border trade. From that year, Greece appears to have been instrumental in persuading Albanian representatives to abandon their distaste for international gatherings, as Albanian representatives began attending Balkan foreign ministers' meetings. The joint communiqué arising out of the February 1988 Belgrade session, to which Albania was a signatory, committed participants to economic cooperation in a number of fields including tourism, transport and protection of the environment (Anon 1987, 1988c; see also Sobell 1988). In January 1989 a successful Balkan deputy foreign ministers' meeting was held in Tirana—the country's first hosting of an international gathering at that level—and was followed up by a full foreign ministers' conference in Tirana in October 1990.

Notwithstanding its constitutional position, Albania appears to have been increasing its level of borrowing from Western banks: from $188 million in

September 1988, the level had crept up to $268 million by the second quarter of 1989 and by the end of that year to $368 million, with the country's liabilities exceeding its assets by $85 million (EIU 1990b, p. 42). The 1990 draft-plan commitment to an increase in imports of consumer goods and food and other reforms was likely to see this trend develop further (EIU 1990a, p. 38).

In the tourism field, evidence that the effects of gradual reform were filtering through to the Albturist bureaucracy could be seen in a number of ways:

1. During 1989, Albturist established a public-relations section: previously, officials would argue that the organisation did not have an active marketing role, but merely awaited holiday requests from approved overseas travel organisations.
2. A new hotel-building programme, albeit relatively modest, was begun, with new structures under way in Vlorë and Berat, and the refurbishment and conversion of an old monastery at Ardenicë (Table 13.1).
3. New itineraries were opened, such as that along the country's south-eastern border with Greece between Korcë and Përmet.
4. As noted earlier, from Spring 1989, day-trippers were permitted from Corfu, as were coach tours from Montenegro and northern Greece, with both Yugoslav and Greek coaches being able to travel with their groups through (a limited part of) the country.
5. Albania's first specially designated tourist map (Albturist, nd) and a new range of publicity brochures were produced in preparation for the 1990 season.
6. Opportunities for individual tourist travel, albeit highly structured and relatively expensive, began to be discussed, with the possibility of visas for such travel being available at Albanian border-crossing points.

Domestically, demands for improved living standards were growing, particularly among the younger generation who, by virtue of past and present demographic policies, represent a large proportion of the total population (the average age being only 26). This generation no longer shares, nor sees the contemporary relevance of, the aspirations of fiercely defended independence and national individuality held by their parents' and grandparents' generations, and which, to a large extent, have sustained but also severely constrained post-war Albania. The post-Hoxha abolition of the ban on watching foreign television broadcasts helped to familiarise Albanians with neighbouring societies' life-styles. This accelerated the pace of growing discontent with life in the People's Socialist Republic of Albania.

As a symbol of changing attitudes, the August 1989 plenum of the Union of Albanian Youth saw participants voicing criticism of the lack of entertainment for young people: a situation which only further encouraged them to watch foreign television. One response to this was the launching of an official social survey—in itself a rare event—undertaken during the last few days of the 1989 summer along the popular Durrës Beach resort.

> One youth was asked where he had bought his 'I love Albania' t-shirt. The answer was: 'At the Egyptian trade exhibition' in Tirana. Another youth said that if 'Durrës were to be printed on shirts, they would sell like hot cakes: but unfortunately such shirts can't be found on the market'. The survey concluded by criticising people who wore t-shirts with slogans in 'poor taste' on them, such as 'Born to raise hell'. [Zanga 1989a, pp. 3–4]

13.8.2 All change? 1990 and beyond

Within the framework of an internal power struggle and hampered by long-term drought, the Albanian leadership reacted to the 1989 events in the rest of Eastern Europe with a series of policy statements during the first half of 1990 which tinkered with the economic, political and judicial system and which downgraded a number of the key policies of the Hoxha years regarding foreign policy, internal political and cultural development (Zanga 1990b, 1990d, 1990e). There were two pressing problems:

1. Economic restructuring within Albania's major Eastern European trading partners required those countries to demand hard currency for their exports. Some 60 per cent of Albanian trade has been with CMEA member countries, and with the January 1991 inauguration of full convertible-currency trading within that bloc, the need to avert intolerable—if not impossible—pressures on the country's financial resources was urgent.
2. There was a need to forestall major unrest within the country likely to be stimulated by the 'demonstration effect' of developments in the rest of Eastern Europe.

Agricultural reforms, based on earlier experiments in selected parts of the country, were aimed at improving urban food availability and raising substantial numbers of rural and urban incomes. But after another mild and relatively dry winter, the water level in the country's reservoirs remained critically low. In 1988 a similar situation had disrupted food supplies and prompted urban demonstrations.

The Ninth Plenum of the party's Central Committee in January 1990 outlined a range of political and economic measures designed to strengthen democracy at the grass roots, reduce bureaucracy (a recurrent theme) and emphasise a commitment to the provision of foodstuffs. In April, at the Tenth Plenum, this was followed up with emphasis on improving the economic mechanism by introducing elements of self-financing enterprise. The possibility of establishing 'friendly' relations not only with the European Community—something which the Albanians had been working up to for some time—but also with the two former deadly enemies (the United States and the Soviet Union) confounded a central tenet of the previous 30 years' foreign policy (Zanga 1990c). Further inroads into the country's diplomatic isolation were indicated by the re-affirmation of the desire to participate in the CSCE process: Albania had been the only European country not to sign the Helsinki Final Act in 1975. All of this would help to provide a more congenial context within which to develop international tourism.

In May 1990, the People's Assembly approved a number of economic and judicial reforms, consolidating the earlier declarations of intent. Of particular significance were the indications that:

1. All Albanian citizens would be eligible for a passport. The ability to pay for travelling outside the country was, of course, quite another matter. They would either need to apply through the official travel agency or prove that friends or relatives abroad would pay all their costs. In practical terms that new 'freedom' appeared largely academic for most Albanians.

2. The offences of leaving the country without official permission, of creating foreign or joint companies and of receiving credits from abroad would no longer be regarded as treasonable and capital offences: the crime of attempting to flee the country, for example, was downgraded to 'illegal border trespassing'.
3. The administrative restriction of residential rights would be abolished: such restrictions in future would only be applied to persons convicted of a penal offence by a court.

Such declarations substantially raised public expectations: the continuing internal power struggle stifled them. When it became painfully apparent that certain measures were clearly not to be carried out—particularly the question of access to passports—the storming of foreign embassies in Tirana and subsequent exodus of several thousand Albanians followed, in early July.

While media attention was being focused on the embassies, the Central Committee's hastily convened Eleventh Plenum approved further reform measures, and, crucially, the Presidium of the People's Assembly declared that direct foreign investment in the country would now be permitted, thereby overturning Article 28 of the 1976 constitution which for a decade and a half had embodied Albania's steadfast ideological and economic stance towards the rest of the world.

As an indicator of change, both in foreign relations and in the former fear of domestic contagion, official attitudes towards foreign tourism are instructive. Signals just prior to the July exodus had indicated moves towards a much more flexible and expansionist approach, after almost a decade of relative stagnation and the overall post-war policy of extreme constraint. Important signals indicating the new approach included:

1. The Yugoslav cruise liner, *Dalmacija*, disembarking some 240 Italian tourists in Durrës port for a day-tour to Tirana and Krujë, but placing no little strain on Albturist's somewhat meagre infrastructural resources (April 1990).
2. For the very first time, official tourism statistics, albeit minimal, being published, in the daily paper *Zeri i Popullit* (February 1990).
3. Negotiations said to have been taking place with foreign companies interested in developing tourist centres along the country's Ionian coast.
4. Road improvements, suggesting to some observers the development of a 'super highway', running the length of the country.
5. United States' citizens, formerly excluded from the country (unless of ethnic-Albanian origin), now being able to apply for entry visas.

At the time of writing it was too early to digest the longer-term implications of these changes in constitutional position. An early announcement was that of a joint venture arranged with a consortium of Greek construction companies to build a 'motorway' from Durrës to Thessalonika, a development which portends a number of likely trends;

1. Increasing foreign-tourism levels, and implicitly, greater freedom for those tourists.
2. A new programme of hotel construction to accommodate them, most likely led by inward investment from Western Europe.
3. The need to upgrade transport and communications infrastructure to meet these new demands.

4. The need to upgrade and expand other, already hard-pressed infrastructural elements such as water supply and sewerage, as well as catering and general tourism staff training.
5. Increasing socio-economic disparities between hosts and tourists, as affluent Germans, Scandinavians and others penetrate hitherto untouched areas of the country.
6. Increasing socio-economic disparities within the host population as the role of the private sector in tourism development and other areas of the economy develops, as internal and international labour migration is generated and as personal ownership of motorised vehicles and other symbols of inequality is permitted.
7. The inevitable degradation and loss of some beautiful, still relatively natural environments.
8. Albania seeking a closer relationship with at least one of its neighbours in the medium term, to avoid the spectre of a totally dependent economy, while in the longer term being inexorably drawn into an appropriate supranational organisation, possibly a restructured European Community.

13.9 Conclusions

The 'prescriptive' Albanian model of tourism development has remained unique in Europe for several decades, reflecting the country's particular if anachronistic circumstances. How far these could survive external and internal pressures has long been a matter of some debate. The assumption that a greater emphasis upon foreign tourism can now be seen as a symbol of Albania's 'opening up' and retreat from dogma still requires careful examination. Until the mid-1980s, the country's leadership had concluded that strictly controlled and stringently planned tourism could positively aid national development by both providing hard currency and gradually stimulating the provision of facilities to the benefit of the host population as well as presenting a positive propaganda face to the outside world.

A continuing power struggle after Hoxha's death in 1985—led principally by his widow against forces for reform within the party—has not made for a clear or coherent policy for tourism development. Certainly increased domestic freedoms have been gradually attained, and the fear of ideological contagion from foreign tourists has commensurately diminished. Economically, Albanian leaders have appreciated, as did their Eastern European neighbours in the 1960s and 1970s, that (Western) technology was required to break a number of vicious circles and to open bottlenecks in their industrial processes and other developmental strategies. A revision of the 1976 constitution to permit Western credit, and an increase in tourism to gain further hard currency, have long seemed likely outcomes of this process. Now it appears, the time has arrived. Albania's beaches, mountains, lakes and rivers hold enormous potential for recreation and tourism. Winter sports in the Alpine north, rambling in the central hills, fishing in clear upland streams, bathing in the blue Ionian Sea and reposing on many of the country's sheltered sandy beaches may all possess mass appeal for a European market ever searching for new playgrounds. For such a small country, with hitherto limited and controlled relations with the outside world, minor changes can have major impacts; major changes can produce upheaval. The implicit understanding that each country's individual situation must be determined by the wishes of its own citizens should see Albania evolving an approach to tourism development, alongside political and economic change, appropriate for a small proud nation. Mindful of continuing instability within the Balkans, Albania must seek harmony with its neighbours. Within a stable national and regional context, tourism development could play a critical role in the country's economic modernisation programme. Without that stability, the future remains uncertain.

Part three: Into the 21st century

14 Contemporary challenges

Derek R. Hall

14.1 New context—old constraints?

14.1.1 The demonstration effect of Western Europe

The great lure of the place—the wonder of political renewal, the zest of building a country's institutions afresh, the energy of a culture reborn . . . The beds may not always be comfortable, but in warmth of human spirit and vitality of hope, Eastern Europe today is the most luxurious place on earth. [Greenberg *et al.* 1990, p. 17]

In the restructuring economies of Eastern Europe and the Soviet Union, substantial tourism development is now being stimulated by:

1. The easing of entry, exit and currency restrictions, tempered by varying degrees of difficulty for citizens of these countries to gain access to convertible currencies for the purposes of travelling abroad.
2. An improved 'image' of the region, but one which, for tourism purposes, will need to be reinforced by each country emphasising its own individuality and attraction to create the tourism 'product image' (Gilbert 1989, p. 87).
3. Economic restructuring processes, emphasising privatisation, devolution and local initiative and innovation.
4. Increased Western involvement in aspects of infrastructural development, in its turn related to:
   (a) a recognition of profitable returns on investment;
   (b) a significant reduction in CoCom restrictions;
   (c) the availability of Western aid, being provided with the explicit aim of hastening the restructuring of economies to market orientation;
   (d) the fashionable attraction of Eastern Europe.

How far will the new economic, political and social attitudes and circumstances encourage East Europeans to follow the recreational and tourism patterns and experiences familiar to West Europeans? With the Czechoslovak and Hungarian governments declaring that tourism will be their most import foreign currency earner by the turn of the century, what lessons can be learnt from the West European experience?

The tourist industry is one of the most important growth sectors within Western Europe, with both the number of international tourist arrivals and tourist movements within the region more than doubling between 1965 and 1986 (Shaw and Williams 1990). Factors responsible for such a growth have included an increase in real incomes and leisure time, a broadening of life-style expectations, the development of mass tourism and package holidays. However, socio-economic variations among individual countries have shifted the balance of emphasis to produce very complex patterns of development within a relatively small region. Such growth has been matched, somewhat belatedly, by a heightened awareness of the economic importance of tourism and an increased appreciation of the tourist industry's potential for creating employment opportunities. Unhelpfully, however, Shaw and Williams (1990, p. 140) conclude that: '. . . there is still no clear consensus as to tourism's role in economic development. The picture is clouded not only by the different assessments of economic development, but also by its socio-cultural and environmental implications . . .'

This problem is certainly no less true for Eastern Europe and the Soviet Union. However, one can at least point to a number of characteristics arising out of the Western European experience which could be replicated in the region:

1. A movement from the northern, industrialised and urbanised countries and regions to the warmer climates of southern Europe. In Eastern Europe, such asymmetrical spatial relationships developed to some extent within the CMEA framework of economic development and cooperation, with the more developed northern countries sending aid and technicians to the south.
2. A highly segmented tourism market: this has only taken place to a limited extent, although new 'niches' are opening up (Table 14.1). One might expect such segmentation to become more pronounced. In particular, conference and business tourism is set to increase significantly, given the new economic and political circumstances. In Hungary, for example, conference tourism is seen as by far the most lucrative aspect of the industry on a per capita basis, with each participant spending an average of $150 a day within the country, compared to health and activity holiday visitors' expenditure of $70–90 and the average tourist's $40 a day in Budapest and only $20 in the provinces.
3. Complex and dynamic tourist flows have partly reflected technological and political influences on transport. Increasing levels of car ownership and mobility across the continent have been matched by improved air technology allowing larger numbers of tourists to travel longer distances in larger numbers at reduced costs. Future technological changes and governmental attitudes towards transport deregulation and privatisation will have a substantial impact on Eastern Europe and the Soviet Union given the poorer technology and rigidity of governmental restrictions hitherto experienced.
4. A significant proportion of the population will fail to participate in growing tourism development: in 1985 it was estimated that 44 per cent of the European Community's population did not go on holiday, a figure hiding

Table 14.1 Examples of post-revolutionary 'niche'-tourism development

Czechoslovakia	
	New Travel 2002 business enterprise specialising in arranging stays in Czech and Slovak homes for travellers with special interests such as wine-growing in Moravia, cross-country skiing or pot-holing.
	Čedok's 'Beer Hunter Tour' for guided imbibing in Pilsen and Budweis, the two Bohemian cities renowned for their brewing prowess.
Former GDR	
	'Berlin Homestays': a specialist firm offering holidays with 'carefully selected' English-speaking families in East Berlin.
Hungary	
	Ibusz's special wedding package, whereby couples visit Szirak, 90 kilometres north-east of Budapest, to undertake matrimonial vows wearing authentic Renaissance costumes.
Poland	
	Polorbis's 'Jewish Tour' includes visits to the former Auschwitz and Treblinka concentration camps, as well as to synagogues, ghettos and cemeteries.
Romania	
	NTO's $1,600 Dracula's Castle tour through the mountains of Transylvania. The nine-day journey features visits to the birthplace, castles and grave of 'Vlad the Impaler', the medieval Romanian prince who provided the inspiration for Bram Stoker's fictitious vampire. A special Halloween excursion encourages horror-mongers to deck themselves out in black capes and plastic fangs.
Soviet Union	
	Concorde supersonic excursions from the United Kingdom to Moscow and Leningrad.
	Special 'space trips' to see the headquarters of the country's space programme at Star City, 40 kilometres from Moscow, where cosmonauts live and train, and to the flight control centre at Kalinigrad which is responsible for the control and monitoring of Soviet manned missions.
	Hiking tours organised by the French travel organisation Terres d'Aventures, using camels, reindeer or horses for portage and local villagers as guides, trekking the snowy Pamir Mountains, the steppes and tundra of Siberia and the Caucasus.

Sources: Greenberg 1990; *The Independent* 2 June 1990; *The Sunday Correspondent* 1 and 29 July 1990

distinct national and socio-economic variations. As appears to have been the case in Eastern Europe and the Soviet Union, the 'tourism poor', whose size and characteristics may vary among countries, are particularly characterised by older people, those with large families and rural dwellers (Shaw and Williams 1990, p. 244). Access to tourism is an important element of access to quality of life. How societies avail their citizens of such access says a great deal about their internal democracy.

5. Eastern Europe and the Soviet Union will now be participating in and contributing to a growing concentration and internationalisation of tourism industry financing. Transnational hotel ownership will act as the most

obvious outward symbol of increasing vertical and horizontal structural linkages within the industry, entailing air and surface transport operation, travel agencies and tour operation.

14.1.2 A new heritage industry?

How these countries use their newly won freedoms will be as important to us in Western Europe as to Eastern Europeans themselves. Tourism will forge but one link between the two halves of our substantially enlivened common European home. In the short term at least, those newly won freedoms have not only opened the doors on more and wider ranges of tourism opportunities, but the process of their attainment has in itself become a tourist industry. A 'new breed of vacationer is seeking excitement, novelty and a taste of the thunderous upheavals that rolled across the region last year' (Greenberg 1990, p. 12). For the 1990 season, Saga Holidays advertised their East European tour as 'a remarkable opportunity to see the places you saw on TV brought to life. The euphoria remains and you, too, can become a part of those cheering crowds as the warm hand of friendship is extended to all fellow Europeans' (quoted in Greenberg 1990, p. 12).

The immediate past state-socialist period has quickly become the source of a new heritage industry. Former leaders' hunting lodges, luxurious villas and other extravagances, political prisons, security police headquarters and military memorabilia of all sorts—particularly east German—have all been opened in various ways to the depredations of tourists. The most striking symbol of change was, of course, the breaching of the Berlin Wall, and the East Berlin authorities threw off their past and joined the spirit of '89 by promoting 'piece of the wall' tours, included in which was the provision of a hammer and chisel (not sickle!) to enable each participant to take part in, and take home, a piece of modern European history. In Poland, Warsaw's Sports-Tourist travel agency were the first to offer tours of places connected with the Solidarity struggle, most notably the Lenin shipyards of Gdańsk, and the grave of Father Jerzy Popiełuszko, who was murdered by the security police in 1984. In Romania, one post-revolutionary entrepreneur provided a 'Last steps of Ceauşescu' tour, taking European and American student groups to the former leader's bullet-riddled palace, to memorials for those who died in the fighting and to the city of Tîrgoviste, where the former Romanian leader was captured trying to flee the country.

> In January [1990], France's Club Med—better known for poolside than political frolicking—organised a tour that whipped through seven revolutions in seven days. The pilgrimage included a visit to the spot where Prague policemen savagely beat demonstrators near Wenceslas Square last November; in Romania, the tourists found themselves snapping away in the midst of an unscheduled demonstration against the National Salvation Front government (Greenberg 1990, pp. 12–3).

And what future for ideological tourism? The embalmed remains of Lenin in Moscow's Red Square are the Soviet Union's most popular tourist attraction, with 3.2 million people filing by annually. In April 1989 some intellectuals dared to suggest that the 'immoral' display of Lenin's body be ended.

Certainly in Sofia, the Stalinist Bulgarian leader Georgi Dimitrov has now been decently cremated after lying in an embalmed state for 41 years. Even in Albania, after the death of Enver Hoxha in 1985, the country's wonderfully eccentric atheist museum in Shkodër, a notable stopping point on tourist itineraries, was closed on the grounds that it was no longer relevant.

Socialist statuary and iconography—red stars, hammers and sickles, busts, statues and plaques dedicated to socialist worthies—are rapidly being consigned to history's out-tray. Tourists wishing to travel to Gorky, Gottwaldov or Karl Marx-Stadt will now have to go to Nizhny Novgorod, Zlín and Chemnitz instead, as these and many other cities, towns, villages, streets and squares throughout the region have reverted to their pre-socialist nomenclatures. With the likely growth of the heritage industry in the region, what price a Stalinist theme park set in re-named Gottwaldov or similar?

14.1.3 *Spatial implications*

After almost half a century of state control, little emphasis on personal initiative and limited material incentive for innovation, it may take some time for the region's citizens to exhibit an unrestrained embracing of free-market principles within the context of tourism development.

Certainly a great deal of potential exists at the lower end of the market—particularly in the accommodation sector—for local, private and joint private-public initiative. In Poland, for example, local provincial capitals and small towns could provide substantial small-scale (private) accommodation to generate local tourism earnings.

With freedom for indigenous privately owned companies to enter into the tourist industry, and for entrepreneurs to undertake joint ventures with foreign operators in a wide range of tourism and leisure activities, an enormous absolute increase in both foreign and domestic tourism can follow.

As Dawson suggests in his chapter on Poland in this volume, if economic regeneration in that country was sufficient to raise living standards permitting Poles to spend more on holidays, coupled with the removal of currency and passport restrictions, there is a strong likelihood that such developments would see Poles preferring to take holidays abroad, in Western-style packages, to such countries as Greece, Turkey or Yugoslavia. He further observes that the citizens of chief sources of foreign tourists to Poland—east Germany and Czechoslovakia—will now be seeking unshackled holidays outside of the former socialist bloc, precipitating a potential rapid decline in Poland's foreign-tourism industry.

One could take this a stage further at a more generalised level and suggest a number of hypotheses. The first, pursuing Dawson's line of argument, could witness a considerable spatial polarisation of tourist activity both within and among the countries discussed in this volume. This is based on several assumptions;

1. Following the law of intervening opportunities, large cities, particularly national and regional capitals and those urban centres with strong historical and architectural attractions, will continue to be the focus of interest for a certain proportion of domestic—particularly rural and provincial—

tourists. They will also act as regional and national exit and re-entry points.

2. Such foci will also retain a certain degree of interest from tourists of other countries of the region for their intrinsic merit as European centres; this role could be further enhanced by the encouragement of conference and convention tourism.
3. With the loosening of restrictions, in terms of visa requirements and geographical constraints, more Western tourists are likely to visit these countries. But while the absolute spread of numbers may be greater than before, their concentration in a limited number of specific locations may well increase as a consequence of: (a) more package holidays being organised (reaching those who were previously put off from visiting a 'Communist' country); (b) economies of scale for host countries being realised; and (c) any lingering ideological requirement to spread the benefits of economic activity across the country becoming a much lower imperative. Such polarisation will also concentrate the problems as well as the benefits of tourism such as traffic congestion, pollution and tourist 'saturation'.
4. Conversely of course, with the imperative of controlling tourists no longer paramount (except perhaps in Romania and Albania), the adventurous minority will gain greater spatial access within the region, especially in the Soviet Union. But compared to mass tourism to selected 'packaged' centres, the numbers involved in such individual and dispersed tourism will remain relatively small except perhaps in Central Europe.

Overall, therefore, one might expect a greater spatial polarisation of tourism activity within individual countries; in Hungary, for example, focusing on the already overcrowded Budapest and Lake Balaton. But additionally, with the perceived differing levels of tourism attractiveness between countries, held by both foreign and domestic tourists alike, an international polarisation may take place at the expense of certain countries. Dawson refers to the attraction of Poland remaining small for foreign tourists (except for the not inconsiderable number of expatriate Poles scattered throughout the diaspora). Eastern Germany, Czechoslovakia and Hungary being far more geographically accessible to Western Europe will bear the brunt of increased tourist numbers, sustaining the dominance of road transport as the region's main tourist transport mode (Table 3.7). By the very nature of their front-line position in relation to Western Europe, these countries previously played an important strategic role in the military disposition of the Soviet bloc, and in reaction to over 40 years of constraint and inhibition, local residents and foreign tourists will be wishing to make up for lost time by generating increasing levels of travel and tourism. German unification has considerably intensified that process.

There is a possibility, however, that Eastern Europe and the (newly independent former?) Soviet territories could easily slip into a dependency role as the cheap playground for West Europeans (particularly Germans). A number of tourist regions could rapidly experience increased overcrowding, infrastructural strains and environmental deterioration. They would be equally vulnerable to changes in tourism fashions, which could quite easily see Eastern Europe abandoned for more novel regions of the globe within a relatively short period of time. Additionally, those countries such as Bulgaria and Romania which have experienced a high dependence on the captive regional tourism market could be doubly debilitated by the ability of East Europeans to travel relatively freely outside of the region and by their own continuing domestic instability.

14.2 Future research agendas

14.2.1 Key issues

That this book has been produced in a context of uncertainty is no overstatement. While the political and economic consequences of the 1989 upheavals were still being unravelled when this volume went to press, a number of key issues were also being raised which require far greater examination than has been possible in this text. Some of the more important of these would appear to be:

14.2.1.1 Tourism's role as a vehicle for economic restructuring

For those economies with hitherto small service sectors moving away from a high dependence on centrally planned systems, there is virtually no prior experience to draw upon and even less appropriate literature to refer to.

14.2.1.2 The likely pivotal role of a unified Germany

For European tourism development in the twenty-first century this will be expressed in terms of financing and joint ventures, tourist generation and as a symbol of European integration.

14.2.1.3 The nature and predictability of changing tourism fashions

As this volume was being completed, Eastern Europe was very much the place to be, but the smaller economies of the region could render themselves vulnerable to the changing whims of tourism fashion. More research is required on the factors influencing changing international tourism fashions and how individual tourism economies can positively influence such forces. Even in mid-1990, three factors were emerging which could impose a deterrent effect on tourism in the region:

1. Continuing political instability, particularly in the Balkans and the Soviet Union. While the 1989 revolutions had unique novelty value for attracting visitors to the region, long-term political uncertainty and short-term political upheaval could both act as deterrents. For example, during one week in August 1990 which witnessed an armed uprising of minority Serbs, the Croatian tourism industry suffered losses estimated at $200 million as a result of cancelled holiday bookings and physical damage to roads and public transport.
2. Significant increases in (reported) crime and traffic accidents in the region have received much publicity. In the Soviet Union, for example, crime increased by 32 per cent in 1989, with one in three felonies remaining

unsolved. Over 6,000 crimes were committed against foreigners, 70 per cent of which were burglary, especially of hotel rooms and parked cars.

3. Substantial oil price rises resulting from the 1990 Gulf crisis would have a twofold negative effect on tourism to the region:
   (a) by making holidays more expensive, although this would apply to most holidays anywhere—to varying extents;
   (b) more significantly, by hitting the Eastern European economies, already handicapped by a reduction in Soviet crude supplies. It was estimated that if the world market price of oil was $25 a barrel, this would consume 30 per cent of Poland's annual hard-currency earnings and possibly all of Bulgaria's. This might lead, on the one hand, to an ever-increasing emphasis upon tourism to generate hard currency, and further calls to Western transnationals to develop tourism infrastructures. With continuing domestic shortages, deteriorating indigenous infrastructures and declining living standards, the perceived gulf between tourist and host, emphasising social and economic inequalities, will be exacerbated.

14.2.1.4 The role of global marketing

The region has an obvious appeal to other Europeans who share facets of culture, geography and history, and this has been reflected in the European dominance of the region's tourist market (Table 4.3). However, Japanese tourists, ubiquitous elsewhere—9.7 million travelled abroad in 1989 and by 1995 the figure may rise to 20 million—appear to have been unenthusiastic about new travel opportunities to Eastern Europe. Substandard accommodation and service, linguistically inappropriate tour guides, a drab night life and a dearth of good shopping—elements endemic to the old state-socialist system—continue to project a poor image of the region in important and emerging non-European markets. The extent to which a robust marketing of the region can overcome preconceptions of the region for the purposes of tourism generation will be an issue requiring close scrutiny in the months ahead.

14.2.1.5 The role of 'green'/'alternative' tourism within the region

The notion of 'alternative' tourism developed slowly during the 1980s (Dernoi 1981; Farell 1985; Krippendorf 1986; Britton and Clarke 1987; Richter 1987) and was seen to be a response particularly to the hegemonistic thrust of much international tourism in developing countries. Yet by the late 1980s, an international conference on theoretical aspects of alternative tourism (held in Poland) (Eadington and Smith 1990) concluded that the term 'alternative' remained ambiguous and confusing and in this context appears to have little or no intrinsic scientific value (Nash and Butler 1990). The notion of 'sustainable' tourism, by comparison, was preferred in the sense that it has a far greater explicit relationship with environmental elements and notions of 'carrying capacity' and 'saturation' (however difficult they may be to quantify in reality). Such concepts and debates have tended to concentrate on the developing world, but given Eastern Europe's very fragile environmental condition coupled with the current burgeoning pressure of tourism within the region, sympathetic approaches to the tourism environment and to tourism within the environment will be required. Much work therefore needs to be undertaken on the nature and role of 'green' tourism in the region.

14.2.1.6 The likely impact of global warming

An Intergovernmental Panel on Climate Change was set up in 1988 by the United Nations Environment Programme and the World Meteorological Organisation to investigate the warming of the world's atmosphere through the emission of industrial gases. Of three scientific reports from United Nations working committees, the second argued that in Europe by the year 2020, average temperatures will have risen by between 1.3 and 2.5 degrees centigrade. Sea levels will rise by up to a metre, sufficient to have a significant effect on European coastlines, inundating a hundred metres of beaches and coastal resorts and ruining coastland agriculture, as in the Neretva Delta (an important producer of food for the Yugoslav tourist industry), with salt deposits. Stormier winters and drier summers for Europe as a whole are forecast. Mediterranean temperatures will transform parts of northern Europe—'turning Manchester and Minsk into sun-soaked holiday centres'. (Nagaitis and Delgado 1990)—while soaring temperatures further south could extend desertification substantially northwards.

Wall (1990) has argued that tourism planners need to turn their minds to the consequences of this likelihood with some degree of urgency, although there continues to be both scientific and political debate concerning the evidence of, and need for, response to 'global warming'. Indeed, that last phrase has even been consciously excluded from American official publications so much does big business fear a slowdown of economic growth if the notion is taken seriously.

Rhodes (1990) offers the following scenario for the year 2030:

> The Costas del Sol and Brava, now desert wastelands, have been hit by North African locusts . . . The Spanish economy has suffered a complete reversal since tourists have looked to Eastern Europe for their holidays. Hungarians have reaped the rewards . . . Owners of once defunct cafés and bars on the shores of Lake Balaton have been celebrating their profits this year. After the prized Italian lakes of Como and Garda became too hot for even the most diehard sunbathers, Balaton has found its niche as the most popular holiday resort in Europe.

Which rather begs the question: if sunshine and warm temperatures are to be readily and reliably available during the summer months in the northern industrial tourism generating countries of Europe,

1. Will Europeans wish to travel very far for such a holiday if they have the appropriate climate on their own doorsteps?
2. With this ubiquity of holiday weather in northern climes, and given the likely increased risk of melanomas and skin cancer as a result, will simply lying in the sun for a holiday lose its appeal, such that tourism becomes a much more varied, segmented and potentially sophisticated activity?

Either way, European tourism managers north and south, east and west may have a great deal of rethinking to do in the next quarter-century. Under such circumstances, tourism could even go out of fashion altogether!

Appendix

Derek R. Hall

Supplementary literature sources

The meagre academic literature

Specific research on tourism and recreation in the region—often only accessible in the original language—is cited in appropriate chapters. In the more general academic literature there have been notably few appraisals of tourism as an income generator either within the context of state socialism or as a subject worthy of academic study in Eastern Europe and the Soviet Union. This situation was due in no small part to the pejorative view (if any) of tourism within 'traditional' interpretations of socialist development paths, a theme taken up in a number of the country chapters and one which has been passing through a period of comprehensive reappraisal in recent months. A few selected texts are cited below to emphasise this point.

Virtually all general academic works on communism and development fail to address tourism, although Bideleux's text offers a passing comment in a chapter on Cuba where, in the context of joint ventures, tourism is seen as a peripheral activity, alongside offshore oil exploration, and as a parenthetical inclusion in a passing reference to comparative cost advantages in a section on Yugoslavia (Bideleux 1985, pp. 175, 179); these references are considered insufficient to warrant a 'tourism' entry in Bideleux's index. Shivji's (1975) edited volume on tourism and socialist development is set within the African development context.

Of the standard geography texts on Eastern Europe, Hoffman's (1971) collection of essays includes a chapter on regional spatial planning in Yugoslavia which takes several pages to address the question of tourism (Fisher, 1971, pp. 314–20), but the overall significance of tourism for the book is reflected in the fact that it does not merit an independent entry in the index. Mellor (1975), in another standard text on the region from the 1970s, could argue that

> Tourism is beginning to develop, with large numbers of east Germans vacationing in Carpathia, Lake Balaton and the Black Sea resorts, while some spas such as Karlovy Vary have an international clientele. Usually movement is in parties and 'delegations', while considerable flows of officials take place between the industrial and political centres. Travel to the non-Socialist (sic) world has been made difficult by financial restrictions and other formalities, though a considerable movement has begun to develop since the later 1960s. On the other hand Western tourists and visitors are

welcome on the hosts' terms in most Comecon countries as a source of hard currency. Jugoslavia is an exception in allowing a remarkably free movement of its own nationals into Western Europe and in having developed a successful tourist industry in the Adriatic littoral, [Mellor 1975, pp. 247–8]

Turnock, in a volume dedicated to industrial development in Eastern Europe, briefly discusses tourism potential as an adjunct to his section on the region's physical background (1978, pp. 16–8, 21, 23–4) but concludes that although tourism is not recognised as an industry for the purposes of the volume, it merits 'acceptance as part of any analysis of living conditions and foreign currency earnings' (p. 233). In a later standard text on the region (1989a) he devotes 17 pages to elements of the phenomenon with a further 14 pages to a case study of Romania. In the companion volume, Turnock (1989c) provides a complete chapter on problems of pollution and conservation, focusing on the recreational and tourism dimensions of the problems with a further section on the scope for recreation and tourism in rural planning. Rugg (1985, pp. 305–9) devotes three pages to the topic, but concentrates almost wholly on the experiences of the Dalmatian coast—by no means typical of Eastern Europe thus far—citing the earlier work of Poulsen (1977).

On the Soviet Union, of the standard geography texts, Symons (1983, 1990) has a handful of brief passing references to the tourist industry; Cole (1984) includes a section on 'leisure activities and tourism', but this runs to less than three pages of text. In Bater's (1989) most recent work, the 'tourism' entry in the index refers us to 'recreation and leisure', where some four pages of text, three maps and a table are to be found. On economic development, Hutchings' (1971) standard work makes no mention of tourism, nor does Lavrishchev's (1969) official economic geography of the country.

In academic tourism texts, Boniface and Cooper (1987 pp. 115–24), in the wide-ranging and essentially introductory text on the geography of tourism and travel, devote a chapter to Eastern Europe and the Soviet Union, comprising six and a half pages of text and three maps. Of Pearce's two most accessible works, the earlier (1981, p. 38), looking at the structure and process of tourism development, cites Vedenin and Miroschnichenko (1970) in their evaluation techniques for assessing the Soviet Union's natural environment for recreational purposes. Research by Barbaza (1970) in the classification of types of coastal development along the Mediterranean and Black Sea is cited, along with a brief evaluation of Black Sea coastal development in Bulgaria and Romania (Pearce, 1981, p. 14). Andric *et al.*'s (1962) estimate of the carrying capacity of Yugoslav beaches is noted, as is the reported low-import content of Yugoslavia's tourist industry (IUOTO 1975; Theuns 1976) and that country's local tourism planning procedures (Vukonic *et al* 1978; Pearce 1981, pp. 37, 58, 83). In a second text, Pearce (1987b, pp. 125–6, 132–4) notes work undertaken on Eastern Europe in tourism type classification (Molnar *et al* 1976; Swizewski and Oancea 1978a), regionalisation (Jackowski 1980) and spatial polarisation (Barbaza 1970; Gueorguiev and Andonov 1974; Poncet 1976; Turnock 1977). Some of these themes are taken up again in the second edition of his earlier work, where additionally the Soviet research of Vedenin and Miroschnichenko (1970) and Nefedova *et al.* (1974) on resource evaluation is cited, and Benthien's (1984) study of recreation in the former German Democratic Republic is mentioned in passing (Pearce 1989, pp. 175–7, 5).

Cambau (1976) and Vuoristo (1981) provide two of the few accessible earlier works on the characteristics of international tourism flows to Eastern Europe.

Of the current authors' earlier work in the field, particularly notable has been Allcock's (1983, 1986) research on tourism and social change in Yugoslavia, Carter's (1978, 1982) work on environmental and conservation issues in the region, Shaw's (1979, 1980) interest in Soviet recreation planning and Turnock's (1973, 1977, 1990b) research on tourism, economic development and rural planning in Romania.

General tourism sources from the region

The quality and content of more general tourism-related material emanating from Eastern Europe and the Soviet Union have varied considerably among individual countries. Perhaps seven types of written sources can be cited.

Pre-socialist publications

Much material was produced in inter-war Central and Eastern Europe by tourism-related societies and organisations, and relatively little by national governments. Of the surviving literature, Bureš' (1929) piece on Czechoslovak spas and Jarosławiecka and Gąsiorowski's (1924) illustrated pamphlet on Kraków are notable.

General descriptive texts from the early socialist period

Where mention is made of leisure and recreation, it is invariably within the context of the enhancement of the working people's lives and therefore wholly within the realm of 'domestic tourism'. For example, Halász's (1960) national handbook of Hungary, issued 'to mark the fifteenth anniversary of the liberation' (p. 7) of that country, addresses the question of recreation within the book's section on public health. Guides for foreign visitors which date from this period, include Crawford's (1956) state-sponsored 'impressions of Czechoslovakia'.

Guides produced for foreign tourist consumption

These may be translations of indigenous productions into at least one foreign language, or may be completely new texts, providing a different emphasis for foreigners compared to that for the home market. Such guides have, of course, been produced by all the countries under discussion. At a national level, they include Albturist (1969), (Albania); Mihailov and Smolenov (1985), Zhelev (1986) (Bulgaria); Chyský *et al.* (1965), Rybár (1982), Ludvik and Mohyla (1989) (Czechoslovakia); Anon (1990) (former GDR); Wichrowski and Wojnowski (1980) (Poland); Florea (1969) (Romania). The Soviet Union's series of small, generally well-illustrated handbooks on each of the country's republics produced in the mid- to late-1980s (for example Stoylik, 1987), may also be regarded as being aimed at the interested tourist.

Again, most countries have produced tourist guides on specific towns, cities and resorts such as capital cities: Budapest (Pap *et al*, 1964; Tőrők 1989),

Prague (Flegl 1988), Sofia (Mihailov and Smolenov 1981), Warsaw (Budrewicz 1974); or specific elements of capitals, such as Prague Castle (Formánek *et al.* 1965); specific resorts or resort regions such as the Romanian Black Sea coast (Dunareanu *et al.*, 1967), the Danube Delta (Panighianţ 1967), Hungary's Lake Balaton (Sebestyén and Vajkai 1982; Wellner 1985) or Dubrovnik and its surroundings (Beritić and Suljak 1972), the latter being one of a number of guides to towns and coastal resorts in Croatia. Of note are a series of some fifty 'pocket tourist guidebooks' published in Romania in the late 1960s and 1970s, such as that on Bucharest (Berindei 1966) and the spa town of Băile Felix (Munteanu and Grigore, 1975). A series of at least a dozen volumes was in production in the mid- to late-1980s on tourist regions in Croatia, perhaps updating the earlier series noted above, including volumes on the River Krka (Friganović 1987a) and the Kornati Archipelago (Friganović 1987b) national parks.

The Poles translated a number of their local tourist guides into both German and English such as that for the Bieszczady Mountains (Izbicki and Suminski 1968) and for Kraków (Dobrzycki 1968), two of a series of illustrated monographs produced in the late 1960s. In the same decade, the Romanians published a series of pocket books on 'historical monuments' in English and French translation. These largely consisted of a detailed examination of religious buildings such as St. Michael's Church of Cluj (Marica 1967), the Căluiu Monastery (Bălan 1967), St. Nicholas's Church in Curtea de Argeş (Musicescu and Ionescu 1967) and the Stavropoleos Church (Theodorescu 1967) and Patriarchate Hill monuments (Miclescu 1967) of Bucharest. Each contained a detailed text, well illustrated with monochrome photographs, together with a short bibliography. In the mid- to late 1980s, the Moscow publishing house of Raduga began producing a range of tourist-orientated material, ranging in scale from the specific, such as the text on the Lenin Museum at Gorki (Ganzha 1984), to whole republics.

Foreign language magazines

Some countries have produced periodicals directly aimed at hard-currency tourists, while most produce 'glossies' which often include articles on aspects of both domestic and international tourism and recreation. Of the former category, one of the most notable has been *Holidays in Romania*, produced by the Ministry of Tourism of that country in French and German as well as in English. Latterly used as a barely concealed propaganda sheet for the Ceauşescu family, at the time of writing it remained to be seen how this periodical and others of its ilk would perform in the post-revolutionary 1990s. The last issue under the old regime (November 1989) ironically extolled the virtues of a rebuilt Bucharest (Focşa 1989), and applauded the facilities of the Hotel Continental in Timişoara (Docsănescu 1989). *Travel to the USSR*, published bimonthly by the Soviet State Committee for Foreign Tourism, acts essentially as a publicity sheet for Intourist, covering both systematic topics such as the construction and modernisation of hotels (Anon 1988d), and regional themes, for example focusing on Russia's 'golden ring' (Moscow, Vladimir, Suzdal) (Anon 1988e). Of the more general magazines, those such as *Czechoslovak Life* often feature short illustrated pieces on aspects of both domestic recreation and international tourism. During 1989–90, for example, a series of articles entitled 'Travelling across Czechoslovakia' was published, including a number focusing on tourist regions such as that by Miškufová (1989) on winter tourism in the High Tatras. Magazines with a geographically more constricted coverage such as *Belgrade Review* also offer informative pieces such as Krstić (1990), examining a major recreational area on the Sava river.

Publications aimed essentially at the domestic market

These are works which cannot be found in translation and therefore must be assumed to be aimed specifically at the domestic market or thought unattractive to, or inappropriate for, foreign visitors or potential visitors. This group includes the series of pocketbooks, numbering over two hundred, produced in Hungarian under the series title of *Tájak Korok Múzeumok Kiskönyvtára* (literally 'small library of landscapes, times and museums') each looking in detail, with text, photographs, maps and diagrams, sketches and a small bibliography, at specific elements of Hungary's tourist and cultural centres, such as Visegrád (Héjj 1988; Szőke 1986), Szentendre's open air folk museum (Balázs 1984; Kecskés 1987), Esztergom (Horváth 1986; Cséfalvay 1987), and Vác (Galambos 1985; Dercsényi 1985). An illustrated guide to Bucharest's village museum published more than two decades ago (Focşa 1970) has yet to be fully translated, although an English-language pamphlet was produced in the same author's name some time later (Focşa nd). Far less explicitly aimed at leisure and recreation is the Albanian series of regional monographs, published under the generic title of *Almanak*. These volumes, such as those on the coastal resort area of Sarandë (Toçka 1982) or the northern centre of Shkodër (Kraja 1976), usually provide an annual summary of political, economic and cultural activities and achievements within each of the country's local administrative areas over 12-month periods.

Publications in translation on folk art and cultural treasures

A vast assortment of publications fall into this category, including those produced in conjunction with Western publishers in order to reach a wider market,such as Fél *et al*, (1971), on Hungarian peasant art, and Venedikov (1976) on Thracian treasures from Bulgaria which was produced in conjunction with the eponymous British Museum exhibition. Trifunović's (1988) well-researched and beautifully illustrated work manages to fuse elements of academic endeavour into a very well-presented tourist guide of the architectural and archaeological treasures of Yugoslavia. In the mid-1970s, the Albanians published a number of multicoloured booklets in French translation on such artefacts as icons (Popa 1974), religious murals (Dhamo 1974) and Roman mosaics (Anamali and Adhami 1974). More recently, 'coffee table' volumes have appeared featuring the museum cities of Berat (Strazimiri 1987) and Gjirokastër (Riza 1978).

Ethnographic and archaeological publications

Usually only found in the original language, although often with translated summaries, such works may provide a wealth of ethnographic, architectural and archaeological detail of specific items and localities. For example, Focşa (1975) is a two-volume ethnographic study focusing on the material culture of the Oaş region, in north-west Transylvania. With hundreds of photographs, diagrams and sketches, even for the non-Romanian reader these volumes provide a wealth of visual detail from the region in question. Also from Romania, in foreign-language translation, are various series of local studies undertaken on regional museum exhibits. For example, the series of at least 15 studies in the series *Collections of the Regional Archaeological Museums of Dobrudja, Scientific Reference and Popularisation Books*, were published in the mid- to late-1960s, each with apparent print runs of about 500. Canarache (ndb), for example, deals with Roman mosaics from the town of Tomiş unearthed below railway lines of the present-day Black Sea port of Constanţa. The same author also provided a guide to the archaeological museum of Constanţa (Canarache, nda). At the height of the country's Stalinist heavy-industrialisation programme, Zachwatowicz's (1956) *Protection of historical monuments in People's Poland*, makes somewhat ironic reading, but does reveal the high priority given to the restoration of national monuments—most notably the market square of Old Warsaw—as symbols of a Polish national continuity. Ethnographic and archaeological journals are also a common feature and useful sources such as Albania's *Iliria*, published by the Archaeological section of the Academy of Sciences, *Monumentet*, from the Institute of Monuments of Culture, Committee for Culture and Art, *Ethnographie Albanaise* and *Culture Populaire Albanaise*, both produced by the Academy of Sciences' Institute of People's Culture.

'Peripherals'

While not published within the societies under discussion, literature has been produced for tourism markets generated by the impacts of these societies' activities on their neighbours. Of particular note are the illustrated critiques of the Berlin Wall published in the western half of that city (Hildebrandt 1969, 1982), now relegated to the role of historical documents. These served the demands of large numbers of tourists attracted to West Berlin to experience the most tangible component of ideological division and feel a *frisson* of cold-war surrogacy.

Bibliography

Albturist, 1969, *Tourist guide book of Albania*, Naim Frashëri, Tirana.

Albturist, 1989, *Hotels and tourist centres in Albania*, 8 Nëntori, Tirana.

Albturist, nd, *The tourist map of Albania*, 8 Nëntori, Tirana.

Alisov, N.V. *et al., 1985, Economic geography of the socialist countries of Europe*, Progress, Moscow.

Alkjaer, P., Eriksen, J.L., 1967, *Location and economic consequences of international congresses*, Einar Harcks Forlag, Copenhagen.

Allcock, J.B., 1983, Tourism and social change in Dalmatia, *Journal of Development Studies*, **20**(1): 35–55.

Allcock, J.B., 1986, Yugoslavia's tourist trade: pot of gold or pig in a poke?, *Annals of Tourism Research*, **13**(4): 565–88.

Allcock, J.B., 1990, Tourism and the private sector in Yugoslavia, in Allcock, J.B., Milivojević, M. (eds), *Yugoslavia in transition*, Berg, Oxford.

Allcock, J.B., Counihan, J., 1989, *Two studies in the history of tourism in Yugoslavia*, Bradford Studies on Yugoslavia, No. 14, University of Bradford, Bradford.

Allcock, J.B., Przecławski, K., 1990, Introduction, *Annals of Tourism Research*, **17**(1): 1–6.

Anamali, S., Adhami, S., 1974, *Mosaiques de l'Albanie*, 8 Nëntori, Tirana.

Anan'yev, M.A., 1968, *Mezhdunarodnyy turizm*, Izdatel'stovo 'Mezhdunarodnyye Otnosheniya', Moscow.

Andrei, V., 1972, Inceputurile turismului în Munţii Carpaţii Moldoveni, *Buletin Societăţii de Ştiinţe Geografice din RSR*, **2**: 217–21.

Andric, N, et al., 1962, Aspects regionaux de la planification touristique, *Tourist Review*, **17**(4): 230–6.

Anon, 1947, *Czechoslovakia: old culture and new life: at the crossroads of Europe*, Orbis, Prague.

Anon, 1964, *Czechoslovakia: a handbook of facts and figures*, Orbis, Prague, 2nd. edn.

Anon, 1982a, Tourist Albania: an interview with the Director of the Albturist enterprise, *New Albania*, **3**: 34–5.

Anon, 1982b, World tourism—still going places, *The Economist*, 16 October: 92–3.

Anon, 1983, *Czechoslovakia camping 1983*, Merkur, Prague.

Anon, 1987, A lot of Balkan questions, *The Economist*, 24 October: 50.

Anon, 1988a, A majestic balcony on the side of the mountain, *New Albania*, 2: 6–9.

Anon, 1988b, Albania and Greece: a door now ajar, *The Economist*, 23 April: 60.

Anon, 1988c, In the interests of good neighbourliness and cooperation in the Balkans, *New Albania*, **2**: 4.

Anon, 1988d, Intourist hotels, today and tomorrow, *Travel to the USSR*, **126**: 23–6.

Anon, 1988e, The three gems of Russia's golden rim, *Travel to the USSR*, **126**: 20–2, 27–30.

Anon, 1989a, Czechoslovakia for development of international tourism, *Information from Czechoslovakia*, **11**: 19–20.

Anon, 1989b, The holiday places, *New Albania*, **4**: 26–7.

Anon, 1990, *Travel guide: German Democratic Republic*, Berolina Travel, London.

Archer, B.H., 1982, The value of multipliers and their policy implications, *Tourism Management*, **3**(4): 236–41.

Ascherson, N., 1988, Albania's dam against time, *The Observer*, 7 February: 9.

Ashworth, G.J., 1989, Urban tourism: an imbalance in attention, in Cooper, C.P. (ed.) *Progress in tourism, recreation and hospitality management*, Vol.1, Belhaven, London.
Ashworth, G.J., Tunbridge, J.E., 1990, *The tourist-historic city*, Belhaven, London.
Azar, V.I., 1972, *Ekonomika i organizatsiya turizma*, Ekonomika, Moscow.
Baçe, A., Çondi, D., 1987, *Buthrot*, 8 Nëntori, Tirana.
Bachvarov, M., 1970, Za ikonomgeografskata s'shnost na turisticheskija raion, *Godishnik na Sofijskija Universitet*, **62**(2): 337–56.
Bachvarov, M., 1975, *Geografija na turizma v sotsialisticheskite strani*, Nauka i izkustuo, Sofia.
Bachvarov, M., 1979, The tourist traffic between the Balkan states and the role of the frontiers, *Frankfurter Wirtschafts- und Sozialgeographische Schriften*, **13**: 129–38.
Bachvarov, M., 1984, Les relations tourisme et arrière-pays sur le littoral de la Bulgarie, *Méditerranée*, **14**(3): 3–10.
Bachvarov, M., Apostolov, N., 1982, *Geografija na turizma*, G. Bakalov, Varna.
Bajcar, A., 1970, *Poland: a guidebook for tourists*, Interpress, Warsaw.
Bălan, C., 1967, *Le monastère de Căluiu*, Meridiane, Bucharest.
Balázs, G., 1984, *Szentendre: Szabadtéri Néprajzi Múzeum I*, TKM, Budapest.
Ban, N. *et al.*, 1973, Aspects géographiques du tourisme dans la region des vallées supérieurs de la Prahova et du Timiş, *Revue Roumaine: Géographie*, **17**: 165–76.
Bănărescu, P. *et al.*, 1980, Viitorul parc naţional Semenic–Cheile Carasului, Ocrotirea Naturii şi a Mediului Înconjurätor, **24**: 127–33.
Baráth, E., 1981, Az országos terűletrendezési tervkoncepció, *Varosepites*, **7**: 5–18.
Barbaza, Y., 1970, Trois types d'intervention du tourisme dans l'organisation de l'espace littoral, *Annales de Geographie*, **434**: 446–69.
Barbic, A., 1983, The farm worker in Yugoslavia: a bridge between the city and the country, *Sociologia Ruralis*, **23**: 76–84.
Barbier, B., 1984, Montagne, tourisme et aménagement en Bulgarie, *Sociétés et espaces ruraux dans les pays de l'Est*, Université de Montpellier, Montpellier.
Barbu, Gh. (ed.), 1973, *Turismul: ramura a economiei nationale*, Editura Pentru Turism, Bucharest.
Baretje, R., 1982, Tourism's external account and the balance of payments, *Annals of Tourism Research*, **9**: 57–67.
Baron, R.R., 1983, The necessity for an international system of tourism statistics, *International Tourism Quarterly*, **4**: 39–51.
Bar-On, R., 1989, *Travel and tourism data*, Euromonitor, London.
Bater, J.H., 1989, *The Soviet scene: a geographical perspective*, Edward Arnold, London.
Bauerová, J., 1986, *Czechoslovakia in facts and figures*, Orbis, Prague.
BBC, *Summary of World Broadcasts: Eastern Europe*.
BBC, *Summary of World Broadcasts: Soviet Union*.
Bebbington, C., 1990, Managing an uphill task, *EuroBusiness*, **2**(8): 67–83.
Benthien, B., 1984, Recreational geography in the German Democratic Republic, *GeoJournal*, **9**(1): 59–63.
Berbecaru, I., 1973, Turismul: element principal al sistematizării teritoriale a ţării, in Barbu, Gh. (ed.), *Turismul: ramura a economiei nationale*, Editura Pentru Turism, Bucharest, pp. 75–97.
Berezówski, S., 1978, *Geografia ekonomicza Polski*, Interpress, Warsaw.
Berindei, D., 1966, *Bucharest*, Meridiane, Bucharest.
Beritić, D., Suljak, T., 1972, *Dubrovnik and its surroundings*, Turistkomerc, Zagreb.
Biberaj, E., 1990, *Albania: a socialist maverick*, Westview, Boulder Co.
Bičanić, R., 1973, *Economic policy in socialist Yugoslavia*, Cambridge University Press, Cambridge.
Bideleux, R., 1985, *Communism and development*, Methuen, London.
Blaha, J., 1981, Le tourisme en Tchécoslovaquie, *Le Courrier des Pays de l'Est*, **256**: 48–56.
Blaha, J., 1986, Tchécoslovaquie, *Le Courrier des Pays de l'Est*, **309–11**: 131–57.
Blanchard, R., 1958, *Les Alpes et leur destin*, Librairie Arthème Fayrad, Paris.

Bokov, G. (ed.), 1981, *Modern Bulgaria*, Sofia Press, Sofia.

Bonev, V., Trifokova, S., 1988, Po v'prosa za s'shnostta na delovija turiz'm, *Godnishnik Visshija Institut za Narodno Stopanstvo 'Dimit'r Blagoev'*, **2**: 80–90.

Boniface, B.G., Cooper, C.P., 1987, *The geography of travel and tourism*, Heinemann, London.

Bora, Gy., 1984, Environmental management in the Lake Balaton region, in Compton, P.A., Pecsi, M. (eds), *Environmental management: British and Hungarian case studies*, Akademiai Kiado, Budapest, pp. 91–108.

Böröcz, J., 1990, Hungary as a destination 1960–1984, *Annals of Tourism Research*, **17**(1): 19–35.

Borrell, J., 1989, A boom in Western tourism, *Time*, **134**(15): 49.

Borza, A., 1978, Construcţiile hidroenergetice şi turismul, in Glavan, V., (ed.), *Studii de turism: turism montan*, Institut de Economia Comerţului Interior şi a Turismului, Bucharest, pp. 99–109.

Bramham, P. *et al.* (eds), 1989, *Leisure and urban processes*, Routledge, London.

Britton, S.G., Clarke, W.C. (eds), 1987, *Ambiguous alternative: tourism in small developing countries*, University of the South Pacific Press, Suva, Fiji.

Buckley, P.J., 1987, An economic transactions analysis of tourism, *Tourism Management*, **8**(3): 190–4.

Buckley, P.J., Witt, S.F., 1987, The international tourism market in Eastern Europe, *Service Industries Journal*, 7(1): 91–104.

Buckley, P.J., Witt, S.F., 1990, Tourism in the centrally-planned economies of Europe, *Annals of Tourism Research*, **17**(1): 7–18.

Budrewicz, O., 1974, *Warszawa/Warsaw*, Agencja Wydawnicza, Warsaw.

Bureš, P., 1929, The Czechoslovak spas and tourist traffic, in Horak, B. (ed.), *The yearbook of the Czechoslovak Republic*, Orbis, Prague.

Burg, S.L., 1983, *Conflict and cohesion in socialist Yugoslavia: political decision making since 1966*, Princeton University Press, Princeton.

Burkart, A.J., Medlik, S., 1981, *Tourism: past, present and future*, Heinemann, London, 2nd. edn.

Business Eastern Europe.

Butler, R.W., 1974, Problems in the prediction of tourist development studies in the geography of tourism, *Frankfurter Wirtschafts- und Sozialgeographische Schriften*, **17**: 49–64.

Cambau, D., 1976, Travel by westerners to Eastern Europe, *ITA Bulletin* **40**: 883–99.

Canarache, V., nd a, *The Archaeological Museum of Constantza*, Regional Archaeological Museum of Dobrudja, Constanţa.

Canarache, V., nd b, *The mosaic floored edifice of Tomi*, Regional Archaeological Museum of Dobrudja, Constanţa.

Carter, F.W., 1978, Nature reserves and national parks in Bulgaria, *L'Espace Géographique*, **1**: 69–72.

Carter, F.W., 1982, Historic cities in Eastern Europe: problems of industrialization, pollution and conservation, *Mazingira*, **6**(3): 62–76.

Carter, F.W., 1984, Pollution in Prague: environmental control in a centrally planned socialist economy, *Cities*, **1**: 258–73.

Carter, F.W., 1985a, Balkan historic cities: pollution versus conservation, in Collins, L. (ed.), *Anglo-Bulgarian Symposium 1982*, University of London School of Slavonic and East European Studies, London.

Carter, F.W., 1985b, Pollution problems in post-war Czechoslovakia, *Transactions, Institute of British Geographers*, **10**: 17–44.

Carter, F.W., 1990a, Czechoslovakia, geographical prospects for energy, environment and economy, *Geography*, **75**(3): 253–5.

Carter, F.W., 1990b, Bulgaria: geographical prognosis for a political eclipse, *Geography*, **75**(3): 263–5.

Carter, F.W., 1990c, Recreational planning in Bulgaria, *Proceedings of the Third Anglo-Bulgarian Symposium in the Humanities 1988*, University of London School of

Slavonic and East European Studies, London.
Carter, F.W., French, R.A., 1975, New era in Slovenia, *Geographical Magazine*, **47**: 556–60.
Castle, T., 1990, East rings the changes for telecoms, *The European*, 27 July: 20.
Cerovsky, J., 1988, *Nature conservation in the socialist countries of Eastern Europe*, Ministry of Culture of the Czechoslovak Socialist Republic for the IUCN, Prague.
Chamber of Economy of Montenegro, 1989, *Possibilities for joint investments in the construction of tourist facilities*, Chamber of Economy of Montenegro, Cetinje.
Charvat, J., 1948, *Rozbor štatistiky cestovného ruchu na Slovensku 1947*, Študijny ústav cestovného ruchu, Prague.
Chase-Dunn, C.K., 1980, Socialist states in the capitalist world-economy, *Social Problems*, **27**(5): 505–25.
Chib, S.N., 1977, Measurement of tourism, *Journal of Travel Research*, **16**: 22–5.
Chojnicki, Z., 1972, An economic approach to some problems in using the geographical environment, *Geographia Polonica*, **20**: 42–7.
Chyský, J. *et al., 1965, A guide to Czechoslovakia*, Artia, Prague.
Cianga, N., 1981, Considerations géographiques sur les ville-stations balneoclimatiques des carpates orientales, *Revue Roumaine: Géographie*, **25**: 269–73.
Cicvarić, A., 1980, *Turizam i privredni razvoj Jugoslavije*, Informator, Zagreb.
Ciobanu, R-S., 1979, The population of the Upper Prahova valley with special consideration on the town of Sinaia, *Revue Roumaine: Géographie*, **23**: 131–42.
Ciulache, S., 1979, A scale of favourable climatic conditions for tourism in Romania, *Revue Roumaine: Géographie*, **23**: 65–74.
Cleverdon, R., 1979, *The economic and social impact of international tourism on developing countries*, Economist Intelligence Unit, London.
CMEA Statistical Yearbook, Moscow.
Cocean, P., 1980, Valorificarea turistică a carstului din Munţii Apuseni, *Terra*, **12**(2): 25–9.
Cole, J.P., 1984, *Geography of the Soviet Union*, Butterworths, London.
Coley, A., 1985, *The development of the Triglav National Park, Slovenia*, University of Bradford, Bradford Studies on Yugoslavia, No. 8, Bradford.
Coltman, M.M., 1989, *Introduction to travel and tourism: an international approach*, Van Nostrand Reinhold, New York.
Compton, P.A., 1987, Hungary, in Dawson, A.H. (ed.), *Planning in Eastern Europe*, Croom Helm, Beckenham, pp. 167–94.
Compton, P.A., 1990, The Republic of Hungary bids farewell to Marxism–Leninism, *Geography*, **75**(3): 255–7.
Constantini, O., 1969, Bulgarien einst und heute, *Zeitschrift für Wirtschaftgeographie*, **13**(8): 253–6.
Crawford, A., 1956, *East of Prague: impressions of Czechoslovakia*, Orbis, Prague.
Croatian Chamber of Commerce, 1989, *Your opportunity to invest in tourism*, Croatian Chamber of Commerce, Zagreb.
Cséfalvay, P., 1987, *Esztergom: Keresztény Múzeum*, TKM, Budapest.
Current Digest of the Soviet Press, weekly, Columbus, Ohio.
Dann, G.M.S., 1977, Anomie, ego-enhancement and tourism, *Annals of Tourism Research*, **4**(4): 184–94.
Dann, G.M.S., 1981, Tourism motivation, *Annals of Tourism Research*, **8**(2): 187–219.
D'Amore, P.L., Jafari, J. (eds), 1989, *Tourism: a vital force for peace*, First Global Conference, Montreal.
Darinskiy, A.V., 1979, *Voprosy turizma v shkol'nom kurse geografii*, Prosveshcheniye, Moscow.
Dawson, A.H., 1984, City profile: Kraków, *Cities*, **1**: 449–56.
Dawson, A.H., 1990, Tides of influence and the economic geography of Poland, *Geography*, **75**(3): 258–60.
de Kadt, E., 1979, *Tourism—passport to development*, Oxford University Press, London.
Demek, J. (ed.), 1975, *ČSSR—příroda, lidé a hospodářství*, Studia Geographica, Brno.

Demek, J., Střída, M., (eds), 1971, Geography of Czechoslovakia, Academia, Prague.
Dempsey, J., 1988, A 'workers' paradise' opens its doors, *The Financial Times*, 27 October: 18.
Dempsey, J., 1989, Hungary sells travel stake to West, *The Financial Times*, 18 December: 27.
Dercsényi, D., 1985, *Vác: Székesegyház*, TKM, Budapest.
Dernoi, L.A., 1981, Alternative tourism: towards a new style in North–South relations, *Tourism Management*, **2**(4): 253–64.
Dhamo, D., 1974, *La peinture murale du moyen age en Albanie*, 8 Nëntori, Tirana.
Diack, H., Mackenzie, R.F., 1935, *Road fortune: a cycling journey through Europe*, Macmillan, London.
Dienes, L., 1973, The Budapest agglomeration and Hungarian industry: a spatial dilemma, *Geographical Review*, **63**: 356–77.
Dienes, L., 1974a, Environmental disruption and its mechanism in Eastern Europe, *Professional Geographer*, **26**: 375–81.
Dienes, L., 1974b, Environmental disruption in Eastern Europe, in Volgyes, I. (ed.), *Environmental deterioration in the Soviet Union and Eastern Europe*, Praeger, New York.
Dinev, L., 1974, Konseptsiya za turistichesko raionirane na N R Bulgarija, *Godishnik na Sofijskija Universitet*, **66**(2): 10–24.
Dinev, L., 1978, Urbanisation and problems of tourism in Bulgaria, *Wiener Geographische Zeitschrift*, **51/52**: 164–182.
Dinev, L., 1982, Regionalizace cestovního ruchu v Bulharské lidově republice, *Sborník Československé Společnosti Zeměpisné*, **87**(2): 132–9.
Dinev, L. *et al.*, 1973, *Geografiya na turizma*, Narodna Prosveta, Sofia.
Dirlam, J., Plummer, J., 1973, *An introduction to the Yugoslav economy*, Charles E. Merrill, Columbus, Ohio.
Dobrzycki, J., 1968, *Cracow*, Arkady, Warsaw.
Docsānescu, N., 1989, Rest, relaxation, amusement . . ., *Holidays in Romania*, **215**: 8–9.
Dogaru, R., 1972, Staţiunea balneară Olăneşti, *Analele Universitatea din Craiova: Istorie–Geografie–Filologie*, **1**: 135–44.
Dohnal, V., Malá, V., 1964, Rozvoj zařizení cestovního ruchu na příkladu územního celku Špindlerův Mlýn v Krkonošich, *Opera Corcontica*, **1**: 121–37.
Dolzhenko, G.P., 1988, *Istoriya turizma v dorevolyutsionnoy Rossii i SSSR*, Izdatel'stvo Rostovskogo Universiteta, Rostov.
Dragomir, V. *et al.*, 1981, *Romania: atlas rutier*, Editura Sport-Turism, Bucharest.
Dragomirescu, S., Nicolae, I., 1980, International tourism of the Balkan countries, *Revue Roumaine: Géographie*, **24**: 175–83.
Dubey, V. (ed.), 1975, *Yugoslavia: development with decentralization*, World Bank/Johns Hopkins University Press, Baltimore.
Dunareanu, I.I. *et al.*, 1967, *The Romanian Black Sea littoral*, Meridiane, Bucharest.
Dunning, J.H., McQueen, M., 1982, *Transnational corporations in international tourism*, United Nations, New York.
Durham, E., 1909, *High Albania*, Edward Arnold, London.
Eadington, W., Smith, V. (eds), 1990, *Theoretical perspectives on alternative forms of tourism*, International Academy for the Study of Tourism.
East European Markets, London.
East European Newsletter, London.
Economic Commission for Europe, 1976, *Planning and development of the tourist industry in the ECE region*, United Nations, New York.
Economic Commission for Europe, 1988, *Economic survey of Europe in 1987–1988*, United Nations, New York.
Edwards, A., *International tourism forecasts to 1995*, Economist Intelligence Unit, London.
EIU (Economist Intelligence Unit), 1989, *Czechoslovakia: country report No. 1*, EIU, London.
EIU (Economist Intelligence Unit), 1990a, *Romania, Bulgaria, Albania: country report*

No. 1, EIU, London.
EIU (Economist Intelligence Unit), 1990b, *Romania, Bulgaria, Albania: country report No. 2*, EIU, London.
Elkins, T.H., 1987, The Fair city, *Geographical Magazine*, **59**(4): 208–10.
Elkins, T.H., 1990, Developments in the German Democratic Republic, *Geography*, **75**(3): 246–9.
Engel, R., 1990, A view of three cities, *Eurobusiness*, **2**(8): 24–6.
Ensminger, S., 1978, Državni organi društveno–političkih zajednica nadležnih za hotelijerstvo, in *Simpozij: 'Hotelska Kuća '78'*, Hotelijerski fakultet, Rijeka, i Opšte udruženje turističke privrede Jugoslavije, Opatija, pp. 25–34.
Eperon, A., 1969, Tourism opens frontiers in Bulgaria, *New York Times*, 2 March: 2–3.
Ernst and Whinney, 1988, *Doing business in the USSR*, Ernst and Whinney, London.
Ertz, W., 1979, *Katalog der Naturschutzgebiete in der Bundesrepublik Deutschland*, Institut für Naturschutz und Tierokologie der Bundesforschungsanstalt für Naturschutz und Landschaftsplege, Bonn.
Etherton, P.T., Allen, A.D., 1928, *Through Europe and the Balkans: the record of a motor tour*, Cassell, London.
Eurobusiness, London.
Farrell, B.H., 1985, Cooperative tourism and the coastal zone, *Coastal Zone Management Journal*, **14**(1/2): 113–30.
Farrell, B.H., McLellan, R.W., 1987, Tourism and physical environment research, *Annals of Tourism Research*, **14**: 1–16.
Fél, E. *et al.*, 1971, *Hungarian peasant art*, Corvina, Budapest/Constable, London.
Filip, D., 1981, Tradiţii şi potenţial turistii în Munţii Parîng, *Studii şi Cercetări: Geografie*, **28**: 135–41.
Fisher, J.C., 1971, The emergence of regional spatial planning in Yugoslavia: the Slovenian experience, in Hoffmann, G.W. (ed.), *Eastern Europe: essays in geographical problems*, Methuen, London, pp. 301–64.
Fisher, L.J., 1917, The Bohemian Sokols, in Zmrhal, J.J., Beneš, V., *Bohemia: a brief evaluation of Bohemia's contribution to civilization*, Bohemian National Alliance, Chicago.
Fitzpatrick, A.L., 1990, *The great Russian fair: Nizhnii Novgorod, 1840–90*, Macmillan, London.
Flegl, M., 1988, *Prague*, Olympia, Prague.
Florea, V., 1969, *Getting to know Romania*, Meridiane, Bucharest.
Focşa, Gh., 1970, *Muzeul Satului din Bucureşti*, Meridiane, Bucharest.
Focşa, Gh., 1975, *Ţara Oaşului*, Muzeul Satului, Bucharest, 2 vols.
Focşa, Gh., nd, *The Village Museum*, Muzeul Satului, Bucharest.
Focşa, P., 1989, The Bucharest of today, the Bucharest of tomorrow, *Holidays in Romania*, **215**: 4–7.
Formánek, V. *et al.*, 1965, *Prague Castle*, Olympia, Prague.
Foster, D., 1985, *Travel and tourism management*, Macmillan, London.
Foster, J., *et al.*, 1984, Protected areas in the United Kingdom, in McNeeley, J.A., Miller, K.R. (eds) National parks, conservation and development, Smithsonian Institute Press, Washington DC, pp. 426–37.
Franzoni, R. *et al.*, 1990, *Yachting in the northern Mediterranean*, Automobile Association, Basingstoke.
Fratu, I., 1986, *Poteci şi cabane în Munţii Făgăraşului*, Editura Sport–Turism, Bucharest.
Frechtling, D.C., 1986, International tourism forecasts to 1995, by A. Edwards, *Annals of Tourism Research*, **13**(3): 497–500.
Friganović, M., 1987a, *River Krka*, Privredni Vjesnik RJ Turistička Propaganda, Zagreb.
Friganović, M., 1987b, *The Kornati Archipelago*, Privredni Vjesnik RJ Turistička Propaganda, Zagreb.
Fujii, E.T., Mak, J., 1980, Tourism and crime: implications for regional development policy, *Regional Studies*, **14**(1), 27–36.

Fullenbach, J., 1981, *European environmental policy: east and west*, Butterworths, London.

Fundamentals of USSR land legislation, 1990, *RSEEA Newsletter*, **12**(1): 27–36.

Galambos, F., 1985, *Vác: Műzemlékek*, TKM, Budapest.

Galasi, P., György, S., (eds), 1985, *Labour market and second economy in Hungary*, Campus Verlag, Frankfurt am Main.

Galla, G., 1989, *Spas in Hungary*, Hungarian Tourist Board, Budapest.

Ganzha, L., 1984, *The Lenin Museum at Gorki*, Raduga, Moscow.

Gardavský, V., 1969, Recreational hinterland of a city taking Prague as an example, *Acta Universitatis Carolinae, Geographica*, **4**(1): 3–29.

Gardavský, V., 1975, Geografie individuální víkendové rekreace v ČSR, *Acta Universitatis Carolinae, Geographica*, **10**(1–2): 123–8.

Gardavský, V., 1977a, Rekreacñí nároky městských obyvatel (na příkladu Chomutova, Litoméřic, Duchova), *Acta Universitatis Carolinae, Geographica*, **12**(2): 25–38.

Gardavský, V., 1977b, Second homes in Czechoslovakia, in Coppock, J.T. (ed.) *Second homes: curse or blessing?*, Pergamon, Oxford, pp. 63–74.

Gardavský, V., Ryslavý, I., 1978, K metodám výzkumu rekreace (na příkladu Liberecka), *Acta Universitatis Carolinae, Geographica*, **13**(2): 43–75.

Gardiner, L., 1976, *Curtain Calls*, Duckworth, London.

Gavrilescu, C., 1973, Turismul international: activitate economică de mare eficienţa, in Barbu, Gh. (ed.), *Turismul: ramura a economiei nationale*, Editura Pentru Turism, Bucharest, pp. 61–74.

Gee, C.Y., Makens, J.C., Choy, D.J.L., 1989 (2nd edn) *The travel industry*, Van Nostrand Reinhold, New York.

Geneshki, M., 1989, *Teritorialnite obshnosti v N R Bulgarija*, Universitetsko Izdatelstvo 'Kliment Ohridski', Sofia.

Geografiya rekreatsionnykh sistem SSSR, 1980, Nauka, Moscow.

Gershuny, J.I., Miles, I.D., 1983, *The new service economy*, Pinter, London.

Gilbert, D.C., 1989, Tourism marketing, in Cooper, C.P. (ed.), *Progress in tourism, recreation and hospitality management Vol. 1*, Belhaven, London, pp. 77–90.

Gilewska, S., 1964, Changes in the geographical environment brought about by industrialization and urbanization, *Geographia Polonica*, **3**: 201–10.

Giurgiu, V., 1980, Pădurile şi lacurile de acumulare, *Revista Pădurilor*, **95**: 309–13.

Glavan, V. (ed.), 1978, *Studii de turism: turism montan*, Institut de Economia Comertului Interior si a Turismului, Bucharest.

Gołembski, G., 1990, Tourism in the economy of shortage, *Annals of Tourism Research*, 17(1): 55–68.

Gorman, B., 1979, Seven days, five countries: the making of a group, *Urban Life*, 7(4): 469–91.

Granville, A.B., 1837, *The spas of Germany*, A. and W. Galignani, Paris.

Greenberg, S.H. *et al.*, 1990, Freedom trail, *Newsweek*, 14 May: 12–17.

Grigorov, N., 1980, Teritiorialnoustroistveno razvitie i upravlenie na vilnija otdih v Bulgarija, *Information Buletin*, 7–8: 3–100.

Grbić, Č., 1984, *Socijalizam i rad privatnim sredstvima,* Biblioteka Socijalističko Samoupravljanje i Suvremeni Svijet, Zagreb.

Gueorguiev, A., Andonov, M, 1974, *Développement et perspectives du tourisme international sur le littoral Bulgare de la Mer Noire*, Cahiers du Tourisme, Series B., No. 11, Centre d'Etudes du Tourisme, Aix-en-Provence.

Gurashi, A., Ziri, F., 1982, *Albania constructs socialism relying on its own forces*, 8 Nëntori, Tirana.

Hadač, E., Gottlieb, M., 1982, Rekreace a lidské zdraví, in Hadač, E., *Krajina a lidé*, Academia, Prague.

Halász, Z. (ed.), 1960, *Hungary*, Corvina, Budapest.

Hall, D.R., 1984a, Albania's growing railway network, *Geography*, **69**: 263–5.

Hall, D.R., 1984b, Foreign tourism under socialism: the Albanian 'Stalinist' model, *Annals of Tourism Research*, **11**(4): 539–55.

Hall, D.R., 1984c, Tourism and social change: reply to Romsa, *Annals of Tourism*

Research, **11**(4): 608–10.

Hall, D.R., 1985a, Problems and possibilities of an Albanian–Yugoslav rail link, in Ambler, J. *et al.* (eds), *Soviet and East European transport problems*, Croom Helm, Beckenham, pp. 206–20.

Hall, D.R., 1985b, Yugoslavia and Albania link up their railway systems, *Journal of the British–Yugoslav Society*, Summer: 23–7.

Hall, D.R., 1987a, Albania's transport cooperation with her neighbours, in Tismer, J.F. *et al.* (eds), *Transport and economic development—Soviet Union and Eastern Europe*, Duncker and Humblot, West Berlin, pp. 379–99.

Hall, D.R., 1987b, Berlin turns on, *Town and Country Planning*. **56**(12): 334–5.

Hall, D.R., 1988, The sickness on the Danube, *Town and Country Planning*, **57**(3): 80–1.

Hall, D.R., 1989a, Planning Bulgaria's uncertain future, *Town and Country Planning*, **58**(12): 347–8.

Hall, D.R., 1989b, Planning for a new Central Europe?, *Town and Country Planning*, **58**(9): 253–4.

Hall, D.R., 1990a, Albania, in Sillince, J.A.A., (ed.), *Housing policy in Eastern Europe and the Soviet Union*, Routledge, London, pp. 359–401.

Hall, D.R., 1990b, Albania: the last bastion? *Geography*, **75**(3): 268–71.

Hall, D.R., 1990c, Eastern Europe opens its doors, *Geographical Magazine*, **62**(4): 10–15.

Hall, D.R., 1990d, Introduction: geographic dimensions of change, *Geography*, **75**(3): 239–44.

Hall, D.R., 1990e, Planning for a united Germany, *Town and Country Planning*, **59**(3): 93–5.

Hall, D.R., 1990f, Stalinism and tourism: a study of Albania and North Korea, *Annals of Tourism Research*, **17**(1): 36–54.

Hall, D.R., 1990g, The 'Communist World' in the 1990s, *Town and Country Planning*, **59**(1): 28–30.

Hamsher, W.P., 1937, *The Balkans by bicycle*, H.F. and G. Witherby, London.

Harrison, D., (ed.), forthcoming, *International tourism in the Third World*, Belhaven, London.

Havrlant, M., 1968, Problémy rekreăcního zázemi pro obyvatelstvo Ostravské průmyslové aglomerace, *Sborník Československé Společností Zeměpisné*, **73**(2): 143–8.

Havrlant, M., 1973, Vlív Ostravské průmyslové aglomerace na rekreační zástavbu v Beskydech, *Sborník prací Pedagogické Fakultet v Ostravé*, **35**: 63–92.

Havrlant, M., 1974, Hodnocenie rekreačního ruchu na příkladu rekreační zástavby v beskydské oblastí, *Sborník Československé Společností Zeměpisné*, **79**(1): 20–8.

Havrlant, M., 1975, Nízky Jeseník a Oderské vrchy jako rekreační zázemi Ostravské průmyslové aglomerace, *Sborník prací Pedagogické Fakultet v Ostravé*, **40**: 43–94.

Héjj, M., 1988, *Visegrád: Királyi palota*, TKM, Budapest.

Heller, M., 1969, *Ski*, Faber, London.

Herold, L.C., 1981, Chata and chalupa: recreational houses in the Czech Socialist Republic, *Social Science Journal*, **18**(1): 51–68.

Hildebrandt, R., 1969, *It happened at the Wall*, Haus am Checkpoint Charlie, Berlin.

Hildebrandt, R., 1982, *The Wall speaks*, Haus am Checkpoint Charlie, Berlin.

Hodgson, A. (ed.), 1987, *The travel and tourism industry: strategies for the future*, Pergamon, Oxford.

Hoffman, G.W. (ed.), 1971, *Eastern Europe: essays in geographical problems*, Methuen, London.

Hoivik, T., Heiberg, T., 1980, Centre-periphery tourism and self-reliance, *International Social Science Journal*, **32**(1): 69–98.

Holloway, J.C., 1981, The guided tour: a sociological approach, *Annals of Tourism Research*, **8**(3): 377–402.

Horna, J.L.A., 1988, Leisure studies in Czechoslovakia: some East–West parallels and divergencies, *Leisure Sciences*, **10**(2): 79–94.

Horvat, B., 1976, *The Yugoslav economic system*, International Arts and Sciences Press,

White Plains.

Horváth, I., 1986, *Esztergom: a vár története*, TKM, Budapest.

Horwath & Horwath, 1989, *Tourism: a portrait of the hotel and tourism industry*, Horwath & Horwath, London.

Hospodářské Noviny, Prague.

Hudman, L.E., 1979, Origin regions of international tourism, *Wiener Geographische Schriften*, **53/54**: 43–9.

Hudman, L.E., 1980, *Tourism: a shrinking world*, Grid Inc., Columbus.

Hudman, L.E., Hawkins, D.E., 1989, *Tourism in contemporary society: an introductory text*, Prentice-Hall, Englewood Cliffs, NJ.

Hungarian Central Statistical Office (annual), *Idegenforgalmi Statisztikai Évkönyv (Yearbook of tourist statistics)*, Budapest.

Hungarian Central Statistical Office (1989), *Idegenforgalmi Évkönyv (Tourist yearbook)*, Budapest.

Hutchings, R., 1971, *Soviet economic development*, Basil Blackwell, Oxford.

Hyman, S., (ed.), 1988, *Edward Lear in the Levant*, John Murray, London.

Iacob, G., Ianoş, I., 1987, Potenţialul turistic al Munţilor Apuseni şi valorificarea acestuia, *Terra*, **19**(4): 27–30.

Iancu, M., 1967, Citeva consideratii asupra geografiei turismului, *Studia Universitatis Babes-Bolayi, Series Geologia-Geographia*, **2**: 371–5.

ICCE (Institut Central de Cercetări Economice), 1983, *Progresul economic al României socialiste concepţia preşedinţelui Nicolae Ceauşescu*, Editura Politică, Bucharest.

ILO (International Labour Organisation), *Yearbook of labour statistics*, ILO, Geneva.

Institut de Géographie, 1974, *III-ème colloque de géographie du tourisme: resumés*, Institut de Géographie, Bucharest.

Iordan, I. *et al.*, 1984, Geografia turismului, in Cucu, V., *et al.*, (eds), *Geografia româniei: geografia umană şi economică*, Editura Academiei R.S.R., Bucharest, pp. 461–99.

Istrate, I., 1988, Dezvoltarea turismului in R.S.R.: realizări şi perspective, *Terra*, **20**(2): 24-31.

IUCN (International Union for the Conservation of Nature), 1986, *1985 United Nations list of national parks and protected areas*, IUCN, Cambridge.

IUCN (International Union for the Conservation of Nature), 1987, *Protected landscapes: experience around the world*, IUCN, Cambridge.

IUOTO (International Union of Official Travel Organisations), 1975, *The impact of international tourism on the economic development of the developing countries*, IUOTO/WTO, Geneva.

Izbicki, R., Suminski, T., 1968, *In the Bieszczady Mountains*, Interpress, Warsaw.

Jacková, A., Herberová, D., 1973, Koncepcie rozvoja cestovného ruchu v hlavnom meste SSR Bratislave a jej rekreačnom zázemi a v okresesech Košice, Prešov a Stará L'ubovňa, *Ekonomického Revue Cestovného Ruchu*, **3**: 132–48.

Jackowski, A., 1980, Methodological problems of functional typology of tourist localities, *Folia Geographica, Series Geographica–Oeconomica*, **13**: 85–91.

Jarosławiecka, M., Gąsiorowski, St. J., 1924, *Cracow: its antiquities and museums*, Gebethner and Wolff, Warsaw.

Jordanov, T. (ed.), 1981, *Geografija na Bulgarija*, Bulgarska Akademija Naukite, Sofia, 3 vols.

Jowitt, K. (ed.), 1971, *Social change in Romania 1860–1940: a debate on development in a European state*, University of California Institute of International Studies, Berkeley.

Jugoslavija, 1919–1988: Statistički Godišnjak, 1989, Savezni Zavod za Statistiku, Belgrade.

Karbuczky, I. *et al.*, 1990, *Tourism in Hungary*, ECHO (Hungarian Economic Information Service), Budapest.

Karrasch, H., 1983, Transboundary air pollution in Europe, *Heidelburger Geographische Arbeiten*, **73**: 321–44.

Kaspar, C., 1990, A new lease on life for spa and health tourism, *Annals of Tourism Research*, **17**(2): 298–9.

Katona, S., 1979, The assessment of anthropogenic effects on environment in the Budapest agglomeration, *Geografický Časopis*, **31**(1): 12–27.

Kecskés, P., 1987, *Szentendre: Szabadtéri Neeprajzi Muzeum II*, TKM, Budapest.

Kerpel, E., 1989, *Czechoslovakia*, International Tourism Report No. 2, Economist Intelligence Unit, London.

Khristova, T., 1988, Sotsialnopsikhologicheska kharakteristika na potrebnostta i motivite za turiz'm prez 80—te godini, *Godishnik Visshija Institut za Narodno Stopanstvo 'Dimit'r Blagoev'*, **2**: 112–20.

Kilian, P.P., 1985, Bulgarien—Kernland des Balkans, *Mitteilungen der Geographischen Gesellschaft zu Lübeck,* **56**: 73–118.

Kobašić, A., 1980, Lessons from planning in Yugoslavia's tourist industry, *International Journal of Tourism Management*, **1**: 233–9.

Kobašić, A., 1987, *Turizam u Jugoslaviji*, Informator, Zagreb.

Kohl, H., *et al.*, 1978a, *Die Bezirke der DDR*, Haack, Gotha.

Kohl, H., *et al.*, 1978b, *Ökonomische geographie der DDR*, Haack, Gotha.

Kóródi, J., 1976, Regional development policy and regional planning in Hungary, in Compton, P.A., Pecsi, M. (eds), *Regional development and planning*, Akadémiai Kiadó, Budapest, pp. 25–34.

Kotrba, M., 1968, *Rajonizace cestovního ruchu v CSSR*, Merkur, Prague.

Kotrba, M., Přikryl, F., 1964, Rozvoj cestovního ruchu a rekreace v ČSSR, *Architektura ČSSR*, **23**: 232–40.

KPS (Komisioni i Planit të Shtetit), 1989, *Vjetari statistikor i R.P.S. të Shqipërisë*, KPS, Tirana.

Kraja, E., 1976, *Shkodra almanak*, 8 Nëntori, Tirana.

Král, K., 1955, *Czechoslovakia: land of work and peace*, ROH, Prague.

Král, V. *et al.*, 1968, *Czechoslovakia: land and people*, Academia, Prague.

Král, V., 1983, Metody hodnocení estetiky krajiny, *Prace i Studia Geograficzne*, **4**:17–22.

Kramer, J.M., 1983, The environmental crisis in Eastern Europe: the price of progress, *Slavic Review*, **42**: 204–20.

Kreck, L.A., 1989, The semantics of the word 'peace', *Annals of Tourism Research*, **16**: 429–30.

Krippendorf, J., 1986, The new tourist—turning point for leisure and travel, *Tourism Management*, **7**: 131–5.

Krippendorf, J., 1987, *The holiday makers: understanding the impact of leisure and travel*, Heinemann, London.

Krstić, M., 1990, Ada Ciganlija—Belgrade's recreational centre, *Belgrade Review*, **29–30**: 64–7.

Kruczała, J., 1990, Tourism planning in Poland, *Annals of Tourism Research*, **17**(1): 69–78.

Kurortnyy putevoditel', 1915, St. Petersburg.

Kushman, J. *et al.*, 1980, Political systems and international travel, *Social Science Quarterly*, **60**(4): 604–15.

Kusiński, W., 1983, Urbanizacja a ochrona i kształtowanie przyrody, *Prace i Studia Geograficzne,* **4**: 91–9.

Labasse, J., 1984, Les congrès activités tertiaire de villes privilèges, *Annales de Géographie*, **520**: 687–703.

Laboutka, M., Výlita, B., 1983, Mineral and thermal waters of Western Bohemia, *GeoJournal*, **7**(5): 403–11.

Lampe, J.R., 1986, *The Bulgarian economy in the twentieth century*, Croom Helm, Beckenham.

Latham, J., 1989, The statistical measurement of tourism, in Cooper, C.P. (ed.), *Progress in tourism, recreation and hospitality management Vol. 1*, Belhaven, London, pp. 55–76.

Lavrishchev, A., 1969, *Economic geography of the USSR*, Progress, Moscow.

Law, C., 1988, Congress tourism, *Built Environment*, **13**(2): 85–95.

Lea, J., 1988, *Tourism and development in the Thirld World*, Routledge, London.

Lear, E., 1851, *Journals of a landscape painter in Greece & Albania*, Hutchinson, London.
Leisure News, London.
Leisure Opportunities, London.
Lemeshev, M. Ya., Shcherbina, O.A., 1986, *Optimizatsiya rekreatsionnoy deyatel'nosti*, Ekonomika, Moscow.
Licinska, D., 1985, *Geographia: Polska*, Interpress, Warsaw.
Lockwood, W., 1973, The peasant worker in Yugoslavia, *Studies in European Society*, **1**: 91–110.
Logoreci, A., 1977, *The Albanians: Europe's forgotten survivors*, Victor Gollancz, London.
Losanoff, E., 1968, Geographische Aspekte der Auslandstouristik in der Volksrepublik Bulgarien, *Geographische Berichte*, **13**(2): 125–36.
Lovenduski, J., Woodall, J., 1987, *Politics and society in Eastern Europe*, Macmillan, London.
Ludvik, M., Mohyla, O., 1989, *Czechoslovakia, Prague*, Olympia, Prague.
Ludz, P.C. *et al.*, nd, *Handbuch DDR*, Bundesministerium für Innerdeutsche Beziehungen, Verlag Wissenschaft und Politik, Cologne.
Lyall, A., 1930, *The Balkan road*, Methuen, London.
Lyall, K.C., 1968, *Inter-republic flows of investment in tourism—Yugoslavia, 1967*, American–Yugoslav Project in regional and Urban Planning Studies, Working Paper, Urbanistični Institut SRS, Ljubljana.
Lydall, H., 1984, *Yugoslav socialism: theory and practice*, Clarendon Press, Oxford.
Lydall, H., 1989, *Yugoslavia in crisis*, Clarendon Press, Oxford.
Maciu, M. *et al.*, 1986, *Mac dictionar enciclopedic*, Editura Stiintifica-Enciclopedica, Bucharest.
MacKenzie, D., 1989, Alpine countries seek control on skiers, builders and roads, *New Scientist, 124(1686): 22.*
Mały Rocznik Statystyczny 1939, Warsaw.
Mandi, P., 1980, Tourist Albania, *Albanian Foreign Trade*, **123**: 6.
Marica, V., 1967, *St. Michael's Church of Cluj*, Meridiane, Bucharest.
Marinescu, F., 1973, Consideraţii asupra locolui şi rolului turismului în societatea socialistă multilateral dezvoltată, in Barbu, Gh. (ed.), *Turismul: ramura a economiei nationale*, Editura Pentru Turism, Bucharest, pp. 21–30.
Mariot, P., 1971, *Regionálna analyza západného Slovenska z hl'adiska cestovného ruchu*, Bratislava.
Mariot, P., 1976, Objekty individuálnej rekreácie na Slovensku, *Geografický Časopis*, **28**(1): 3–22.
Mariot, P., 1977, Die Grundzuge des Verlaufs der Besucherzahl in den slowakischen Hohlen, in *International Speleology 1973*, VII, sub-section Fc, Academia, Prague, pp. 221-6.
Mariot, P., 1983, *Geografia cestovního ruchu*, Bratislava.
Mariot, P., 1984, Geography of tourism in Czechoslovakia, *GeoJournal*, **9**(1): 65–8.
Marković, S. *et al.*, 1980, *Osnovne srednoročnog i dugoročnog ravitka 'Atlasa'*, Institut za Ekonomiku Turizma, Zagreb.
Marmullaku, R., 1975, *Albania and the Albanians*, C. Hurst, London.
Marx, K., Engels, F., 1964, *Sochineniya*, Gos. Izd. Pol. Lit., Moscow, vol. 26, 2nd edn.
Mason, K. *et al.*, 1945, *Albania*, Naval Intelligence Division, London.
Mathieson, A., Wall, G., 1982, *Tourism: economic, physical and social impacts*, Longman, London.
Matley, I.M., 1968, Transhumance in Bosnia and North Hercegovina, *Geographical Review*, **58**: 231–61.
Matley, I.M., 1976, *The geography of international tourism*, Resource Paper 76–1, Michigan State University, reprinted in Mill, R.C., Morrison, A.M., 1985, *The tourism system*, Prentice-Hall, Englewood Cliffs, NJ, pp. 175–200.
Matthews, R., 1937, *Sons of the eagle*, Methuen, London.
McCulloch, J.I.B., 1936, *Drums in the Balkan night*, Putnam's, New York.

McIntosh, R.W., Goeldner, C.R., 1990 (6th edn.), *Tourism: principles practices and philosophies*, John Wiley, New York.

McIntyre, J.F., 1987, The USSR's hard currency trade and payments position, in *Gorbachev's economic plans*, Joint Economic Committee of the Congress of the United States, Washington DC, vol. 2: 474–88.

Mellor, R.E.H., 1975, *Eastern Europe: a geography of the Comecon countries*, Macmillan, London.

Mellor, R.E.H., 1979, *The two Germanies*, Harper & Row, London.

Meyer, B., 1990, Russians on holiday at home, *Geographical Magazine*, **62**(4): 16–8.

Miclescu, P.E., 1967, *The monuments on the Patriarchate Hill*, Meridiane, Bucharest.

Mihailov, D., Smolenov, P., 1981, *Sofia: a guide*, Sofia Press, Sofia.

Mihailov, D., Smolenov, P., 1985, *Bulgaria: a guide*, Collets/Sofia, Press, Wellingborough.

Mill, R.C., 1990, *Tourism: the international business*, Prentice-Hall, Englewood Cliffs, NJ.

Mill, R.C., Morrison, A.M., 1985, *The tourism system*, Prentice-Hall, Englewood-Cliffs, NJ.

Miškufová, H., 1989, Winter in the High Tatras, *Czechoslovak Life*, December: 5–7.

Mišunová, E., 1988, Hodnotenie přiordných predpokladov dynamického cestovnĥo ruchu v Slovenskej Socialisticket Republike, *Geografický Časopis,* **40**(4): 364–78.

Molnar, E. *et al.*, 1976, Types de localités touristiques dans la République Socialiste de Roumanie, *Revue Roumaine de Géologie, Géophysique et Géographie, Série de Géographie*, **20**: 189–95.

Morris, A.E.J., 1973, Four towns in a Bohemian setting, *Geographical Magazine*, **57**: 77–81.

Morritt, J.B.S., 1985, *A grand tour. Letters and journeys 1794–96.* Century, London.

Motka, L., 1962, *Touring Czechoslovakia*, Sportovni a Turistické Nakladatelství, Prague.

Movčan, J., nd, *National Park Plitvice*, Touristkomerc, Zagreb.

Mukic, M., 1982, Tourism's contribution to the Yugoslav economy, *Tourism Management*, **9**(4): 301–16.

Munteanu, L., Grigore, L., 1975, *Bāile Felix*, Publishing House for Sports and Tourism, Bucharest.

Muranský, S., 1974, Krajinářské hodnocení území, *Sborník ČSSZ*, **79**: 82–93.

Murphy, P.E., 1982, Perceptions and attitudes of decision-making groups in tourism centers, *Journal of Travel Research*, **21**: 8–12.

Murphy, P.E., 1985, *Tourism: a community approach*, Methuen, London.

Musicescu, M.A., Ionescu, G., 1967, *The Princely Church of Curtea de Argeş*, Meridiane, Bucharest.

Myrdal. J., Kessle, G., 1978, *Albania defiant*, Stage 1, London.

Nagaitis, C., Delgado, M., 1990, Leading scientists call for urgent action, *The European*, 25 May.

Naidenova, R., 1989, Turizmit-rezultat i faktor za razvitieto i teritorialnoto razpredelenie na proizvoditenite sili, *Geografija*, **43**(2): 1–6.

Nallbani, H., 1989, *The Onufri Museum Berat*, 8 Nëntori, Tirana.

Narodnoye khozyaystvo SSSR v 1988g, 1989, Finansy i Statistika, Moscow.

Nash, D., Butler, R., 1990, Alternative forms of tourism, *Annals of Tourism Research*, **17**(2): 302–5.

Nashi zdravnitsy, 1965, Fizkul'tura i Sport, Moscow.

Neef, E. *et al.*, 1977, *Sozialistische Landeskultur*, Edition Leipzig, Leipzig.

Nefedova, V.B. *et al.*, 1974, Techniques for the recreational evaluation of an area, *Soviet Geography*, **15**(8): 507–12.

Newby, E., 1985, *On the shores of the Mediterranean*, Pan, London.

Nicod, J., 1982, Canyons et grottes du plateau de Trigrad (Rhodope central Bulgarie), *Revue de Géographie Alpine*, **70**(3): 227–31.

Oancea, D. *et al.*, 1987, *Geografia romaniei: Carpatii romanesti*, Editura Academiei

R.S.R., Bucharest.

Obrman, J., 1989, Tourism: expansion plans are criticised, *Radio Free Europe Research*, **14**(25): 23–8.

OECD, 1972, *Economic Survey: Yugoslavia*, OECD, Paris.

OECD, 1978, *Tourism policy and international tourism in OECD member countries*, OECD, Paris.

OECD, 1980, *The impact of tourism on development*, OECD, Paris.

OECD, 1985, *Economic Survey: Yugoslavia*, OECD, Paris.

OECD, 1987/8, *Economic Survey: Yugoslavia*, OECD, Paris.

O'Hagan, J.W., 1979, *The dispersal pattern of United States tourists in Europe, 1967–1977*, European Travel Commission, Dublin.

Okolicsanyi, K., 1989, Dramatic increase in Soviet-Hungarian border crossings, *Radio Free Europe Research*, Hungarian SR/10: 33–4.

Okolicsanyi, K., 1990, Can Hungary afford the 1995 Budapest–Vienna World Exhibition? *Report on Eastern Europe*, **1**(3): 9–11.

Oldberg, I., 1983, Planned economy and environmental problems: Eastern Europe from a comparative perspective, *Bidrag till Ostatsforskningen*, **11**: 1–64.

Ostrowski, S., 1984, Tourism in protected areas—the case of Poland, *Tourism Management*, **5**(2): 118–22.

Ostrowski, S., 1986, Poland's international tourism, *Tourism Management*, **6**(4): 288–94.

Ostrowski, S., 1987, Polish holiday villages: secular tradition and modern practice, *Tourism Management*, **8**(1): 41–8.

Otrubová, E., 1980, Priestorové rozloženie chát na Slovensku so špecifickým zameraním na chaty obyvatel'ov, *Acta Facultatis Rerum Naturalium Universitatis Comemianae, Geographica*, **18**: 129–46.

Otrubová, E., 1985, Cestovný ruch—aktivizujući činitel' v hospodárskej štruktúre Tatranskej obce Ždiar, *Acta Facultatis Rerum Naturalium Universitatis Comemianae, Geographica*, **25**: 69–78.

Oudiette, V., 1990, International tourism in China, *Annals of Tourism Research*, **17**(1): 123–32.

Pacepa, I., 1989, *Red horizons*, Coronet, London.

Păcurar, A., 1987, Cîteva consideraţii asupra aşezărilor umane de pe terra situate la mare altitudine, *Terra*, **19**(1): 38–40.

Panighianţ, E., 1967, *The Danube Delta*, Meridiane, Bucharest.

Pano, N.C., 1968, *The Peoples Republic of Albania*, The Johns Hopkins Press, Baltimore.

Pap, M. *et al.*, 1964, *Budapest*, Corvina, Budapest.

Pătrăscoiu, N., 1987, *Pădurea şi recrearea*, Editura Cereş, Bucharest.

Paxton, J. (ed.), 1988, *The statesman's yearbook*, Macmillan, London, 125th edition.

Pearce, D.G., 1981, *Tourist development*, Longman, London.

Pearce, D.G., 1987a, Spatial patterns of package tourism in Europe, *Annals of Tourism Research*, **14**(2): 183–201.

Pearce, D.G., 1987b, *Tourism today: a geographical analysis*, Longman, London.

Pearce, D.G., 1989, *Tourist development*, Longman, London, 2nd edn.

Pearce, P.L., 1982, *The social psychology of tourist behaviour*, Pergamon, Oxford.

Pearlman, M., 1986, *Bulgaria*, International Tourism Report No. 108, Economist Intelligence Unit, London.

Pearlman, M.V., 1990, Conflicts and constraints in Bulgaria's tourism sector, *Annals of Tourism Research*, **17**(1): 103–22.

Pehe, J., 1989, Government proposes more liberal travel law, *Radio Free Europe Research*, Czechoslovak SR/20: 25–8.

Pejović, S., 1966, *The market-planned economy of Yugoslavia*, University of Minnesota Press, Minneapolis.

Pellumbi, S., 1988, 'Restructuring'—ideological mechanism to deceive the masses, *Albania Today*, **99**: 48–52.

Penkov, V., 1987, Turisticheski vazmozhnosti v Rodopite, *Turistichesko Delo*, 21 January: 2.

Pertsik, Ye. N., 1973, *Rayonnaya planirovka*, Mysl', Moscow.

Peters, M., 1969, *International tourism*, Hutchinson, London.

Petrov, V., 1981, A country of tourism, in Bokov, G. (ed.), *Modern Bulgaria: history, policy, economy, culture*, Sofia Press, Sofia, pp. 442–66.

Petrujová, T., 1974, Rekreace v okolí měst ČSR, in Blažek, M. (ed.), *K otázkám urbanizace*, Brno, pp. 79–93.

Ploaie, G., 1983, *Valea Lotrului*, Editura Sport-Turism, Bucharest.

Pollo, S., Puto, A., 1981, *The history of Albania*, Routledge & Kegan Paul, London.

Poncet, J., 1976, Le developpement du tourisme en Bulgarie, *Annales de Géographie*, **85**: 155–77.

Popa, T., 1974, *Icônes et miniatures du moyen age en Albanie*, 8 Nëntori, Tirana.

Popovici, I., 1977, Regiunile turistice din R.S.R., *Studii şi Cercetări: Geografie*, **24**: 23–9.

Poulsen, T.M., 1977, Migration on the Adriatic coast: some processes associated with the development of tourism, in Kostanick, H.L. (ed.), *Population and migration trends in Eastern Europe*, Westview, Boulder, Colorado, pp. 197–215.

Pounds, N.J.G., 1985, *An historical geography of Europe 1800–1914*, Cambridge University Press, Cambridge.

Preobrazhenskiy, V.S. (ed.) 1986, *Territorial'naya organizatsiya otdykha naseleniya Moskvy i Moskovskoy oblasti*, Nauka, Moscow.

Prifti, P.R., 1978, *Socialist Albania since 1944: domestic and foreign developments*, MIT Press, Cambridge, Mass.

Prifti, P.R., 1979, Albania, in Bromke, A., Novak, D. (eds), *The communist states in the era of detente*, Mosaic Press, Oakville, Ontario, pp. 189–210.

Prifti, S., 1988, The museum zone of the Shkodra city, in PSR of Albania, *Legacy of centuries*, 8 Nëntori, Tirana, pp. 27–30.

Pritchett, V.S., 1960, Bulgaria today, *Holiday*, **28**(6): 108–9.

Probald, E., 1974, Air pollution and the urban climate of Budapest, in Pecsi, M., Probald, F., (eds), *Man and environment*, Hungarian Academy of Sciences, Budapest.

Probald, E., 1984, Urban climate and urban planning in Budapest, in Compton, P.A., Pecsi, M., (eds), *Environmental management: British and Hungarian case studies*, Hungarian Academy of Sciences, Budapest.

PSR of Albania, 1977, *Constitution of the People's Socialist Republic of Albania*, 8 Nëntori, Tirana.

Putrik, Yu. S., Sveshnikov, V.V., 1986, *Turizm glazami geografa*, Mysl', Moscow.

Quiroga, I., 1990, Characteristics of package tours in Europe, *Annals of Tourism Research*, **17**(2): 185–207.

Rachev, R.P., 1988, S'shnost i sistema na dogovorite v mezhdunarodnija turiz'm, *Godishnik Visshija Institut za Narodno Stopanstvo 'Dimit'r Blagoev'*, **2**: 130–9.

Radio Free Europe, 1972, *Czechoslovakia situation report 3*, Radio Free Europe Research, Munich.

Radio Free Europe, 1973, *Czechoslovakia situation report 8*, Radio Free Europe Research, Munich.

Radio Free Europe, 1976, *Czechoslovakia situation report 17*, Radio Free Europe Research, Munich.

Radio Free Europe, 1977, *Czechoslovakia situation report 30*, Radio Free Europe Research, Munich.

Radio Free Europe, 1980, *Czechoslovakia situation report 28*, Radio Free Europe Research, Munich.

Radio Free Europe, 1981, *Czechoslovakia situation report 25*, Radio Free Europe Research, Munich.

Radio Free Europe, 1984, *Czechoslovakia situation report 15*, Radio Free Europe Research, Munich.

Radio Free Europe, 1985, *Czechoslovakia situation report 12*, Radio Free Europe Research, Munich.

Radio Free Europe, 1986, *Czechoslovakia situation report 3*, Radio Free Europe Research, Munich.

Radio Free Europe, 1988, *Czechoslovakia situation report 14*, Radio Free Europe Research, Munich.

Radišić, F., 1981, *Turizam i turistička politika*, Istarska Naklada, Pula.

Rakadjhiyska, S.G., 1990, Tourism training and education in Bulgaria, *Annals of Tourism Research*, **17**(1): 150–3.

Rakadzhiyska, S., Radilov, D., 1984, Britanskite turisti v N R Bulgarija i vomozhnosti za uvelicharane na valutnite prichodi, *Trudove na Visshija Institut za Narodno Stopanstvo 'D. Blagoev'*, **56**(4): 134–78.

Reiseführer DDR, various editions, VEB Tourist, Berlin.

Reymers, N.F., Shtil'mark, F.R., 1978, *Osobo okhranyayemyye prirodnyye territorii*, Mysl', Moscow.

Rhodes, T., 1990, Europe bakes in the hot-house, *The European*, 25 May.

Richter, L.K. (ed.), 1987, The search for appropriate tourism: focus on the Third World, *Tourism Recreation Research*, **12**(2).

Riordan, J., 1977, *Sport in Soviet society*, Cambridge University Press, Cambridge.

Riza, E., 1978, *Gjirokastra: museum city*, 8 Nëntori, Tirana.

Robinson, H., 1976, *A geography of tourism*, MacDonald and Evans, Plymouth.

Rocznik Statystyczny, various, Warsaw.

Rocznik Statystyczny Wojewódz, various, Warsaw.

Rogalewski, O., 1966, Podstawy zagospodarowania turystyczego Polski, *Ruch Turystyczny*, **2**: 20.

Rogalewski, O., 1980, International tourism originating from Poland, *International Social Science Journal*, **32**(1): 114–27.

Romeril, M., 1989, Tourism—the environmental dimension, in Cooper, C.P. (ed.), *Progress in tourism, recreation and hospitality management*, Belhaven, London, pp. 103–13.

Romsa, G.H., 1984, Comment on Hall's 'Foreign tourism under socialism', *Annals of Tourism Research*, **114**: 607–8.

Ronkainen, I.A., 1983, The Conference on Security and Cooperation in Europe: its impact on tourism, *Annals of Tourism Research*, **10**(3): 413–20.

Rosencranz, A., 1980, The problem of transboundary pollution, *Environment*, **22**(5): 15–20.

Rostow, W.W., 1973, The take-off into self-sustained growth, in Mountjoy, A.B. (ed.), *Developing the underdeveloped countries*, Hutchinson, London, pp. 86–114.

Rot, D., 1968, Jihozápadní okalí Prahy, *Květy*, **16**: 18–20.

Ruble, B.A., 1981, *Soviet trade unions: their development in the 1970s*, Cambridge University Press, Cambridge.

Rugg, D.S., 1985, *Eastern Europe*, Longman, London.

Ruler, J., 1989, *Horse riding in Europe*, Ashford Press, Southampton.

Rybár, C., 1982, *Czechoslovakia*, Olympia, Prague/Collet's, Wellingborough.

Sallnow, J., 1985, Yugoslavia: tourism in a socialist federal state, *Tourism Management*, **6**(2): 113–24.

Sampson, A., 1968, *The new Europeans*, Hodder and Stoughton, London.

Sándor, J., Kárbuczky, I., 1989, Az idegenforgalmi teruletfejlesztesi, *Idegenforgalmi Kozlemenyek*, **89**(1): 11–7; (2): 15–23.

Savezni Komitet za Turizam, 1965, *Mogućnost razvoja turizma u Jugoslaviji*, Materijak Grupe Eksperata Ujedinjenjih Nacija, Belgrade.

Schmidt, C.J., 1975, *The guided tour: insulated adventure*, Travel Research Association, 6th Annual Conference Proceedings, New York.

Sebestyén, T., Vajkai, A., 1982, *Lake Balaton: a comprehensive guide*, Corvina, Budapest.

Senn, H.A., 1982, *Were-wolf and vampire in Romania*, Columbia University Press, New York.

Shackleford, P., 1987, Global tourism trends, *Tourism Management*, **8**(2): 98–101.

Shaw, D.J.B., 1979, Recreation and the Soviet city, in French, R.A., Hamilton, F.E.I., (eds), *The socialist city*, Wiley, Chichester, pp. 119–43.

Shaw, D.J.B., 1980, Achievements and problems in Soviet recreational planning, in Brine, J. *et al.*, (eds), *Home, school and leisure in the Soviet Union*, Allen and Unwin, London, pp. 195–214.

Shaw, D.J.B., 1986, Union of Soviet Socialist Republics, in Patricios, N.N., (ed.), *International handbook on land use planning*, Greenwood, New York, pp. 421–44.

Shaw, G., Williams, A.M., 1990, Tourism and development, in Pinder, D., (ed.), *Western Europe: challenge and change*, Belhaven, London, pp. 240–57.

Shipkovenski, T., 1986, Kurortnijat kompleks 'Shipkovski Mineralni Bani', *Geografija*, **41**(2): 13–15.

Shivji, I.G. (ed.), 1975, *Tourism and socialist development*, Tanzania Publishing House, Dar Es Salaam.

Simons, P., 1988, Après ski le dèluge, *New Scientist*, 14 January: 49–52.

Singh, T.V. *et al.* (eds), 1989, *Towards appropriate tourism: the case of developing countries*, Peter Lang, New York.

Singleton, F.B., 1985, Environmental problems in Eastern Europe, in Collins, L., (ed.), *Anglo-Bulgarian Symposium 1982*, University of London School of Slavonic and Eastern European Studies, London, pp. 58–74.

Singleton, F.B., (ed.), 1987,*Environmental problems in the Soviet Union and Eastern Europe*, Lynne Rienner, London.

Singleton, F., Carter, B., 1982, *The economy of Yugoslavia*, Croom Helm, London.

Sinnhuber, K., 1978, Recreation in the mountains, *Wiener Geographische Schriften*, **51–52**: 59–86.

Sitkina, M., 1985, Mezhdunarodnyye turistskiye svyazi Sovetskogo Soyuza b 1985 godu, *Vneshnyaya Torgovlya*, (5): 43–8.

Slater, T.R., 1988, Lower Silesia, *Urban Morphology Newsletter*, **3**: 5.

Slavkova, I., 1983, Teritorialnoustroistven plan za razvitie na otdiha i turizma v Staroplaninskata chast na Loveshki okrug, *Informatsionen Buletin*, 5–6: 39–40.

Smith, A.H., 1983, *The planned economies of Eastern Europe*, Croom Helm, Beckenham.

Snak, O., 1973, Turismul: activitate cu pondere crescindă în timpul liber al omului modern, in Barbu, Gh. (ed.), *Turismul: ramura a economiei nationale*, Editura Pentru Turism, Bucharest, pp. 109–20.

Sobell, V., 1988, The ecological crisis in Eastern Europe, *Radio Free Europe Research*, RAD/5.

Sobell, V., 1989, Beyond communist economics: postcommunist transition in Eastern Europe, *Radio Free Europe Research*, RAD/224.

Šprincová, S., 1976, Changes in the location of second homes in the Jeseniky Mountains in the period of the 'tourist boom', *Sborník Československé Společnosti Zeměpisné*, **81**(1): 69–79.

Šprincová, S., 1977, Vývoj geografie cestovního ruchu v Polsku a v Československu, in Blažek, M. (ed.), *Ekonomickegeografické Studie*, Brno, pp. 109–15.

Staar, R.F. (ed.), 1989, *Yearbook on international communist affairs*, Hoover Institution Press, Stanford, California.

Stankov, G. *et al.*, 1985, *Geografija na otdiha i turizma v Bulgarija*, Nauka i Izkustvo, Sofia.

Statistické Přehledy, annual, SNTL, Prague.

Statistická Ročenka ČSSR, annual, SNTL, Prague.

Statistički Godišnjak, annual, Central Statistical Office, Belgrade.

Statistisches Jahrbuch der DDR, annual, Staatliche Zentralverwaltung für Statistik Staatsverlag, Berlin.

Statisticheski Godishnik, annual, Central Statistical Office, Sofia.

Statisticheski Spravochnik, annual, Central Statistical Office, Sofia.

Sterev, K., 1985, Perspektivi i problemi v usvojavaneto na mineralnite vodi v Bulgarija za mezdhunaroden zdraven turizam, *Problemi na Geografijata*, 1: 26–36.

Stoica, C., 1986, Turismul periurban de agrement al oraşului Deva, *Terra*, **18**(1): 40–3.

Stoicescu, C., Munteanu, L., 1977, *Natural curative factors of the main balneoclimatic resorts of Romania*, Editura Sport-Turism, Bucharest.

Stoylik, G., 1977, *Moldavia*, Novosti, Moscow.

Strazimiri, G., 1987, *Berati*, 8 Nëntori, Tirana.

Sutela, P., 1989, Economic reform in Eastern Europe, *Unitas: Finnish Economic Quarterly Review*, **61**(2): 42–9.

Svatkov, N.M. *et al.*, 1981, Turistskiye resursy SSSR, *Izvestiya Vsesoyuznogo Geograficheskogo obshchestva*, **113**(2): 105–13.

Swizewski, C., Oancea, D.I., 1978a, La carte des types de tourisme de Roumanie, *Revue Roumaine de Géologie, Géophysique et Géographie, Série Géographie*, **23**(2): 291–4.

Swizewski, C., Oancea, D.I., 1978b, Tipologia ariilor turistice de interes international din România, *Terra*, **10**(3): 22–4.

Sykora, B., 1976, Nektere faktory ovlivnujici rozvoj lyžovani a zimní turistiký v Krkonošich, *Acta Universitatis Carolinae, Geographica*, **11**: 27–36.

Symons, L.J. (ed.), 1983, *The Soviet Union: a systematic geography*, Hodder and Stoughton, London.

Symons, L.J. (ed.), 1990, *The Soviet Union: a systematic geography*, Hodder and Stoughton, London, 2nd edn.

Szöke, M., 1986, *Visegrad: Ispánsági központ*, TKM, Budapest.

Taft, R., 1977, *Coping with unfamiliar cultures*, Academic Press, London.

Tassin, C., 1984, Tourisme et aménagement regional en Europe de l'Est, *L'Information Géographique*, **48**(5): 188–98.

Tassin, C., 1985, Tourisme et aménagement regional en Europe de l'Est, *L'Information Géographique*, **49**(1): 26–34.

Teodoreanu, E., 1981, Le potential baneo-touristisque des monts de la roumainie, *Revue Roumaine: Géographie*, **25**: 35–42.

Theodorescu, R., 1967, *Stavropoleos Church*, Meridiane, Bucharest.

Theuns, D.L., 1976, Notes on the economic impact of international tourism in developing countries, *Tourist Review*, **31**(3): 2–10.

Thomas, C., 1978, Decay and development in Mediterranean Yugoslavia, *Geography*, **63**: 179–87.

Thomas, C., 1990, Yugoslavia: the enduring dilemmas, *Geography*, **75**(3): 265–8.

Thomas, C., Vojvoda, M., 1973, Alpine communities in transition: Bohinj, Yugoslavia, *Geography*, **58**: 217–26.

Thomson, C.M., Pearce, D.G., 1980, Market segmentation of New Zealand package tours, *Journal of Travel Research*, **19**(2): 3–6.

Thomson, I.M., 1988, Alien in the land of Zog, *The Sunday Times*, 5 June: F1–2.

Tichkov, H., 1974, Thermal inversion and industrial pollution of the near-surface air of some depressions in Bulgaria, in Pecsi, M., Probald, F., (eds), *Man and Environment*, Hungarian Academy of Sciences, Hungary.

Toçka, J., 1982, *Saranda almanak 2*, 8 Nëntori, Tirana.

Török, A., 1989, *Budapest: a critical guide*, Park/Officina Nova, Budapest.

Trandafir, G., 1972, Creşterea bunăstarii materiale şi spirituale a poporului, in Moisuc, C., Tamas, S., (eds), *Făurirea societăţii socialiste multilateral dezvoltate*, Editura Politică, Bucharest, pp. 297–318.

TRC (Telecommunications Research Centre), 1990, *Eastern European telecommunications: regional assessment and analysis*, TRC, Chichester.

Trifunović, L., 1988, *Yugoslavia: monuments of art*, Jugoslovenska Knjiga, Belgrade.

Turizm, 1977, *Bol'shaya Sovetskaya Entsiklopediya*, 3rd edn., vol. 26, pp. 332–5.

Turner, L., Ash, J., 1975, *The golden hordes: international tourism and the pleasure periphery*, Constable, London.

Turnock, D., 1973, Tourism in the Romanian Carpathians, *Town and Country Planning*, **41**: 268–71.

Turnock, D., 1977, Romania and the geography of tourism, *Geoforum*, **8**: 51–6.

Turnock, D., 1978, *Eastern Europe*, Dawson, Folkestone.

Turnock, D., 1979, Water resource management problems in Romania, *GeoJournal*, **3**: 609–22.

Turnock, D., 1982, Romanian geography reunited: the integrative approach demonstrated by the conservation movement, *GeoJournal*, **6**: 419–31.

Turnock, D., 1986, *The Romanian economy in the twentieth century*, Croom Helm, London.

Turnock, D., 1989a, *Eastern Europe: an economic and political geography*, Routledge, London.

Turnock, D., 1989b, *Eastern Europe: an historical geography 1815–1945*, Routledge, London.

Turnock, D., 1989c, *The human geography of Eastern Europe*, Routledge, London.

Turnock, D., 1990a, Romania: Ceauşescu's legacy, *Geography*, **75**(3): 260–3.

Turnock, D., 1990b, Tourism in Romania: rural planning in the Carpathians, *Annals of Tourism Research*, **17**(1): 79–102.

Tyler, C., 1989a, A phenomenal explosion, *Geographical Magazine*, **61**(8), 18–21.

Tyler, C., 1989b, Killing the goose . . ., *Geographical Magazine*, **61**(10), 38–43.

Ujedinjenje Nacije—Program za Razvoj (UNDP) i Vlada SFR Jugoslavije: Projekt Južni Jadran, 1968, *Regionalni prostorni plan južnog Jadrana*, Dubrovnik.

United Nations, various, *Statistical yearbook*, United Nations, New York.

United Nations Centre on Transnational Corporations (UNCTC), 1988, *Transnational corporations in world development: trends and prospects*, UNCTC, New York.

USSR Law on Ownership, 1990, *RSEEA Newsletter*, **12**(1), 36–41.

Unković, S., 1981, *Ekonomika turizma*, Savremena Administracija, Belgrade, 5th edn.

Var, T., *et al.*, 1989a, Tourism and world peace: case of Turkey, *Annals of Tourism Research*, **16**: 282–6.

Var, T., *et al.*, 1989b, Tourism and world peace: the case of Argentina, *Annals of Tourism Research*, **16**: 431–4.

Vasiliev, B., 1984, Harakterni osobenosti na turistopotoka v turisticheskija mikroraion Slanchev Bryag—Nesebûr, *Izvestija na Bulgarskoto Geografsko Druzhestvo*, **21**: 125–32.

Vedenin, Yu. A., Miroshnichenko, N.N. (1970) Evaluation of the natural environment for recreational purposes, *Soviet Geography: Review and Translation*, **11**(3): 198–208.

Vedenin, Yu. A., *et al.*, 1976, Formirovaniye dachnykh i sadovykh kooperativov na territorii Moskovskoy aglomeratsii, *Izvestiya Akademii Nauk SSSR, Seriya Geograficheskaya*, (3): 72–9.

Venedikov, I., 1976, *Thracian treasures from Bulgaria*, British Museum Publications, London.

Veyret, P, 1963, Le tourisme en Tchécoslovaquie, *Revue Géographie de l'Est*, **3**(2): 131–6.

Vidaković, P. (ed.), 1982, *Turizam i ekonomska stabilizacija*, Privredna Komora Hrvatske, Studeni, Zagreb.

Vielzeuf, B., 1971, L'évolution du tourisme en Bulgarie, et la conception actuelle des équipements touristiques, *Société Languedocienne de Géographie Bulletin Trimestriel*, **5**(1): 27–59.

Violich, F., 1972, An urban development policy for Dalmatia, *Town Planning Review*, **43**: 151–65, 243–53.

Vlad, S., Truţi, P., 1984, Despre turismul montan în România cu privire specială asupra Munţilor Aousni, *Studii şi Cercetări: Geografie*, **31**: 85–98.

Vladuţiu, I., 1976, *Turism cu manualul de etnografie*, Editura Sport-Turism, Bucharest.

Vodenska, M., 1984, Harakteristika i territorialna organizatsija na kurortno-turisticheskite sredstva za podslon v Blagoevgradski okrug, *Izvestija na Bulgarskoto Geografsko Druzhestvo*, **22**: 115–23.

Vorontsov, Ye. A., 1966, *Yalta: putevoditel'-spravochnik*, Krymizdat, Simferopol'.

Vukičević, M., 1978, Recreation in the self-managing socialist society: contemporary theory and practice in the Socialist Federal Republic of Yugoslavia, in Sinnhuber, K., Julg, F. (eds), *Studies in the geography of tourism and recreation*, Verlag Ferdinand

Hirt, Wiener Geographische Schriften, 51/2, Vienna.
Vukonić, B., Tkalac, D., 1984, Tourism and urban revitalization: a case study of Poreč, Yugoslavia, *Annals of Tourism Research*, **11**: 591–605.
Vukonić, B. *et al.*, 1978, Italy and Yugoslavia: a case of two touristically advanced countries, in *Tourism planning for the eighties*, Editions AIEST, Berne, pp. 174–204.
Vuoristo, K-V., 1981, Tourism in Eastern Europe: development and regional patterns, *Fennia*, **159**(1): 237–47.
Výstoupil, J., 1981, Week-end house recreation of metropolitan population on the example of the city of Brno, *Geographia Polonica*, **44**: 77–80.
Wall, G., 1988, *Tourism in the modern world*, Pinter, London.
Wall, G., 1990, Tourism alternatives in an era of global climatic change, in Eadington, W., Smith, V. (eds), *Theoretical perspectives on alternative forms of tourism*, International Academy for the Study of Tourism.
Wall, G., Wright, C., 1977, *The environmental impact of outdoor recreation*, University of Waterloo, Department of Geography, Waterloo, Ontario.
Ward, P., 1983, *Albania: a travel guide*, Oleander, Cambridge.
Weir, D., 1937, *Balkan saga*, Oliver and Boyd, Edinburgh.
Wellner, I., 1985, *Balaton guide*, Panorama, Györ.
Wichrowski, K., Wojnowski, T., 1980, *Poland: a guide for young tourists*, Interpress, Warsaw.
Williams, A.M., Shaw, G. (eds), 1988, *Tourism and economic development: Western European experiences*, Belhaven, London.
Williams, A.V., Zelinsky, W., 1970, On some patterns in international tourist flows, *Economic Geography*, **46**(4): 549–67.
Winiecki, J., 1988, *The distorted world of Soviet-type economies*, Croom Helm, London.
Witt, S.F., Martin, C.A., 1989, Demand forecasting in tourism and recreation, in Cooper, C.P. (ed.), *Progress in tourism, recreation and hospitality management Vol. 1*, Belhaven, London, pp. 4–32.
Woolfson, K., 1990, East's carriers facing a difficult take-off, *The European*, 15 June: 20.
Wright, C., 1967, Slovakia—seeing the other half, *The Times*, 30 September: 7.
WTO (World Tourism Organisation), Annual, *Yearbook of tourism statistics*, WTO, Madrid.
WTO (World Tourism Organisation), 1978, *Methodological supplement to World Tourism Statistics*, WTO, Madrid.
WTO (World Tourism Organisation), 1981, *Technical handbook on the collection and presentation of domestic and international tourism statistics*, WTO, Madrid.
WTO (World Tourism Organisation), 1988, *Economic review of world tourism*, WTO, Madrid.
Yalta: klimaticheskiy kurort na yuzhnom beregu Kryma, 1910, Yalta.
Young, G., 1973, *Tourism: blessing or blight?*, Penguin, Harmondsworth.
Zachwatowicz, J., 1956, *Protection of historical monuments in People's Poland*, Polonia, Warsaw.
Zajbert, M., 1975, The problem of use and protection of water resources, *Geographia Polonica*, **32**: 63–74.
Zanga, L., 1989a, A freer and more assertive Albanian youth, *Radio Free Europe Research*, **RAD/177**: 20 September.
Zanga, L., 1989b, Alia criticizes reforms and Yugoslavia, *Radio Free Europe Research*, **RAD/118**: 30 June.
Zanga, L., 1989c, Tirana's views on the 'crisis of socialism', *Radio Free Europe Research*, **RAD/183**: 4 October.
Zanga, L., 1990a, A major revision of cultural history, *Radio Free Europe Report on Eastern Europe*, **1**(20), pp. 1–4.
Zanga, L., 1990b, A progress report on changes in Albania, *Radio Free Europe Report on Eastern Europe*, **1**(16): 1–3.
Zanga, L., 1990c, Albania makes overtures to superpowers, *Radio Free Europe Report on Eastern Europe*, **1**(19): 1–3.

Zanga, L., 1990d, Albania's new path, *Radio Free Europe Report on Eastern Europe*, **1**(24): 1–5.

Zanga, L., 1990e, Changes in the 'last bastion', *Radio Free Europe Report on Eastern Europe*, **1**(21): 1–3.

Zečević, M., 1973, *Investicije irazvoj turizma u Jugoslaviji*, Institut za Spolnju Trgovinu, Belgrade.

Zhelev, D., 1986, *With automobile in Bulgaria*, Sofia Press, Sofia.

Zloch-Chrisly, I., 1987, *Debt problems of Eastern Europe*, Cambridge University Press, Cambridge.

Zwozdziak, J.W., Zwozdziak, A.B., 1985, Evaluation of atmospheric trace species in the vicinity of a copper smelter and a power plant, *International Journal of Environmental Studies*, **24**: 97–105.

Index